Beyond Dark Hills

Jesse Stuart

"Just to think, you try to write something to suit everybody and you suit no one. Then you write to suit yourself and be yourself and the people like it!" Jesse Stuart.

(Courtesy *The Courier-Journal*)

Beyond Dark Hills

A Personal Story by
Jesse Stuart

Edited and with an Introduction by
John H. Spurlock

The Jesse Stuart Foundation
1996

Beyond Dark Hills
Copyright © by Jesse Stuart
Copyright © by the Jesse Stuart Foundation

Library of Congress Cataloging-in-publication Data

Stuart, Jesse, date
    Beyond dark hills : a personal story / by Jesse Stuart : edited and with an introduction by John H. Spurlock.
       p.   cm.
    Originally published : New York : Dutton, 1938
    ISBN 0-945084-53-6 (alk. paper)
    1. Stuart, Jesse, date —Biography.   2. Authors, American—20th century—Biography. 3. Educators—Kentucky—Biography.
I. Spurlock, John Howard. II. Title
PS3537.T92516Z52   1996
818'.5209—dc20
[B]   96-4611
                                           CIP

The Jesse Stuart Foundation
P.O. Box 391
Ashland, Kentucky 41114
1996

This edition of *Beyond Dark Hills* is dedicated to the memory of our fathers, Richard Carroll and Joe Shy.

JOE SHY   RICHARD CARROLL

Their dedication to the traditional Appalachian values of hard work, personal honesty, dedication to family, and commitment to education will live on through the accomplishments and lives of their families and friends. Our memories of them will live forever in our minds and hearts.

Stephen and Nancy Shy
Huntington, West Virginia

An early view of Greenup, Kentucky, and the Ohio River
(Courtesy *Frank Dunn Collection, Kentucky Historical Society, Frankfort*)

"I have walked in the silence of the night. I have talked to the stars.
I have tried to be strong as the oak trees...."

Jesse Stuart, 2nd from left on front row, with Plumb Grove School
classmates, 1921   (Courtesy *Irene Griffith, Greenup, Kentucky*)

Contents

Jesse, wife Naomi, and the director of the National Arts Foundation, Carlton Smith of New York City, at Marietta College, where Jesse was awarded one of his sixteen honorary degrees, this one an honorary doctorate of literature, February 1952

(Courtesy *The Courier-Journal*)

Introduction

In a lifetime of speaking and writing, Jesse Stuart (1906-1984) traveled throughout America and in many foreign countries, frequently speaking to various school and civic groups about the importance of education in forming the character of America and Americans. Stuart often stated that he had asked one thing of America—a chance—and that education provided him that chance. *Beyond Dark Hills* is the story of Stuart's educational odyssey from his protective hills of Greenup County, Kentucky, into the outer world.

While a twenty-five-year-old graduate student at Vanderbilt University in 1932, Stuart wrote the first draft of *Beyond Dark Hills* as a term paper in Dr. Edwin Mims' Victorian literature class.* Several years later, Stuart revised the manuscript into its present form. It is one of the greatest American autobiographical novels ever written. Throughout its pages, Stuart recounts the struggle of the Appalachian people for self-sufficiency, from the pioneer days of virgin timber to his own desperate struggle in obtaining an education.

The narrator of *Beyond Dark Hills* chooses a path leading beyond the encircling confines of his dark hills to Plum Grove School, Greenup High School, Lincoln Memorial University and Vanderbilt University. In perhaps the greatest educational odyssey in the history of American literature, the narrator returns to the dark hills of his homeland, but he returns on his own terms as an educated man.

Beyond Dark Hills has had the honor of being published by two of America's most respected presses—E. P. Dutton (1938) and McGraw-Hill (1972). Stuart dedicated both editions to his parents, Mitchell and Martha Hilton Stuart. At the time of the latter edition, J. Donald Adams, writing in the New York *Times Book Review* section, praised the novel as a "chapter" in American history. Adams wrote: "Many an American education has been worked for as hard as Jesse Stuart worked and fought for his, but I don't know where that story has been told with such convincing effect as Jesse Stuart has told it here. *Beyond Dark Hills* is, in its implications, more than a personal record; it is a chapter in the American story." In this sense, *Beyond Dark Hills* is the story of all Americans who overcome great obstacles in obtaining a college education.

Today there remains a great contemporary demand for a new printing of *Beyond Dark Hills*. Such an enduring demand comes as no surprise to those familiar with the book. In this novel, Stuart employs a young narrator who conducts a bicultural odyssey in a search for meaning in two worlds: his Appalachian home-world of simple but treasured comforts and the outer world of American mainstream society, with its emphasis upon rigid schedules, money and contacts. In both worlds, alienation and frustration are fundamental to life, and individuals undergo a lifelong process of defining themselves and their values.

In *Beyond Dark Hills*, Stuart referred to his year of graduate study among the Fugitives and the Agrarians at Vanderbilt University as the most difficult one of his life. He went to Vanderbilt to study creative writing with the Fugitives, whom Stuart mistakenly thought were gentlemen farmers and teacher-writers—men who lived close to the soil and wrote about the experience. Disillusioned when he found this not to be the case, Stuart, nevertheless, persevered in his studies, but a dormitory fire in his second semester proved devastating to his immediate goal of a master's degree. He lost his on-campus job as a janitor (having been assigned to the building now in ruins), his clothes, term papers, the work on his master's thesis, and many poems and short stories. At the end of the semester, he was wearing borrowed clothes and friends loaned him money for meals. Although offered two scholarships—one in academics and another in athletics—Stuart borrowed two dollars and hitchhiked home to W-Hollow, the land of his birth. He felt he had learned all the Fugitives and the Agrarians could teach him, and he was eager to resume the model of life lived in harmony with the soil, a concept which the Fugitives and Agrarians held in high regard, even if they did not practice it in their daily lives.

In the years 1932 and 1933, while helping his parents with their crops and working respectively as superintendent of Greenup County Schools and principal of McKell High School, Stuart began writing poetry and short stories in one of the most creative outpourings in the history of American letters. His *Man With A Bull-Tongue Plow* (consisting of 703 "sonnets") was published in 1934, and that same year he sold three short stories to major magazines, which opened the short-story market for him. As a result of the glowing critical reviews of *Man With A Bull-Tongue Plow*, Stuart was awarded a Guggenheim Fellowship and sailed for Scotland in July of 1937. While in Edinburgh, he made final revisions to the manuscript of *Beyond Dark Hills* and also wrote its concluding chapter. The book was published in April of 1938, by Hutchinson in England and E. P. Dutton in America.

Through the focus of his narrator, Stuart transforms the novel's autobiographical fact into myth by the creation of a particular Appalachian persona and perspective. This magical transformation makes *Beyond Dark Hills* suggestive of the desperate search for meaning in the twentieth century as the reader travels with the narrator, who defines himself in the following vital relationships: to his home-world of Appalachia, to the outer world of the American mainstream society, to his concept of himself as a writer, to his family, and to his concept of his individual freedom versus his social responsibility. The narrator thus becomes a cultural hero in his epic quest for meaning in the world—a far-wandering "I" in the tradition of Ulysses, Beowulf, Ralph Waldo Emerson, Henry David Thoreau, Walt Whitman, and Thomas Wolfe. As has been true of many epic heroes weary of the quest, the narrator decides to return home to the land of his birth.

Leaving Vanderbilt University, the young Jesse of *Beyond Dark Hills* returned to W-Hollow to write of his people and his place. In so doing, Stuart appointed himself the literary spokesman of Appalachia—his source and substance. In his poetry, short stories, and novels (biographical and fictional), Stuart captured fixed points in a turning world—those rare and inexplicable exposures of the intersections where the matter of Appalachian life becomes the matter of literary art. These crossroads of the temporal and eternal he indelibly recorded and framed for us all. The literary legacy of Jesse Stuart's W-Hollow now belongs to the people of the world and to the ages. *Beyond Dark Hills* is a rich part of that legacy. As an autobiographical novel, it has no superior.

John H. Spurlock, Ph.D.
Western Kentucky University

---

*In the Foreword, written forty years following his days at Vanderbilt, Stuart carelessly stated he was age twenty-three when *BDH* was written. In actuality, he was age twenty-five. Stuart was born August 8, 1906; *BDH* was written in March 1932. See *Jesse: The Biography of an American Writer*, by H. Edward Richardson, p. 1, and "Stuart Letters," edited by William Boozer, in *The Register of The Kentucky Historical Society* 80.1 (1982): 10.

Foreword
by Jesse Stuart, 1972

Since *Beyond Dark Hills* is being republished, there has to be
a foreword explaining where and under what circumstances it was
written. To me, now, *Beyond Dark Hills* is far away and long ago.
There is really a big generation gap between the Jesse Stuart when
he was twenty-three—a graduate student at Vanderbilt University—
and the Jesse Stuart of today. Forty years have passed since I did
"Beyond Dark Hills" for a term paper in Dr. Edwin Mim's English
class—my only course at Vanderbilt in which I didn't receive a
grade. Thirty-four years have gone by since it was first published,
in April, 1938.

Except for the last chapter, I have never read this book since I
wrote it—until now. (In fact, I have never read any of my books
after it has been published.) I wrote the last chapter at 8 Viewforth
Gardens, Edinburgh, Scotland, where I lived on a Guggenheim
Fellowship in 1937-1938. Since I was in Scotland, I never read the
proofs of this book. I sent the last chapter over to my publishers,
where it was added to the manuscript and the editors put it together
and did the proofreading.

Reading this book after the passage of so many years has been
an experience. When first published it inspired many a young
person. Since this is a book of time and place, and since it might

relate to the young people of today—especially those who have to struggle—it certainly needs explanation.

When I was an undergraduate student at Lincoln Memorial University, Harrogate, Tennessee, I read books by writers who called themselves The Fugitives of Vanderbilt University, Nashville, Tennessee. Here were writers who had joined together in an organization. Part or all were in the Agrarian Movement—"pro" back to the farms and "anti" industrialization of the South. Being a farmer then, as I am still, all of this was attractive to me.

I graduated from Lincoln Memorial in 1929. I went home, taught in a rural high school so successfully that I was promoted to principal of Greenup High School. Here I was successful too, but I made the mistake of asking for a raise in salary. I had made $100 per month in the rural high school and $1,000 per nine months at Greenup High School. I asked for a $200 raise. I was fired.

I had always had in mind going to Vanderbilt University, where teachers wrote books and farmed. I wanted to be part of this group. Vanderbilt was my dream school. It had to be Vanderbilt.

Money was my problem. But money or no money I was going to Vanderbilt, as I'd gone to Lincoln Memorial University. I entered this school on $29.30. I had a fortune when I arrived at Vanderbilt with a trunk and an old Oliver typewriter. I had $130. Dr. Mims let me register—but he was dubious about me. In my trunk I had more manuscripts than clothes.

But I soon found out The Fugitives was a closed corporation. A stranger and an ambitious unknown couldn't just go to Vanderbilt and join them. And the disillusionment came when I learned about their farming. Their farming was on paper. I went to one professor's home and he had a few tomatoes in a little garden and these plants were poorly cultivated. At my home, we farmed; we knew how to do it. We made a living and some to spare farming our Kentucky hills and valleys. We were not "gentlemen farmers." We did our own work.

Now a Depression was on. I worked first semester at the Wesley Hall Cafeteria for eleven meals per week. (There was a lot of difference between twenty-one meals per week and eleven for a young energetic man, weighing 225 pounds, who could run the hundred-yard dash in ten flat.) I was also one of two white student janitors; the other was a ministerial student. I shared Clem Carson's textbooks with him. I couldn't afford textbooks. Clem and I had the same schedule. Under these circumstances, I didn't do well at Vanderbilt. There were scholarships available but I never asked for one. The head of Nashville's YMCA tried to help me find extra work. I thought my first semester at Vanderbilt was the hardest time I had ever had to endure in my life, but I wasn't about to give up. They had not asked for me at Vanderbilt. I had asked for them. I'd gone there without applying to be admitted.

So, I registered for the second semester. I liked all my instructors: John Donald Wade in American Literature, Dr. Edwin Mims, Head of the English Department, in Victorian Literature, Robert Penn Warren in the Novel, Donald Davidson in Elizabethan Poetry. Here was one of the greatest, if not the greatest, teachers I had ever known. I made straight A's in his course. He changed my life. Vanderbilt was worth the year of suffering and hardships to have this one great teacher.

In Robert Penn Warren's Novel course, I was among classmates who had ambitions to write novels and two, I remember, said they would write "the great American novel." Robert Penn Warren was a very young man, just back from Oxford University (England), teaching at his alma mater and working on his first novel, *Night Rider*. I had no desire to write a novel. I never said that I would write one. I have since written eight novels with the ninth awaiting publication. I believe I'm the only one from that class who has ever written a novel.

In 1940 in New York City at a party given by Amy Loveman at the *Saturday Review*, after my first novel *Trees of Heaven* was published, one from this Novel class who vowed to write the great American novel—one who had a private plane at Vanderbilt—came up to congratulate me. He was living in New York. I asked him if he'd done his novel yet and he told me he hadn't. Being his

Vanderbilt classmate and hearing him talk, an A student, I thought he would have been the one from our class to have written a novel.

I have since learned it's not the grades that count. I received a B or less in The Novel. But I've been the one from that class who has written them.

My eight novels have been reviewed as quality novels and the reviews have been from excellent to poor, but the books have sold a combined total of at least three million, not counting foreign editions.

During my second semester, Wesley Hall burned along with the cafeteria where I was earning eleven meals per week. All my clothes, except what I had on my body, burned. My trunk, and all my manuscripts—poetry, stories, term papers and my thesis for my M.A., which was nearly finished—burned. My old Oliver typewriter I'd purchased from Dr. Henry Morris back in Greenup, Kentucky, for $25 was the only thing of mine I could recognize in the ashes of Wesley Hall.

Old clothing was given immediately for needy students, and there were many of us who had been living in Wesley Hall. I received the best suit because it was too large for anyone else. It was like a suit that had been tailored for me. I sent word back home to a fellow teacher, Lewis McCubbin, asking him to loan me a suit. He'd taught at Greenup High School for me when I was principal. He sent me one of his suits, which was a little small, but I managed. I had ripped two big tears in the crotch of the suit I was wearing when I first saw Wesley Hall on fire. I must have run faster than ten flat for a quarter of a mile toward the building to save my manuscripts and belongings. When I approached I couldn't go up to my room. The fire had spread all through the building.

I wanted to save my almost-finished thesis, but I was too late. All my possessions in Wesley Hall went up in flames.

A former Lincoln Memorial classmate, then working on his D.D. degree in religion at Vanderbilt, purchased for me one meal a day at a boarding house, and I remained in Vanderbilt. Seven meals per week!

Dr. Mims asked us in March to write for his class a paper about ourselves. The minimum was eight and maximum eighteen typewritten pages. We had eleven days in which to write this paper. Students in this class smiled and quipped about their unimportant lives. I had another idea. I thought all lives were important. I knew my life was important to me. It was the most important thing I possessed and I wanted to make my life count.

Katherine Atherton Grimes, on the old *Southern Agriculturist,* gave me paper. I rented a typewriter for seventy-five cents. I wanted to explain to my teacher, Dr. Mims, there was something to me. I imagined he was sitting in my room and I was talking to him with my typewriter. My typing flowed. My typewriter sang. Dr. Mims would know I had had a long journey getting to Vanderbilt University. But I had come and I wasn't about to leave. I never cut a class and I lived on one meal a day. The day our papers were due, I put mine on a piece of cardboard and bound it down with two heavy rubber bands. I had written 322 pages from margin to margin. I wanted the paper to look small when I gave it to Dr. Mims. I let all the other members in my class turn in their papers, which were mostly minimum. I'll never forget how Dr. Mims took my paper and felt the weight.

"There you go, Stuart, you hand me a paper like this when you are failing my class. And you know I read every word of a paper handed to me by one of my students!"

When I saw Dr. Mims again three days later, he had read my paper.

"It's the finest paper ever handed to me in my career as a teacher," he said. "So crudely written and so beautiful and it needs punctuation."

Vanderbilt suddenly became a new place for me.

I didn't know then that I had written my first prose book and that it would be published six years later as my third book and reviewers would question why a man thirty years of age had written his autobiography. I couldn't tell these reviewers I had written it at twenty-three for a term paper, all but the last chapter, and I hadn't passed the course. But Dr. Mims did look at me with keen, piercing eyes and say: "Stuart, I believe you're a genius. If you were my son, I don't know what I'd do with you."

Before leaving Vanderbilt I was offered a scholarship in English if I would return—also, a football scholarship. In football season I'd sold programs in front of the stadium. After I'd sold programs, I'd get to see the rest of the games. I saw the tackles they missed. I'd liked to have been in there playing instead of selling programs. I went out for three days of spring practice—a little weak on a meal a day. But I was good enough to be offered an athletic scholarship. But I decided my higher education was over. I borrowed two dollars and hitchhiked back home—a distance, before new super highways, of approximately four hundred fifty miles.

Things have greatly changed since *Beyond Dark Hills* was written. There wasn't a foot of hard road in Greenup County when I wrote this book. There was not even a Greenup County High School. Now there are schools and hard-surfaced roads all over Greenup County. There is a hard road into W-Hollow, where I still live. There was a cow path over which we walked when I was a student in Vanderbilt over part of the way the W-Hollow hard road now runs. The American Rolling Mills, where I worked in its early formative years, is ARMCO today. If you apply for a job there, you must be a high school graduate. When I worked there, I never knew a rougher place. Today it's one of our finest companies in this area—where young men seek employment and consider themselves lucky to be hired.

My brother James had his problems growing up after he finished high school at fourteen. He finished college, taught school and was school administrator for nineteen years, was an officer four years in World War II and was in the Korean War. At the industry where he works, he has twenty years' experience, mostly as an engineer. How has he packed all this into his fifty-six years, when neighborhood women used to tell my mother her son was heading for destruction? My mother told them her son might preach someday. James is a lay minister in his church. My mother knew her son. She told her sons and daughters we were the best. We believed her. We are one-hundred percent college graduates and we did it without scholarships or money. We worked our ways through colleges and universities. We learned this could be done in America.

Everything in my world has changed since *Beyond Dark Hills* was written. It is certainly a book of time and place, born in the beginning of the Depression and first published in the middle of the Depression.

Now, *Beyond Dark Hills*, a collectors' item in its first edition, will be published again and it will have more readers, I know, than it had before. And some readers will be American young people who seek to make their lives count, as I sought, from a ghetto of poverty, to make mine count.

Family of Mitchell and Martha Stuart. Left to right: Glennis, James, Mary, Jesse, Sophia, Martha and Mitchell

Log Run in Sandy River, Catlettsburg, Kentucky

"He'd get the logs close to the Big Sandy so...he could roll them into the river and take them down the Big Sandy into the Ohio and down the Ohio River to Cincinnati or Louisville."

Grandfather Mitchell Stuart

"I was afraid of him. He was twice as large as my father and had a great long beard.... If I had met Grandpa at night, I would have thought he was the devil."

Chapter I
Tall Figures of the Earth

I do not know authentically when it was that six tall Scottish Highland brothers left the Firth of Forth to come to America. All I know is that they came. For a short time, they settled in Burkes Garden, Virginia. Then for no well-known reason, apparently no reason at all, these six Highland brothers left Burkes Garden and settled in Wytheville, Virginia. It was here the clan was broken. One brother died and was buried at Wytheville; one went to Wyoming; the third brother went to Tennessee; the fourth remained in Wytheville; the fifth pushed into Kentucky and settled on the Big Sandy River, and the sixth brother disappeared, leaving no trace the way he had gone.

And the tall Scotsman, Raphy Stuart, six feet six, I'm told, that came to the Big Sandy Valley, was my great-grandfather. Not one of the brothers was under six feet two. Raphy Stuart's third son happened to be my grandfather, Mitchell Stuart; and Mitchell Stuart's eleventh child, another Mitchell Stuart, is my father.

At this same time, a stubborn English family by the name of Hilton was gradually pushing northward through the Kentucky mountains from the mountains of North Carolina. They were slow to become angered but persistent against force when angered. They loved gaudy colors. They loved their homes and their small hill

Grandfather Nathan Hilton

*"When I asked him what were the best years of his life,
he said: 'Son, they have all been good years. But when I
was the most powerful was between sixteen and seventy-five.'"*

Grandmother Violet Anne Pennington Hilton

farms. They loved books. They were very impulsive but nothing like the Stuarts. The Hiltons were distinguished in the mountains for being good preachers (Baptists), and for being "good larners."

If you were to see a Hilton, the first thing you would note would be the dark and very prominent features that remind one of an Indian. I could prove this better if I could let you see my mother. She is five feet eleven inches tall, straight and strong, brown-skinned with high cheekbones and coarse straight black hair, though in recent years her hair is turning gray. She hates the drudgery of housework but loves the sunlight, the fresh air and the freedom of the open fields. The distance has never been too far for her to walk. And I am very proud to be a son of Martha Hilton.

I would rather not go back and discuss the Stuart family again. I love to talk about the Hiltons. But there is more to say about the Stuarts even if it is often embarrassing and a sad thing to reflect on when I begin to realize that I am only a chip off the old block, to

Martha Hilton Stuart

"I am very proud to be a son of Martha Hilton."

use a woodman's phrase. It was no wonder that my Grandfather Hilton cried out frantically: "My heavens, my daughter is marrying an outlaw when she marries Mitchell Stuart." He had a right to say that, knowing the Stuarts, but it did not turn out to be true. She did not marry an outlaw. Grandfather Hilton knew my father's father and he judged my father by him.

I shall pause here to give you a word portrait of this figure of earth. He was married at eighteen. He joined the Federal Army at the age of twenty. He joined the North because the recruiting station for soldiers for Northern armies was nearer. He just wanted to fight. He always would take sides in the neighborhood wars. He had fought the three bullies that the West Virginia side of the Big Sandy River had put up against the Kentuckians. There was constant fighting between the Kentuckians and West Virginians. And West Virginia had had the bully for a long time. After my grandfather had whipped the three West Virginians one at a time, he would drink booze, go to public gatherings and ask for a volunteer to fight him. If no one volunteered, he offered a dollar. He raised it until he found company. Then the ring was drawn. The two men pulled off their shirts and stepped inside. The boys around knew exactly what to do. They ran for buckets of water. Before that one fight was over, there would be dozens of others and the women there would have to clear out. It is a thousand wonders that he did not get killed. But he did not. He was a hero among them. That was a time when America had her heroes.

My grandfather became one of the best wrestlers in Grant's army. Only two years ago, I talked to Mr. Miller, an old soldier who soldiered with him and saw him win his last bout in the army. He said he was the most powerful man he ever saw—that he broke his opponent's arm before two minutes had passed. He said he was the gamest man he had ever known.

I sometimes think my grandfather was in the wrong army. He was hanged by his own men before the battle of Gettysburg. He had killed a comrade. For this act my grandfather was to be court-martialed. They took him to an old house and tied a rope around his wrists. They kept him hanging to a rafter for two hours, just so his toes could not touch the ground. Then they let him rest four hours. All the food he had at this house was bread and onions. The guards told him: "You don't need food, what you need is prayer. You will be under the earth this time tomorrow night."

Grandpa's General ordered his removal from the old house just before the battle of Gettysburg. "I am sure you will be a better man above the ground than you will be under the ground." Grandpa would say: "When they took the ropes from around my wrists and turned me loose, I felt limber as a cat. The blood from my wrists had run down my arms and down my body. It had filled my shoes and my clothes were soggy-red. There were puddles of blood in the old house. It was a bad fix for a body to be in.

"I was put in front at the battle of Gettysburg. Men's brains were shot out right beside me. I never got a scratch. I was in all three days of the battle. All the scars I got out of the damn war was these scars on my wrists." And Grandpa would pull up his sleeves and show them to his friends. They were almost all the way around his wrists. These deep scars he carried to the grave.

He would tell about during the night at the battle of Gettysburg how he crawled over the hill to get water. At a spring there he met boys dressed in gray. They, too, were drinking from the same spring. He exchanged words with them and laughed. "I met a couple of boys there from home. One was akin to me. Met them there at night and to think that at sunrise we'd start pounding away at one another. I don't know whether these boys were left there or not. Men were lying on top of one another four-deep in some places and the creek there ran blood for two weeks."

He would tell about being captured twice during the war by the Southern soldiers. Each time they let him go free. "Once we went to a dance in Virginia. I was with the boys dressed in gray. One started a fuss and the others made him behave. I danced that night and had a good time while I was their captive. Before daylight they turned me loose." But Grandpa never told about coming back on a furlough and how when he started to treat his comrades to cigars a Negro ran in and said: "If I can't have my share first, I won't have them last." And he scooped up a double handful. Grandpa said: "You won't have them at all." He didn't take time to shoot him. He hit him over the head with a rifle barrel and his brains spilled out on the street. He pulled fifty dollars from his pocket and said to Uncle Marion: "A lot of money. But there, bury the son-of-a-bitch."

He went through all four years of the war. When his first time of enlistment was up, he re-enlisted until the finish of the war at Appomattox Courthouse when Lee surrendered to Grant. He would tell this surrender story over and over again about the meeting of the two armies and how they gave coffee to the Southern soldiers for the parched corn that they were using for coffee. He would tell about how hungry and ragged the Southern soldiers were, some without shoes and many of them "just strips of boys too young to fight," he would always remind his listeners. He never liked to talk about Gettysburg, and when he spoke about getting hanged the tears would come to his eyes, or when he spoke about losing some of his best comrades at the slaughter at Cold Harbor. Once my father and I went to see Grandpa. He lived upon a hill that overlooked the Big Sandy. Grandpa was sitting in the yard in a big split-bottom chair. He said to my father: "What are you going to do with him, Mitchy . . . let him grow up with the weeds?" And he reached out with the handle part of his cane and hooked me around the neck . . . drew me over to him and gave me what he called the "dutch-rub" . . . rubbing his fist over my head. I cried and tried to get away. I was afraid of him. He was twice as large as my father and had a great long beard. And then he pointed to the Big Sandy River and said: "Never no more, Mitchy, will I ever ride the log rafts down that river. That river is as dear to me as my blood. It is all over, Mitchy. See these white hairs in my head. These legs are giving way. Time will get a man in the end." If I had met Grandpa at night, I would have thought he was the Devil.

And when we went down to catch the Big Sandy train, my father said: "Son, you see that rail fence up there on the hill. Pap put that there when I was a little boy. Sister Belle carried me over there on her back. I remember Pap cussing and sweating and giving orders to the boys, and he was doing more work than any two of the men. He was trying to get it finished before a storm. That was in Garfield's administration." The fence was still standing and looked as good as new. The oak rails were seasoned by the sun, stacked-and-ridered, and were the color of a wasp's nest.

When he got on the train, my father said: "I used to ride this old train with Pap down to Catlettsburg when he would get on his sprees. I'd go with him when he got his supply of whisky. Pap drank enough whisky to float a saw log down the Big Sandy River. Once they carried him on past the station and him and old Buck Stump made them back-back the train two miles and put them off. A big crowd was on the train and everybody was fighting. The conductor got his coattail cut off. Soon as Pap got his pension, he got his supply of Old Rock and Old Rye and a brand called 'Old Kentucky.' The last brand mentioned had the picture of a bony horse on the label with these words below: 'She was bred in Old Kentucky.' He wouldn't go to bed at night without the lamp burning. He'd always say: 'I see that nigger. He is after me.' And Pap would keep the lamp burning all night."

And once I asked my father how many men Grandpa had killed besides the men he killed in the war. And my father said: "Don't ask so many questions, Son. Little boys don't need to know too much." But I learned myself about the man hunting to kill Grandpa at the lane where the men used to come to drink and fight. And when Grandpa heard about it, he started hunting for the man who was hunting for him. Grandpa stabbed at his own brother's throat with the knife and thought he was the right man. He hit Uncle Bob's shoulder blade and broke the knife blade. He threw the bloody knife into the Big Sandy. Uncle Bob got well after a long time. The man hunting to kill Grandpa was killed that night. And a man left the Big Sandy and went West and everybody thought he was the one who killed Houndshell. There was never any trial over it anyway.

My father would say: "There never was a worker like Pap. He's cleared more land than any man on the Big Sandy River, and I wouldn't be afraid to bet. He'd take a lease of thirty acres and get it clear in the first year. He'd build a log house on it out'n the trees he cleared from it, split rails enough from the oaks and chestnut trees and fence it. He'd get the land to farm for three years for clearing it, putting a house on it and fencing it. Just as soon as his crop was laid by, he'd start cutting timber. He'd cut timber and the boys would gather the crop at home. Pap would cut timber all fall. And when the ground froze and the snow fell, Pap would start logging with eight yokes of big cattle. He'd log while the heavy snows were on the ground and the ground was frozen. I've seen him come in and feed the cattle and just lay down before the fire. He wouldn't pull off his shoes nor go to bed. He'd sleep from four to six hours. He'd get Ma out'n the bed to make him hot biscuits and fry him ham and make him a biler of black coffee, and then he'd be off again. He'd get the logs close to the Big Sandy so when the snows melted and the land thawed he could roll them into the river and take them down the Big Sandy into the Ohio and down the Ohio River to Cincinnati or Louisville. And after he got the logs sold, he'd come home on a boat and drink all the way home. His spree would be over by the time he got here and then he'd start clearing land again. He'd have out every one of us children working us from daylight until dark. He'd lay out the work for the boys to do while he was gone too. Everybody worked around Pap. A big powerful man with little hands and little feet."

Once Grandpa said: "I'm going to quit my licker, my terbacker, and be a brother to all men. I'm going to be a different man with my family and quit blowing my money." And Grandpa went to the church. It was a Methodist church. He got down on his knees. I don't know whether he confessed all of his sins or not. He had a lot of things to confess. But he got "saved" and stayed in the church one week. Then he said: "I can't stand this sort of a life. I've got to live. I've got to have my licker and my terbacker. And I can't be a brother to a Houndshell." And Grandpa went back to his old ways of living. He'd get his jugs of liquor and go to bed with them. He fought his own battles. He lived his own life.

Once Mom said to me: "I thought I was in a terrible set when I married your father. He took me to his home. And his stepmother didn't like me. She carried an old pistol. After the man your Grandfather had been, not afraid of the Devil himself, why that woman had him afraid to speak. Once he left her and went to his boy's home to live. She followed him and made him walk right back. She tried to bully me after I'd been at the house three days. She started to pull that old pistol. I walked in and gave her the best thrashing she ever got. Your Grandpa Stuart started for me with his cane and I says: 'Just a minute, Mr. Stuart. I have respect for old age and white hair. But you keep coming and I'll give you the same.' And your Pa ran in and kept him back."

When Grandpa was old, his wife was still young. He left Greenup County with her and went back to the Big Sandy. He told my father, "I tell you, Mitchy, I'm going back to the Big Sandy to die. It is my home there. My home is not here. These hills are no good for wheat. This land's not the land we have on Big Sandy. I'm going back there to live the rest of my days and die there, and be buried there." And Grandpa moved back to the Big Sandy. He left the land where we still live today. It was a good place for Grandpa to come and dodge his troubles. But he went back to face them when his hair was white and his legs were getting tottery.

"W'y, old Mitch Stuart is having trouble with that young wife of hissin. That's what happens when an old grandpa marries a young girl. Why didn't he marry somebody his own age? This morning Mort Billings and Eif Fannin carried him into the house and he was stiff as a board. If they hadn't found him when they did, w'y he'd a been froze to death in a little while. Was out there in that old log house by the road with a double-barrel shotgun p'inted through the crack a-waitin' for Lin Hinton. He said Lin had been comin' to see his wife and he's goin' to kill the damn son-of-a-bitch. Old man and his white hair flyin' to the January wind. He must be up in eighty."

And Grandpa did die on Big Sandy. We don't know how he died. We didn't know that he was dead until he was dead and buried. We heard that he was beaten to death. We do not know. Uncle Joe's boys said they knew who did it and it would be his turn next. But his turn came sooner than Uncle Joe's boys expected. It came at the point of someone else's gun, and the suspect sleeps under the Big Sandy clay not far away from Grandpa.

Grandpa had seen others die, perhaps, the way that he had died. It is said: "If you live by the sword, you die by the sword." And I believe that he would be fair enough to say, if he could only speak through the Kentucky clay that holds him: "I have no regrets, for I lived my life. I loved it. I came and spent my years. I didn't grow tired. I just needed a safe place away from my enemies. I have it here. I lived by the sword and by gad I can die by it."

Didn't Grandpa once go to a place in West Virginia where they talked to the dead? He went there to talk to old Jimmie Howe, veteran of two wars, boozer, and friend of Grandpa's, who had departed this life at the age of 102. In the dark room among the spirits and the people who had come to talk with them, didn't Grandpa stand up and say: "Come out, all you dead babies and have a drink on old Mitch Stuart! Come on and have some fun on earth again, for you ain't had none in your damn graves for so long!"

And standing there he shook his bottle of whisky and said: "Don't that make your mouth water, Uncle Jimmie Howe?" Grandpa took a drink standing there in the dark. Didn't that break up the meeting! The woman who ran the place said to Grandpa: "You old drunken sot, you've insulted the spirits! Take your half-a-dollar back and get out of here." Wasn't Grandpa free with his whisky even with the spirits!

Mitch Stuart's first wife was Cynthia Meade, his first cousin. By her he had eleven children. By his second wife he had eight children. Nineteen children by the two. "I can jerk up nineteen children by the hair of the head and not half try." When he came back to Kentucky after the war, he was not satisfied with the peace

among the hills. One of the meanest families of people on the Big
Sandy were the Houndshells. Rank Houndshell shot Uncle Bob
Stuart's boy with a sawed-off shotgun. Later Uncle Bob's two boys
met the three Houndshell boys. Rank Houndshell and Clem Stuart
were clinched on the ground fighting and Rank had Clem on the
bottom. Ennis Houndshell was helping his brother Rank beat Clem
Stuart into a jelly. Young Mitch, Uncle Bob's other boy, knocked
Eif Houndshell down, pulled a pistol and thought he was shooting
Rank Houndshell, but he shot his own brother. And there on the
ground as Clem Stuart's life slowly ebbed away, his knife went in
and out of Rank Houndshell, a little slower and a little slower.
Rank was knifed until he bled to death there. It was a man for a
man. With Rank on the earth beside the lifeless Clem Stuart,
Kentucky drank the blood of both her native sons. Naturally, old
Mitch Stuart took up the fight. No wonder the families thereafter
had no use for one another. The fighting that took place thereafter
would take too long to describe. It is all over now and forgotten
and Uncle Bob and both his boys are dust, for Uncle Bob's last
son, young Mitch Stuart, was killed somewhere in the West, leaving
no heritage behind to carry on that branch of the old tree.

After the war, Mitch Stuart became a staunch Republican and
furnished the beef for the barbecues on "Rally Day." He always
furnished the beef for the "big days," and after the speakers had
got through, Grandpa would always get up and say a few words.

Grandpa said he never wanted to be buried near a Houndshell
when he died. He said if a Houndshell went to Heaven he didn't
want to go and if a Houndshell went to Hell he didn't want to go.
Said he'd had enough of the Houndshells here on earth. If they
meet in the same place, there will be war in either Heaven or Hell,
I fear. It is strange how democratic the Kentucky hill people are in
life and then at death they become aristocratic in their own small
world. They have family cemeteries where they want to be buried.
They have certain ministers to preach their funerals. They make
requests to be buried by So-and-so. It was the request of my
grandfather to be buried beside Jimmie Howe, an old man who

could always drink more whisky than Grandpa. He never mentioned about being buried by either of his wives.

My mother's grandfather, Preston Hilton, an old man and Baptist preacher when the war broke out, enlisted early. He enlisted in the Federal army, while his son chose the Southern army. My great-grandfather started as a chaplain in the army. Later he became an officer. He mobilized a Kentucky company to defeat Morgan's "Wild Riders." The adventure was unsuccessful. He met Morgan near Lexington, Kentucky, and Morgan met him. Great-grandpa Hilton lost every man he had in the battle and had to flee for his own life. He rode a horse twenty-two miles without a bridle, fleeing for safety. And Morgan and Morgan's men went free to roam over Kentucky and to kill and plunder.

After the war Preston Hilton went back to preaching. He was noted for his long sermons. If a man slept during one of his sermons, he went back and woke him up. He didn't use a rabbit's foot to tickle his nose with either. He grabbed him by the collar and the seat of the pants and dragged him out.

Great-grandfather Preston Hilton never liked the Ku-Klux Klan. And in a region where they were strongly organized, he not only preached against them in his four-hour sermons but he went out on the road and clapped his fists and preached against them. Had he not been a Baptist and in a country where the Baptists ruled, his life would have been in danger. It was in danger as it was, and Preston Hilton had a room built in the upstairs of his house for protection. He had every sort of rifle, and he had holes he could shoot from if the Klansmen came after him. He doubly defied them. He invited them to come and get him. And back on a hill in Lawrence County, they took this sturdy hillman and laid him to rest among the soldiers he had led in battle, and among whom he had stood years before and preached their funerals. He was a lover of books, a schoolteacher, a farmer, a warrior and preacher laid to rest.

His son, Nathan Hilton, my mother's father, went to Morgan's camp when he was fifteen. He was loyal to the South. And when

Grandpa started to cast his first vote for Horace Greeley, Great-grandpa Preston Hilton asked him to haul off his coat. Grandpa says: "I'll do it, Pap, but I figure I'm just as good a man as you are."

And Grandpa says: "I've voted the Democratic ticket all my life and never missed but one election. My second wife lay a corpse when Woodrow Wilson was elected the second time." Nathan Hilton is living still, though he is well on to fourscore years and ten. His hair is white as cotton and thick as sheep's wool; his blue eyes are dimmed by time and his sleep each day is just a little longer. He has been a powerful man physically. "W'y, old man Hilton wouldn't take an easy job. Can do more work than any one man I've ever seen."

In Grandpa's eighty-second year, he came into the Baptist fold and was baptized in Coal Branch. He, too, loved his whisky but not war. He helped to cut the timber from the hills and mine coal from the earth. He helped to build the highways and the railroads. When I asked him what were the best years of his life, he said: "Son, they have all been good years. But when I was the most powerful was between sixteen and seventy-five." He ran a big farm and did his own work until he was eighty-eight and his legs gave way.

Now here are the men of earth I am directly descended from—both sides are sturdy mountaineers. On the Stuart side are workers, fighters, heavy drinkers and men of physical endurance. Among the Hiltons are lovers of flashy colors, book readers and people religiously solid as their hills. I can truthfully say that not a Stuart of close kin that I have known or heard of has ever been drafted in the three wars they have participated in.

And now the old generations are sleeping upon the high Kentucky hills amid the primitive lands they cleared and close to the log houses they made. And the stars that I walk under there at night, as I worship the drowsy summer landscape, wet with dew, illuminated by the moon and stars, are the same stars that swarmed over my people in their day—maybe creating the same impulse in them to do something worthwhile in life. That was the day when tall figures of the earth were needed.

And now those stars, brilliant and cold, gaze down upon the old graves that contain dust that I was made from, dust that was powerful in its day, but now unnamed and forgotten lies, eternally sleeping.

Jesse's birthplace   *(Photo by Earl Palmer, Christiansburg, Virginia)*

"Should it matter where a man is born—in a shack, a cottage or a palace?...I pray that it really doesn't matter."

Chapter II
The Destiny Of Hills

Should it matter where a man is born—a shack, a cottage or a palace? Does his environment make him or does his blood tell? This is an old question and we'll not debate it here. The only thing is, I pray that it really doesn't matter.

In a place where miners come to dig coal in the high hills of Greenup County, Kentucky, I was born. The log house had at that time a huge single log room. But now that old house has two rooms. Someone has built a lean-to for a kitchen and dining room. This house is five miles from Riverton, Kentucky, the nearest post office. The spot is a lonely one. The Little Sandy River runs near and the waters can be heard going over the stony riffles on silent nights. But when the wind is blowing through the pine trees, the water cannot be heard. And in the days when we lived there, we could hear the foxes barking from the lonely hilltops. Squirrels played in the tall walnut trees near our home. We could hear the leafy branches of a tree shaking on the early autumn mornings, and that would mean a squirrel. All we had to do to kill a squirrel was to take the gun to the milk gap—to kill several squirrels, we took the gun when we went after the cows. The rabbits played around the house, ate the bark off the apple trees during the winter, and cleaned the cabbage out of the garden during the summer. And snakes often writhed through the tall weeds not far from our door.

Dogs for us were not something to be kept as luxuries. They were essential things. We could not do without good dogs. We kept hound dogs and mountain curs. The hound dogs had good noses and the curs were energetic and vicious. We crossed the two and got the ideal dogs. We always kept good dogs. We began training them young. There was plenty of game near to train them with, for snakes often came and foxes would come in open daylight and carry chickens out of the yard. I have often thought that in the wildlife of the high hills everything was waiting for something to die to eat its flesh. The wild dogs killed the sheep and cows, the buzzards and the crows sailed above and waited for their share of them. The foxes killed the birds, rabbits and chickens. The hound dogs killed the foxes. All forms of animals preyed on the rabbit— even the snake, though man was his greatest enemy, for the rabbit and squirrel are the sweetest of all wild meats. When a man in the hills is sick and cannot eat squirrel, more than likely he is going to die. The squirrel can climb and fight. The rabbit can do nothing but run, and when he is overtaken just gives up. Nearly all forms of wildlife are his enemies—the chicken hawk swoops down out of the air and carries the victim away in his claws.

My father worked in the small coal mines during the winter. He would go before daylight and come back after dark. His clothes would be thick with mud and dirty clay would be stuck to his knuckles. It was hard to wash off. During the summer he farmed the rough hill slopes. There was no other land to farm. He had to use mules, for they could stand up better on the rough hillsides. And a mule did not tire like a horse when breaking roots endlessly all day long pulling a root cutter. The mule would shrug up his body and take it easy. "Ease up against the collar," as my father often said, "and make plowing easy for a man." The tobacco crop, the money crop, was cultivated better than the corn. For we only worked the corn twice in the rich newground soil, and it shot out of the hot earth rapidly. It usually grew tall and eared well in the wet seasons. In the dry seasons it grew up slender and the ears were spindly.

Father, Mitchell Stuart   *(Courtesy Jesse Stuart Collection, Forrest C. Pogue*
Special Collections Library, Murray State University, Murray, Kentucky)

"During the summer he farmed...[using] mules, for they could
stand up better on the rough hillsides."

But the tobacco fields! I can never forget them. Long tobacco rows winding around a steep hillside and the hot sun streaming down. The smell of burdock, pursley, smartweed and cockleburs! The smell of the hot parched soil worming up between the toes. The peck-peck of bright-handled gooseneck hoes all day long! I can hear them now. The slender bodies of girls in motion all day long with the gooseneck hoes—the brown-faced stalwart men tearing up the soil with a cutter—leading the women many paces hoeing the tobacco. In March we sowed the tobacco seedbeds, and the eastern Kentucky hills were lined with white canvas strips over tobacco beds in early spring. Then we caught the early spring rains for tobacco setting.

We cultivated the crop until the broad leaves met across the balk. And from the middle of the season until frost, we had to worm the tobacco plants. That is, pull off the long green worms that love "the weed" the same as man, and pull them in two and throw them back into the furrow—the thin green rinds of their bodies and the amberish fluids within. We suckered the stalks too, pulling out the little sideshoots that tried to grow between the leaves of the plant and the main stalk. In the fall we cut the tobacco before heavy frost hit it and hauled it on a sled to an open-air barn where it would cure well. Then when moist autumn days came, when the leaves were damp, we pulled off the leaves and did them up in hands. So many leaves were put in a bundle, with a leaf tied around the stem ends. It was now ready to market. We hauled it often twenty miles and sold it for three, four, five and nine cents, and ten cents a pound for the best. That was a good price—ten cents—but that was for the best tobacco. The tobacco crop is the farmer's money crop in the eastern Kentucky hills.

Regardless of all the work we had to do, my father always took time to hunt. Hunting was his recreation. All the Stuarts loved guns. They loved to carry them. He would say: "Well, a man's kindly got to keep the brush cut back from the door and the rabbits whipped away." He did his part doing both. He would go out and hunt all day long. When I was big enough, I went with him. When he had killed all the rabbits I could carry, he would laugh. That was my job, to pick up the rabbits after he shot them and carry them along.

"Men from cities don't know how to hunt," he would say, "for all their fine guns, hunting coats and kennel-bred dogs. I can take Black-Boy and the old single-barrel and trim any of them. It only fires one time and I know I have to be sure of that shot."

In the early spring, about the time that crops were getting under way the most, the big revival meetings would start. One of these meetings usually lasted from two to five weeks, it depended on how many people needed salvation. The mountain way is a man is saved or he isn't saved. And every time a new revival is held, some women are saved over again. That is because something is done contrary to the Bible in the meantime, maybe they have said something slanderous about another woman. But anyway, the only thing for them to do is "get right" with God again. And they do it, sometimes by praying hard for three to seven nights successively. When the burden is rolled away, they shout again like they did when they were saved before. Sometimes these meetings last nearly all night. It all depends on how many are wrestling with the Devil and about to win. The next day the men are sleepy and drowse at the plow. The women nod over the churn.

I can remember the cold winter night when my father and my mother wrestled with the Devil. Five Baptists participated in the preaching. I think the Devil was completely whipped that night, and had he been there they would have hanged him to the ceiling and filled him full of holes. Anyway there were many powerful threats made against him that night. I was scared—my sister and I sat on the back seat and wondered what it was all about. But my father and mother wrestled the Devil. They won. The next day a hole was chopped in the ice. They were baptized. "It must be done soon," said one of the ministers. "It is high time we are whipping the Devil." This happened in Kentucky about twenty years ago. "Times are changing," the old men would say back then, "the way people are doing nowadays. I don't know what this world is a-comin' to. Back yander in my day it was different." Oh, if you old men could arise from your graves today and note the change, what would you think? The radio, the automobile and the air mail would all be a puzzle to you.

From the time I began to remember, Cedar Riffles impressed me very much. I can remember vividly hearing the water howling over the stony riffles on the quiet starry nights. I can remember the way the wind howled around the shack and through the cedar tops. These scenes made me love loneliness—the howling wind in the cedar needles and the barking of squirrels and foxes and hound dogs at night; flocks of wild geese going over in the shapes of letters, L's, W's, I's and V's, with their honk-honking cries floating high above the brown autumn fields. These were sounds and sights of beauty but they were things of loneliness. It made one long for something beyond the hills.

I can still see the winter sun obscured by the flocks of crows— black shiny things between one and the sun—great trains of them. They settled on a late ungathered field of corn and wiped it out if the farmer did not shoot into them. They kept many guards in the tall trees around the fields. The guards would exchange places every few minutes with the crows on the ground. These would become guards and the crows in the trees would fly down and eat. But these black birds shining in the icy air and their caw-caws against the wind were things to be remembered. I can still hear the winter wind in the lonesome treetops way back in the hills, where the houses are far apart and the people are few in number. The lonesome wind ties a family together. Men must not be faint-hearted and women must endure hardships along with the men.

And then there are pictures of those snow-covered fields lodged in the album of my brain—the sundowns over the snowy hill that left a red radiance in the sky, maybe with a black snag on a ridgetop caught against it, a snowbird picking in the dead weed tops, a red moon coming up over a patch of autumn-red oak trees—these things I still remember.

I remember my trips to the coal bank with my father—the cap

with a lamp above the bill that sat back on his head. When we went under the hill, I rode in the coal buggy. My father pushed me along. It was great fun to ride in a coal buggy back into the darkness under a hill. The bank rats would come to meet us. Then they would shy away. My father would feed them. He would say: "Don't shoo them away, Son, they are my friends. If it had not been for them, you would have no father today. They warned me when the left entry of this bank fell in. I got out just in time. Then the whole thing caved in."

It was true that the rats had saved him. They are friends to the miners. They warn them when danger is near. They will not stay in the mine. They can be seen running out. He always kept a little drink upon a bank post. The rats noddled over it if he didn't. But after he wrestled with the Devil that night, he would say: "I ain't got no more use for licker. I wiped the slate clean."

After he spent his day in the mine, he would come home and feed and get in wood to last that night and the next day. Then came those fine evenings by the winter fireside—popcorn, roasted potatoes, chestnuts, hickory nuts and walnuts. Mom would be knitting socks and sweaters and the lazy cat would be playing with the yarn. And she pieced many quilts on winter evenings. I remember she taught me a few poems before I knew one letter from the other. One went something like this:

> Mother's knitting stockings,
> Pussy's got the ball;
> Oh, don't you think that winter
> Is pleasanter than all?

II

We moved from Cedar Riffles on a sled. It was a winter day when we moved. Snow lay heavy on the ground and a yoke of oxen pulled the sled with everything we had loaded on it. Swarms of snowbirds flew among the leafless boughs of the oak trees and alighted among clumps of ragweed along the roadside. They were hunting for ragweed seeds to fill their empty craws.

"Cattle are powerful things," my father would say over and over again, "watch old Berry get down there and pull. Lay over there, Buck, and quit that a-crowdin' Berry. That Buck is a lazy ox. I wish I had another one as good as Berry to match. I'd tear down hillsides with them."

" *...a yoke of oxen pulled the sled with everything we had loaded on it.*"
(Courtesy *The Courier-Journal*)

My mother drove a horse hitched to another sled. We moved along behind my father. My sister sat beside me on the seat by my mother. We wanted to sit too close to her and her elbows hit our shoulders when she reined the horse. Straw was around our feet. A lap robe was over our legs and tucked well up around our waists.

The snow hit us in the face. The wind pierced our clothing but we did not care. We had been accustomed to places where the wind whistled through the undaubed cracks of a house.

Our new destiny was a log house in W-Hollow. The creek got its name because it curved like the letter W. And our place was to be on the tip-most of the middle prong of the W. Woods came up to our house on all sides. "We'll have to clear cropping lands," my parents said together. "We must start in a new place and clean it up for somebody else." Well, this is what we always did. Clear up a farm and then move on. I was introduced to the ax and sprouting hoe at six, the plow at eleven. There are no vacations for children on the wooded hillside Kentucky farms.

It was from the new home my sister and I started to school. We walked two miles to and from the old log schoolhouse at Plum Grove. There were wild plum trees all around the schoolhouse, and the thorns there kept getting in our feet and giving the teacher trouble picking them out. So he and two of his larger students brought axes one day and saws. They cut the plum trees down and dragged them into a pasture field, then raked the ground and carried the leaves there too. They burned this pile later.

Our way to school led over a desolate country path. We had to go through two old orchards, two patches of red-oak timber and one long pasture field where we dared not wear red. There was a bull in the pasture. My sister became my boss—too much so. She was three years my senior. I couldn't let my hands get dirty; she told on me. Every time I tried to do some miraculous thing before the other students, she told on me, such as jumping off the highest fence post or eating the most apples. It was a daily thing to hear her tell at home, "Mom, Jesse got a whippin' today. He hit Bill Weaver with an apple core. He tore down the girls' playhouse. He got into Mrs. Collins' apples. He tore down a doodle of Mr. Wheeler's cane hay by running and tumbling over it. He even said a bad word." She was the direct cause of my mother examining my neck and ears every morning before I went to school. And I have heard Mom say so many times: "Son, even if your clothes are a little bad, I'll keep them clean for you, and you must keep your neck and ears and face and hands clean."

Plum Grove School, 1917. Jesse is on the extreme right of the bottom row. His sister Sophia is standing center back row. Miss Elta Cooper, teacher.   (From *Jesse: The Biography of an American Writer*, by H. Edward Richardson, McGraw-Hill, 1984)

The school terms only lasted five months in Kentucky then. And I'll declare it was the finest place to me I'd ever been up to that time. It was a place where I saw a lot of people. Thirty or thirty-five people were a multitude for me to see together. And the things called words and people—there was something fascinating about both. Words are marvelous things. They are something which you can do anything with but take hold of with your hands. You can put them on paper and they mean something. I tried them out first by writing notes. I wrote one to a girl and was severely whipped for it. The girls sat on one side of the schoolhouse and the boys on the other, and I threw the note across to Mabel Jones.

I remember the first poem I ever memorized. It was in an old

primer. I loved these words and they have been with me for the last
twenty-three years:

> Oh, Mother, look at the moon,
> She's riding so high,
> For tonight she looks
> Like a lamp in the sky.
> Last night she was smaller
> And shaped like a bow,
> But now she is larger
> And round like an O.

It was at this place that I saw the seasons come and go. The
spring came. We plowed the soil. My mother and I worked in the
field beside my father. She was strong and had more endurance
than most men. When we were hoeing, I could not keep a row of
corn up with her. She led always many paces even when men worked
with us. My sister did the housework. She was only a child. At
night my father and I did the work around the place. We fed the
hogs, mules and got in wood and kindling. We milked the cows
and drew water out of the well. After the evening meal was over,
we sat around and told stories of fighting men of the past, of ghosts
and places where truthful people had seen them. We talked about
the old hunting days and the big game our people had killed. Now
it was not here for us to kill.

At an early age on one of my walks in the Kentucky hills, I
thought a great thought. I believe today it was a great thought. It
was this: People last only a short time. Nature plays a trick on
them. She stays young forever. The leaves come forth on the trees
at spring's rebirth. They flower during the summer season. They
wither in the autumn and tumble to the ground. Then the trees rest
for a night—winter. Again they awake with spring's rebirth and
flower in their season. Not so with man. His youth is springtime—
middle age his summer. He flowers then. Autumn comes and his
flesh begins to wither, his shoulders lower, his beauty decays, and

then the winter comes when he sleeps. He awakes to flower no more. His work is done. Night comes when man works no more.

Well, the seasons came over and over again in the hills and these thoughts returned just as often to me. They have inspired me. They have told me to flower in my season. To bear in mind autumn would come and winter would follow, the time when man would work no more.

I have said the seasons came over and over again in the hills. We farmed the same land each year and cleared just a little new land. We all worked hard because existence in the hills compels whole families to work hard. When the grim outlines of the hills cut sharp against the sky and the ground lay white with snow, it was Mr. Cricket: if you dance all summer, you'll starve all winter. Go, thou sluggard, like the ant and be wise. Remember the fable of the ant and the grasshopper. Better lay up something for a rainy day.

If early frost blighted the berries and killed the fruit, food was more scarce in the hills. If corn crops and potato crops were short during the same season, existence was terrible. I can remember years when such things happened and the table never held any too much food. If the seasons passed over without mishap, we had food to feed the hogs. The way of hill life—feast today and famine tomorrow.

Rent was raised on my father. Twelve dollars in cash was too much to pay a month for the use of one-hundred acres of land and pasture for his cattle, and all the land he wanted to cultivate. Again we were ready to go. We had cleared that farm for somebody and we were ready to move on. We were willing to move away from our neighbors. One house was in sight down the creek from us. We were living too close. "This place is too much like town to suit me," said my mother. It was true our chickens had mixed with our neighbors'. Their Plymouth Rocks and our Gray Games had actually crossed. We were ready to go. Our family had increased three new members while we were living here. It was early January when we were getting ready to go, but we were delayed. Herbert, the boy next to me, "took down" with pneumonia. I recall vividly the January day with a little bit of sun when my father sat on a box under a leafless apple tree. He wrung his hands and said: "It is too unbearable to stand. If we could have only had a doctor here in time to have saved him."

Another scene I hate to recall was seeing a spring wagon with a pine box roped to the bed and two mules hitched to it. And then the short train of buggies and wagons and spring wagons that followed. We had to go five miles to my grandfather Hilton's farm for burial. He was there, his hair white and tousled by the blowing wind. He called to the driver who drove the leading team, "Right this way." The driver drove out across a little field and all the other teams followed. It was the best way to get to the top of the hill. My grandfather had cut the wires of his pasture fence. We saw the fresh dirt thrown up near some pine trees. I remember the songs they sang, some of the words the preacher said. I remember how cold my feet got standing in the mud and how the people cried. All of the others in the family cried but I did not. I cried when I went back home and he was gone. Many people offered consolation. The preacher offered the most. Blessings be on the country preacher even if he is sneered at for being uncouth and his sermons often full of loopholes. Many of these men work for no pay. They will not take money for their services. That shows their heart is in their work.

That night at the fireside Mom said: "Well, I feel free in moving on now. Herbert is buried on land that belongs to my father. He will not sell it while he lives. It will be part mine by inheritance at his death, and for my part I shall take the place where the grave is. You know I just couldn't stand to move on and leave his grave on property owned by other people. It is foolish to be that way but that is the way I feel. We don't own any land to bury him on, but I can rest tonight knowing that his body lies on my father's soil. We have to move now. I can stand this place no longer."

III

The same spring wagon that hauled my brother away took our furniture on the road again. I led the cows, called the hounds and later came back for an express-load of chickens. Our new place was the last log house in the head of W-Hollow. It was the most desolate place I have ever seen. Those were the darkest days I have ever seen. Another brother was born there the spring after we arrived. My mother was not able to work much. My father "took sick" there. Our corn rotted in the cold wet ground, for spring was late that year. Heavy rains fell on the lowlands which we were to cultivate. And the young corn that did get up through the sour earth was cut down by the crayfish. The fruit was killed that year. The cattle took murrain. It was a bad season, but we didn't give up; we battled on. My mother would never give up. There was no such phrase in the language for her as "give up."

She picked the scattered berries—gathered a few apples that escaped the spring frost and made jelly from the wild grapes. We cut the tall grass along creek banks for the cows that winter. We made a supply of baskets from the tall oak timbers. I cut the timber and split it. My mother wove the baskets. I sold them. When I sold them, she always requested that I tell the purchaser that my father made the baskets. She was an artist at work. There is no question about it. Some of those baskets were built so endurably that years later, after I had finished college, I saw one I had sold when I was a boy. It had been used as a feed basket too. I had unpleasant thoughts of a hard winter and a woman's hand when I saw it. All the time my mother labored on baskets she would say: "This is going to be a hard winter and your father is sick." It was a hard winter too. This was the winter of 1917. Snow lay on the ground all winter and an icy crust was frozen over its top. Birds died by the hundreds and rabbits became so lean they shrank to the bone. Cattle became lean. The dark days—the soldier trains passing through on the other side of the bony ridge of hills. Men would shout from the windows: "We are going to get the Kaiser."

The spring of 1918 came. The winter was breaking. My

youngest brother was the victim of pneumonia fever and lasted only a few days. He had died the same way that Herbert Lee had died. I had said viciously that I would never return to that pine grove on my grandfather's farm. I had said I would never go back where Herbert's grave was. But I did return. I followed for six miles through the mud this time. It was in February. The mud was deep in many places and the wagon went in to the hubs. I drove a team of black horses. We went up the same old road to the pine grove. Grandfather was standing by the fence again with the wires let down. The same preacher was there. He was the Reverend Oaks. There were two mounds beneath those pines now. We left the hill. My horses ran away for they were turned towards home. I let them run. After they were willing to quit running and became very tired, I made them run more.

Some of you will remember the heavy snow that fell in April that spring. My father and I were walking to the barn. I refused to step in his tracks any more, as I had done before when there came deep snows. I made a path of my own. I said to myself: "You are a man of the hills. You have let them hold you in. You were born among them—you'll die among them. You'll go to that pine grove where we went less than two months ago. You will lie there forever in that soil. Your night will then have come when man's work is over. Since You have brought us into the world, isn't there some escape from fevers? Can't we move to a place where we can get a doctor easier? Two of my brothers are dead and sleeping over there by that pine grove. Don't they have the same right as I have to be here? Now they are gone, I repeat. Life for them was a tragedy. They had better not have cost my mother the pain of birth—dying young when it can be prevented. I have had pneumonia twice and typhoid twice. I was able to survive them. It was because I was strong. Now these hills will not always hold me. I shall go beyond them some day."

Again my mother said: "I cannot stand this place any longer. We must move on." My father rented another place. We had cleaned this farm up and run some new fences. We had made it possible for other people to live there. So it was time for us to move on.

IV

The spring wagon was loaded again and we moved to another part of W-Hollow. The house was a log house upon a steep bank. There was a sulphur spring under some beech trees in the front yard and hollyhocks grew all around it. It was a flower garden surrounded by rabbits and sassafras. But we had no time to play with flowers. Spring was on us and we had to get land cleared for spring plowing. We had to get corn and potatoes in the ground. They were the staples and other things mattered less—corn and potatoes mean life in the hills.

Our crops that year did exceedingly well for the amount of time we had to get the ground ready. We filled a large crib with corn. The potatoes yielded abundantly. We had to rush the corn over the last time and lay it by so we could enter school on the 25th of July. But we always hurried the corn over the last time to get to school the first day. Our road had to be mown out to keep us from getting wet by the dewy weeds. It took my father several days to mow three miles of country path with a scythe.

We started off to school early in the morning to get there in time. On our way it wasn't anything strange to meet a fox on the road. They liked to travel our path, it seemed. Squirrels would ramble through the heavy-leafed branches over our heads and bark. Pheasants would wallow in a sand hole in our path and quails would call from the weed fields. Usually when we got home on winter evenings, the stars would be shining. And usually I would have to stay in for fighting, and Mary and Sis would be afraid to go home without me. It happened that I was never the teacher's pet. We only had one teacher and he taught all the grades from the first to the eighth.

In the autumn months when we went to the country schoolhouse three miles away, during the heavy autumn rains when the creeks were swollen, I would have to carry my sisters across the streams. My eldest sister was delicate. She didn't look like a girl used to the hardships of hill life. Mary, my second sister, was brown-skinned and could walk and climb like a boy. She was tireless when it came to pinches of life that called for endurance.

My eldest sister was one of the best students in the school. It is a sad reflection but a true one when I say that at the age of eleven I knew as much about nouns, adjectives and adverbs as I know today. Those parts of speech appealed to me. I loved grammar and argued with my teachers over the way words were used in sentences. I nearly memorized my grammar book.

During the summers when I was nine and ten, I worked for the man we had rented our farming land from. I got twenty-five cents each day. I worked all the week until Saturday at noon for $3.15. This I took home and gave to my mother. She got many little things with it that she had to have. This was before 1918, however. My work was digging sweet potatoes carefully and sacking them in sawdust for seed potatoes. Then too, I dug many strawberry plants and cleaned them for resetting. I used a short-handled mattock. I had to do much stooping and it kept my head dizzy. There was the rule the old farmer made to me when I went to work: "You must not sit down on the job. The minute you do and I see you—you quit."

Nearly every Saturday, Fielding Flaughtery would get drunk. He would see that he had too much. He would climb up on the express bed and ask me to haul him home when he passed out. He knew that I could never lift him there and he knew he was getting dead drunk, so he always climbed into the express bed himself. I would go and unhitch the mules from the willows beside the creek and fasten them to the express. I would throw several sacks of sweet potatoes into the express bed beside Fielding, throw in the sacks of wet strawberry plants, the mattocks, spades and hoes. I would run the mules over the bumpy potato ridges and laugh when the sacks of potatoes rolled against him. I rode upon the spring seat and laughed and laughed. I would haul him to the cottage where he lived with his mother. If she was not there, I would back the end of the express down and slide him out onto the grass carefully, as I would a barrel of salt or any dead weight. I would go into the house and get a quilt to spread over him. If his mother was there, we would both lift and tug to get him down to the ground from the express bed without hurting him in any way.

Many of the old men would say to me: "Son, don't let him get you to drinking licker. I remember him when he was a young man. He was the best thought-of man in this country. Now look at him. He's got to be a sot. He used to have plenty of money. Now he has nothing. He drinks it all up. Now, don't you let him fool you." This was true. At one time he owned over five-hundred acres of fertile hill land. He had money in the bank. But he spent his bank account for whisky. He began to sell the timber off his land to buy whisky, and finally he began to sell off his land to buy whisky after all the timber was gone. "That man will die drunk," the old men would say.

We had felt obligated to Fielding when we lived on his place. I worked for him then. When we moved I quit work. When I knew I was going to quit, I sat down on the job before him. "Up!" he said. I remained still. He didn't fire me. I heard him tell another workhand before the day was over that I was a strong youngster for ten years of age. He said he hoped to hold me to work for him the next summer. But he called me "lazybones" part of the time and "contrary bones" part of the time.

At twelve years old, I was cutting corn in the Riverton bottoms, in the fertile Ohio River valley. We got war prices for the work, twenty-five cents a shock. When that job was over, I found work that winter in a timber job. I could saw and chop equal to any of the woodcutters. I worked with my father first. Later I worked with Wilburn Crump, a Negro. We first cut saw logs. After the logs were cut, we made the smaller timber into crossties. We got eight cents for making a number-three tie, ten cents for making a number-two, and twelve cents for making a number-one. Two men would average about thirty ties per day for six days a week.

The war came on now. My father got work with the C. & O. It paid him big money. He could hardly believe that he was making four dollars per day. He contracted us a fifty-acre farm. There was no house on it. We were to pay the three-hundred dollars by part payments.

The last place we had moved to was getting too well cleaned up for us to remain longer. We were getting ready to leave again anyway. And now we would go to a home of our own. When we cleaned it up, we would stay. We would build a house on it and keep making the house better.

Grandfather Hilton and I (with the aid of a carpenter to build the foundation, put in the windows and hang the doors) built the house. It took us from July until December. It is the house we live in today. I remember the sweat and curses that went into that house better than anybody else, unless it is Grandpa. He was seventy then and I was fifteen. He would get mad and throw his tools over the hill and I would have to go and get them. The hard thing for us was to make two stonemasons out of two supposed-to-be-carpenters. Grandpa changed the plans of the house to suit himself. He said if he was to build it he had the right to make it the way he pleased. He wanted to build a chimney in the center of the house. There was a place where men had quarried sandstone for chimneys. We went to this sandstone, drilled a hole in it, and dynamited. We picked out the stones and smoothed them off with dull axes. Then we hauled these quarried stones into the floorless house. We used a block and tackle to lift them up to build the chimney. Sometimes four strands of new rope would snap like shoestrings and the stone would fall. We would get new rope and do it over again. Two of us erected the chimney. It was work, too. Though the house was unfinished, we moved into it in November. We were glad to leave the place where we had been living. We were ready to go again. Just before we made this last move, my mother gave birth to her seventh child, a girl, Glennis Juanita.

V

Mom was able to move after the birth of her last child. And we were all anxious to move. We loaded the old spring wagon for the last time. We moved to where we live today. It is a place back in the hills with no houses near. We began to work on land of our own. There was a great difference, too. My father would say: "I've spent my strength on other men's land. Now I am old and I've got land of my own." We cleared the thickets. We farmed them two years. Then we sowed them in grass. We set fruit trees on the south hill slope. We set strawberries in new land. We made improvements on the place that was a wilderness before we moved there.

Home at last. And it was good to have a home. It is a place where wind blows off the pine tree tops and passes over our house. We smell pine fragrance in the winter wind there. It is a lonely place. It is desolate. But it is home. And it is good to have a home on a little piece of land where one can bury his own dead. It is good to hear the chickens cackle and see the wrens coming back each year to build in the smokehouse. It is good to hear the martins building in a box in early spring. And best of all it is good to see the hollyhocks blooming in the front yard.

I still like to see the fields of corn and hear the blades rustle in the wind. These things make a home. The pumpkins in the field, the hay stacked on the hill. And the smell of the hot July soil is good for the senses. The smell of sour vines, smartweeds, ragweeds and cockleburs. The smell of silking corn and of feathery tassels.

There are scenes where we live now that I have not forgotten. The white clouds drifting high above the pines. The radiance left after sundowns over the black-oak ridges. There is the tall grass and the sassafras sprouts rustled by the wind. The friendly pine-tree fingers greet one. There is something about it all—this drowsy place—something ghostly about the sound of rustling leaves and the song of the wind and the crickets. There is something about the floating of white clouds above pines and sun flares behind the oak trees. There is something to it that leaves an image on the album of the brain and, like the yellow flame of an old lamp, it flickers often but will not go out.

Chapter III
Opossums and Poetry

After the first crops were laid by on our own land, there was part of the summer left. I would go and find a job. I needed the money. I went four miles over the bony ridge to the little town of Greenup. The town was in the process of being overhauled. There were electric wires being put upon poles. The alleys were being paved and the main streets of the town. The contractors were crying for help. They wanted farm boys, I heard. Well, this was the place to get work.

I began to work for John Pancake. My work was taking a pick and tearing old stones out of the street. They were buried under dirt that had been smeared with oil every July to hold down the dust. The work paid well, I thought. I made thirty cents an hour. I worked ten hours a day and on Saturday until noon. That was really hard work and the walk back home made my legs stiff at night and my hands hurt. One day we were working under an elm shade. Three husky farm boys "white-eyed" on the job and asked the boss for their money. An old man seventy years old working beside me said: "Look at that, won't you. Them big strong devils won't work when they can get it. That's what's a-matter with our country today—jist sicha fellers as them. They need their blocks knocked off. Then they'd have a little sense maybe."

It was on the following day some extravagant man bought a watermelon and shared it with the crew. A boy standing on the street said to me: "Hit me on the nose. I dare you." He put his finger on his nose. I hadn't finished the melon but I let the piece I was eating cover his whole face. "You are fired!" shouted the boss. He was standing behind a tree. Then the old man that had talked about the men that "white-eyed" the day before said: "What is this world a-coming to, anyway? They didn't act that a-way when I was a shaver a-kicking up my heels." In two hours I was working for the concrete gang. They didn't know I had been fired from the other gang. I told that boss the other fellow had sent me there—said he was working too many men as it was. "W'y hell! I can't work any more men. Oh, let me see. I can use you over there dumping sacks of concrete into the mixer. How is your flesh? Can it stand concrete against it in July? You know that damn cement is hard on the skin when you sweat. It takes off the hide." "I can stand it if the other men have stood it," I told him. I got the job.

September came and the wires had been tied to the tall poles. "Them are live wires," said an old man, "touch one and your soul will be blasted into eternity. Funny how smart people are getting to be. This world can't last much longer." The main street was a white walk of smooth concrete, and the yellow elm leaves were skipping along on it. The concrete mixer was moved around in front of a schoolhouse. When I saw that schoolhouse, I had many thoughts. I would go home and get my sister and we would come to this place to school. It was a beautiful place, a bluish-gray brick building with a spire shooting above the tops of the elm trees. I saw the children going there and they were all well-dressed. I wanted to go there. I told the boss to pay me off.

The next Monday morning Sis and I walked under the tall door when the bell sounded. I remember hearing a red-headed girl say, "I get mixed up when I talk to the teacher about the bell. You know, when I sleep late of a morning and have to talk to her about it. I don't know how to say that ring, rang and rung. I get them all mixed up. Oh, what is the use of all this schooling anyway? I'll clerk in the old man's store someday anyway!" I thought that was funny. She was afraid of three words. I would just say one. What did it matter, right or wrong? I wouldn't be afraid, at least.

The students did not take to us very well. I remember a boy saying, "That Stuart girl is right good-looking if she had good clothes to wear." One day a skinny boy asked me what I knew about the price of eggs. I asked him what he knew about the length of mattock handles. The students standing near all laughed. That was a great place, I thought. I saw many boys wearing fine clothes I envied. I wanted a long red sweater like Burl Mavis wore and a necktie like the one I had seen Fred Mansfield wear. I wanted many things I could not get. When I ate my lunch that I brought wrapped in a newspaper, I always got away from the other boys. I went around by the old flour mills. I didn't want them to see biscuits with meat and mustard between, and the corn bread.

1922-23 Greenup High School freshman class. Jesse is seated in window on far left.   (Courtesy *Irene Griffith, Greenup, Kentucky*)

Schoolwork was not hard for me. And I would hear the boys by the houses along the streets tell their mothers that the work was terribly hard at school. Some spoke of the teachers being unfair. That was funny too. We walked eight miles each day and helped to do the work at home. When we had an algebra test, Burl Mavis sat beside me and called me Stuart. At other times he told me to get the hayseed out of my hair. The greatest enjoyment I could have was to work a problem when the rest of the class had failed. I did this a few times. One day Miss Hamilton said: "There is a Patrick Henry in this room. Now you just wait and see. To whom do you think I refer?"

"Oh, you are referring to me," shouted many of the boys.

"No," said she, "there he is."

She pointed to me. After that the students would pass me and giggle: "Patrick Henry, how about 'Give me liberty or give me death'?" they would say. That year I made three B plus's and one A. My sister made four A's. But that place was great, I thought, and I'd like to be a teacher in a big school like that. A teacher there was something.

I asked some of the old men about how old the schoolhouse was. I had noticed that the steps were wearing thin. "I don't know," said one. "My Grandpa Jake Filson went there. It is mighty old, Son. I just can't tell you. But I know things have changed mightily since I was a boy and went there." I learned later that it was one of the oldest schools on the Ohio River. Then I asked Miss Lykins one day about the oldest college in America. She said it was Harvard. I told her I wanted to go there to college someday. She looked at me in a funny way. Then I asked her more questions. She was very kind.

My father would say now: "Yes, go on to school and get an education. I want you to do something with your head as well as your hands. I don't want you to have to work like I have. Go on to school." And my mother would say, "My oldest children are in high school," when she wrote a letter to one of her brothers or to her sister.

The bell rang the hour school closed. Miss Lykins met us in her office and gave us our report cards. She said: "The school year is over now. I hope you have enjoyed it. Here are your report cards."

That summer I went back to the farm. It was not the same place. I wanted to think about the town over the bony ridge—Greenup. I could see that white concrete and the yellow leaves drifting over it. I could see the happy, well-dressed girls going along talking about nothing in particular. There was that flashy red sweater Burl Mavis wore. I could see Fred Mansfield's pretty necktie. Lord, there was lots to live for and the world was big.

I plowed in the oats early that spring before school was out. They were green on the hillsides now. The young rabbits played among them. The cows that had been used to woodland pasture stepped out on timothy and orchard grasses this summer. The martins came back to their boxes. The honeybees played over the wild plum trees that grew in a cove at the back of the house. But these things were not the same. When I turned the furrows on the hillsides, I did not think of the tall corn that would soon be growing there—nor did I dream of the snow on the ground and the big white ears of corn in the crib with a split-bottom feed basket at the front door. I didn't care much about the crows and the cowbirds that followed the furrow after me. "Them cowbirds are funny things," said Uncle Rank Larks. "They lay their eggs in other birds' nests. The other birds hatch out their young and raise them. They are durn funny things."

My father worked away now. I was the boss on the farm. I planted the corn. I planted the potatoes. I sowed the cane hay. I prepared the land for tobacco. It was a big job for me. My mother, my sister Mary, and my brother James worked in the fields with me. I did the plowing and I selected the grounds for certain grains. And since I was boss my orders were to clean the corn and tobacco well the first time—get every weed. "Don't leave a weed in any row. Clean the stumps well. I like to see the fields clean. The corn isn't smothered then."

"There is a hurricane of weeds in that piece up in the hollow. We must get to it soon, Son," my mother would say. My father would say: "That boy of mine is tearing that place all to pieces. I'd put him against any man in the country. He's worked them mules down lean." Uncle Rank Larks would say, "Mitch Stuart, with a family to work like yourn, you ought to be independent rich." When I sat down at the table at home, it was: "Now children, eat something that will stick to the ribs. Don't mince around over the sweet stuff too much. You'll be hungry before night comes."

I wanted to get the corn laid by as soon as possible this summer. I had heard of a military camp where boys got their way paid there and back and all expenses while they were there. I put in my application. I was fifteen and the first boy in Greenup County to try it.

That summer was a hot one. But we had plenty of rain and plenty of weeds. The corn shot up out of the earth. It was a fine season. The beans covered the cornstalks and the pumpkins lay over the fields. It was all over and the season was a glorious one. Mom would pickle her beans now, can the peaches and berries and later make apple butter and wild grape jelly. There are so many things for a woman to do on a farm about this time of year. And my mother was called over the country to help in time of sickness. She would get out of bed at midnight and go. It did not matter, rain or shine, when a child was sick she would go. And with all the time it took to do this work, she found time to work on her quilts. She would go out and find a wild flower she liked. Then she would make the same kind of flower with quilt pieces. She loved to do it. She would sit far into the night looking at the beauty in a new design she was creating.

After the season was done with, I took the mules to the pasture and gave them their freedom. Their manes and tails could grow out now and their hoofs grow long. I did not care. I was ready to leave for a place below Louisville, Kentucky. I wanted the trip. I had never been fifty miles away from home before, and this was three hundred. And I collected the mattocks, spades and plows and hoes and put them in the shed. The season was over.

The trip to Camp Knox was the trip of my life. I took the longest way possible on government money. I went to North Vernon, Indiana, then I turned directly south to Louisville. At Camp Knox I found that a fifteen-year-old farm boy, six feet tall and weighing one-hundred and ten pounds, was too much out of place. "Did you bring a bottle along, Gawky?" said a gentleman from a north Ohio town. "I don't know whether you would call it a bottle or not," I said, "we'll see." I pulled a blank pistol from my pocket, which I had brought for curiosity. He made his way rapidly through the crowd. When the other boys saw the gun was a fake, they laughed. But Camp Knox was a torture to me. I was put in the awkward squad for throwing my rifle to a captain when he asked for one. I was kept there three days for that offense. I was given a cold mud bath for throwing a bucket of water on the corporal in charge of the barracks. I was placed on K.P. for coming to reveille with my shoes unlaced and leggings left in the barracks. I did not conform very well to military rules and regulations. Then the fellows tossed me up and let me fall back on a blanket. I went through the blanket to the ground. I was sore for weeks. They only laughed about it. That was why I threw the water on the corporal. He had a hand in it. I actually cried when I was put on the awkward squad for speaking at attention. But it did no good. The army is no place for tears. But I excelled in doing exercises and shooting. I loved to do them. I learned them all and the counts they were done in.

Jesse at Camp Knox
(From *Jesse: The Biography of an American Writer*,
by H. Edward Richardson, McGraw-Hill, 1984)

When I reached home again, I was glad to see the hills. I went out and looked over the corn. And I said: "My, how this corn has grown! It is as big as it will ever be. The cane hay is ready to cut. The potatoes are ready to dig. And it will soon be time to start off to school again." I was glad to get back home and hold my brother and sisters spellbound about Camp Knox and Louisville. I had only been in Louisville twice and that was passing through both times. But I had big tales to tell about everything but K.P. and the awkward squad. I never mentioned them.

Autumn came again. The oak trees in northeast Kentucky were shedding their leaves. The flying leaves were of many colors. The crows began to fly in pilfering trains over the country. And wild geese went southward with many a honking cry. It was all beautiful back there and the best place in the world after all. The corn was getting ready to be cut now. The brown fields of heavy corn looked very pleasant. It was the victory of hard labor.

My sophomore year in Greenup High School was a happy time in my life. When I went back to Greenup, I felt just about the equal of Burl Mavis. "I would be better than Burl," I let myself think, "if I only had some clothes." I had an idea—two of them. I could buy my own books, my sister's books and buy myself some clothes. I would ask my father's permission to make crossties to sell from the timber on the farm. I would hunt the fur-bearing animals in those surrounding hills with old Black-Boy. I could make money. I was too tall now to wear knee pants. And I was getting too old to wear them now.

I started making crossties in our barn lot. I could make them well, I found out. I would cut down a black-oak tree. Then I would measure eight and a half feet. I would hack that place with the ax, trim the branches from the tree and measure another length and so on. Then, I would measure the thickness of the crosstie on the body of the tree—hack little lines to score by. Then I would smooth down the sides with a broadax. My brother would help me to saw the ties apart. I would bark them and they would be ready for market. On a bet one day, I made twenty-two crossties and got them ready for the wagon. Many people doubt that but it is an actual fact. If you know anything about timber, you'll know that is a day's work. I made my father's timber up so rapidly that he stopped me. But I had fifty dollars now. I went to Ironton, Ohio, and bought myself a long suit of clothes. It was a gray tweed suit and cost me eighteen dollars. I bought shirts, ties and socks. I gave my sister some money and bought our books.

There came a frost and hit the corn. The blades turned white and began to fall. "Save that feed, Son. The cattle will need it this winter. You will have to miss school long enough to cut that knob piece of corn." "I'll cut it all on Saturday," I said. That Saturday I dressed well to keep the blades from cutting my face and hands. I "railroaded" the corn from daylight until four o'clock that afternoon. I cut it twelve hills square on a steep hillside. I tied one middle band around the shocks and two outward bands to make it stand well. My father would not believe that I had cut fifty-four shocks until he counted them. He opened his eyes wider when I went back that night and cut twenty-four by moonlight. "Go to the store and get anything you want. My credit is good and nothing I've got is too good for a boy that will work like you." The corn was out of danger now. The frost-bitten blades were safe for the cattle. It is a great thing to have a strong body, I have often thought.

I would take Black-Boy and go into the woods at night. I would go alone for miles and miles. I would trust Black-Boy quicker than I would any person I knew. Black-Boy was a powerful cur. He had hound blood in him. "A little hound blood gives a dog a good nose." He had strong front legs, a heavy pair of shoulders, a thin body near his hips. He was built for speed, power and endurance. He was as vicious as he was powerful. I was not afraid to go anywhere with Black-Boy. I knew the kind of affection he had for me in a time of danger. Though he was nine years old now and his face was getting gray, his teeth were still good. On a night's hunt, I would take a lantern, a coffee sack, a mattock and a couple of books. I would go off in a silent dark hollow and tie the lantern to a tree. I would sit at the base of the tree and study plane geometry and read English—especially the poetry of Robert Burns. I would get interested and Black-Boy would tree. If he barked fast, I knew I must hurry. If he barked slowly, I took my time. When I got to him, sometimes he would be fighting an opossum. I would put it in the coffee sack and move on to another patch of woods. He would run and bark in an old field. I knew what that was. It was a skunk. I hated to handle them but there was the money. A skunk hide would bring from one to seven dollars.

This would go on some nights all night long. I have caught as many as eleven opossums with Black-Boy in one night. That was on a night when he didn't find a skunk. The scent of a skunk always hurt his nose. He could not smell as well afterwards. For miles and miles around my home, I knew where every persimmon tree of any importance was. I knew where the pawpaw patches were. I went to those places for opossums. I got them there. Black-Boy went just as strong at three o'clock in the morning as he did when we started, if he didn't run across a skunk. And one night I remember getting four skunks and one opossum. I made money that night. I hunted over those hills night after night during the autumn season.

There was loneliness in the dark hills when the wind stirred the withered leaves on the trees. It was music to me. It was poetry. It hangs to me better than a piece of clothing for it fits me well and will not wear out. Black-Boy's bark grew to be beautiful to my ear. It was the assurance of something in the darkness of a night. A dog's voice that you know out in a lonely place does you good to hear. Persimmon tree leaves and the yellow leaves on a poplar tree are beautiful at night when a dull moon is shining barely over the hilltop. A gray opossum in a persimmon tree is something you like to shake to the ground with a shower of small reddish leaves falling like a little shower of rain. And then when the rain fell it was the time to hunt. The forest is so silent. Opossums love quiet woods. They are afraid of wind in the brush or the rattle of dead leaves. And when the rain thug-thugs—slowly at night—the skunks come out to root their noses into the dirt in the old fields. But skunk scent at night will knock one down if it is raining, it is so strong.

Many boys asked me to let them hunt with me. I would not take them. They wanted to bring guns and shoot. They wanted to build fires in the woods and go away and leave them. I thought they didn't know how to hunt. I knew old Black-Boy wouldn't hunt with a bunch like that. He was too old at the trade. He would go back to the house. I would not hunt with any of them.

I sold the opossums. I sold them to the Negroes and I got the hides back. One shipment of fur I recall getting forty-three dollars for. Then there was the fun of hunting. The boys would say to me: "Where do you find all them opossums? We can't find them." "For two reasons," I would answer. "First, you don't know how to hunt. Second, your dog isn't any good. His nose is not made right. He has no hound blood in him." On windy nights man must seek the low quiet valleys for opossums. On still damp nights, the hilltops and the old fields. Again, you must keep your mouth shut and never crowd a dog. Go quietly like an Indian. Always keep in mind the pawpaw trees and the persimmon trees.

I would take Black-Boy when game began to get scarce in the black-oak hills and go into the old fields near the town of Greenup. There I found plenty of game. I sat down to figure it out. Fur-bearing creatures are not fools. They learn the fields that are molested less by man and dogs. After I had hunted a valley out, I would tell the boys where I had been getting the game. They were always silly enough to follow where I had gone.

This was the year that I began to try writing poetry. It was because of the wind I heard in the dead leaves and the loneliness of sounds at night, not to mention the influence Robert Burns had on me. This was my first year to study literature. I had the course under a Southern woman, Mrs. Robert Hatton. She read poetry well. She stressed Robert Burns because she loved his verse. I would read his poetry every spare minute I had. I carried his poems wherever I went. I thought I had never heard words more beautiful than those in "Flow Gently, Sweet Afton." It was sung in school once or twice each week. The sentiment of that song choked me, for I loved it deeply. And there was "Highland Mary," "John Anderson, My Jo," and "The Cotter's Saturday Night"—I feasted on the poetry of Robert Burns. It seemed as if something big in life had taken hold of me. I wanted to write poetry like Robert Burns. He was a Scottish plowboy. I read all about his life. I knew it didn't always take the boys that wore sweaters like Burl Mavis to do things. And my prayer, if I ever prayed one then, was to write poetry that would endure like the poetry of Robert Burns.

I would go home at night and tell my mother that I wanted to do something in life. I told her my plans at the milk gap every evening after spring came on and the cows were turned out on the grass. The second year of high school had taken hold of me tremendously. My mother would be surprised at the things I said to her. She would say: "You know, sometimes I have felt like I would just like to get out and go and go and go. I have felt that these hills could not hold me. And if I had been a man, I would have gone. But now, you see, I am a mother tied down with a family and I cannot go. I want to stay and take care of my children. They are all I have that I care anything about. I want to see them well-raised to be young men and women. And when they go out into the world, I want people to say there is a respectable family of children—the children of Martha Stuart. She tried her best to raise them right and she did."

We would talk on at the milk gap. I would try to milk a cow, and it would kick the bucket out of my hand. I would want to hit the cow with a stick. "You mustn't hit one of the cows. They feed you half you eat. The way you like milk and then hit a cow! Here, put my apron on and you can milk that cow. My cows are not used to men folks." I put the apron on. The cow stands perfectly still. Now I set the bucket on the ground and zig-zag two streams of white milk into the zinc two-gallon water bucket. "You are ruining these cows feeding them middlings and cow feed when the timothy is knee-high." "They are always right at this gap morning and night for the handful of middlings I feed them. I do not have to go through the wet weeds to hunt them. No one is here to get them since you go to school in the springtime now and your father works away. It is so lonesome to hunt the cows and hear the whippoorwills a-callin'."

It is lonesome to hear the whippoorwills calling and walk over the new-plowed fields in April. When I came in from school, I would pull off my shoes and slip into the silence of the evening woods. I would steal quietly. I would watch the young rabbits play in the pasture. I would hear the crows caw-caw in the pine trees. I would take a paper and pencil and go to the pine grove over from the house and write my themes. The teacher would say: "There is a flavor of the soil and a picture of the sky and the trees in your themes."

The time was here to sow lettuce and tobacco beds. It was the time to take the mules and go into the fields and plow all day long. James was big enough now to keep the stalks and sprouts cut ahead of the plow. But he was only six and when night came he would be very tired. We took our lunch to the field in a gallon lard bucket and tied it up to a locust limb with a string, to keep the ants out of it. We brought two bottles of milk and put them in a deep blue hole of creek water to keep it cool. When night came the sweaty mules were glad when they heard me say, "Whoa-ho, Jack and Barnie, whoa-ho." They stopped breathlessly still. Then I would unhook the rusty trace chains and wrap them around a rump piece of the harness to keep them from dragging on the mules' heels. James would ride one mule and lead the other. I would carry the dinner bucket and milk bottles and a load of stove wood back to the house. "It don't look right and it ain't right for a man to work a brute all day and ride it home at night," my father used to say when we worked in the fields together.

When the red worms came to the top of the ground around the hog pen, it was time to go fishing. We would dig red-worm bait and then go to the branch and seine minnows for bait with a coffee sack . "Them craw-dads ain't very good bait. I can't have any luck with them," Uncle Rank Larks would always say. James and I would go to the W-Hollow creek. I would teach him how to fish before we went to Little Sandy River. I would take a minnow hook. I would catch a fly with my hand—put it on the hook and drop it with a little thug into the water. The minnows would fight over it before one could swallow it. Finally the bottle cork would go under the water and I'd flip the string tied to the end of a short pole. A silver-colored minnow would gape and wiggle in the wind. "Stand back here so a minnow can't see you. It is always better. Go silently and never shake the brush along the bank. It will be better, you'll learn later. But this doesn't have anything to do with fishing in Little Sandy—only you must learn to keep quiet when you fish and wait a long, long time for a bite sometimes. But keep at it. Change your bait when they don't bite. Different kinds of fish have different tastes. Try many foods on them. And whatever you do, don't drink water out of these streams. They are dangerous to human flesh." James learned to catch minnows first. He later learned to fish.

But against what I warned him about the treacherous streams, one hot June day he drank from a stream. Typhoid fever was the result and it lasted for five weeks. One leg was left lame. "The water was clear as the sky," he said, "and it looked good to drink. It was pretty water and it tasted good." Do not be deceived by the crystal clearness of high hill water. It is full of thousands of germs that will put you flat on your back in less than seven days after you drink them. You will want to die. But you can't die sometimes and sometimes you do die against your will. But your bones ache and your flesh is hot. I have been that way twice because I drank of that beautiful liquid—cool to the parched lips and fine to the taste, yet treacherous as a copperhead.

Once I drank of blue mountain water under the shade of beech trees. I went above and found a dead horse in the stream and two spotted hound dogs pulling carrion from his flanks. I wanted to vomit but I could not. The buzzards sat upon a dead oak limb in the sun and waited for their share. The buzzards are worth thousands of dollars and save many lives by cleaning the carrion off the land. I know of nothing but a copperhead's head that they won't eat. A copperhead's head is the most poisonous of flesh. A hog will eat all of a copperhead but its head. This is the way of mountain streams. When beasts of the land and the birds of the air know they are sick enough to die, they go for water. Water has a great healing power for a feverish body. When they come to the stream, they gorge on water and die by the stream. If a skunk gets his leg cut off between the steel jaws of a trap, he will die by a stream of running water if he is to die at all. The same is true of the fox and the rabbit.

This was the time of year I would go to the old orchards near home. I would see the apple trees white with blossom. The wind would blow through their tops and blow the blossoms to the ground. In the springtime, a thought about man and the seasons would always return to me. These apple trees were only treacherous. They would bloom again next April. But I would never be as young again as I was that day. My season only came once. I would bloom but once, and then I would go back to the earth and be silent and cold forever. I would walk under the trees and hear the wind blow. I would see a buzzard fly over the trees in bloom, and then I would think of carrion—dead horses by the sky-blue streams. The shoe-makes would be leafing now—those little red sticky leaves with a sour smell on damp days. "It looks like a hound dog with a good nose will get his nostrils filled with the scent," I liked to think.

Later the blackberry briars bloomed beneath the apple trees, and the wind off the blackberry blossoms is enough to make man jealous of bees. It is enough to make him want to live forever. It is enough to make him want to write poetry. It is enough to make him want to shout to the wind, the sky and the stars: "I have something to say. Won't you listen to me for a moment? My voice is not strong, but won't you listen? I tell you again and again I have something to say. I have walked in the silence of the night. I have talked to the stars. I have tried to be strong as the oak trees I have leaned against and on whose bark I have put my hands. I have clenched my teeth to keep from crying when the wild geese flew over the brown autumn fields with their honk-honking cries. I wanted to follow them. I have lived among the things I loved. I have put my hands on them. I have talked to them but they could not understand. Now I have something to say to you. I want to say it in words beautiful as the stars. Can't you listen to my voice while I am still beneath these blooming apple trees?"

During the second summer of my high-school career, I farmed. And again the corn crops were heavy. We cleaned new land each spring and sowed the old in grass. "It pays a body not to run his land too long in corn in these hills. They are never the same any more." The fruit trees grew faster than the corn—long, healthy-looking slick-bark appletree branches and smooth-bodied cherry trees. The peach trees looked like rank red switches in the wind, for the leaves are small and the body of the tree shows well. The crop was all done a second season since I had been boss on the small place. I didn't set out much tobacco. It took all the time between July and September when I wanted to be free to hunt and swim and ride the mules. I would not go back to that army camp at Camp Knox. I didn't want to any more. "You do this. You do that. You are in the army. Bristle up. This evening comes parade. You'd better watch about not saluting an officer. It is the uniform and what it represents that you salute." This summer I took a supply of Tennyson's poetry and the songs of Robert Burns and went to live at Carter Caves. I went with Tillman Cartwell. We took a small tent and lived in a place called Horseshoe Bottom. That was a drowsy place there.

We would fish all day long. We made a raft to sit on and fish. But the turtles were vicious and would take our bait. We could not swim in the clear waters of Tygart for turtles. I would sit upon the banks and knock them off logs and rocks down in the river with a .22. "Where did you learn to shoot that way, Stuart—Camp Knox last summer?" "Hell, no. Not in any army. They don't teach you to shoot. I got it shooting squirrels out of the tall walnut trees near home. Hunting by myself. I take pride in my shooting and hunting. Watch me knock that little turtle down on the rock." Tillman would let me use the rifle after he saw me shoot. I killed bullfrogs, squirrels and several ground hogs. We ate the squirrels and bullfrogs but Tillman wouldn't touch a piece of ground hog and they were fat on the earing corn. They make a great dish but Tillman couldn't cook them. I tried to show him how Mom rolled them in meal and baked them. But I had forgotten how myself if I had ever really learned. "Them ground hogs are clean things and man won't eat them," said Farmer Rankins, who lived nearby. "Yet they eat hogs and chickens. There ain't anything dirtier than a chicken."

Often in my walks around the caves, I found old bones. I shall never forget the hum of the bees around Carter Caves. They were feeding on buckwheat. My, how they love buckwheat blossoms! The fields were filled with blossoms and the blossoms were filled with bees. The black-locust trees were blooming too. The bees were working on them and on the shoe-makes, but not like they were working on the buckwheat.

I would sit at the mouth of a cool cave and read Tennyson for hours. When I left there, I left my books in this cave. I never went back for them. I wrote and told Farmer Rankins he could have them for the many good meals I had eaten with him. In the letter, I directed him to the cave. "Upon a shelf of rocks when you first go in at the entrance," I said, "you'll find them, away from the dripping water."

When the last food we had was eaten, we started the twenty-mile walk to the railroad station. We were on our way back to Greenup. Tillman Cartwell would enter school that year as a freshman. He would get along fine.

Tillman's people had graduated from the school. He said to me: "You must come to visit me, Stuart. I want my mother to know you." "You must come to visit me, Tillman," I said, half hoping that he would never come. My home was not what he was used to and my people were only educated to the soil. Tillman was one of the boys who had once asked me to hunt with him. He asked to go into the woods with me and Black-Boy. I thought he was giddy like some of the fellows there. I always got around taking him. Now I was sorry I hadn't taken him with me before.

Back to school again. The pigskin was flying in the air again. I had always thought I would play when I put on some weight. The big fellows had graduated off the team. I was getting to be one of the big fellows there now. Tillman said, "Get in there, Stuart. You can make the team. You're tough as Spikey. He made it his first year out."

I was introduced to Rawl Briswell. He was the bully of the town and the school's bad boy. It wasn't anything uncommon to see a boy with blood running out of his nose. Ask what was wrong, and a boy would say, "W'y, Rawl Briswell hit him." Rawl was six feet two and weighed nearly two-hundred pounds. The boys in school were afraid of Rawl. He knew it too. He would slap them around anyway he pleased. If they didn't like it, he would slap them again. Nothing was said for there was nothing to say, only that Rawl Briswell did it. There was nothing to do about it. This was his fourth year in school and he would have one more year to finish. He stayed to play football and fight, everybody thought. "John Briswell's boy don't go to that school for any good. He just goes there to bully the boys around and to fight. It's a bad streak running through his blood."

1924-25 Greenup High School junior class. Jesse is standing 2nd from right on back row.   (Courtesy *Irene Griffith, Greenup, Kentucky*)

Tillman Cartwell told me one day that he had heard Rawl talking about me coming in from the country and getting cocky. He told Tillman he was going to take some of it, if not all of it, out of me with his fist. He said he thought he would do it before the day was over. Tillman warned me to watch him. I knew that he was foul in a football game. He would spit his opponent's eyes full of tobacco spittle. The next time, he would slug him under the chin with his fist. I have seen boys carried from the field when Rawl hit them. The referee was not wise enough to catch Rawl. Often he would yell he had been slugged to hide his own foul play.

We were all in the room—a crowd of boys and girls. Rawl came in. He said: "Fee fo fum." I never knew any more until I arose perhaps five minutes afterwards. Rawl laughed and chewed his tobacco in the schoolhouse. I never said anything. There was nothing for me to say. I was weak. My eyes were blackened and my right eye was closed. I felt ashamed. That was the first time any fellow had ever done me like that. I wanted to sneak out and never come back to the school. That night when I was going home, I was mad. I thought I ought to conceal a pistol on me and walk up and shoot Rawl down.

I told my father about the way it had happened. He said, "You are big enough to take care of yourself. But no man would ever do me that away." But I wouldn't kill Rawl, I concluded. It was weeks before the black rings left from under my eyes. I could hear people in the town saying: "There goes that boy John Briswell's boy hit. They said he shore beefed him. Hit him right under the eye and the next thing that Stuart boy knowed they's a-pouring water on him. I tell you John's got a bad boy. He'll go to the pen if he don't mind out—that boy will." Then flashes of madness would return to me and I would want to kill Rawl Briswell. At least I made up my mind to hit him and hit him hard. "Always get a man the first lick. That does the work. Hit him hard too. Stand on your toes and throw your weight behind your fist. Hit him hard the first time. That's the way your Uncle Rank always did."

When I went home that night, I got a coffee sack out of the

corncrib. I went up in the gap and filled the bottom of it with many pounds of sand. I took it inside the smokehouse and fastened it to the pole where we had kept the middlings hanging. Then I took a brush and drew the nearest likeness of Rawl's face I could. I made a long mouth like his. He had a big mouth with corners that dropped and I made this big mouth on the sack. That afternoon when I came home, I practiced hitting that face with my fists. I would try it with a left and then a right. I was trying to get where I could swing the sack over the pole with my fist. This was in the spring of the year. One day a crowd of us were in the same school-room where I got hit by Rawl. Rawl was in the room. He started to say "Fee fo fum—" but, before he had said his battle song, I drove a left into the flesh of Rawl Briswell's face he'll long remember. As he was sinking to the floor, I followed it with a right to his left jaw. The girls in the room began to scream. The boys closed the windows and held the door—so that there would be no excitement. Rawl came to himself in a room filled with students who were wishing that the two licks had been fatal ones. "Did you hear about that Stuart boy beefing that Briswell boy? I took the wad of tobacco out of his mouth and that was the whitest boy I've ever seen. He hit him hard enough to kill."

When Rawl came back to school with his eyes blacked, the teachers never said a word. They were glad it had been done, but they hadn't wanted to have the trouble of blacking his eyes. It was a greater task than teaching the school. I know I didn't want to do it at the cost of the lick he struck me. When he passed me in the schoolhouse one day, he gritted his teeth and said: "I'll get you yet." I snapped, "Rawl, you won't get any boy your size. You won't get me. I'll whip you so quick you won't know that you are whipped." I determined to do it.

The last of the third year passed. I went back to the farm. One more year and I would finish school now. The summer before my senior year in high school, I farmed another heavy crop. The new land on our farm was productive. During crop time I sat for the teachers' examination and got a second-class certificate. That was good when only twenty-two passed out of forty-four and for one with twelve credits in high school. After the crops were laid by, I went out and taught in a country school. Sixty-eight dollars a month beat making crossties and opossum hunting. It was easy-made money. I paddled a few girls for cursing and chewing tobacco behind the schoolhouse. The old women talked about that young man teacher putting young girls across his lap and using a book on them. "I don't think that is right to paddle a girl. He ought to take a willow switch and tickle her legs. I am afraid my man John will go around there to him if he paddles Jessie again." I had a great time with the hill children. I knew them. I was one. They didn't know it and I didn't tell them. I let the little children play all the time they didn't have to recite. It took play and association to make them keen and alert as well as it took books. They were starved for association. I turned them loose. It did them good. When I left there,

From left, Jesse with senior classmates Oscar Sammons, Thurman Darby and James D. McCoy   (Courtesy Jesse Stuart Foundation)

I gave the kids a bucket of mixed candy. It was their treat. Several of them cried and said: "We'll never see you again, Mr. Stuart." Well, they were right. I never went back.

When I returned to Greenup High School, I had confidence in myself. I had nearly two-hundred dollars now. I bought two new suits of clothes. I stepped out. I was a senior in high school now. I was invited to parties by the friends of Burl Mavis. When a substitute teacher was needed in mathematics or history, I filled the place. And time after time, I served for days as a substitute teacher in the grades, making up my high-school work at night. I played football that year and did some punting—something I liked very much to do. I was elected president of the Y.M.C.A. and of the Hi-Y Club. I tied for the highest honors in my class. Burl Mavis had dropped from school now. He flunked his final exams when he was a junior. He went back to work in the store. The red-headed girl who had trouble saying ring, rang and rung was married.

That fall I went with hunting parties of town boys into the fields and woods near home. I would laugh and be gay with the crowd. I could laugh as loud as any of them, shoot as well and hunt better than most of them. We would go from field to field and not get any rabbits. I would say: "I must kill a rabbit. Don't anybody speak to me. Don't anybody follow me. I am afraid I may shoot you." I knew I wouldn't shoot anyone but I wanted silence. I would look for the rabbits' ears around stumps, in leaf beds and up against little clay banks. I would get down and look up under the edges of turf where the dirt was sliding down. I would see a rabbit. I would take the gun quickly and clip off its head. I found them that way. I never trusted trying to find a rabbit by looking for his tail. His tail is too often under the leaves. The ears were the things. Then the tail would fool one so often. Life-everlasting has gray-looking leaves and tops that look like a rabbit's tail. I would explain to the boys how I found them. But it was not in many of them to know how to hunt. You know, I think a lot of these things are born with us. The first time I ever went into the hills hunting, I killed two rabbits. I stole silently through the brush and found them. I found them for my father. Once I saw a rabbit crouched beside a stump fifty feet away. I went to the house, got the gun, and killed the rabbit. My father stepped the distance. "You have an eye for finding rabbits a-setten. I was never like that."

My high-school days were over now. I had walked the eight miles per day with ease but during my senior year I stayed one third of my time in Greenup. I was a welcome member of many families. "You know right where the bed is. Now come anytime and make yourself at home," said Mrs. Darby. "The key will always be above the door. Remember you are welcome here."

Now what was there for me to do? I was out of school. Must I go back to the farm? I remembered that on a snowy day in April 1918 I had broken a path for myself through the snow. I would not step in my father's broken path. I had said that I would not live among the hills forever and die among them and go back to the dust of the hills like my brothers had. I said my father would live his life among them and his life would be an empty life. He would give all of himself to the hills and in the end the hills would take him back and protect his bones against the elements. And briars and trees would soon cover his grave, and the dead leaves from the trees would soon hide the prints of his grave. Now must I follow the footprints of my father? "Son, I'm in debt for part of this land yet. I'd like for you to go ahead with the work this summer. You know I am not able to hire help and James is too small to plow."

I thought it over. I told him I would stay for a while. But all the time I thought of the vows I had made to my mother at the milk gap. One day we took the mules to Greenup. It was the last time they were to see our farm. It was the last time I would follow them at the plow. We traded them for a team of horses. "Horses can stand up on this land now. It is pretty well worn and there are not many roots in it. Horses are not so dangerous either. They're not half so bad at kicking as mules. I got a little afraid of that Barnie mule when I went to put hay in his manger by lantern light at night. Mules are bad to kick." But a mule hates to leave a place he has learned to love. He hates to leave a place where he has given the best of his strength to get the land ready for corn and tobacco each spring. We had been fighting for a home of our own. Why not keep one for the mules? We had moved from place to place getting farms in good condition, then we moved on and left them. Among those cornfields and tobacco fields, we had left strength and youth. We moved on and left the land in better shape than we got it from the landlord. Now the mules moved on, older and with less strength maybe, to a new home, and the land that they had given their strength to help get in shape went to the horses. "Ain't it funny that a horse in the hills gets a quarter a day for his work and the man gets seventy-five? The horse does more than the man. Ain't it a queer thing? Now you take these country roads, what could we do without horses?" said Uncle Rank Larks.

I would get on the fastest young horse and ride as fast as the wind. I tried to outrun the wind. I would ride the ridge roads—out under the oak trees and the pine trees. Fred would jump drawbars and gates with me. I would laugh and say, "Do it again, Fred." One day Mom said: "Jesse, teach Mary and James to ride. Make them take it barebacked."

I put Mary and James on Kate. They rode barebacked. I would get in front with Fred and he would set the pace for Kate to follow. We would ride the ridges. We would go to Cedar Riffles. I would point out to them the house where I was born. No one lived there now and a skunk denned under the floor. Birds built their nests under the eaves. Tall weeds grew beside the shack. The roof was leaking. We would ride beneath the oak trees and the pines. I would let Fred jump gates. Then Kate would follow. At first the children screamed. Then they began to like it. "Them Stuart youngins is plum fools. I seed them back over yander from Morton's Gap jist a raising hell with them horses. That little girl was with 'em. If them was youngins of mine, I'd whip their tails with a hickory," said old John Hackless.

But we worked hard in the fields together. We played hard together. But things to me were not what they once were. I dreamed of something beyond the hills. I wanted to go and go and go. I wanted to do something.

One night I was sitting in the chip yard talking to my father. I told him fifty acres of land was not a big enough place for me. He sat silently and gazed at a bunch of hollyhocks in the moonlight.

Chapter IV
God: And the Evening Sky

When I think of God, I think of the evening sky in Kentucky. When I was a child in the hills of northeast Kentucky and living in a log shack near Cedar Riffles, I would ask my mother, "Can God ride on one of the white clouds up in the sky?" I would see a white cloud in the shape of a bear's head or a mountaintop or in the shape of a scaly monster. My mother would say: "Yes, God can do anything." "Can he see through that plum tree out there in the garden?" She would say: "Yes, God can do anything." Then I would say: "Well, God is a great man if he can do things like that. But I am afraid some of these days he will fall off the clouds and hurt himself when he falls to the ground. Then without God the earth will come to an end."

Then I would wish I was God. I could ride on the clouds. I could see through the trees. I could do things then that my cousin Glenn Hilton could not do. I would see through the log house the Hiltons lived in and watch them sitting around the table eating supper. None of them would know my eyes were watching every forkful of food that went to their mouths. I would turn hills over and leave them upside down so that people could see what was under the hills. When the horses stuck in the mud with a wagonload of corn, I would go out and pull the wagon from the mud. I would be stronger than horses. If I could only be God! I wanted to be God. I would ride the white clouds and take a long-handled broom and knock them down to the earth and let the sparrows build their nests in the clouds instead of in the barn. The boys would come along seeing me do big things, and they would feel ashamed. They would want to go off and hide in the weeds. And if they did, I would see them through the weeds and trees. They couldn't hide from me.

On winter days when the snow lay white on the barren Kentucky hills, I would go out in the yard with a broom and sweep a place in the snow. Then I would throw cane seeds there, and the hungry snowbirds would fly down and pick them up. They would crane their necks and eat and eat. I would go back to the house and look through the window at the birds eating cane seed. Then I would say to Mom: "Did God make the birds?" She would get tired of my questions and nod "Yes," and go ahead piecing quilt tops by the fireside. "Well, does God love the birds?" She would drowsily nod: "Yes." "Would he kill a cat for catching the birds?" She would nod again.

I asked her no more questions about God. I went to the corncrib and got more cane seed for the birds. I threw more seed back on the place I had swept in the snow. Over the seed I put a screen box with the bottom out of it. I lifted the front end of the box and put a stick there to hold it up so that the birds could go under. Then I tied a string to the stick and pulled a rag out of a hole in a windowpane and put the string through. I stood by the side of the fire and waited for the birds to come. When they went under, I pulled the string and let the box fall over them. Then I went out and ran my hand under the box and put the frightened birds in my cap. I showed them to my mother. "God didn't kill me and I caught his birds like the cat. Now what is he going to do about me catching these birds?" She said: "You are not accountable for all the sins you do now. But you will be when you are twelve years old. All of the sins you make now, me and your father will have to suffer for them. You are accountable to us and we are accountable to God." "Then I'll turn the birds loose for I don't want God to get after you and Pa about it like he would a cat."

I turned the birds back into the icy air and put the rag back in the broken windowpane. The cool air came in and the house was getting cold. But I had come to know my first lesson about God. He was a man one could not get away from. If you did not walk on a straight line, God did not want you, and the Devil got you with a pitchfork. There was no getting away from a man that rode the clouds and saw through a tree. I was afraid to lie. I was afraid to steal. I was afraid of God. I thought God was hidden somewhere and looking on and listening to everything I did and said. I was always looking for him to jump from behind a tree and hit me with a stick. I remember a twin set of chestnut trees upon the bank from the house; I thought God hid behind them to watch me.

II

When I became twelve years of age, the time that "my accountability" began, I dreaded to do what the hill preacher told the people they would have to do before they would get to Heaven, the place God kept for his people. The preacher said one would have to fall to one's knees at the altar, in the cornfield, in the apple orchard, in the woods—just any place, but on the knees to show humbleness. There underneath the heavens, cry out to God and say: "God, I've stolen sheep. God, I've loved my neighbor's wife. And God, I talked about Tessie Holbrook. God, I carried a pistol for Wayne Wright. Won't you forgive me for these things, Lord, and many others? I've been a mean man. Make me a soldier of the Cross." God would say then, "You are saved, Young Man. Get up out of the dust and follow me. Take up the Cross and follow me." There would be a light upon the young man's face. He would be happy. Now I dreaded to do this. I knew I had to do it. The preacher was right. He knew, for many times he said he was the chosen one of God, gone out to preach God's word. He knew about God—maybe he had talked to God.

When I got right with God, I would go out on the hilltop. I would put my face down against the wet oak leaves on the ground.

I would get rid of the wheelbarrow load of sins I had done. I had broken Aunt Viola Hilton's eggs. I threw them against a slick beech tree to watch the yolk run down the bark. I had stolen Mr. Wheeler's sweet apples. I had called boys bad names. I would get rid of all this. But I must get out in a lonely place—away from everybody. I wanted to get down against the leaves.

I knew there was a Heaven. I knew the kind of place it was. Granny Flaughtery told my mother over and over again about going to Heaven. She said: "I went up a long ladder. I was tired and weary. But finally I got to the gate. My mother and father met me there. Then they escorted me to the Throne. There I saw God same as I see you sitting in that chair. He smiled at me. I saw angels as far as I could see, with harps. The streets were made of gold there. After I had looked over this beautiful place awhile, I found a horse trader that people back on earth prayed over and thought he went to Hell. I saw one-arm Dave Perkins. But he had two arms there. I saw that man, ah, what is his name anyway?— you know, that went around over the streets in town without legs and told stories for his living. Don't you remember? ["Tim Sneedley," said my mother.] Yes I saw him there on two good legs. I saw many people I knew there. Oh, it pays to be good. Then the Lord said: 'Go back, and come again.' I could not help it. I had to leave. I wanted to stay. My mother and father came back as far as the gate with me. They said they could come no farther. Then I choked all the way down that long ladder. When I woke up I said: 'Bring me a glass of water and I will tell you where I have been. I have been to Heaven. Take the water away.' People were crying in the room and there was the coffin I was to be buried in. It makes a person feel funny to wake up and see her own coffin. I told them to haul it back to town. They took it out of the house then loaded it on the express, and there was much rejoicing. But I was unhappy to come back to this old world."

Granny Flaughtery told this story over and over again. She would tell other stories I cannot tell here. When I was too small to understand things and sat under the quilt my mother and Granny were quilting, I listened to all of these stories. I did not know what they meant then, but I remembered them and have interpreted the stories since I have grown older. Mama would say, "Ah Granny, go on and talk. He's too young to know what we are talking about." But I'll say Granny Flaughtery knew life and knew what she was talking about in some of her stories. She had married a vagabond and he would come and go—leave his family and travel until he became ragged. Then he would slip back through the woods to hide his nakedness. Granny would have to keep the family. But her man would always return even if he did follow the sun.

One day I was down in the W-Hollow creek. I would wade out in the water, lift up a rock, and catch a crayfish. I would put him in a wash-pan. Then I would get another and another. I went down the creek lifting rocks like this. When a water snake would fall off into the water with a thug, I would stir the sand with a stick and muddy the water. I would wait silently with my stick. The snake, when submerged, can stand muddy water only a short time. When the snake lifted its head above the water for air, I hit it across the top of the head with the stick. The water would turn milky and the snake would float on the water. I would go on catching crayfish and killing water snakes. I knew about where the snakes were by the snake feeders flying around.

There were many wild blue flags and yellow flags growing along W-Hollow creek. I would climb out of the water and catch a bumblebee between flag petals and listen to him buzz for his freedom. When I let him go, he would fly away into the green treetops. But once when I had a bumblebee between the petals of a yellow flag, I heard a rustling in the weeds. I went toward where I saw the weeds shaking. I looked and saw a man and woman on the grass. It was the preacher I had heard tell about what a man had to do to be saved. I shall not tell all of this story. He gave me twenty-five cents and told me to go down to Baker's store and buy myself something. He told me not to say anything about seeing him there. I did not understand then. I took the money, threw the crayfish back into the water and went to the store. I never understood that until I grew older. But I didn't want to go into the silence and do what he said. Something told me not to follow his words. God could find better men than he.

III

When I was twelve, I started going to Plum Grove Sunday School. The days for Sunday School there had a season. It kept going as long as the roads were not impassable. When the roads thawed out in March and the wind and the sun of April dried up the mud, Sunday School would get under way. Then autumn would come and the heavy rains would fall that swayed the shocks of corn to the ground and filled the country streams. A long siege of cool falling rain that took the dead leaves off the treetops and pinned them to the ground. Then the wagons would be buried to the axles on the soft marshy roads. Drivers would yelp at their horses and lash them with whips. It was no time for a family in a jolt wagon to venture to Plum Grove Sunday School. That was the way many of them came. They would drive down to the foot of the hill and unhitch their horses and tie them to the wagon bed. The horses would munch on the straw in the wagon beds while the family went to the little church house on the hill.

The church house was set out on a grassy hilltop facing a black-oak grove. Under the shadow of the oak trees it faced, sat the old Plum Grove schoolhouse where I first attended school. My first memories of that place were the big boys and the teachers cutting the wild plum trees and raking the leaves where they had once stood and carrying the whole works out in Wheeler's field. I remember the teacher picking thorns out of the children's feet. He would say: "Charlie, the skin on the ball of your foot is as thick as sole leather." Once Jimmie Welch came to him and said: "Look here, Mr. Thombs, at this thorn in my foot." The thorn had gone in under the bottom of the foot and was standing out half an inch above. "Hold still, Jimmie. Now don't cry. I'll yank it out. Walter, you go and look in my desk and get that bottle of turpentine. It may smart a little but turpentine is good for soreness."

I had gone to school here to Professor Iron Hand long before

The traditional one-room schoolhouse
(Courtesy *Cora Wilson Stuart Collection, University of Kentucky*)

"...it was the finest place to me I'd ever been up to that time."

I began to attend Sunday School. I remember the honey-locust switches he whipped us with. He would send a boy up through the scuttle hole in the attic to get the seasoned switches. The boy would hate to go, but Professor Iron Hand made him climb a pole that he called a ladder. It had notches on it where the branches had been trimmed a little and the stubs left.

And when we played ball in the schoolyard, the heavy batters would knock it into the churchyard. It was against the rules to go into the churchyard. But a boy would slip in and get the ball. (We located Professor Iron Hand first.) It was too hard to save twine and make a ball. We usually put rags in the middle or a steely marble. When I went over after the ball, I had thoughts about a story I read. It was called "Roland in the Dark Tower." The story said a boy went over into a churchyard someway in opposition to the sun. I went over opposite the setting sun after a ball like he did. A cave opened to him and he found himself under a big hill. He had trouble getting out. I wondered about all of this as I watched the sun setting in the west over the black-oak ridges. I wondered too if Iron Hand was watching me get the ball. Those were my thoughts when I went there once to school. But now I had left school and had gone to work cutting corn in the autumn time, farming at home during the summer.

When my sister and I went to Sunday School after the roads dried in April, we had to cross many fields and wood patches. We had to go through two old orchards and over long strips of yellow country roads. I remember the smell of the oak buds bursting in Wheeler's woods in April. I remember the white flowers on the bloodroot and the spindly windflowers springing under the tall oak trees. The red and blue sweet williams growing around old stumps—a tuft of blue violets where the wind had idly shaken the dead leaves from over them. I remember the May apples growing by old logs in the woods. My sister would say: "Jesse, that patch of May apples over there by that log looks like all fourteen of the Larkins family going to town with green umbrellas over them. That little slender one looks like Mrs. Larkins' little legs, and that big stubby one looks like Martha Larkins' legs."

It was then that something stirred deep within me. I don't know what it was. It may have been God. Those were the sunny springtime days when the coloring of sunshine was on my face. I walked barefooted across wide expanses of broken fields, and a silver wind would tousle my unkempt hair. I was free as the winds were free. I was free as a colt unshod. My sister and I both walked with God. What did we care for the bull in Wheeler's pasture?

Summer would come. The corn would grow tall and tassel in the fields. The crows and the ground hogs would come to the fields and eat. The tobacco leaves would lazily shake in the wind across the balks—great broad leaves with a stinky smell in the hottest part of the hot days when the wind was idly blowing. I wondered if God ever came to the tobacco fields and watched people hoe tobacco and wipe sweat with big red handkerchiefs. God's men preached against tobacco. At least, they said they were chosen by God to preach. They had heard his voice and they meant to talk for God. It was an evil weed they all preached. But I wondered if God would come down off his white throne and walk in the tobacco fields in the moonlight. I wondered how he would like the smell of green tobacco in the hot July sun when a light wind was idly blowing. Then I would think: "What is the use of this weed? The preacher said God made everything and made it for a purpose. Why did he put this weed here then? Did he do it so that country people would toil and sweat and make a little living out among the lonely hills? Or did he do it so that rich men could pass the evil weeds as a token of friendship, of courtesy to men in making a big deal easier to go over?" I knew what I would do. I would go and ask the preacher about it. I would not ask the preacher I had found in the weed field. I would go and ask the Reverend Finnis. I was certain he knew. He said: "Son, don't you use that weed. It is an evil weed. It is the Devil's own work. The Lord didn't make the tobacco plant. It was the Devil. Before the Lord ever saved me, that stuff had rotted out all my teeth and took lots of my nickels and dimes."

Tobacco fields—Kentucky tobacco fields and Sunday School and God. My mind is in a muddle. Man has to raise the wicked plant for a living. God doesn't want him to do it. It is a plant of the Devil. Yet what better does God offer among the hills? The timber is disappearing. The moonshine still has been partly closed. The corn and cane sell for low prices. Where is the money? Man has to live. The crows fly over the tobacco fields but they do not alight. They go flapping in the bright air and cawing. They are going to the cornfields. Crows don't like tobacco. Man likes tobacco. Crows like corn.

Then my sister and I went on through the hills on the Sabbath morning to Sunday School. We would see the birds in the bright blue air above the oat fields. They would fly down and peck the oats from the shocks and fly up again into the blue air. Birds flying, and I would say to my sister: "You can't fool me about Kentucky oat fields. I know about them. They are hideouts for copperheads. Old Black-Boy killed twelve in that two-acre oat field back of the house. Black-Boy tears blacksnakes into little pieces of tough skin. But he takes his time on the copperheads. He bays the copperhead and teases it until it becomes tired. He makes the snake uncoil by striking at him. Then he runs in and takes it by the neck. Black-Boy is a smart dog." "Yes, Jesse, I'm afraid of copperheads. You ought to carry a stick along here. You know Mom was bitten by one once but not in an oat field. It was in a tobacco field. Haven't you heard her tell about the snake being 'quiled' under a broad tobacco leaf—one of the ground leaves?

"She was cutting the weeds from around the plant and pulling off the suckers and worms. The copperhead bit her on the foot. She was a barefooted girl in the Kentucky tobacco fields then. Grandpa was plowing. He heard her screams when she saw the snake and hopped off down over the loamy earth. She thought a wasp had stung her until she saw the snake. She never screamed until then. She knew the bite of a copperhead was terrible where there were no doctors. But Grandpa took her to the house on a mule as fast as it would carry double. He took a bottle of turpentine and held it to the bite. The green venom could be seen going up into the turpentine bottle. Another way is to take a knife and cut a place over the bite. Suck the poison blood into your mouth and spit it out. That is a good way to do in the hill country. You know the place where the snake bit Mom never rotted and fell out like it does on lots of people."

We could often hear the rusty bell sounding over the hot lazy countryside before we got to the Sunday School house. My sister, then fifteen years of age, would often carry her shoes all the way and put them on just before she got there. The slippers got terribly muddy and the little skin surface got knocked off if she did not. As for me, it did not matter. I never wore shoes until late in the fall.

One pair of shoes during the year was all I got. I went to Sunday School barefooted like all the other boys.

I loved to hear the people sing. I thought it was wonderful to be able to play an organ. I admired all this. It was great to me. I thought all the preacher said just had to be true. I was not muddled about anything. God was there in the house looking on us all. He would take us home in the end. There would be no trouble about it. God would take us. Everybody there had the same picture of God. He was a strong man that rode the clouds. He saw through a tree. He took the good people home and sent the bad people to the Devil. God and the Devil were at war. They had many fights there at Plum Grove.

The greatest fights the Devil and God had at Plum Grove were on Sunday nights at church and at the spring revivals. When the summer moon rode slowly up the sky over the summer hills and the evening was filled with insect sounds—the katydids and the jar flies buzzing—then there would be the frogs croaking along the streams and in the little swamps, the whippoorwills calling from the pastures around the church house—this was when the old women and the old men would come walking in to church. The women would wear shawls around their shoulders—black shawls used for church purposes. The men would come dressed in overalls and denim-jackets. Their faces were colored by the wind and the sun to a brown leather tan. They were hard men. They were strong men. They had worked in the tobacco fields and the fields of tall corn. They had come to help God fight the Devil. They came like they did in the days of old—a little Puritan band.

"Now gather up around the mourners' bench—all of you praying mothers and fathers—come right up. If God was here, you wouldn't wait." A long line of mothers and fathers would gather before the long S oak fence in front of the rostrum. There would be much noise in getting there. The heavy thug of coarse shoes on the rough floor—shoes of a strong people, made to endure the hardships of hill life. "Sister Gibson, lead us in prayer. When she is through, everybody pray."

The house would be held spellbound and many serious people brought to tears by the prayer of Sister Gibson. Finally, she would cease. She would lean over and cry. She had given out. She could pray no more. Then a mighty sound of inharmonious voices would fill the room. Prayer, and no one could tell what they were all saying. But the congregation could always hear Brother Tobbie yell above the other voices, "We'll whip the Devil tonight." There would be "Amens" going up all over the house. There would be cries: "Yes, Lord, help us to whip the old Devil." There would be shouting. Benches would go over. The Devil would flee.

The next day there would be much talking among the people of the neighborhood. "Well, Mrs. Fort came through last night. Yes sir, she got religion if ever a woman did. She finally told the Lord what was the matter with her. She told him she had killed a lot of young babies. She had never had but three children—Dan, Oscar and Essie. When she said these words, she began shouting." "I want to tell you Sy Mullins got religion last night. He's been trying for years. But he could never get right with the Lord. Last night, he told all he'd ever done. Since Hilder Kameen's wife died, Sy confessed being with her down in the cornfield one time. He would never confess when she was living—afraid of old Hilder I guess. But last night he came clean. He wiped the slate clean— Sy Mullins is a saved man." "Charlie Stigall had an awful fight with the Devil last night. But when the Lord did give him light he tried to climb the stovepipe. That was after he confessed going over to Mart Wilder's place—going under his porch and boring a hole up through the floor and into the barrel. He took all he could carry and never plugged the hole. The whisky all ran out on the ground. You remember hearing people talk about it when it happened. They thought Mart was the one who did it. He stayed drunk for a month." "Reverend Doubty is shore a good preacher. When he preaches, he never takes his left hand offen the Bible. That man is shore a good preacher. Now he is a man called by the Lord to preach. He won't take anything for his preaching either. Nowadays that's what most of these preachers are out for—the money and not to save the souls of men. When I die, I want Brother Doubty to preach my funeral." "Did you hear about Ezekiel Boggs getting saved last night? He went and told all the men he owed money to. He threw his tobacco and his knucks and pistol out in the crowd. The boys grabbed for them. But Zeke came clean. He wrestled a long time with the Devil. But Zeke threw him. Then he went home and cut his green tobacco down with a tobacco knife in the moonlight. I'm just wondering what he is going to do this winter. His children will go hungry."

But on the outside of the house, the Devil had his gang. There would be dark ghostly figures of earth prowling around over the churchyard and looking in at the windows. They would come to church to shoot and drink and fight with knives and razors in old dirty work clothes. The fronts of their shirts would be open and one could see their hairy chests—figures of earth—grim and daring—they feared not man, nor God, nor the Devil. There would be quarrels and wicked curses and sour smells of rotten breaths and whisky fumes in the night air. And one could hear whispers— low whispers: "There's going to be hell here tonight. I see it a-brewing. Them bad Tarters and Larkins have met here tonight. There'll be blood before this thing is over." "They say 'Shooting' Mack Fundy's out there with two guns on him tonight and a razor. He'll stir up trouble too. Mack ain't afraid of hell or high waters." "Hell, that bunch has got a jug hid over there some'rs in the cockleburs. I seed them coming from it. Let's hide and watch 'em to it. Then when they leave, slip over there and empty the damn thing for them." "Not me stealing any whisky. You know what some fellers did one night to a jug. Don't you remember what they did in the jug? It looked like charred licker—red whisky—but it turned out to be something else when we tasted. And one man would not tell the other what was in it until they all tasted. Each would spit and wipe his mouth and say it was good until we all got fooled. I ain't stealing no more licker." "Say, what are these smart fellers doing out here from town? Let's show 'em the way back to town. Out here after Murt, Liz, Birdie, Nora or Kate, I guess. Well, they'll get fooled for once. They'll get a little lead in their pants—a load they can't carry."

One night rocks came through the church house windows. Glass fell over the floor. Mack Fundy was in the house that night. He jumped to his feet, pulled a long gun and said: "Brother Bill, must I get them?" We all ran to the doors and they were locked. Mack Fundy stepped back and hurled his body through one door. Another man broke the other door with the back of a seat. The congregation swarmed out into the moonlight like a mad swarm of bees. The boys were running at the foot of the hills. Mack leveled his pistol. The preacher took hold and raised his arm before the gun went off.

When officers were sent to church to keep order, men had respect for the High Sheriff. They had some respect for deputy sheriffs. They had no respect for constables. They would shoot them like rabbits. "What the hell's a damn constable! He's a low lifer or he wouldn't be a constable. Look at old Yokum. Never was a lower down man. Think I'd let him arrest me? I'd shoot him so quick it would make your head swim. Bill Taylor's got four notches on his gun. Three are for constables."

The big revivals would be held in the springtime. Men and women would get saved over and over again each year. "There is great rejoicing in Heaven tonight. A sinner here at Plum Grove has repented. This ain't no mourners' bench call—this is a funeral. Sing the last stanza of 'Nearer My God To Thee!' O won't you come? God may let a tree fall on you before morning. O won't you come? The Lord and the Devil are waiting to see how this meeting is a-comin' out. That's right, Sister. Come right up. Now don't be afraid. Others want to come but the Devil won't let them. The Lord is knocking at all their hearts. O won't you come? Praise the Lord they are coming. The Devil is going. Sing more of that song. Oh glory to God—Oh Glory to God—the strong people keep comin'. They are not afraid."

They would fall at the altar. They would cry and jerk. They would cry again and again: "Oh Lord, be merciful to me a sinner. I want to go to that beautiful place you have prepared for me. I want to see my loved ones in Heaven tonight. Oh Lord, be merciful to me tonight—be merciful on a sinner." There would be many souls saved. There would be great rejoicing.

Many of us left before the sinners prayed through. Sometimes church would go on far into the night. And in the morning around two o'clock, the house would shake by much shouting and the dim oil lamps on the walls inside the church house would be burning low. But the rusty church bell would sound out across the night fields through the silence of the night. We in our beds sleeping knew that the sinners had pulled through and there was great rejoicing at Plum Grove.

On the outside of the house, there would be a yellow moon up in the sky and a cold white glitter of thousands of summer stars. There would be moonlight on the hayfields and the tasseled corn. And there would be darkness in the little patches of oak trees. The air would be filled with the voices of frogs, katydids, whippoorwills and beetles. And there would be the white slabs gleaming in the moonlight where hundreds of dead lie buried on Plum Grove Hill. I had stood at the sides of these graves when many of them were buried. The graveyard was behind the schoolhouse and Professor Iron Hand let us out of school for the funerals. When the moonlight reflected on the marble gravestones, it made me have sad thoughts.

I would think about what the preacher had said: "Get right with God. Right out there on that p'int back of the schoolhouse is what the Devil has done. The Lord didn't do nary bit of it. Go out there and look at them tombstones and see for yourself—people eternally sleeping. The moon rises over them and the sun, over and over again. But they do not rise. They will not rise—they sleep. The wind blows over them and the grass whispers to them but they do not hear. Go out there and look at what the Devil has done. He keeps his big ears in everything. I tell you children it pays to get right with God."

After the big spring revivals were over and the Little Sandy backwaters from the heavy spring rains and ground thaws had subsided and left the black debris over the lowlands, and sticks and grass in the birch tops along the banks, the time would be set for the spring baptizing. It would be, maybe, the third Sunday in June or the second Sunday in July. It was never delayed late into the summer season. If it were, there would be backsliders, and many of them. Men would get mad and curse their horses at the plow and someone hearing them would get mad and tell. Then they must be saved over again. Women would talk about each other. They are hungry for things to say and there is nothing to talk about but the earth around them. They grow hungry for association with other people. And they talk about something.

"I seed John Hix going—going to town with a new saddle on his mule."

"Murt Peasly's hens are laying eggs to beat the band this spring. She carries off that big willer basket full twice a week."

"Ephraim Dials's wife had a baby last week that weighed eleven pounds. She's a little woman too. But she's right pert now—and the baby's the worst thing to cry I ever seed in all my born days."

"Did you hear about Owl Skinner getting a corn thief by the hand in a steel trap? Well, old Owl's a smart'n. He kept his crib locked all the time. And he said he kept saying: 'Boys, you're feeding a little too heavy on that corn. Now you must go lighter or we won't have enough to last us all winter.' But he said the boys said, 'Pap, we ain't feeding corn that way. We don't feed the cattle anything but roughage. And the mules are going down on what we are feeding them. They're weak on pulling a little drag of wood into the yard.' Then Owl goes out to the crib and finds a hole worn slick as a ground-hog hole. He gets him a heavy-jawed steel trap and sets it right at that hole. He puts a little corn silk over it so the jaws won't show. He fastens it to a crib log with a trace chain and locks the chain. The next morning when he goes out, there stands old Pete Woodrow with his sack at his feet. Owl didn't say a word. He went right on and done up his feeding. Then he comes around and says: 'Now let this be a lesson to you, Pete, you won't forget.' He goes in the crib and unlocks the trace chain and lets Pete's hand out of the trap. 'Come on and get you some breakfast now, Pete.' He makes Pete go in, wash the blood off his hand and eat breakfast with him. Pete looks from shameful eyes ever since then. But don't you know Old Skinner said: 'Now, Pete, I am the law here in this case. What I want you to do is go out there and fill up that sack out of my best corn and take it home with you this time.' It hurt Pete to take the corn but he went and done it. Owl Skinner ain't lost any more corn since."

And the baptizing was talked about by many people before it came. The converts bought clothes to be baptized in. The girls bought white dresses. The men bought flashy pants and loud neckties—silk shirts with attached collars. The long-anticipated day arrived. On the banks of Little Sandy, the birches and the sycamores waved heavy green clouds of leaves in the lazy summer wind. The devil shoestring vines ran over the loamy overflowed land. The elderberries were white in bloom. The water poured over the rocks at the ford. There were the crickets singing in the cornfields and the jarflies singing in the trees. The mud thrush would fly through the dark foliage of the water birches and hit her wings against the leaves. The snake feeders would fly up and down the brown stretch of water and sometimes would dart down and skim the surface and leave little lead-pencil waves on the water.

The wagonloads of people, sometimes two and three families in one jolt wagon drawn by two huge mules, buggy loads and express loads, would drive down to this appointed place—Put-off Ford. The birches would soon be a livery stable for horses. They would be tied to the trees far enough apart so that they could not kick and bite each other. So that the spans of mules couldn't part, a bridle rein was unsnapped from the bridle and snapped into the rings of the bits that went through the mules' mouths. Their heads were held together now. Then their tails were tied together to keep their rumps close together and to keep them from getting away. In many places corn would be laid down on a coffee sack or in a wooden box for the mules. When they left, the ground looked like

a barnyard by the corncobs and manure left there. Many of the
horses would squeal and kick. Horses and mules are like men. There
are many figures of earth among them. "What do you know about
a brute like that! He just laid his ears back and squealed. He jumped
and bit my horse's ear off—plum off—clean up against that knot
on the base of his head." One thing that makes them mean is that
they are free to roam the hills at home. Then put them in strange
company and you can bet they are aware of all that is around them.

When the horses were placed in the woods in safety, the wagons
were parked upon the bank. Rocks and pieces of driftwood were
carried and put back of the rear wheels. Many of the strong men
took the tongues of the wagons and cut the front carriages around
so that the wheels couldn't roll. Everything was got ready before
the baptizing came off. If a wagon got started and rolled down the
bank full of people and among the people, someone was sure to
get hurt. Sometimes one would start and a strong man would lock
a wheel until other men could assist him in getting it solidly and
safely placed.

The girls, many in number and all dressed in white, the old,
fewer in number, and the young men, still less in number and dressed
in flashy clothes, all got down near the river. Some sat on wagon
tongues, many on logs and others on rocks. They awaited their
turn. "Say, Mart, what ever made them call this Put-off Ford? Do
you know?" "Yes, Cy, it was in my Pap's day when it got its name.
I've heerd him tell it over and over again. Old Silas Woodberry
bought all the land around here in the early days. He was awful
wicked. But Silas was a good worker. He took a notion to put a
mill in right here. He put in a big milldam across where you see
them rocks there. When he had finished the dam, Brother Tobbie
came along here and said to him: 'Silas, don't you know they ain't
no use for you to do all these big things? You can't take them to
Heaven with you. Why don't you build big mansions and milldams
for God?' Silas, he up and says: 'Brother Tobbie, I doubt if there is
a God Almighty.' Then Brother Tobbie he says back to Silas: 'Now,
Silas, did you know God Almighty could clear this dam right out

of here in twenty-four hours? Now, you defy God and see if he don't.' Silas lifted his eyes to the heavens and he said: 'Lord God Almighty, if there is one, sweep out this dam in twenty-four hours. You can't do it. If you do, I'll believe in you.' Gentlemen, of all the rains that mortal eyes have ever witnessed, it fell that night. It cleaned that dam right out. Just them few rocks you see scattered across there is all's left. The place has been a ford since that time. Silas Woodberry got down on his knees some'rs right along here on this sand. He lifted up his eyes to the God in Heaven. He said, 'Now, God, I want to build milldams to catch the drifting souls. Take me on to help you in your work. I believe, God, that you are a living God and could strike me down this minute. Oh, God, I want to carry your heaviest cross.'

"And old Silas caught many souls in the dam he built for the Lord. He bore a heavy cross. But now he lies sleeping out yander on the ridge where you see them pines waving in the wind. And many pieces of broken dishes have been carried there by little children that loved him and put them on his grave. Some blue vases hold old dried stems of flowers. The boards at his head have rotted down. There ought to have been a stone put there, Cy, saying:

> 'Silas Woodberry
> 1810-1905
> He built milldams for the Lord
> to catch the drifting souls. He
> bore the heaviest cross. Now
> here he rests in the lap of this
> cold earth.'"

The preacher walked out into the muddy waters of Little Sandy. He took two strong men with him. In his hands he carried a light chestnut fence rail. He would measure the water here and there. He was trying to find a place free from snags and rocks. The water was the color of faded gold—a yellow ribbon of rippled water flowed under the water-birch trees. The sunlight could only fall at midday when it came directly downward on the water. The trees spread far over the banks and their tops nearly met over the middle of the stream. There was only a long clean line through the tops where the sky could be seen from the riverbank. The preacher would go on searching for a safe place. "Funny crick—you just can't never see no bottom. It's muddy all the time. Must be them mud turtles and water moccasins always stirring it up." The preacher has found a place.

Sister Tister is the first to follow the preacher into the brown swirling water. The water makes her clothes cling tight to her body. When the water is close under her arms, they stop. He waves his hand for the choir on the bank to sing:

> "Yes, we shall gather at the river
> Where the saints of our fathers trod,
> Yes, we shall gather at the river,
> The beautiful, the beautiful river
> That flows by the throne of God."

There is a splash of water. Words have been said. Sister Tister is up and she is shouting. The two strong men keep her from running into the deep water or from hitting a snag. Women on the riverbank are sobbing and shouting. She comes out of the river shouting. She shouts all over the bank. She goes down exhausted. She begins to jerk, lying stretched out in her wet clothes on the sand. The clothes fit tight against her body.

Then Sister Wilburn is called. She rises from a stone at the edge of the stream and wades out to the waiting preacher. The song goes on as he lowers her beneath the water. Then Sister Wilburn emerges shouting and clapping her hands. The stream surface is churned by little eddies where the bodies jump up and down in the water. Brother Peasly is called. "Say, Brother Tobbie, are you right shore they ain't no mud turtles or water moccasins out there? I'm a little shaky about it. They bite a man's fishhooks in two purty bad here when he is fishing—them and mud turtles does." But the flashy pants and the loud necktie of Brother Peasly are soon clinching his

skin. His shape is ugly, his spindly legs and his rough log body. He jumps higher and whoops louder than any woman. He comes down and his big hands hit the water like johnboat oars.

When one by one they have gone into the water and have been immersed, the last song to be sung is "Where the Healing

"[T]he 'Spring Baptizing' ...was never delayed.... If it were, there would be backsliders...." (Courtesy *David Greene Collection, Special Collections and Archives, Eastern Kentucky University Libraries*)

Waters Flow." It is all over now. Many of the wet go into the bushes and change their clothes. All of the men do and some of the women. Now they hitch up their horses to buggies, expresses and wagons and head home. It is a long line of teams leaving Put-off Ford. Men on horseback race on ahead, leaving behind the wagons with the big loads of people, toiling across the Little Sandy bottoms. They are on their way to the E.K. turnpike. The teams strain, pulling the heavy loads of people across the sand.

On the wagons, talks between people are going on—and comments are passed between wagonloads of people. "Say, Ike, how is yer tobacker crop this year?" "Ah, Fred, is your hens a-layin' many eggs since the worms went in the ground?" "I seed your bottom piece of corn over there on the Shultz's place and, Gentlemen, God Almighty don't let better corn grow out'n the earth than that corn." "Say, Dolly, I killed a chicken the other day, and it didn't have anything in its craw but a June bug. A body orta feed their hens a little cane seeds or cracked corn through July and August." "And boy, that old Sister Wilburn got right with God and don't you doubt it." "Don't Brother Cy tickle you when he is happy! He can't stand up. He just lays down and shouts and jerks." The teams would move on—slowly, rolling along over the yellow strips of country roads. There were many chugholes the drivers couldn't miss and the wagons would sink to the hubs.

The big baptizing day would be over. It would go down in community history to be talked of and talked of for years yet to come. Many men and women saved now would be saved over again the next spring. Religion would be on the decline after the heavy rains in autumn came and made the roads impassable, then it would be over until April came again. Religion in the country is hard to keep the way it has to be kept. The men get lonely and curse in their loneliness. The women's lives become empty and they talk in their emptiness. All these things, such as curses and gossiping, are against the word of God and when this is done, the people have backslidden.

These are my people moving in the caravan of wagons from the ford. I am of their flesh and blood. I am one of them. I am a product of the hills and the tobacco fields upon the steep hillsides and down in the lonely hollows between the hills. I have watched them and felt as they felt about religion. But I have finished high school now and it has changed me some. I see no use in it all. Though I stand not against it, I can never join my flesh and blood in their worship. I am not half as happy as they. I am not contented with my lot on the Kentucky soil. I told my father in the chip yard one night that fifty acres of land could not hold me.

I have often lain under the blooming apple trees and looked at the blue sky on April days. It was then my body wished to be left alone—lifeless—lazy—my brain wished for something. I thought, what if a dead man could return to me and tell all about where he had been? Then the thing would all be settled for me, and I would know exactly what to do about the whole works. If he had gone to that place called Hell, he could tell me all about it and how he had got there and so on. If he had gone to the place called Heaven, he could let me in on the secret as well, and I could go about preaching it and get nailed up like Jesus did. But dead men do not return. They lie forever with the earth.

After I had seen my brothers hauled to my grandfather's farm, I was afraid of Death. He was an evil thing to me—Death—something that takes the breath out of a body and stops the beating of a heart and changes the red and white corpuscles to blue and black. Death, something that changes the color of the face and closes the eyes. Death, sometimes coming as a friend—sometimes an enemy—but in all respects impartial to man. I had no use for Death. I hated him. Someday he would take my last brother. I would have to follow the pine box to Grandpa's pasture hill. Then, he would take my sisters, mother and father, and I'd have to follow them there. Then, he would take the girl I loved. And Death would get me. Maybe he would get me before he got them. And when I began to think about all this, I said: "To hell with Death! To hell with Death! I would fight you back but there is no way. I cannot see you. You just come."

But then I went out on the lonely hills alone. "What does it matter about all this stuff that muddles a man's mind?" I said. "Here are the woods in autumn now. The yellow poplar leaves look good in the starlight. Here are the pine trees, green through all the seasons. Here is a stream of water murmuring lonesome-like in the silence of this night. Why is it that my mind is muddled? Isn't God around me tonight? How could he make a place so lovely and so lonely and stay away from it himself? He just couldn't do it. I know that he is here. I am going to speak and if he hears me, all right, and if he doesn't, all right." And I said a prayer in my own words to God in the silence of the night around me. "God, if you can create a universe and if you did create this one, you can give me a backbone like this Kentucky black oak I am leaning against. You can give me two fists like sledge hammers I drive fence posts with. You can give me a body that is as endurable in its season as this hill I am standing on. You can give me a sound brain. Surely you will do this much for one individual. And when you have given me these things, I will not go about shouting your Holy Name, for I know you have grown tired of that already. But I will make use of these strengths in a different way. I shall not tell about Heaven and Hell. I am sure people have heard enough about them already. I know I have. The black-oak backbone will make me felt among the worthless. With the sledge-hammer fists, I shall slap down kings and constables. With a body like a hill, I shall take all the flying missiles and bullets harmlessly into my flesh. The brain will have a strong body and I shall warp it to do the things that need be done. I shall live a life that is worth the effort and the time. With my neighbors I shall live on the square. If they rebel, I shall slap a face. I shall be felt. I shall not be afraid of the Devil. I shall not be afraid of Death." I have grown strong since that night. I did not hear a voice. I got consolation from the silence of the hills.

And now in the end when I meet Death, if I am still young or if I have grown old, I shall not be afraid. Millions and millions have met him before, and I am no better than they. I know it will at least be something new. It is something I have wondered often about. I shall think of my young friend, Alton Felch, that went to meet him. Alton was forced by poverty to leave school and become a section laborer. The motorcar he was riding in was struck by a freight train one foggy morning. Two days later on Hill Cemetery, I was one of the eleven baseball players that he had played with, in a line going up to see him in a coffin with a glass lid. I paid my last respects to him with a handful of wild flowers and a baseball— things I knew he loved in life.

I remember how he had once taken long trips over the country. Then he would come back with a smile on his face and say to us: "Goody, I've been someplace you ain't been. I've seen something you ain't seen." And now I saw Alton in much better clothes than he had been used to wearing. He was dressed neatly and clean.

And on his face was a smile—and his curved lips seemed to say: "Goody, I've been someplace you ain't been. I've seen something you ain't seen." Then why should I be afraid? I shall meet Death as I have met Life—unafraid and ready for the change—ready for something new—ready to tackle and to fight!

The Mitchell Stuart family home, built by Jesse and Grandfather Nathan Hilton   (From *Jesse: The Biography of an American Writer*, by H. Edward Richardson, McGraw-Hill, 1984)

Jesse with sister Glennis—the oldest and youngest of Mitchell and
Martha Stuart's children—ca. 1926   *(Courtesy Jesse Stuart Collection,*
Forrest C. Pogue Special Collections Library,
Murray State University, Murray, Kentucky)

Chapter V
The Merry-Go-Round

We walked beneath high floating clouds and across the windy fields. Maria was the daughter of a Sandy River bottom farmer. Her home was in a little plank house at the foothills, under some oak trees. But I had vowed that I would marry Maria Sheen. She was strong as a sapling and as restless as the wind. Her long, wide, dark eyes with heavy lashes, her dark skin, her curved lips and her rows of white teeth made her beautiful to me. The first time I met her at the Plum Grove schoolhouse, I vowed I'd marry her. Professor Iron Hand would not let us look at one another at school. I hated him for it. We had a girls' side of the schoolhouse and a boys' side. And the playground was divided as well.

Behind the schoolhouse, we played together. The boys played London Bridge with the girls. Two girls would stand facing each other clasping each other's hands, held high. We formed a circle and marched under the arch of the bridge they formed. In the meantime we would be singing:

> London Bridge is falling down, falling down,
> London Bridge is falling down, falling down,
> Oh, London Bridge is falling down, falling down,
> Falling down, falling down, is falling down,

Falling down, falling down, so merrily.
Build it up with sticks and stones, sticks and stones,
Build it up with sticks and stones, sticks and stones,
Oh, build it up with sticks and stones, sticks and stones,
Sticks and stones, sticks and stones, sticks and stones,
Build it up with sticks and stones, so merrily.

We would circle under the two girls' arms that formed the bridge and keep singing "London Bridge" until the two girls would select either a boy or girl. The arms of the London Bridge would close around him, and the two girls would take him out to one side and ask him who he loved. The rest of us in the circle would be anxious to know, and we would wait until the two girls returned with him. Once the arms of London Bridge fell around Big Andy Howell. And when the girls came back, one said: "Maria Sheen." Big Andy was the biggest boy in school. And when we played Fox and Dog, Big Andy was always the Fox. He could outrun the rest of us over the big meadows on the uplands, through the woods and down the hollows. Sometimes we would start away from the schoolhouse as soon as we ate our lunch, and that didn't take long. We got an hour for noon, and many times we chased Big Andy for an hour and then never caught him. We would come in, wet with sweat, after school had begun for the afternoon. We'd miss our first recitation and have to stand for a long time as punishment. We could never trap Big Andy and catch him. I was one of the fastest hounds, and it killed me because I could never catch Big Andy, the Fox.

One day in the schoolhouse, I climbed upon a seat and leaped off around Big Andy's neck and twisted him to the floor. He had on a new pair of overalls and a new shirt. He said: "I'll get you going home over the hill as soon as school is out." He had two sisters and two brothers in the school, and I had two sisters and one brother. We walked a path together, just the nine students from the two families. I knew Big Andy would get me. But he had always liked my eldest sister. I always liked him until he started to claim

Maria Sheen for his own. I just couldn't stand that.

When we started across the hill that afternoon, Big Andy, Little Eif, and Ennis Howell and James and I were on ahead. Big Andy said: "Here is the place I'm going to get you. You are not big enough for me. I could break you in two. My brother Little Eif can whip you. Take him on, Little Eif." Little Eif did everything Big Andy told him. Little Eif made a rush for me on the hill. I stepped aside. He missed and sprawled on his belly down the hill. James and Ennis took up the fight. James was much younger but when they fought they always mixed it up, and it was a good fight. The girls came running up through the apple orchard. Big Andy's eldest sister, Murt, got a dead apple-tree limb and started to come over my head with it. My eldest sister grabbed her arm just in time. My youngest sister Mary and Linnie Howell started pulling each other's hair.

Sis said: "There's not going to be any fight here. I'm going to tell your Professor Iron Hand on the whole pile of you. Jesse, you are always starting something." We stopped the girls from fighting and our brothers. My, how the hair was flying! James was getting the better of Ennis. He had his nose bleeding. He was handling his fists like a man but crying. They were fighting like hound dogs only they were not snapping, they were really fighting. Sis said: "I'd be ashamed if I were you boys. Andy, I thought you were too much of a man to be fighting with a bunch of boys." Andy looked pleased when Sis called him a man among boys. He said: "I'm sorry about it all. Your brother over there started this fight. Look at my clean clothes how dirty he made them when he threw me down in the schoolhouse. Now don't you tell my Mom on us, and we'll not tell your Mom on you. And don't any of you tell Professor Iron Hand." It was all agreed that we wouldn't tell anybody about the fight.

Little Eif was still rolling on the ground and crying with his stomach. The hard rocks that he had fallen on had grained and bruised the skin on his stomach. He was in much pain and misery.

Every time I went to the Put-off Ford to swim, over where

Maria Sheen lived, Big Andy would come over there lurking around.

Once I said to Sis: "You know I think Big Andy is a fine boy. Why don't you go with him? I think he claims you. I saw your initials 'S.S.' on the bottom of his dinner bucket. He can outrun any boy in school. He is our Fox at school. I believe you can take him from all the rest of the girls." She saved my head from more than one dead apple-tree limb, but she would not sacrifice herself in my love affairs to remove a dangerous rival. I always wanted to whip Big Andy with my fists but never could. It was always an honor in our school to be the Fox. Big Andy was always the Fox.

I would make excuses to Maria's mother and father when I went there that I had come to play with her brother. I had it all fixed up with him. He helped me along and for compensation I helped him with a girl over in W-Hollow. His girl was named Nettie. I would go and get the cows with her. I would say: "Nettie, you're going with the best boy in the hills, Antis Sheen." She always said the same thing in reply, "Yes, I think so." "And we'll be sister-in-law and brother-in-law someday. You see, I'm going to marry Maria. We are going to live in Ireland in a mud house and eat potatoes. She said she would go with me." Nettie would laugh and laugh.

The cowbells would sound on a far hill. We'd have to hurry to get the cows before dark. "Nettie, your father has left your mother and you have no brothers. How would you like to claim me for a brother—you and Virginia? I'll take care of you, and if anybody says anything about either one of you, I'll whip them or they'll whip me. All I want you to do is talk to Maria Sheen for me." "Yes, I'll talk to her." Darkness fell around us. The cows were still far away. We had lingered in the woods talking about our lovers. We were two children far back in the hills. But we were children with dreams.

I went to Sheens' house every Sunday. I always asked for Antis. Maria always came to the door. We would slip off down the dusty pasture lanes. The cowbells would tinkle on the green hillsides. The cow flies swarmed over the horseweed tops. We walked together and laughed and laughed. It was great to be with my Maria even if we were barefooted and the dry clods of dirt around the old wagon ruts hurt our feet. "When we get to Ireland, we'll not have to sneak out like this. We'll go anywhere we please. It will be all right then." "When we get to Ireland, you'll buy me some shoes, won't you? You'll buy red ribbons for my hair. You'll buy me new clothes to wear." "Yes, I'll get you anything you want and then something besides." "You may be like a man my Papa told about. He said there was a young man and a young girl in a buggy. They were going to get married. The horse stumbled and fell over a stone. The man said: 'Poor old Kate! Did it hurt you, poor horse?' Five years later he drove across that place and Kate fell again. He had the same girl with him and they had four children. When Kate fell, he said: 'Get up there, Kate, damn your old looks! Can't you stand up!' He said a lot more bad words that I'm not going to say." "No, I'll not be like that and if you think I will, I'll not marry you. I'll marry some other girl and take her to Ireland and live in a dirt house." "You're not going to do it. You've got to marry me. You've done said you would."

From the pasture land, we stole off down through the tobacco field, out across the cane patch and down to the ford. The chain that fastened the johnboat to a birch was locked but could be slipped off the birch root. I slipped the chain off the root. "Climb in and we'll go down to Shackle Run and back. If the boat turns over going over the rapids, could you swim to the shore?" "No, I can't swim across Little Sandy." "Well, that won't make any difference whether you can swim or not. I can save you. I am the boss of everything." "My Mama said not to let any man boss me." "Well, your Mama hasn't got anything to do with this." "I know she has too." "Well, you'll not get to Ireland with me. I'll marry—let me see—oh yes, I'll marry Quadroon Mott." "No, you'll not do it. You are going to marry me. You've done said you would."

The boat dipped and swirled over the eddying stream. Maria caught leaves drifting on the water. She said about the leaves: "These leaves on this water are strange ships. They are going to faraway lands. Watch them drift and drift. There goes one to England, there goes one to Japan, and over there, that poplar leaf is going to China. But the big red oak leaf over there is going to Ireland. We are going to take a ship for Ireland. We'll get to see fields of water bigger than these hills and a strange land when we go to Ireland."

When we rowed back against the current and tied the john-boat back in its moorings, darkness was settling over the Sandy Valley. The yellow moon was riding in the clear sky above the tobacco fields. Dew was glistening on the cane tops. The corn blades were rustling in the slow-moving wind. I took her hand and we ran across the sand bottoms together. We went in by the potato patch at the back of the barn. Antis met us before we got in sight of the house. "Say, Maria, Mama's been hunting all over the place for you. She said she was going to tickle your legs with a switch for staying away so long. She thought maybe you had gone over to play with Sis Womack. But Runyon said he couldn't find you there. She's worried about you, Maria." "Listen, Antis, I'll tell Nettie a lot of good things for you. Now don't you tell Maria's Mama about us being out together. You go away for a few minutes and then I'll leave." "If Mama ever sees you two a-kissing, there'll be more than one with switched legs."

Antis goes on about his work. We linger in the potato patch just for a minute. Then I slip off down through the tobacco patch and out through the cane to the road. We did this over and over again. I gave myself happiness by saying I'll marry Maria. I'll drive her in a big automobile. I'll get one so big that no other car can pass it on the road. All that people can see of us will be a big streak and dust following.

When I went to high school and started studying Robert Burns' poetry, I thought more than ever about marrying Maria Sheen. I read where Robert Burns and Highland Mary dipped their hands under the water together and held Bibles in their other hands. This was a token of eternal engagement. Maria Sheen and I must go to Sandy and do the same thing under the shade of the birch trees. We were still going to marry, but I had changed my dream and was going to write many poems for Maria. We would not go to Ireland.

Now together we walked before her mother. We went in the afternoons down to Put-off Ford. We walked through the grain fields and the pasture fields where horseweed and milkweed grew in waves. It was a lonesome place. The katydids sang in the dark places. The crickets sang in the sunny weed fields. It was a dreamy, hazy land of the long long ago. It was our Kentucky land of Robert Burns. The Little Sandy was the River Ayr. Maria was my Highland Mary. She was tall, strong, slender and beautiful. The dark skin and the curved lips and the white teeth, and the laughs and laughs we had together. We were happy. The water fell over the rocks at the ford, and the sound of water falling would make us stand a long while in silence. Then we went where the water was falling and sat on the stones and watched the foam gather on the turf.

We got the johnboat again and went upstream to a little riffle below the deep hole and two little islands where green twisted grass with a little yellow bloom grew to be waist high. There the marsh hens were nesting. They flew from their wild haunts with many terrifying screams. There were young marsh hens in the nest with little feathers on their wings and tails and their bodies were covered with soft feathery down. We took the johnboat back and moored it at the roots of the birch tree. We went back across the Sandy bottoms. We went back along the garden filled with sunflowers along the palings. Morning-glories and gourds vined out of the garden and over the palings. The gourds had long crooked necks and little round plump bodies. "These are to make drinking gourds out of." "Well, how many drinking cups do you need?" "By the time we give the neighbors all they want and Father lays out all he needs to use in salting the cattle, there'll not be many left."

"Maria, tomorrow night the *Cotton Blossom Showboat* will be anchored at Greenup. Would you like to go?" "Oh yes, but my father will not let me." "Yes, but your aunt lives in Greenup. Make an excuse to go there and stay all night. Then I'll meet you there and we'll go on to the show." "That is the thing and we'll do it." I parted from Maria. She haunted me all the time. Her beauty was impressive and striking.

The next day we were planning for the show. We could hear the calliope playing "Dixie." If ever there is a time when my feet want to move, it is when I hear the immortal "Dixie Land." Many Southern melodies were sent out over the town and nearby villages. "Old Kentucky Home," that sinks deeply into the heart of every Kentuckian, was the last number played.

I went to Maria's aunt's home for her. We tripped together down the streets of Greenup, under the shade of the maple trees and under the flare of electric lamps hanging above the streets. "Did you know I helped to build all the streets? It was pretty white concrete then. But now it is dark and the concrete is broken." "No, I didn't know that you helped to build these streets. What did you do?" "I worked at the mixer. I threw in the cement. I had an easy job. The boss gave it to me because he liked me."

We were soon on the gangplank and inside the boat. The boat was a gay place and we did love the acting. I loved to see the girls

Showboat *America* on the Ohio River, 1932

"The boat was a gay place.... I loved to see the girls come on the stage and dance."

come on the stage and dance. Maria loved the music. We enjoyed the boat. When we left the boat, I said: "Let us take in all the coming attractions on this river—the *French Sensational*, the *Water Queen* and the *America* are billed to follow soon." "Yes, it will be great to get out and go and go, but you know, Stuart, it is hard for me to get away from home." "Ah, well, we'll fix that all right. And street carnivals are coming here too. One will be here next week. Let's take it in. Let's go in big fashion."

High school was over now. I was working on the farm and going with my Maria. We went together and laughed together because we were happy. The days went rapidly by. At home, on the farm, the crops were planted again and the corn was bursting through the soil. The oats were green on the hillsides. "Mitch, that boy ain't what he used to be any more. I worry a lot over him. Some mornings I get up and walk the floor because he does not come home. He gets in here at one and two in the morning, and three and four some mornings. I don't know what is wrong." "Yes, and much of the corn land is lying idle this year. He don't take any interest in his work any more. He used to be as good a worker as I ever saw go in the field. But I can't say that now. He's getting trifling about his work. I found him asleep at the plow the other evening when I came in from work. He has got it in his head to leave the old place here." "Yes, I hate to see my children go."

I wanted something I could no longer find in the hills. I wanted to go away and leave and stay years and then return to see the change. I wanted flashy colors, gay clothes, parties, romance, the splash of the Ohio River water against the shore—the darkness—the red lights reflecting on the oozing and splashing waters. These things appealed to me more than any farm with all its trains of crows, hawks, hounds, rabbits and buzzards—more than all the dark woods and the white clouds floating over. There was beauty in dancing women on a showboat, their bodies swaying to lively music. I thought I would get a job on the boat. I asked the manager about it. "What kind of acting can you do? Can you sing or dance?" "Sing a little, but can't dance." "I'll give you a job shoveling coal

down in the engine room for your board and seven dollars a week."
"You'll play hell. I want something different to that. I'll stay on the
farm where I am first before I take it."

The next week Maria and I were at the carnival in Cole's Field
on the west side of Greenup. There were farm boys there standing
back grinning. The girls at the stands were shouting:

*"All right—right this way—win something each and every time.
Come right this away, Boys, and win something for your sweetie.
Come on, win a baby doll—come on, Boys—don't be bashful!
Come and spend a nickel—a dime—a quarter."*

The tents were pitched in the shape of the letter U. The Ferris
wheel, the merry mix-up and the merry-go-round were out in the
center of the U. At the open part of the letter, was the entrance. At
the entrance was a stand to allure the farm boys:

*"All right, Big Boy—you with them big brown arms—come right
over here, Sweetie. Come over here and show these boys how to
knock the kitties off the bench. Come right this away. Three balls
for a dime, and three kitties knocked off, a quarter! Right over
this way, Boys, for the big payday!"*

The farm boys would first stand off and grin and then they
kept coming closer. One picked up the courage to throw three balls.
Then it was a race among them to keep the bench and throw. After
a few minutes, one could hear the boys talking: "Boy, I lost every
damn cent I had over there at that stand. Them cats are weighted at
the bottom and light at the head. They're hard to knock off. They
are loaded cats. Hell, I threw my arm away and lost my money
too—damn sawdust baseballs!"

The street carnival was a fascinating place to me, the painted
showmen, the dancing girls, the vagabond life and the old dull
music of the merry-go-round—the whole thing was fascinating!
The whole works was a merry-go-round. I made up my mind to get

a job and follow it. I didn't tell Maria what my intentions were. I heard people say: "Damn cheap bunch following a fair, ain't they? Look at them women with painted lips after the greenhorn boys. They're taking the bait set for them too. Damn ornery people. They ought to all be shot." I didn't feel that way about them. I felt as if they were people getting a satisfaction out of living by going from town to town. Where a man settles to one place, his life would someday become empty, I thought. I would follow the merry-go-round.

I walked with Maria that night through the entanglements of

*"I wanted
something
I could
no longer find
in the hills....
flashy colors,
parties,
romance...."*

A frustrated young Jesse

*(Courtesy H. Edward
Richardson Collection,
Ekstrom Library,
University of Louisville)*

human beings. The white and red streamers of confetti were flying through the crowd. The clowns and the people threw it. It was a great life to me. I wore a gray suit and a gray felt hat. My dark-skinned Maria wore a combination of blue and red. We never laughed more than we did that night together. I took her home after the night gayness at the carnival. It was the last night with my Maria Sheen.

I walked three miles after I left Maria's aunt's home. It was three miles back over the lonely hills into W-Hollow. My whole life was empty. I hated the hills. I had a desire to leave and never return. That night a whippoorwill called lonesome-like by the meadow lands near the house. A fox barked on the ridgetop. My horses neighed to me as I passed the barn. It was about the time my father got up. It was four o'clock and he left for work about five in the morning. I slipped to the water bucket and gorged on water. I put the gourd on the table so that he could not hear me. I slipped upstairs. I said to myself: "You ought to see me, Pa, I'm leaving here sometime today. My life is too empty here. I can stay no longer. I can stand it no longer . . . Mom, this is the last meal you will cook for me for a long time."

Upstairs in my room, I never went to bed. I lighted the old oil lamp on the table where my books were. There were my old friends there in three little rows. I didn't like them now. I was tired of books. I was tired of everything. As far as I was concerned, every-thing could go to hell. Why was I ever born? I gathered all the clothes I had now, which were few in number, and packed them away in an old yellow pasteboard suitcase. I hid the suitcase be-hind the dresser. Then I took the books one by one and threw them out of the window. They were all deceitful things. I would burn them all. They did not give me life. Life can be put into a book but life cannot be taken from a book. The man that gets life must get down and put his hands on it. He must hide his face in the wet leaves of the earth. What good had the books done me? I had even acted crazy over them for a little while. Little Sandy River, the River Ayr—Maria Sheen, my Highland Mary? W-Hollow, the land of Robert Burns? It was all a joke. It was all a big joke! A brown-skinned farm boy put his face against the quilts his mother had made for his bed and cried.

"Jesse, roll out! It is work time! I've fed the horses and harnessed them for you. Get James up when you get up." I had never gone to bed. I got James out of bed. We ate breakfast together. I drank three cups of strong coffee. "What is the matter, Son?" "Oh, a little headache is all. It'll wear off soon." I slipped out behind the house after I had eaten breakfast to where I had thrown my books. I carried them to the wash kettle under a hickory tree by the edge of the chip yard. There I blew life into the old embers from a yesterday's fire where my mother had washed clothes. I put the books on the fire—tearing the pages out of the thick books so that they would be sure to burn. James must not read my old books. I would not leave them behind for him. I wanted him to grow up and be happy and live without the knowledge of many books. He would not be restless then. He would settle down to the soil like my people. After the flare of the flames from my old friends, I went toward the barn after the horses.

James rode one horse out through the pasture under the pine trees and led the other. The corn ground was tough plowing. I used one horse awhile and then the other. I was plowing corn. James was thinning the corn and chopping the weeds. We worked until nine o'clock. "James, unhitch old Fred from the pine tree by the gate. I'll bring old Kate." "You ain't going in this early, are you?" "Yes, I'm going in for good. I'm quitting, James, for good. I'm leaving the hills not to return. If ever I come back, it will not be to stay." "What will we do here without you? No one is left to plow." I said nothing but I thought of Mom. She worked too hard as it was. Here I was going off and leaving my parents with all the fields to plow and hoe. I was rotten for doing it. But I was going to do it. We rode the sweaty beasts around the hillside path under the pine trees. I left James unharnessing the horses. I went to the house. I went upstairs and put on my gray suit and gray felt hat. I got my suitcase and went down to say good-by to my mother. She was cutting the weeds from around her currant vines in the garden.

"I'm leaving," I said. "Well, be a good boy and when you come back the key will be above the door where we always keep it. The door might be unlocked when you come back. I trust that you will take care of yourself. I think you will. You know I would not hold you here. But remember, chickens come home to roost. I have told you often that I would like to get out and go and go and go."

I was leaving the old home now, the house my hands had helped to build. Every stone in the chimney I helped to place, the logs, the weatherboarding, the roof and everything. I had cleared the land, set out fruit trees, and made fences. I had helped to put the farm in shape and now I was going on. Would I go on and help to clear another farm as my people had done? No. My life was made empty by the farm in the hills. I was through.

I went up the path under the peach trees—out town ridge and down to Greenup and out to the fairgrounds. I wanted to follow the merry-go-round. With the carnival, I would be free from the soil and able to keep traveling. I was through with plowing the sweaty horses, cutting sprouts from around the stumps and worming the smelly tobacco on hot days.

There was much throwing of confetti in the crowd. The men would angle up to the girls. One would step out and say something. Then they would all laugh. They would all pair off and go out to a car. They would climb in and drive away into the darkness. Very soon they would return. These men would not angle up to any other women for that night. Other men would come and take out these same women. They would keep going out with fellows until far into the night. It all looked very interesting to me. It was fascinating to follow the lure of a showman's life. I was going to see if I couldn't get work with them and leave town with them the following day.

The boss was a grouchy man with a black mustache. He slapped my shoulder and said, "Young Man, you're the very feller I'm looking for. That pinhead that I had over there taking tickets at the merry mix-up got sore and hauled his freight this morning, and

I can put you right over there." "What all do I have to do?" "The big job is keeping them back when they try to run through on you without paying for a ticket. Punch the first one that tries. Hear? Well, you can go on tomorrow." "It suits me. I am your man. Now this is something I've been wanting for a long time." "Oh, you may like it and you may not. It all depends. I've been at it myself for twenty-five years. I couldn't do anything else if I wanted to."

My tent-mate that night was Lonnie Whitt. He was the fire-eater for the carnival, and after he had eaten fire he was converted into a clown. Then Lonnie ran everywhere to attract attention and make the farm boys spend their money. Lonnie came in after he had performed and got ready for bed. He pulled off his clothes and threw them on the straw. Then he pulled a pint from under his mattress. "This life's hard as hell. Boy, you'd better stay out of it. Hell, this rotten licker a man gets here! Then everybody tells us about the good moonshine licker we'll get when we get to Kentucky. Say, where are you from anyway?" "I'm from out in the Greenup County hills." "The hell you do say! What did you do before you got with this goddamn dump?" "I farmed and went to high school."

"Well, you'd a-better stayed there if you could get your bread and clothes. This ain't no place for a young feller like you. But live and learn like I have. I didn't have anybody to tell me about it. I could have probably been a rich man today a-sitting back in my own home and taking life easy. But look at what I am a-doing! I'm eating fire to make people wonder and laugh. Then I go out and act a damn fool in a clown's clothes. Well, I am a clown. I am something to be laughed at. I am a goddamn fool. Say, have a drink. I forgot to offer it to you a minute ago." "Thanks. I don't drink." "You from Kentucky and don't drink? Well, I don't believe it."

"Where do we go from here?" I asked. "We go to Longsville. It's down in the tobacker country and there ain't no money there, the boss said. You know the price of tobacker was rotten last winter and they just ain't got no money." "What kind of women does this carnival have?" "Well, that's something else I want to warn you about. Lay off of 'em. They're what's ruined me. They are mighty nigh all burnt. And they've burnt nigh all the fellers that have come on here to work. They like to get hold of the farm boys."

The next morning the carnival trucks were rolling over the gravel road along the Ohio River. I rode with the carnival cook and his helpers in an old Ford sedan. One of them said, "Greenup was a hell of a hole. I was glad to get out of there. I didn't know whether I was going to get out of there alive or not. The rotgut licker they sell there just simply set my guts afire. They're burning yet. Hell of a dirty hole!"

Longsville was a dirty little Ohio River town. When we rolled along down the cobblestone streets—our heavy trucks lumbering along and our touring cars pepping up a little—we could see old women and old men gazing at us from the streets and in front of the stores. There were little benches placed around over the town where old men would sit and whittle and talk about the presidents and the women that passed along the street. A swarm of dirty-faced children followed us out to the grounds where we were to show.

It is a job to set the tents up and get ready for the show that night. It works the whole show gang nearly to death. When the time comes to take in the nickels and dimes, the carnival workers are tired. But then to the dead, thrumming music of the merry-go-round and the throwing of confetti—the laughs of the people, and the mingling of words and milling of almost every kind of people—there is some sort of a consolation to one that has grown weary of the hills. It is association. The place is not an empty place. But the body I fear will grow empty if it remains there. The hard work of pitching tents and the late hours at night. The little sleep on rough beds and out in the night air and the poor food—all these things have a tendency to wear strong bodies down.

My first night was great fun: "Right this away, Men, right this away—take your sweeties a fifteen-minute ride for fifteen cents! All right! All right! Come right this away! This wheel is absolutely safe! Come right on and give the girls a ride! Right this a-way—right this a-way—and have a look—have a look—right this a-way—this a-way!"

The boys would stand out in the flare of dingy electric lights and grin. They would whisper something to their girls like this: "Hell, it won't hurt you! Come on—let's try it once anyway." They would come over and buy tickets. The boys would act domineering and the girls bashful. The boys would put their arms around the girls on the Ferris wheel when it left the block where they climbed into the seats to go over and over in the air like a water wheel. When the wheel went up, the people riding for their first time acted scared. When it dropped over and they started coming down, they acted as if they were thrilled. They yelled and threw things down on the couple riding on the seat below, such as chewing gum wrappers and tin foil off candy bars. In many instances the boys would look up at the girls' legs when the wheel was bringing them down. The girls would spit down on them and call them names. They would pull their dresses close around their legs and act ashamed and think the whole crowd was staring at them. They were nearly all country girls. This was something new to me. I really loved this work. There I saw empty faces and bright faces—morbid—solemn—funny—all kinds of faces. I met all kinds of people. Some would argue with me about fifteen cents being too much to pay for the tickets. I'd tell them to go and see Cap, the boss, about it—that he was standing right out there by the gate. I would be friendly with the people riding there, and when a couple of good-looking girls got on I told Nick Larmar, the engineer of the works, to let that couple stay on for twenty minutes.

Nick was from Augusta, Georgia, and a lively old boy. He always understood what I meant when I whistled, stuck up two fingers and pointed to a certain seat on the Ferris wheel. Nick rode them as long as I asked him to. "Ah, what to hell does it matter anyway, Stuart! W'y, let the poor girls have a good time up here in these hills once in a while. This is a hell of a lonesome place, I'm telling you." I got to feeling the same way. I wanted to ride beside some of the girls there. I had left Maria and I thought of her dark skin, her white teeth and curved lips often. I thought of the grain-fields around her home and the quietness there, nothing but the sound of the whippoorwills and katydids and of waters falling and crickets singing. Now this was all different. I saw many girls. I heard different sounds from those made by the whippoorwills and the water and crickets. I heard voices all day long. I heard cries of anger and fits of laughter. Voices all day long and part of the night. It was a gay place. It was a place for love-making.

I made arrangements with a youngster there in Longsville to take up the tickets for me when I rode on the wheel, and then I would let him ride all he wanted, free. This worked splendidly. It gave me a chance to ride with the girls and laugh and enjoy myself. I was rebelling against the silence I'd known in the hills. I spent most of my work hours riding with the girls and let Wiley take up the tickets. If I saw a girl that I thought looked as if she wanted to ride, I motioned for her to come over to the wheel. "Now, I'll let you ride free, Good-Looking—just all you want to ride. We have to watch Cap. I'll get myself in Dutch if he catches me doing this."

I would ride with her. Or perhaps I'd wait for another one I'd rather ride with. The girls soon began to flock around the wheel for free rides. It was great to have so many girls—just for a night. Then they would go away and I would go on with the carnival the next week. It was always good-by. If I thought it did them any good, I told them I loved them. But deep within me I did not. I thought of Maria Sheen. I was just having a good time with these girls. I intended to marry Maria. I would go back there someday, driving a new car and dressed in fine clothes and get her.

At night when the lights blinked for the carnival to close, I went out to my tent to sleep. Many nights I could not go to sleep. I would go to bed and then get up and write poetry. I was not mastering poetry but it was mastering me. I just couldn't help writing poetry. I thought now that only little soft men wrote poetry. I wrote poetry about the cornfields since I had left them. Before, when I was working there, they were ugly. But now they had become beautiful to me. They were in my blood, I could not forget them. I thought about my brother and sisters at home and what they were doing. I wondered what they were doing for somebody to plow since I had gone. I wondered if the weeds were taking the corn and the suckers were out long on the tobacco and if the worms had eaten holes in the broad leaves. I was not sorry I had left but I pitied them back there with all the work to do. I knew just how much there was to do. I often thought of Maria Sheen. I wanted to write poetry to her and about her. She was more beautiful than the cornfields. I had a feeling for the cornfields the same as I had for Maria Sheen. I wrote these sonnets for her in the tent one night.

I

I hear the lapping of the Sandy water,
I hear it lapping—lapping night and day,
And I go down and sit beside this water
And throw in sticks and watch them float away.
Long years ago barefooted I walked there,
Unlocked the old johnboat and let it glide
Down the birch-shaded aisle of lapping water . . .
I had sweet Maria Sheen close by my side.
And how we mingled happy words and laughter!
The raincrow croaked for a downpour of rain,
The lizard roved the scaly bark for sun
While Maria Sheen sat closer by my side.
I do not know if water kissed the grain
And if that lizard found his patch of sun,
But I do know who said she'd be my bride.

II

And when I hear the lapping, lapping water,
I think of her whom I still love so dearly;
It all comes back in music of the water
The childhood Love I know I'll marry surely.
Her skin is milkweed dark, her eyes sky-blue,
Her teeth are bloodroot white, her hair is black
As thick rainclouds . . . her lips are soft as new
Bark peeled from a slippery elm and her back

Is straight as a horseweed upon the shore.
Her legs are brown as the buff-colored corn.
As I hear water lapping on the shore,
And as I see the sun rise up this morn,
I think of her that I shall see once more,
The sweetest mountain girl I've ever known.

One afternoon the girls were lined up waiting to get their free rides, and I was standing out in my gray suit and gray felt hat yelling: "Right this way, People, for the next big ride! Right this way—this way! Have a look! Have a look! Come on, now, and ride your sweeties!" Cap walked around biting on the stub of a cigar. "Stuart, you are through with me. I want you to get the hell off this ground by four o'clock. That's giving you one hour." "All right, Cap. I'd like to have my money before I go." "You have lost money for me on that Ferris wheel. Out there riding them girls free all afternoon and night! W'y, you are a hell of a guy." "This is a hell of a rotten place too. This whole fair is a joke. Now you give me what money I have a-coming to me and I'll go."

"The best thing for you, Kid, that ever happened." "Hell, Lonnie, I hate to get canned." "That shows there's something to you. Most of the damn rats with this outfit would beg to get back. They don't have any homes, you know—a lot of rusty pickups and some old wenches. I heard you a-talking to Cap. Well, good luck to you, Boy—and good-by." "Good-by, Lonnie. Don't swallow too much fire."

I was free to go again. But I would not go home. I didn't think much about losing the job I had. I was getting tired of it anyway. I wanted to go to Harvard. But I laughed when I thought of the jump from a street carnival in the hill towns of Kentucky to Harvard. Then I thought about the sea.

Harvard Or The Sea
I have lived my youth in one unsettled state
And months of barren earth is life too much for me.

The glorious close will bring me Harvard or the sea.
Nine months earth-prisoned! How can I bear to wait?
Since I was twelve, I have been foot-free to the soil;
Pocketless a dime, I've rambled through many a town
When the winter moon and silver stars slanted down;
Bunked with toughs; did with them a tremendous toil;
Met pals, forgot; stopped and took my school life stay.
Now within Harvard's halls there is one life for me.
Another life is on waste waters' blue immensity
That will make me turn my back on home, forget the day
My feet were bound to earth. Then Great Seducer Sea,
Be last to pant and lick your wet lips over me.

I wanted to go to an old college. I wanted to go to Harvard--a school with a heritage to follow. But I could not go anywhere to school. I didn't have much money. What I had I was spending freely. I knew of nothing to do. These were the thoughts I had when I was in the depot waiting for a train to take me back to Greenup.

When I reached Greenup, there was much excitement among the boys. They were all excited about Camp Knox. Twenty of them were going. Mack, the gun man and the razor man from Plum Grove, was there drunk as a lord, but he was going to Camp Knox. "Hell, Stuart, come on and go to Camp Knox with us." "W'y, that's what I'm doing here. I'm in Greenup to go to Camp Knox." I had made my mind up to go with the crowd.

Mack was drunk all the way there. He wasn't sober when he reached the camp. He could barely write his name. He had an old razor on him and an Owl Head pistol. "That damn thing'll outshoot purt' nigh anything you ever seed." When we got to Camp Knox, I had five cents. I would have had more but it took nearly every cent I had to buy a ticket for Mack. When he was crazy drunk on the streets in Greenup, he said somebody robbed him of ten dollars, all the money he had. I'll always believe he wasn't robbed at all but spent the money for more moonshine whisky.

There wasn't anybody in Company I who didn't know Mack

before he had been in camp one week. Down at the latrine one day, he stood four fellows in the corner with a razor. They were all taking a shower bath and a dispute arose among them over the water. Mack went over where his pants were hanging on a nail and got a long black-handled razor. The next day Mack was on a coal truck and three guards looked down into his sweaty collar and told him to throw the coal faster. He shoveled coal for three days. He was put in the awkward squad because he could not learn to do about-face. He hit a boy with a pair of knucks down at the Haymarket one night. He worked six days for that. Before the six days were over, Mack got sick and spent the rest of the time in the hospital. Then he came back to camp and asked for a permanent place in the kitchen. He drilled about three days, all told, before the shooting practice began. Mack went to the range. He was the best marksman in Company I. Mack had found his place. He would borrow all the cartridges he could to shoot. He would shoot for other fellows when the officers were out of sight. He would bring up the low scores. Mack was a man that meant business when it came to the use of firearms. He had carried a pistol from the time he was eight. When boys at camp asked him where he was from, he would say: "I'm from Greenup." They would laugh and say: "Where's Greenup?" "Well, hell, you been a-living this long and don't know where Greenup is!"

At Camp Knox I began to grow hungry for poetry to read. I had burned all my books at home. I obtained permission to go to Louisville one weekend. I bought everything I could find on Edgar Allan Poe. I bought another volume of Robert Burns' poetry. I kept these books stacked in the window at the foot of my bunk. I read poetry in the afternoons and swam in the pool. We drilled from six till twelve in the mornings. I thought several times I would join the army when the camp was over. This was a great life, I thought. Every Sunday I walked back over the artillery ranges and looked at the holes torn out in the earth and the sapling trees ridden down by the tanks and tractors. Old houses on the ranges had been torn to pieces by the seventy-fives. Old apple orchards had been destroyed. Old rusty barbwire fences had been torn to pieces by tanks. The place was one of complete devastation. All of this had been caused by practice on how to kill men. It all seemed queer to me. Officers showing me how to kill a man. I would have to get mighty hard to run a bayonet through a man's heart, knowing he had the same right to live that I had. I didn't like the idea of it at all.

One day I asked an officer: "Why is it man is shown how to kill man? He is taught the scientific use of firearms and how to charge in hand-to-hand combat and run a bayonet through a man's guts. Yet, out around a bar, two hours before he killed him, he would sit down and talk with the man if he had the chance." "Our country has to have protection," he said. It looked pretty damn foolish to me. I made up my mind to salute no more uniforms. Protection of a country! Many men had fallen and bled because a few told them to fight. Everybody ought to rebel and there would be no wars. It all looked so futile to me. Men fighting for presidents and kings and big holders of ammunition plants! It was a time of wiping out whole masses of people. The World War had been over seven years now. Many of the fellows in camp were World War veterans. Nearly all the officers had seen service and none of them seemed enthusiastic about war. The officers who had been graduated from military schools were the patriotic men, the fellows who tried to put patriotism into us.

One day I failed to salute one. He asked me the reason why. I did not answer. I was charged with insubordination to an officer. Had I been in the regular branch of service and not a training camp, the penalty would have been imprisonment. As it was, I carried logs and split kindling with a dull ax for one day. Another day I pulled weeds, and the third day I hauled garbage and cleaned the latrine.

One morning when the barracks were inspected, my Edgar Allan Poe books and the book of Burns' poetry were in the way. "This isn't a place for a library. We have an Army library down at Stithton. Go down there if you want to read. Be sure and keep books off your bunk when we have inspection. I shall lower the grade of this whole floor for that one thing." This seemed as crazy as hell to me. I rebelled against the whole works. At ten o'clock we were supposed to be in bed. It was hard for me to get back to the barracks from down at the Haymarket Theatre by that time. I had been running to do it all the time before. I would not do it again. I would take a dishonorable discharge first. To hell with it all!

One Thursday night I came in after taps. The officer of the day met me at the barracks door. "Halt." I halted. "Advance to be recognized." "I'm only Private in the rear rank, Sir—Sir—Sir. I'm Private Stuart." "Explain why you came in at this hour." "I went to the Haymarket to see *God's Country and the Woman*. It was a good show too." "Never mind about the show. I don't want to know about it. You be in on time from this on." I did not promise.

The next night I went to the Haymarket. I saw *The Vanishing American*. When I got to the barracks door, I was halted by the officer of the day. I made a promise to him that, if he would release me, he would never catch me out again. I didn't want to get a dishonorable discharge, much as I hated the place. He let me go on my own word. I went up on the second floor of the barracks and went to bed. I thought as I went upstairs that it was a funny thing to do—to call an officer that went snooping around at night to catch somebody an "officer of the day." But that was like the whole system. It was all wet and all wrong, or I was a misfit. I didn't like that word misfit. The boys it applied to around the camp were fellows like Mack from Greenup and Goofey somebody from Beaver Dam, Kentucky. But I was out of place at Camp Knox.

I determined to go to the Haymarket the next night. I tore the screen loose at the bottom of the window by my bunk. A ladder ran up the corner of the barracks right by this window. When the officer of the day caught me again, he would have to outrun me. I knew there were no guards in that part of the camp—nothing but snooping officers of the day. And I determined to walk from the theater again. To hell with them! Saturday night I saw *North of '36*. When I got back to camp, the officer of the day cried: "Halt!" I started running around among the barracks. He gave chase to me.

I got a good lead on him by dodging among the buildings. The last time, I made a great gain by fooling him the way I went around the latrine. He thought I went into it. But I was heading for the back of the barracks. I climbed up the ladder on the back wall of the barracks—under the screen and into the bed with my clothes on. He came up just a minute later and came to my bunk. He turned a flashlight on me and said, "Little Innocence." He went back down the stairs.

I got up in the dark and pulled off my clothes. I fooled the officer of the day three times like this. But on the fourth night he came to my bunk. I was panting hard. The sweat was running down my face. I pretended I was sleeping. He looked for my clothes at the foot of the bunk. There were none. He looked for my shoes. Then he pulled the blanket from over me. There I was dressed in uniform—in bed with my shoes on. "Well, you've got me this time." "Yes, get out of there and undress."

I got out of bed and took off my clothes. "Now, don't think you are going back to bed. Come on outside without a stitch of clothes on your body or shoes on your feet. You must run around the barracks seventeen times, and that is a light sentence."

I went out with him. My pace around the barracks was little better than a walk. The boys in the barracks woke up when they heard the racket. They began to stick their heads up against the screens and make all kinds of noises. Some crowed like chickens, some neighed like horses and others bawled like cows. In five minutes the whole outfit on the second floor was out going around the barracks seventeen times.

On the rifle range was a great redemption for me. The officer that made me run around the barracks gave me orders to fire and how to shoot. I made a sharpshooter with ease and points to spare. He took a different attitude when he saw me go up and shoot calmly and crack the bull's-eye when a heavy wind was blowing across the long space between the target and me. We stayed on the range for three days. It was a great life. I pitched up tent with Bill Taker. And the first night we did not sleep until past midnight. We talked and looked out at the stars and the thousands of fireflies on the rifle range.

After three days on the range, we marched the eight miles back and carried fifty-pound packs, including the weight of our rifles. The first time I had been to Camp Knox, I gave down on marching the eight miles and carrying the heavy pack. A fellow by the name of Harlan Staggers would carry my pack and rest me when we were on the march. But I weighed 145 pounds now and could carry two such packs as Staggers had done. And another thing, no group of boys ventured to toss me about in a blanket. I had changed completely from the boy I had been four years before. When I was a kid there, I was very humble. Now, I was older and had become, to a certain degree, rebellious. I thought for myself. In the foot drills I excelled. I was one of the four men selected as the best soldiers in the camp, though two boys out of that four rated higher than I did. The day the prize winners were called to march up and get their medals, I had to salute an officer. I did not rebel then. I took two first-place medals like a little hungry boy takes candy. I was proud to get them, one for track, the other for shooting. I thought the camp was a very good place after all. But the one thing about Camp Knox that still lingers in my mind was the three days' battle we fought. It was called "the Maneuvers."

Maneuvers was the time when every man in camp was used. There were about thirty-six hundred of us. We were divided into two equal armies. The infantries were divided, the cavalry troops were divided, the machine-gun companies and the artillery battalions were divided. One army, under the supervision of World War officers, maneuvered on one side of the thirty-four-thousand acres of camp reservation. And the other army, the same in number, just as well equipped and under the same type of officers, maneuvered on the other side of the reservation. The two armies met in the woods and on the old blackberry fields on the artillery range.

The planes drummed in the air overhead and dived under and over the bombing planes. The artillery battalions were constantly echoing like low thunder from their places in the woods. The machine gunners were shooting from nests in the woods and black-berry briars. "What if they were using ball ammunition instead of blanks?" I thought to myself. "We would not last long out on this open field. The blackberry briars now black with berries would be red with blood. The old apple orchards would be torn to pieces, and the white draft horses with flaxen manes and long flaxen tails and broad rumps that drew the artillery along would have their guts ripped out and hanging down from their sides." War must be hell on white horses. They are good targets. But this was not really war—we were only boys out there getting a lesson on what war is like.

When I saw a rifle grenade shot into the air, I wanted to run. I could not help it. I knew it would not fall within range of any of us, but I was afraid. I would try to run under the edges of banks and get behind trees for fear one was going to fall on me. I thought of the horses all the time. Man could find places to hide in. He knew what to do. But a horse just has to stand and take war as it comes. He is slaughtered and, like the men in most wars, for no reason. Anyone knows a horse has nothing to do with man's troubles. Then why drag horses into war? There ought to he a universal law against it.

We had to crawl on our stomachs through the saw-briars when we were facing our enemy's line of fire. It was a hot day and our uniforms were wet with sweat. We fired all day without food and then part of the night. Dog-tired, we went back to camp and were glad to get there. We threw ourselves on our bunks any old way for sleep that night. The next morning at 5:45 reveille was sounded. We were a sore and sleepy bunch of men. But the maneuvers are the last thing in Camp Knox, and we are going home. We give our uniforms back and get our civilian clothes from the storeroom. I am glad to leave that place. I want to see people in civilian clothes. I want to see women in flashy dresses. I want to just see women. I don't care who they are, just so that I see them.

We are all saying good-by now. We are comrades and we drink the wine together. We carry heavy suitcases, with some of our belongings tied on the outside. I carry a little slip of paper that says "is Honorably Discharged on this day" and so on. Mack tells us that he got a D.D. "Hell, it's all the same to me—a dishonorable discharge is as good to me as a honorable one." I stop at the Army Library at Stithton and find a book called *Carlyle's Essay on Burns*, edited by Edwin Mims. I ask to buy the book. "We can't sell any of the library books." "Well, no one here is reading it for the book is in mint condition." "That doesn't matter. You'll have to buy one someplace where they sell books." I put the book back and when the librarian was not looking I put it under my sweater and carried it out. I found out, going back on the train, that the book was great reading for me.

I now thought of how my people loved to fight in wars. I thought of how they enlisted. None of them was ever drafted. Back on the Plum Grove Hill, down among some briars, was the grave of Uncle Bob Stuart. The only thing on his thin white stone was his name, date of his birth and death, and the words "43rd Kentucky Infantry." But I couldn't see where the glory was in taking chances of killing a man or getting killed myself. And before I got to my destination that night, I thought about a cousin killed in the World War. When he left the Big Sandy Valley, he said he would send back the Kaiser for a souvenir. But he never got the Kaiser. Someone got him. Jim's mother, long returned to dust, will tell you the story.

Jim

Kentucky gave my father to the Blue,
Kentucky gave his brother to the Gray;
My own Jim charged the San Juan with Teddy
And malaria fever put him under clay.

And I remember what my Grandma said,
So many years my Grandma has been dead:

"A bird flew in
At th' head o' my bed,
It told me that
My man was dead
And it flew out again.

"The bird came back
To th' head o' my bed,
And told me that
His brother was dead
So early in the morning."

And Grandma said:
"This was a sign of warning.
My man fell at Cold Harbor
And left me home a-mourning.
The news of his own brother,
The one who wore the Gray,
Came only two hours later . . .
He fell there the same day.
I wondered if their mother
Thought brother had killed brother . . .

Not men, but women have
The price of war to pay."

II

And I have been a widow to this day,
Since Jim sleeps high upon the mountainside;
He has gone back unto Kentucky's clay,
And Blue and Gray, my Jim now sleeps beside.
I've kept a flag above his through these years,
And I have kept his resting place so clean;
I have gone there and shed so many tears
When I would think what our lives could have been.

And I just think what Grandma used to do,
Hoe in her hand and basket on her arm,
Alike, she kept their graves of Gray and Blue
Where only sheep-bells rang to do them harm.

III

I got a pension and I raised my boy,
Much like his father and was named for him;
He was a man of strength, my pride and joy,
And all I had was none too good for Jim.

He would come home after the way he plowed,
And cut stovewood and help me wash a dish;
On Sundays he would laugh above the crowd,
And how he always loved to hunt and fish.

And Jim was strong and had the finest looks,
And all the girls were kindly after Jim;
His teacher said he was so smart in books,
He used to come and talk for hours with him.

I remember how Jim plowed that April.
I can't forget, it hurt in such a way
When he came home from plowing on the hill . . .
The call to France took my last son away.

So good to work, so big and fine and strong!
Jim marched away—he was a volunteer!
And at the train Jim says: "Don't worry, Mom,
You'll get the Kaiser for a souvenir."

IV

And when he went away my heart was stone.
I got a letter every day from him,

And living in the old house all alone,
I set the table just the same for Jim.

I just pretended that I saw his face,
And just pretended that he talked to me;
I kept his guns right in the same old place,
And all his clothes just like they used to be.

I kept the mules unharnessed in the field
While all the plows were rusting in the shed,
Weeds grew on slopes where always we had yield
Of corn to feed the mules and make our bread.

And Jim was rushed across to No-Man's Land . . .
It was so long before I heard from him . . .
And all this war so hard to understand...
Leaves turned . . . no rabbit hunting now for Jim!

V

Jim wrote once more: "It's strange this fighting here.
We rabbit-hunt such different way in France.
We'll hunt the entire season of the year
With gas and gun, man hardly has a chance.

"Not fair as hunting rabbits on the hill,
 When rabbits find a hole we let them be;
 But we get in a hole and still they kill...
 We blast each other to eternity.

"W'y, Mom, these men we kill we seldom see,
 If not in war we'd sit and talk like brothers,
 And why we fight's beyond the life of me
 And leave clean beds, our hills and dogs and mothers."

VI

Snow left the hills and winter was a-breaking,
And straths of green were spreading up the hollows;
And poke-stalks in the silver winds were shaking
And tender leaves were coming to creek willows.

"A bird flew in
At th' head o' my bed,
So early in the morning.
It told me that
My Jim was dead,
My Jim was dead . . .
I knew the sign of warning.
My Grandma used to say:
*'Not men, but women have
the price of war to pay.'*"

The letter says: "He fell, but not in vain,"
When I'm too old to bear another son!
Briars will grow from Jim's heart, trees from his brain,
His heritage is doomed to carry on.

My Jim so big and proud and strong and tall,
They sent him in a coffin back to me;
My Jim, so smart and good to work and all,
Must now be planted like an apple tree.

Only the tree bears fruit and Jim will not . . .
Wrapped in the stars and stripes his cold, cold clay,
We planted him today to be forgot,
My Jim, who volunteered and marched away!

VII

I got the crosses later that Jim won
But what could all these crosses mean to me
For taking lives of other mothers' sons
And planting them for worm and briar and tree?

Spring has come back and sprouts grow up again,
The mules run in the pasture fields unshod;
No one to plant the corn and sow the grain,
Nor break a furrow, nor to disk a clod.

I set Jim's plate as I have always done
And talk to him a-sitting in his chair;
The old house here, the dog and me alone . . .
I just pretend that my son Jim is there.

As much as I have said against war, no country could invade
my country and slaughter my people unless they'd do it over my
dead body. If a country is not worth fighting for, it is not worth
living in. Just to think, my home and my people among the hills
that I have always known, the trees, briars, brush, rocks and wild
flowers thereon, are these not worth fighting for? The cornfields
on the high hill slopes growing in the silver showers of spring and
the creamy-colored wheat fields on the uplands in July beneath the
great expanse of white clouds that float across the wide blue heavens,
and the loamy sags with the heavy tobacco crops where the broad
leaves flop-flop in the wind . . . these timber-covered hills, are they
not worth fighting for? Isn't the rugged earth that holds my dead
and feeds me with bread worth fighting for, and these hundreds of
acres of elbowroom? The golden autumn hills and the full bins of
ripe harvest from the slopes, I would fight for these.

The American Rolling Mill Company, Ashland, Kentucky
(Courtesy *The Courier-Journal*)

"They were all men of bronze. Their faces had been tanned by fire heat."

Chapter VI
Cool Memories of Steel

Tonight a cool summer rain is falling. I am standing in front of the Raeburn Hotel. I have sixty cents in my pocket. I cannot get a room and a bed for sixty cents. I need forty more. I shall be here for a couple of hours, and then I shall spend a couple of hours out on the corner of the square at a poolroom. I know one boy that works at this poolroom. From the poolroom, I shall go to the railroad depot and spend the night sleeping on one of the long seats there as if I am waiting for a train. I must not go to sleep and let someone steal my suitcase. It is all I have. Early in the morning, I shall go to the Armco employment office and see John Findlay about a job. I shall be the first at the office to see if I can get work. If I do not get work, I shall join the Navy. One must be twenty-one years of age to get work at the Armco plant. I am eighteen but I shall not lie to them when they ask me if I am over twenty-one. I shall be over twenty-one.

I am leaving the lobby of the Raeburn Hotel. A man approaches me. He wants something. "Say, Pal, how about helping a fellow out of a pinch, will you? I just want enough to buy a loaf of bread with. I am a war veteran. I fought in the World War and a German run a saber in my left lung. I'd like for you to help me along if you can. A loaf of bread won't go bad for an ex-soldier standing out in a rain like this." "Sure, here's thirty cents. It's half of what I've got. But you are welcome to it."

The man took the money. I went on towards the poolroom. I stayed at the poolroom awhile. The boy I knew had been discharged from there. The manager looked at me rather strange for coming in fairly well dressed with a suitcase, saying not one word nor buying anything. He thought I was a "dry-clothes" man snooping around to see if he was selling liquor.

I slept in the C. & O. railway depot until dawn. The heavy puffing of the early outgoing trains woke me. On my way to the Armco employment office, I had to pass the Raeburn Hotel. When I passed there, I saw the fellow I had given the thirty cents to. He was still pulling the same gag about the German running the saber through his lung, and that he wanted a loaf of bread. He was too wise to have begged in the one place all night. He had been out over the town and had just happened to come back to the Raeburn Hotel at daybreak. "I think I'm one that gave you thirty cents to buy bread with. You haven't bought thirty cents' worth of bread and eaten it yet. Now, you are just a professional bum. You can give back the thirty cents I gave you last night. Give it back quick too. Now you know who I am. Right at this place last night is where I divided what I had with you." He pulled a roll of bills from his pocket and a handful of change. He gave me back thirty cents.

Before I got to the Armco employment office, I cut out a piece of paper and wrote 21 on it. I put it in the heel of my shoe. Now I was over twenty-one. If John Findlay asks me if I'm over twenty-one, I'll tell him the truth.

There is a long line of men at the employment office. One man has beaten me there. He is at the head of the line, I am second. We go in one at a time. One fellow in the line behind me says: "John, they tell me this Armco plant only hires the best of men any more. You know it kindly looks to me like work is a-fallin' off. Hell, I hope I can get on here and work out enough to buy me some clothes anyway. They can 'can' the hell out'n me if they want to after I get me some winter clothes."

"Well, Stuart, just where are you from? Tell me a little about yourself and how long you intend to stay with the Armco plant and the kind of job you ever hope to hold with Armco." "Well, Mr. Findlay, I'm from Greenup, Kentucky. I lived on a farm there. I worked on different farms until I finished Greenup High School. I'm over twenty-one now and I have set out to do for myself. I want to get in with some big company and work myself up to a good job like you have here, Mr. Findlay." John stopped me then. He began to talk. The boys back on the bench laughed and laughed. But the flattery I gave Findley helped to get me a job. Out of the forty-two men in line that morning, seven were hired. Men from the farm, I learned later, had a much better chance of getting work at the mills than the other fellows. They were better workers. If I had told John Findlay the last work I'd done was with a street carnival, he would have told me he had no work for me. If I had told him I was eighteen, he would have said that I was too young.

I took a physical examination that morning, a more rigid examination than is required to join the American Army. Around the pit of the stomach, the doctor examined me carefully to see if I had rings. That is, if I could stand heavy lifting without rupturing myself. So many men become ruptured in the mills with heavy lifting. Then I was examined carefully to see if I had any kind of venereal disease, or had ever had any kind of venereal disease. I made B on the medical examination. It was a tough examination. There were many men to select from and only the best physically were chosen to handle steel. I would have made A on the examination, but I was too much underweight for six feet tall. And on my card was marked: "Not too much heavy lifting."

I was supposed to go to work at noon. I would take the sixty cents and get myself a square meal before I began working. I must find a boardinghouse too. I walked out of the office and found a forty-cent meal at a little restaurant on Eighteenth and Winston. Then I began trying for a boardinghouse to return to that evening after my day's work was done. I found many places with signs in the windows and on the doors, "Boarders and Roomers Wanted." I would go up and ask about board and room for one week on credit. "I have a job at the steel mills. I begin work at noon today. I wonder if you could room me and board me for one week only on credit." "No, we can't do that here. We'd go broke if we did. People have to pay in advance here. They come and work and draw their money and skip out. I'm sorry." And she would close the door.

I found a place called the "Radner Home." Henry Hanover was the owner and proprietor. He was a Dutchman that stood back and laughed and smoked fat cigars. "W'y, hell yes, we'll take you. We take 'em all on here. Money or no money. You've got a pretty damn good-looking face. I ain't afraid to trust it. Take that suitcase over there and set it down until I get you fixed up. Now, I can give you room and board for seven dollars a week, that is, if you'll take a room down in among them small rooms on the first floor. Rooms are all right. Some of the boys have nightmares and say rats run across their beds. I can give you a room on the second floor and your board for nine dollars a week. It's a pretty damn nice place. I've only got one room up there vacant now. Or, I can give you a room on the third floor for eight dollars."

I was thinking all the time I would take the seven-dollar-a-week fare. We went on each floor. I looked over them all. I took the room on first. I would make only three dollars and a half for ten hours on the gin gang, and that's where they tried out all the new men to see if they'd work. If they worked well, they soon got a job on the inside. With this much salary, I could not afford a nine-dollar-a-week room fare. When Henry gave me the key to my room, I unlocked the door. I saw a black man in the double bed. I went back and told Henry about it. "Oh, hell, Stuart, he's only a greaser. A Mexican, damn it! He may be black but damn it, Boy, you'll find out Fidelas Gonzoloas has a heart white as yourn." Then Henry laughed and blew rings of cigar smoke from between his ugly lips.

My first work was with the gin gang. The "bull gang" it was called by many. We cleaned out manholes and laid sewer lines from the new privies the firm was building. We unloaded coke and coal by the trainload. We picked up scraps of rusty steel and sent it in on trucks to be worked over again. We pulled ragweed and crab grass from beside the long bright metal sheds with tops of glass. We worked ten hours each day. "Goddamn, I wish them peckerwoods'd call me inside. I'm tired of this damn hot sun. I've been out here a month now. Hell, I'd just a-soon they'd fire me." "Hell, Stuart, you're damn lucky to get under the shed this soon. You've only been out here a week and one-half day. You're a lucky damn peckerwood. They must be agoin' to make a damn boss out'n you."

When I was finally moved into the shed, I was put on the shears. It was a long machine that trimmed the edges off the thin slabs of steel. It was a place where, when you went to sleep on the job, you lost a foot or a hand. I was glad when "Red" came back and took his place. Then I was put permanently on the "oilers." It only took a man and two helpers to run this. It was light work after one learned how to flip the heavy sheets of steel. There was a sleight to it that made it easy after about five or ten days of practice, but some men never learned how. The trouble with that job was that not many men wanted it. The oil played havoc with a man's skin. When the first two weeks had passed, my legs became a solid mass of little sores. The oil had hit my flesh and soap and water could hardly take it off. The pores of the skin were closed. Then the sores came. My hands were getting the same way. "Yes, we'll change you. Men never hold that place long. We just keep a man there until he gets sore, and then we send him to another place. You've held the job down about as long as any of them."

Next, I began loading steel into the boxcars. That took lifting and skill on flipping steel. I worked here until the regular came back. Then I was transferred down into the hot part of the mills. I stood by a track and took a long steel hook and kept the white-hot slabs of steel from running off the track. "Now, Boy, if you can't sweat, you'd better keep your tail out of this place. If you can sweat, you'll never leave. They'll keep you here shore as hell. I've been over on this track for fifteen years now. It will be sixteen next March.

I couldn't sweat very well at first. I kept a little salt in my pocket. I'd lick salt about every hour, and talk about drinking water—I funneled it down. And don't you know sweat begin to break out on me and run off like water. The sweat was enough to drown a grass-hopper—damn'd if it wuzn't. But hell, it had to go someplace. I'd go out to piss and I couldn't piss a drap."

I didn't have to drink water. I sweated freely. My face soon lost the color the sun had given it. It became a reddish-brown, the color of burnt bacon. It was a fire tan. And all I could hear when I went to the Radner Home to sleep at night was the sound of steel battering steel and the cries of working men, the zooming cranes and the tractor motors pulling steel. The deadly rumble of the shears cutting steel and the soft oozing sounds of the oilers.

"Get the hell from under that crane! The hook on the left there has slipped! She's coming down! Get the hell out of there! Clear out, Men! Watch that load of steel coming down! Oh, hell, it got a man's foot. Poor devil! One of these five cranes here gets a man a day. You see it pays to be careful around here. Look out for yourself first, then others." The man is carried to a hospital. When he gets well, the Armco will have no more use for a man with one foot. They'll pay him, say, five-hundred dollars for his foot. No, they'll not give him a job the rest of his days. That's too much on the company to give a job of sweeping floors for a lifetime just because his foot and his sweat and blood went into the steel. Hell no, tell him he needs an education now and get him off to school. That's the way they work it at the mills. He's been with the company fifteen years, and after they took his foot they want him to get an education. They tell him he can make it easy then. "The world needs men trained in books. There's just plenty of big jobs waiting on you. Get an education. You know the world don't need men trained in steel. The world needs men trained in books."

Sometimes, I would go out of the shed for a breath of fresh air. That would be when a belt broke and threw the whole works out of order. When I went out into the night air in clothes as wet as sweat could make them, the summer wind felt like a February wind blowing from the north. But the sound of the Ohio River lapping against the bank down by the dwarf willows was more pleasant than the din of the ever-rolling machinery— wheels, hooks, slides, cutters, motors and cranes. The moonlight on the Ohio and the boats moving cat-like through the water, their reflections whipping and slashing, with red lanterns on the deck, and men waving green lanterns and signaling were pleasant things. I could stand out all night in the cold summer air for things like these, but the machinery is going again. The belt has been fixed.

I work all day, and every other night I work part of the night. I need money. I have debts coming due in Greenup. I need clothes. And some day, I am going to school. I had it in mind to go to school when I talked to John Findlay. I knew that I didn't want a job like he had. I had a higher aim than that. Just slave for a company and in the end die! Maybe in the meantime I had married and was the father of five children and to each of them I would will a part of what I had saved and the rest to my wife. This money would have to be made by sweat and blood. Hell no, I would never do it. I was going beyond the iron claws of machinery, and why not? Others had done it. They had had less sense than I had. Others had done it and they had had more sense than I had. But I was young and I would not give my body to steel. Too many strong bodies and brains were being interwoven every day with the stuff steel was made of. And their dreams were being worked into steel and fashioned into short endurable things.

Get Carl Sandburg to tell you about it. He knows. He's the singer of steel. And I am almost positive that Carl Sandburg has never worked a day in the steel mills in his life. Yet he gives you an idea of their beauty—the beauty of steel—the beauty of blood and sweat and cinders. Carl Sandburg saw beauty there. He saw the beauty. He had felt the beauty. Carl Sandburg, I've got a question to ask you: "Have you jerked hot slabs of steel on a track with a long hook and licked salt like a cow to make you sweat? Have you singed your eyebrows with the heat of steel and the wisps of hair that fell over your forehead when you stooped down? Tell me, Carl

Sandburg, have you? I am reading your books because I work in steel now. I know you have never worked in steel.

"If you have worked there, you had a snap. Carl Sandburg, you don't know anything about steel. You got your ideas from walking around the mills at night or talking to the Mayor of Gary, Indiana. Go on and write your excellent poems about the wheat fields and the sunflowers in the wind and the great open spaces of the sundown west, but Carl Sandburg, lay off writing about steel. Don't disillusion people about the beauty of steel and about the steel birdman that drones and drones high in the blue, blue sky. Keep steel out of the sky. And whatever you do, quit singing about the beauty of steel."

I go to the Radner Home to sleep. I hear the rumble of steel all the way. Like a bullet the sound is shooting through my head. But I am out in the night air walking toward the Radner Home. There is nothing but a pillar of fire over the mills I have left, and the stacks from the furnaces look like pop bottles. I'd like to have a hand big enough to pick up the pop bottles and break them against the earth. I'd do it. I'd like to have a toe big enough to kick the white metal sheds over. I'd do it. I'd tell the men to go back to the soil and make their bread. Lay off this steel game for a while and rest their bodies.

There were forty-five men living at the Radner Home and six women. Five of the women were married. Mattie was single. The men were Russians, Swedes, one Mexican (my roommate), one German, Englishmen and Americans. They kept going and coming all night long. Some worked ten hours at night. Others worked eight-hour shifts. There was moving through the hall all night long.

The Mexican that was my roommate stank so badly that I could hardly stand to sleep with him. One day I heard some men talking in the lobby. "By God, I'm going to put the skates under that Mexican. The sour-smelling bastard. I'm going to lift his heels higher than his head if he don't know it. Old Henry's going to run all his men off keeping a damn greaser 'round here. By God, I'll see that he goes. See this old sledge hammer. Well, when I put this against his eye once, he'll be glad to go. God damn a greaser anyway."

I heard loud cries in my room one afternoon and strong curses. I ran and opened the door. A fellow by the name of "Old Kentuck" from Letcher County in Kentucky had raised the window and thrown Fidelas out. He had thrown all his clothes out on top of him and was saying: "Now, don't ever let me catch you back here. You stink like a rotten pig. If I ever catch you back here, you'll not be able to leave the next time. You'll have to go away in a wooden overcoat." He turned to me and said, "The next to go will be that damn old Pete the Russian. And I ain't got much use for them damn Englishmen. All the time talking about winnin' the war. I helped win that damn war. English soldiers was rotten as hell. Stick their hands above the trench to get shot in the hand so they could go to the hospital. Damn sorry bunch of English. I'll go right upstairs now and get old Slater. I'll make this a fitten place to live in. I'll show 'em who won the war. I'll throw him offen third floor. I'll break his damn neck. That's what I'll do."

Old Kentuck's breath smelt like a whisky bottle. His shirt was torn loose at the collar. His chest was hairy. He looked like a madman. He went upstairs after Slater. After five minutes had passed, I heard a fight on the stairway. I saw Old Kentuck coming down the stairs dragging the tall Slater by the heels. Henry Hanover met him at the stairs. "What in the hell are you doing anyway, Kentuck?" "I'm cleaning this damn place up and maken it a fitten place for Americans. Got a bunch of these damn foreigners in here makin' our wages low. It's for us to put 'em all outen America." "Now, you can this stuff right now 'er git out yourself. Slater, you go on back to bed." "No, Sir, I won't stay here another hour. I'm too much of a gentleman to fight an old beast like him. I'm leaving." The Englishman leaves. Old Kentuck stays on at the Radner Home. The Mexican does not return. He went off owing Henry for a month's board.

My next roommate was a piano player. He puts a coat across the keyboard and then he plays "Yankee Doodle" over the coat. He lets the men blindfold him and he plays "Yes Sir, She's My Baby."

They think he is a genius and the farm boy from South Carolina who plays by note and studies music at night is pushed aside. The stranger is quite the stuff.

We go down to the room together. He unpacks his clothes and makes himself at home. "Say, Boy, is there any women around this joint? I'm just aching for a woman. I'll have my wife up here in a few days. But I want me a woman before she gets here. You know I'm married and I live in Canton, Ohio." "No, I don't know any women here at all. I know a few of the men's wives here at the house." "Say, come over here, Bud. Let me show you something. Now, here's what women's done for me. I ain't a-tellin' you what I've done to them. Now, ain't this a hell of a shape for the 'siff' to leave a man in. It don't hurt me a bit though. I'm well of it. I've been well of it for years. But I tell you it like to ruined me before I got it stopped." He has made me fear women. He was a sight to look at. I would not want to be left like that. I'd rather be dead. I'd never marry and be in that shape. Wonder what his wife thought about it. I wonder if she knew. I wonder if she noticed. I wonder if she has ever known another man so that she could make the comparison. But that fellow didn't mind it a bit. He was still hunting women and playing the piano.

One day I needed two dollars. I didn't know anyone I'd care to ask for money unless it would be Mattie. She was the friendliest person there. "Mattie, could you loan me two dollars until next week?" "Sure, Kid. I can let you have more if you want it."

Mattie unrolled her stocking and pulled out a roll of ones, fives, tens and twenties, big enough to choke a horse.

"My heavens, you are a rich woman," I said. "You've got to know how to get by in this old world," she said. I took the two dollars and they were quite warm where they had been against her leg. I thought about her having all this money and working for only one dollar a day. But that night when I was up on the second floor I passed Mattie's room, and I understood. I saw Mink Leadingham come out of her room and Tim Stevens go in. They were married men. Mink lived in Ferton, West Virginia. He had a wife and one child. He was twenty-six and had to be careful about lifting steel. He had been ruptured. Tim Stevens lived in Canton, Ohio. He had a wife and four children. He was forty years of age.

The next day in front of the Radner Home, I heard Mink say to Tim: "Listen here. Ain't I told you about going in there? I'll cut your damn heart out if I ever catch you in there again. Now, you get me? Well, you had better. I'll cut you in two and throw you out at the window if I ever catch you in there again."

One day when I came in from work, Mattie came around where I was sitting in a rocking chair. She said to me: "Listen, Kid, I've got something I want to tell you. I knowed when you passed my room the other night. I could see you when Tim opened the door. I don't want you to say anything about that. Now, I want to give you some advice. You are the youngest man at this place. How old are you anyway?" "Eighteen." "Well, I didn't think you was that old. But what you saw the other night is the way I make my money. The men that work at the mills don't care to throw their money. They work hard, you know. And they think, 'Ah well, what does it matter anyway?' And I take in a lot of money. Did you know I've been married? I've got two of the prettiest children you ever saw in Cincinnati, a boy six and a girl four. They are staying with my father. I never want them to know what I'm doing. I want to raise 'em right and never let them know that I've throwed myself away. I don't think I can ever let them come back here. I'll have to leave this town if I do. Too many people know me here. I am called 'Red Hot Mattie.' But I get their money. I take them on. Some of them I can hardly stand."

I worked down at the Third Division shops for three months. The Second Division shops needed a man that could stand heat. I was transferred there. It was within eleven blocks of the Radner Home. I could go home for a hot lunch now. The overtime I'd been working was cutting my weight. Little dark circles were under my eyes.

When I first walked into the Second Division shops, I found there was a foundry, a machine shop, and blacksmith shop combined under one huge metal shed. And over across the street toward the river was a huge furnace. And then toward one of the valley foothills and off to itself was the pattern shop. My place was in the blacksmith shop, working at the furnace where the heavy pieces of steel were heated for the air hammer.

When I walked into the shop, all the men began to wave their caps. They all said together: "Look who's come!" Then they all laughed. The boss, Ruddy Flannery, a short stocky man, weighing about two-hundred pounds, stood at his office door over in the corner of the shop and laughed. He was chewing tobacco and the tobacco had made his front teeth yellow except the front gold teeth. It had stained them. He came over to me and put his hand on my shoulder. "How old are you, Bud?" "I was over twenty-one when I hired in at the office over three months ago. Don't you suppose I'm still over twenty-one?" "You'll do damn well to be over seventeen," he says. "I asked the office yesterday for them to send me a man up here. They sent you. Well, hell! Now what can you do? I want men. Look at these fellers around me here. You see they are men. Let me just see how heavy you are anyway. Stand in that shovel there."

I got in the shovel. "Steady now as I bring you up. Hold onto my shoulder." Then I sailed through about ten feet of space and hit headlong into a slack tub filled with water where the steel was cooled. I thought every man in the shop would go into hysterics. It was their idea of fun. The boss showed his yellow teeth. I came out laughing a forced laugh. I didn't like it. There was nothing I could do about it but quit the works. I wanted money to pay off debts I had contracted to buy good clothes with when I was a senior in Greenup High School. I had wasted borrowed money going to parties too. The notes were at the bank. They would soon be due. I couldn't quit the works. I was tied to the place. I laughed with the crowd. I was dripping wet.

"Let me feel of your muscles," said the boss. I was a little leery of him. But he felt of my muscles. "I'll put some muscles there where them little strings are," he said. "Now, you feel of them in a month from now." My first work was striking with a sledge hammer. I was very inaccurate at first. But different blacksmiths showed me twist after twist in handling a sledge hammer. I never knew before that there was any science in using a sledge hammer. But I found it out soon.

All day long in the blacksmith shop, there would be sparks flying, very beautiful sparks flying and all colors of fire blazing from the coke. The air hammer would come down with ten-ton thugs and flatten out the white-hot steel into thin pieces. There was a two-ton air hammer in the other end of the shop, used for lighter work. There were about thirty men working in the shop. They were all men of bronze. Their faces had been tanned by fire heat. Their faces looked like burnt strips of bacon. The blacksmiths were grouchy with the strikers. They would fly mad and throw their cleavers away. Then they would go and get them and come back smiling. That was the way my grandfather had done when we were working on our house. I thought there must be a reason for this. They were old at this work. This was the only reason I could ever find.

One afternoon I saw the men laughing. I smelled something burning. I felt an intense heat in the seat of my pants. I twisted around and my pants were on fire. I ran and sat down in the slack tub. All the men laughed. One of the fellows had slipped a cigarette butt into my hip pocket. It burnt a place larger than a man's hand out of the seat of my pants and scorched the skin. It made me too sore to sit down at the table unless I put a cushion in the chair. I knew who did it. I would get him someday. I looked at the seats of all the men's pants, and I found that all the hip pockets were ripped off. Even the boss had his pockets ripped off.

I talked to Buster Meadows, the ten-ton air-hammer boy one day about the blacksmith gang. He said: "Boy, don't you know this is the damnedest bunch in the whole mills? Now Old Ruddy Flannery likes his men to do all these pranks. He's the biggest devil in the bunch hisself. Don't you know how he picked you up in the shovel and throwed you in the slack tub? Hell, Old Flannery's a bad 'un after his licker and women. You know he has a lot of trouble with his wife. Hell, I don't blame him for 'monkeying' a little. You know that blonde you saw out there in front of the card clock the other day—well, she was his wife. She'd come down here to report him to the superintendent and get him canned. Oh, she's a slick 'un, they tell me. She raises hell with Flannery for doing the things she goes out and does herself when Flannery's down here at work. And when Ruddy takes his men down to the First Division to help 'em out, you ought to see them boogers down there run from us. When we catch a candy-ankle going between the sheds, a couple or three of us fellers grab him and away we take him to a barrel of oil. We souse him under too. Now don't think we let him off. Hell, we're the meanest bunch in these mills."

One afternoon Perry Rodden came rolling a baby carriage into the shop. Everybody took off their hats. They laughed and said, "Say, Perry, how is your wife and my child?" Then the men would argue among themselves who the child belonged to. "I know that baby right there in that buggy is mine." "No, that baby is mine, ain't it, Perry? You know your wife said it was anyway." Perry went out at the other door, pushing the baby carriage. He worked on the night shift. He had the hip pockets torn off his pants.

Flannery called me into his office. He said: "Kid, are you any good at figures? I've got some stuff here to make tomorrow and it's got me puzzled." "I may be able to help you." "Here is what it is. Now this piece of steel is to be cut up like this. There are to be four pieces. The first is to the second as the second is to the fourth. The first is five feet. The second is ten feet. The third is ten feet. Now, what is the fourth going to be?" "Twenty feet, of course." "Now, are you right sure you're right?" "I know I'm right." "Well, here's a little tip, I want to use you in the office a lot. Would you like to help me out once in a while? Can you use a typewriter and write letters for me?" "Yes, I'll be glad to."

That was one reason why I never left the shop. Flannery needed me to help him. He often called me out to figure the weight of a piece of steel or to write a letter—or to carry a message to the

Second Division shops' superintendent. But now I was working on the air hammer—the ten-ton vertical air hammer. The work was strenuous for my weight. I weighed only one-hundred and forty-five. But it took somebody that could remember the kind of cleavers to use. There were about sixty different shapes and sizes. The white-hot steel blocks had to be lifted from the furnace with the long metal tongs—suspended from overhead on block and tackle—and placed upon the work-anvil block beneath the big air-hammer. Then, while holding a cleaver by its long handle over the hot steel, I drove it through the steel with the air hammer. It took quick thinking and accurate thinking. A mistake might mean the death of a man. It didn't look like a responsible position but it was.

Flannery held me at it regardless of my weight. A hand crane, suspended in the middle of the shop, was used to lift the heavy steel work-anvil blocks onto the stool beneath the air hammer. He would have the stronger fellows help me wedge them onto the stool. The twenty-pound sledge hammer got my wind and weakened my arms after a few strokes. I didn't have the power to swing it many times. But I kept that job. I had an assistant helping me. The hardest job was getting the hot steel out of the furnace. I always dreaded to pull down the weights and open the furnace doors. The flames threw out an intense heat. They singed my eyebrows and my eyelashes. They burnt my hair to a singe in front. My face was often made sore by the flesh getting so hot. And after the furnace heat hit the face, one had to stand within six feet of a piece of steel six by ten inches, white hot through and through, and use the different kinds of cleavers. I would have to think fast. Sometimes my pants would get hot enough to smoke. But they were wet with sweat and couldn't burn. After the hurry at the air hammer and after the steel had got too cold to work more, it was put back in the furnace, and we usually went after water to drink and then stood out in the cool air. I'm telling you it took guts to stand that work. I had helper after helper come and go. They either couldn't stand the work or wouldn't stand it. It was one of the two things.

I went home for my lunch. And we only took thirty minutes

for lunch. We didn't wash our hands and faces. They would be black as the dirt on the blacksmith floor. And when we touched food, we got black on it. But that did not matter around the mills. Eat coarse food and gulp down black coffee and dream of steel. Many times when I lifted a slice of white bread from the plate, my fingerprints were left on it. That did not matter. I ate my fingerprints with the bread. I didn't know the difference. The other fellows did too. Sometimes we threw the bread across the table. I ate the other fellows' fingerprints then. What did it matter? We cleaned up the table usually. We ate like real he-men. We were he-men. It takes a he-man to handle steel. I could see why the medical examination was so rigid. I could understand why they asked about the venereal disease. It was a mighty good place to lift and strain and bring gonorrhea back on you if you thought you were cured of it. Steel mills and venereal diseases among the employees don't work well together.

For three months I didn't read any poetry or prose or even a newspaper. I held my nose down against steel. Then after the first three months, I bought a new book every week. I read it in my room at night. I marked the passages. Then I went over it again and again. I read all of Carl Sandburg's poetry. It was about steel. I read and reread and marked and reread again. I loved Carl Sandburg's poetry of the soil. Then I went in for more poets. I read Rupert Brooke, Alan Seeger, Amy Lowell, Robert Frost, Sara Teasdale, Edna Millay and Edwin Markham. I began to write poetry again. Luke Bancroft and I rented a typewriter for three dollars a month. He worked on the night shift and used the typewriter during the day. I worked during the day now and used the typewriter at night. I was trying to write poetry like Carl Sandburg's, and Luke Bancroft was trying to reform the nation by writing critical articles against capitalists. He had only a grammar-school education, and I was only a high-school graduate. His prose was so terribly written that no magazine could use it. My poetry was only a jumbled mass of words. I tried to write poetry like Carl Sandburg's but not about the beauty of steel. Songs like Sara Teasdale's—I can never forget this little song:

"When I am dead and over me
  Bright April shakes out her wind-drenched hair;
  Though you shall lean above me broken-hearted,
  I shall not care.

"I shall have peace as the trees are peaceful
  When wind and rain bend down the bough;
  I shall be as silent and cold-hearted,
  As you are now."

(Sara Teasdale, *"I Shall Not Care"*)

When the rain would be falling by my window at night, and
the green maple leaves were stirred by the wind and the rain, I
would sit down and try to write poetry. I would read it and appreciate
this new poetry. I had read only a smattering of the new poetry
while in high school. We studied the poets of the past. When I had
written many poems, and articles in favor of the new poetry, I put
them away in my suitcase. But one day I told myself I was an ass
even to have dreams about writing poetry. I got the poems and
articles out of my suitcase and put them in the cookstove at the
Radner Home. Later I found a one-stanza poem in my coat pocket
that had escaped the fire. It was published years later in *Harvest of
Youth*. I called it "Stanza on Leaving College." But I had never
been to college. I only dreamed of the day when I could go. I was
homesick and I thought of the people I had left at home, instead of
friends at college.

Stanza on Leaving College
Written in Dejection

My room lights sink, outside the night winds moan;
The hour approaches I strike the world alone.
Then forget me not for I shall think of you,
And this my last dear friends, adieu! adieu!

I took my books down to the blacksmith shop. I put them on a shelf in Flannery's office. Sometimes instead of going outside to cool between heats, I went inside and read the new poetry. Buster Meadows would say: "That damn boy's going to be President of the United States someday. Like hell—all but what he likes!" Then he would yell: "All right, the next heat. Lay off that damn poetry long enough to do your work here. The Super'll fire the hell out'n you one of these days if he catches you in there a-readin' that a-way."

One night at my boardinghouse, I heard Jerry and Sam cursing loudly out in the hall. The curses got louder and louder. I got up and opened the door. "Well, Kid, we got rolled last night." "Rolled," I said. I didn't know what they meant. "Yes, we got rolled. They took everything we had. All of our money, clothes, watches, rings and even our suitcases. They went off owing Henry a big board bill." "Who did it?" "Oh, it was that Jeff Rainwater and Bud Trevis. And I'll bet my hat they went to the coal fields up in Kentucky. Well, we'll follow 'em anyway. Go get Old Kentuck. We'll take him along. He's the man that'll bring 'em back." They borrowed clothes to wear on the trip. Jerry, Sam and Old Kentuck put a couple of pistols in a suitcase and started for the coal fields that night.

In three days they came back with Jeff Rainwater and Bud Trevis. Old Kentuck brought them back to the Radner Home so that the boarders could look at them. Then Old Kentuck turned them over to the officers of Ashland. "Here they are," he said to the law—two policemen wearing blue uniforms with two rows of bright shiny buttons.

The piano player, my roommate, was shifted from the First Division shops to the blacksmith shop. "That bird ain't worth the powder it'd take to kill him. Watch him get around. Stuart, come over here. I got a job for you. I got to get rid of that pianer player. They sent him here for me to can him. So I've got to have a little fun about doing it. Here's half a dollar. Go up to that little she-bang up on Nineteenth and Winston. You know where it is, don't you?"

"Yes." "Well, get me one of the largest loaded cigars you can get, then buy five five-centers not loaded and hurry back. I want to put the skates under that guy as quick as I can. We want to have the fun before Superintendent Whitley comes through to inspect."

I gave the good cigars to the men and held the loaded one until last. I gave it to my roommate. Not a single man in the shop but Flannery knew that one of the cigars was loaded. He had planned it all. The men smoked and worked. They thanked me for the cigars. Piano Player was working beside the furnace. He was stacking brick. I heard a scream. The men saw pieces of the cigar flying. Piano Player was stretched out flat on his back on the shop floor. "My goodness, Boys, take him to the slack tub." The fellows threw their cigars down in a hurry as soon as they saw what had happened. They took Piano Player to the tub against his will. They carried him there and soused him up and down in the water. Then they turned him loose. He left cursing the shop. He left the whole works. He never returned. He went out cursing and wet as a drowned chicken.

Sunday was a great day at the Radner Home. The men got their pay on Saturday afternoons. On Sunday morning one man had all the other fellows' money. The men would get drunk. The more sober fellows would lock the drunker men in their rooms to keep them from getting arrested out on the street. The bootleggers brought the whisky, wrapped in brown sugar sacks, to the boys. The cops would see them pass. They, perhaps, would think they were carrying home groceries. The boys would carry the sacks into their room in front of Henry. He never dreamed there was whisky in them. One day a tall boy came to the door. He wore a striped shirt with a blue collar and a red tie. "I want to see Jerry and Sam." Jerry came to the door. When the stranger handed Jerry the sugar sack, Jerry fumbled and dropped it on the stone doorstep. The stranger disappeared down a back alley running as fast as his skinny legs could carry him.

Henry came running to the door. "Was that whisky?" he asked. "I don't know," said Old Kentuck, "but here, take this match and stick a little fire to 'er and you can tell." Henry struck the match and threw it on the steps. The flames leaped high. They ran over the ground. They caught the woodwork on fire in the front of the building. Henry was scared. He called the Ashland Fire Department. A charge was brought against Henry for trying to burn his house for the insurance money. Several men sitting in the lobby testified that they saw Henry set the house on fire. They were the fellows who often brought in brown sugar sacks.

The first floor of the Radner Home was known as "The Hell Hole of Ashland." One morning I got up to find two of the windowpanes above my bed had been shattered by bullets. There were little holes about two feet above where I had been lying. I knew they were bullet holes. I began to look in a cherry tree that was in line with my window and the door that led out of my room into the hall. I found the bullets lodged harmlessly in the soft cherry-tree wood. Someone had just had too much and shot his pistol to hear it rattle. Had he shot a little lower, it wouldn't have been any fun for me.

Men would get dead drunk down in the "Hell Hole." I'd help to put them to bed. I hated to see the cops get them. They'd lose their jobs. They had no money from one payday to the next. They couldn't pay a fine. They would have to lay it out in the Ashland jail—maybe have to pay their fines by breaking rocks on the county roads. I hated to see them doing that. They were not such bad fellows. Steel had taken the good there was out of them. That game of steel is a game of pure hell. When I think of steel, I have cool memories. When I think of furnaces, I have hot memories. There wasn't anything any of these fellows wouldn't do for me. Many Saturday nights I was the only sober fellow on the floor. I would drag to bed the men with bodies limber as a rag until I'd give out. Maybe I'd tell them about how drunk they were two days afterwards, and they wouldn't remember being on a drunk.

Their lives were cramped. All the poor devils knew was steel, furnaces, the deadly rumble of machinery all day long. Steel, sweat, blood, and steel! Life was monotonous. Why not drink whisky and shoot out the windowpanes? Why not do something for a change? Tear up the place—fight each other, fight the Law! Life was ugly and dirty and dwarfed as the little ragweeds growing at the edge of the metal sheds. They were covered with soot and grew weakly in a place where the rain could hardly fall. Those men's lives were just dwarfed like the ragweeds. Their faces wore the blank expression of the Armco plant's shotgun dwelling houses. It was a terrible mess.

Whisky, women and gambling were the three escapes the men found at the Radner Home. I found one escape in books, another in the consolation of thinking I would go to college someday. I would be a college graduate. I would quit the mills. I would marry a different woman to Mattie. But sometimes I despaired. I had three-hundred dollars to pay and clothes to buy. It looked almost impossible for me to enter college.

I got a catalogue from Vanderbilt University. I wanted to go there. It was impossible for me to enter Harvard. But Vanderbilt's expenses were only a little under Harvard's, I found. Then I started to see what I could do at the University of Virginia. But the expenses were too heavy there. I must go to a small school. I tried to gain admittance to Berea College. It was my choice of the small schools. They informed me that the college enrollment there was limited to five hundred and that quota had long been filled. I would pack and go there someday and see if they wouldn't have me. There was nothing left for me to do but stay in the mills until I paid off the three-hundred dollars, then set out and find a college where I could work to cover my expenses.

If I stayed on in the mills, my body would soon become ruptured and my blood would become steel. My mind would go no further than the little world I knew. The little world where smoke clouds obscure the sun by day and pillars of fire from the furnaces illuminate the sky at night. I would stay there and maybe marry. I might get a woman like my boss Ruddy Flannery had married. Then I would be dissatisfied like he was. I would live an empty life like most of the men lived there. I would be hauled out on a poor point where the wild gooseberries and the huckleberries grew. I would be laid there to rest forever. I would be no more. I would have died and would have never lived at all. I could not bear the thoughts of steel.

There is a cry down near my room. I go there. The curses are going freely in an adjoining room. It is Murt, the maid, and Bill Thomas in a quarrel. I hear her say, "Now, you've done enough to me already. And I want you to leave my daughter alone. She's the only child I got. I won't have her mistreated." "Who's mistreating your daughter? I know I'm not." "Didn't I catch you in her bed Sunday morning? You was drunk as a lord." "Well, I wasn't mistreating your daughter. I was only sleeping with her." "Well, you stay away from my house. Don't you ever step your foot inside my door. Do you hear me! And you bring back that watch you stole, too."

And now the summer has come again. Money is hard to save when one is making four dollars a day. I have nearly all my debts paid. I never go back home. My mother has written and told me that she would like to see me. She thinks that it would be all right for me to come home. She said Pa was terribly mad at first and thought I would soon be home. But now he had begun to think I was going to stay away forever. She said he'd be glad to see me too if he'd only admit it. But she said: "You know how contrary your Pa is." But I do not plan to go back until he sends for me.

One day in the shop, Spike McCartie came up to me. He said: "Wasn't that old Mitch Stuart your grandpap that used to live up in Lawrence County?" "Yes. Why?" "You know what I think about him. I think he was just a goddamned old son— My first wife was a Lathrop, and I ain't nigh over the way your grandpap treated them. He stood in the bushes and shot everyone he killed. He ambushed 'em." "Spike, every time you say he ambushed a Lathrop you are a liar. You know you are. No man was ever a fairer scrapper. He stood in the open and took it fist and skull. You know he did."

Before I could say another word, he had staggered me with his fist. He hit like a sledge hammer. The men quit their work. They all swarmed around. They were cursing and sweating and betting. "By God, old Spike'll beat the hell out'n him easy. Look how his mouth's bleeding now." "W'y damn it, Spike's stiff. If he'd go in and clench him, he'd have more of a chance." Spike looked like a hairy gorilla when he was mad. He struck another glancing lick at my face. My shoulder caught his arm as it came down. I backed off. He followed me waving one fist, holding the other as a guard. Spike was thirty-eight-years old. There wasn't anything left to do but clench him and throw him. Any man who has worked fifteen years in the steel mills at hard labor is stiff, I don't care who he is. When I clenched Spike, my eye caught a blow from him that closed it.

I threw him to the ground and pinned his arms down. The crowd was frantic. He was easier than a boy to throw. He was clumsy. "Now if you move, I'll break your ribs into sticks," I told him. Many of the fellows in the crowd took up for Spike. After I had him down, I felt sorry for him, though he had closed my eye and burst my lip. I got off his hairy body. Where his rough hands hit my face in the scuffle, they had grazed the skin. We stood up face to face again. He was silent. I was silent. The fellows began to throw tens and fives at my feet, saying: "You may handle old Spike, but by God, here's what I got to say you can't handle me." I went over to the far end of the shop and sat down on an anvil.

Daddy Farris, the oldest man in the shop, said: "Hang with 'em, Young Man. You're just as tough as any of 'em. I'll bet the last cent I got you'll whip old Spike McCartie in a fair fistfight." "I know a boy that's lighter'n he is'll pin his tail to the ground. I'll bet any man money he will. He'll be in here just in a few minutes. It's Neil Caudil. He's the night forgeman. He's a man." "Well, I'll bet you Neil can't put him down. I'll put up a twenty he can't. You can't bluff old Daddy Farris like that."

Neil came in. A ring was drawn. We stepped into the ring. The money began to fall all around. Men came in out of the other shops.

I stepped back out of the ring. "What's a-matter, coward?" "I'll wrestle with Neil when you take up the money and not before." "You're just a coward." They refused to cancel the bets. I refused to wrestle. He might have thrown me, but I wasn't afraid to try him a round.

Flannery called me into his office. "Kid, I'm going to put you on night turn from now on. I'm afraid to work you and Spike under the same roof at the same time." "Yes, but I'll never start anything with Spike." "That's just it. He'll start it with you. He's liable to come up behind you and hit you over the head with a wrench or something. He never forgets when anything's been done to one of his people. He asked me the other day if your people was from Lawrence County. I told him I thought they was."

I made up my mind to get the best of Spike first if he ever came toward me. I watched him closely as we went out of the shop. He was still mad. When he looked at me, he gritted his teeth. When I looked at him, I gritted my teeth. I made up my mind if we ever fought again he'd lay me out or I'd lay him out.

I rested the next day. I went on that night to work ten hours a night and seven nights a week, for three months. I went to work at dusk and went to bed at dawn. It was hard for me to adjust myself to night work. This was a summer in my life that I hardly saw the sun. It was darkness during the day. I was tired and I slept as if every day was my last sleep. I slept so soundly after working all night in the shop at the air hammer that one morning in the shop, I wrote something about sleep.

Sleep

There are seconds in our lives that pass
Us down like long dark alleyways of dreams.
We drift like leaves on currentless streams
Out beyond all time and whirling mass
Of space. Softly we sink, and strangely deep
Beyond all time, and where all time is vain,

Where we give up the body and the brain
And lie in peace in our long night of sleep.

Then what is sleep when only seconds take
Us to the long dark night that we must face
Without the body's will or strong embrace
Of mind? Whether this night of sleep shall break
Or last, there is no one here to tell,
We only know we sleep and then, farewell.

After I had the fight with Spike, I wrote a poem one Sunday morning in the shop when the bell was softly calling for the good folk to come to prayer at the Catholic Church in Ashland. It was early Sunday morning and the dawn was breaking. The fires were burning low in the shop and I wrote on a Hershey bar wrapper:

Batter Me Down, Life
Batter me down, you who are strong, I plead.
I who am weak, in the little ways I know
Will learn to battle young and soon take heed.
Batter me down, as rain beats grasses low!
I know when cherry buds learn to obey
The gusty April raindrops' stern command;
I know that night will usher into day
Sun gems of dewdrops to bestrange the land.
I know the lark will rise in afterglow
Of storm . . . proud wings above the scarlet lea;
And a river young will wear a way to go
Until it cuts a channel to the sea.
Batter me down, Life! Give me blow for blow!
I'll take the bleeding lips and liberty!

Felix Hendrix was in charge of the shop at night. He weighed two-hundred and sixty. He was six feet six. He was the strongest

man I have ever known. He could tell more tales than any fellow I
have ever known. Some nights we would let the steel burn, listening
to Felix tell his yarns. He would say, "Ruddy Flannery knows
better'n to say anything to me about this shop. I've forgot more
about blacksmithin' than Ruddy ever knowed. I learned Ruddy all
he knows, out at Middletown, Ohio. Ruddy and me's both from
the same place."

Ruddy would leave his orders on his desk in the office. Felix
would take the order and say: "Now, if you'll strike like hell
tonight, we'll get done by two in the morning. You can take a little
nap and I'll slip over here to see a woman. Or, you can go with me
to see a woman. I can find you one. They all come here, you know.
They know where the money is. Now, you be careful around my
wife. Don't you ever say anything to give her a hint. She's a little
woman but she can raise a hell of a stink."

When it came to making things out of steel, Felix Hendrix
was a genius. He taught me enough to make a smithy out of me.
I got to be an expert on heating steel. Ruddy Flannery told Felix
Hendrix that he was going to make a blacksmith foreman of me.
Ruddy and Felix talked the thing over between themselves, that I
would have great possibilities to advance in the forging of steel.
One advantage I had over the other fellows was a high-school
education. Flannery told the superintendent, Charles Whitley,
about the plans they had worked out for me. "Hell, that boy is
young and he's picking up steel fast. We want to make somethin'
out'n him. No use to always hold 'em down to a striker and an
air-hammer man. We'll give him a little more experience and put
him on a fire."

There was one fellow I had worked with at the "oilers" down
at the First Division shops by the name of Charlie Wampie. He had
been my helper flipping steel. I had never seen Charlie again from
the time I left the First Division. One day he came walking into the
shop. He saw me. He came up and we shook hands. "Don't tell
Ruddy Flannery you know me," he said. "Don't tell him about me
working at the First Division shops. I got canned down there and

I'm going to try for a job here with old Ruddy. I'd like to work with him." "You were a good worker. Why did you get canned?"

"Well, it was like this. You know when I first came to this joint I just took on any kind of women. I got tired of working seven days a week and nothing else to do. So I began to take on the women. You know I messed around with nearly every 'Weedmonkey' in this town. I know 'em all. And God knows they're thick as snowbirds in this joint. Well, I got tired of going around by myself and I asked Foreman Sheff out with me. We got to 'Weedmonkeying' together. We took my Chevy roadster, a couple of blankets, and a little licker and how we did get them. But we got a whole lot of them rotten stinking kind. And God, when one of them 'Weedmonkeys' smells, she's enough to vomit a buzzard. But hell, me and old Sheff took 'em on together. So one time I told Sheff I was tired of old stinking 'Weedmonkeys' and I was going to have something pretty good. So I went out by myself, and I shore as hell did cull 'em. I found me a pretty blonde. She's just the right size, you know. Boy, that woman was built like a brick barn. Now that woman, she took my eye and she took my pocketbook. We had our fun together. We went up in that holler at Flint Wood. You know where it is. Nearly everybody that knows about it calls it Flint Wood. When we's up in this holler together, I told my blonde about my partner over at the mills. I didn't tell her his name. I told her he was a boss and a swell guy. She told me to bring him along and she'd bring her girl friend for him and we'd all go to Flint Wood and have a rip-snorting good time together. To make a long story short, here's just what happened. When we all met down on Sixth and Winston to go to Flint Wood, Sheff cried out: 'My God, it's my wife—my wife—what th' hell are you doing here?' I didn't know what to do. I just grabbed his wife's girl friend by the hand and we went down the street. I left them quarreling by a lamppost. They were nearly fighting.

"The next morning Sheff told me he wouldn't need me any longer. He said the company was through with me. You know old Sheff's got a big drag with them big bosses at the plant. And don't you know, them fellows blackballed me. That's what they done. I can't get a job anyplace if I tell them where I worked.

"And now, I'm going to get one on old Sheff. I'm going to get back with the Armco plant under a different name. I am a good blacksmith, you know. I used to shoe horses at the lumber camps up on Black Beaver. You see, Ruddy is the only man in this whole damn works who is allowed to take a man and not have him examined by a doctor. And if Ruddy takes me in, I'll only work about five months. Just long enough to finish paying for my car. And then I'm going to kick that goddamn Sheff so high that the bluebirds won't build in him. Damn him to hell, anyway. I'll fix him. You mind what I say. You just keep quiet. Here comes Ruddy now."

Dennis Harkreader had gotten work at the steel mills with strong intentions of working upward to obtain a foreman's position. Dennis was a youth that fought his work. The bosses had to watch him to keep him from doing too much. He would do his part and help the other fellow. He was a tall handsome youth with a shock of bright curly hair.

One night Ruddy came into the shop. He said: "Dennis, I'm going to put you on the hammer tonight instead of Stuart. You are nearly thirty pounds heavier and you can swing the crane better. You can swing the twenty-pound sledge in putting the blocks upon the stool. But you must be very careful and remember the right cleaver to use. You know that was where he was good. I'm going to put him on one of the fires tonight. Now go to it, Dennis. Take your time tonight and do the very best you can."

It was two o'clock that Sunday morning and the ten-ton hammer was chug-chug-chugging away. The hammers were clanging at the fires, as men pounded and shaped the hot steel. But they were the hammers swung by the strength of man. They were the ten- and sixteen-pounders. The little noises in the shop were drowned by the cries of Jack Brown, the night air-hammer boy. "Hurry over here! Dennis is hurt! Hurry—he's hurt!" The men rushed to him from all over the shop, the machine shop and the foundry. Two men pulled the cleaver out of his intestines. The blood oozed and spurted. The dirt floor around the hammer was red. The blood was clogging with the dust into round soft balls of amalgamated blood and dust. We picked Dennis up, four of us, to carry him out of the shop and send him to the hospital. "Boys, just let me alone. There's no use doing this. I'm gone. Look at that gut torn open there. I know I'm gone. Take me home. I don't want to go to the hospital. I want to die at home. Stuart, don't let 'em take me to the hospital. Make 'em take me home. And for God's sake, don't you ever go back to the hammer. It wasn't Jack's fault. It wasn't my fault. It wasn't anybody's fault. It just happened."

We have him at the ambulance. The blood is all over our clothes. "Well, good-by, Men, you've been a swell bunch of fellows to work with." Strong men turn aside and shed tears. They are not ashamed of their tears. Dennis Harkreader, one of the finest men in the shop, is gone. Two young men are left. The night forgeman and I are left.

All of the crew go with the ambulance but four. We go back into the shop where the air hammer is silenced and where the fires are burning low. I don't feel like working. I tell Blair that I cannot do any striking the rest of the morning. I am weak. I am nervous. I have never felt like this before. He says that he feels sick. We sit down together on a bench by the slack tub. "Go over there and get a shovel and cover up that blood." I take a shovel and shovel dry dirt off the blacksmith floor and put it over the blood. It keeps soaking through. I tell Blair. He says to wet the dust with the hose and put the mud over it. I do. It does not soak through any more.

The inspectors come the next day. Flannery comes with them. He is afraid he is going to lose his job. He comes with them to explain. They spend about three hours at the hammer. These two inspectors are Armco plant men. They make the bosses step and the bosses make the men step. They talk viciously to Flannery. He is very silent. Buster Meadows steps up and says: "It wasn't Flannery's fault. It wasn't Jack's fault. It wasn't Dennis's fault. It wasn't anybody's fault. It was the fault of this whole damn steelworks. Fire me if you want to. Don't fire Flannery. Hell, I'm ready to quit the goddamn place anytime."

Then they go on talking to Flannery. "We'll take the cleaver to the general superintendent. We'll draw a picture of the hammer. We'll give every little detail and let him decide." They draw at the air hammer for a couple of hours. That evening it was announced that the fault was not one of Flannery's. It was regarded as just an "accident." But Dennis was dead. He would sleep now forever under the cold clay upon the hill above the mill where the wild gooseberries and the huckleberries grew.

With Dennis gone, the place was lonely for me. It was lonelier than it had ever been. Now there was Dennis Harkreader that had died in my place. I had just gone off the air hammer that night. I went on a fire with Bill Blair because Felix Hendrix was in jail. He had got drunk and tried to take the town. Bill Blair was a fine fellow to work with. We talked about Dennis very often. "You know, Stuart, you was a lucky fellow. You got away from there just in time. The general superintendent said that it didn't matter who'd a-been at that hammer that Sunday morning, they'd a-been killed. You ought to thank your God you got off'n there."

"Blair, I don't thank my God that I got off. I was no better than Dennis. It is all a game of chance here. It is a gamble. I happened to get 'a straight' and Dennis 'a pair.' It makes me feel pretty tough to think about Dennis being sacrificed for me. It may not have been like that, but it just feels that way to me. Again, I think if I'd been at that hammer, regardless of what the superintendent says down at the First Division shop at his office desk with only maps to go by, I could have gotten by. It may have been that Dennis used the wrong cleaver. He hadn't had much experience at the hammer and I've been over there a long time. I know it pretty well. I know there's been a lot of times when a cleaver has been snapped in two and the hammer didn't knock it out of my hand. And when I was holding one under the hammer, I never let the end point toward me. If I had, I'd already have been dead and forgotten about. I've made mistakes in there and turned loose of everything and ran out of the shop. And Jack Brown would run behind the hammer and reach up and cut the air off. But I always tried to play the safe side. Dennis wasn't used to it. You see where he is now. If I'd been left on the hammer, it might have been a life saved." "Get that out of your head. If you'd a-been on that hammer, you'd a-been on some poor p'int sleeping like Dennis Harkreader."

The next night Felix Hendrix was back with us. "Boys, I drinked a quart. I got pretty well stewed. But they'd never got me if they hadn't caught me up there trying to pour a little down Reverent Huff. The boys told me old Reverent liked his licker. I thought I'd try him out. But if I'd had him in a woodshed someplace or out behind a tree, he'd a-just soaked it. Hell, it cost me a hundred dollars to get out of it. If I hadn't had a pull with the Judge, they'd a-railroaded me shore'n hell, Boys."

I worked on with Felix Hendrix night after night. I hardly saw day. There was one hill that I memorized better than any poem I have ever said from memory. Here is the hill: "A hill in the shape of a half-bushel split-bottom feed basket turned upside down. The rocks around the sides were the slats and the high-tension wires strung over the top was the handle. The little patches of dwarf trees growing among the rocks on the sides were corn silks and blades of fodder caught on the side of the basket at the crib door. The yellow moon that rode above the hill and lodged in the trees was a yellow grain of corn lodged in the corn silks and fodder blades on the basket. And the horse that I saw come out every night and pick grass on top of this hill was a big slow-moving bug crawling over the basket."

Every time I had a chance to walk out of the shop, I went out for a breath of the night wind and to look at this hill. I grew lonely staying in the shops at night. Felix grew lonely too. One night he called me over to him and said: "Now, My Boy, I'm a lot older than you and I could tell you many things. Here is one I do want to tell you. I'm drinking like hell again. Now don't you ever say anything to Old Flannery about it. We're damn good friends and I hate to make it hard on him. No drinking is allowed around here. If Flannery gets hold of it, he'll have to report me to Whitley. He'll have to fire me."

Night after night Felix came to the shop drinking. One night he got Brown drunk and Brown tried to tear the air hammer up with a sledge hammer. "Goddamn air hammer—damn black monster! I'll break your slats out with a sledge hammer. Damn you, you killed Dennis Harkreader but you'll never kill another man. Goddamn you."

When we took Jack off the air hammer, he'd damaged it almost beyond repair. Felix then called us all together and began telling us a chapter of his past. "My three brothers are in the pen. My father, dead now, served twenty years there. I'm the only one that never had to go. But I've drinked licker till it's nearly got the best of me. Now, Boys, when they see that hammer over there, they'll fire me. I'm going to tell them I done it. You know last summer I got on a spree. I got crazy. I carried a hammer and I pounded the walls. Snakes were after me. I thought I could feel them running down my pants legs. I would break down and cry. I couldn't help it. Then I would pray a long prayer. Then the snakes would come back and I would curse and fight. None of the doctors in this damn joint could do me any good. My wife knowed what to do. She sent for my brother. He come and he made everybody stand back. He took some licker and heated it just as hot as I could stand to drink it. He done it time after time. And I begin to come back to my senses. I swore right then I'd never drink any more. But look at me now. I'll go to seeing snakes again if I keep it up."

The next night Ruddy Flannery came to the shop. Felix Hendrix's wife came with him. They were looking for Felix. He had never been home that day. I didn't have a partner that night. I cleaned up the shop. About ten o'clock Felix drove his car into the blacksmith shop and around between the anvils until he bumped one and had to stop. "Come over here, Stuart. How're you gettin' along? I'm drunk as a lord. I ain't eat nothing for three days and nights. My wife's a-huntin' for me, they say. She'll never get me. You want to go over here with me? It ain't more'n three blocks away. I've got two of the prettiest women over there and they're cooking a turtle for me. Come on and go with me. Well, if you won't go then and if you ever see my wife, you tell her you ain't never seen me. Tell Old Flannery I said for him to go to hell and take his job with him." When Felix backed his car out of the shop and turned toward the highway, two Armco plant police halted him. One stood in front of the car. Felix bumped him off and kept going. The other policeman turned to his unconscious partner. Felix went on after his women and turtle.

September would soon come round again. The nights were getting cool. The corn in the fields up and down the river had reached its maturity, and soon it would be turning buff-colored in the autumn sunlight. I had paid all the debts I owed. I had thirty dollars ahead. But I was going to leave. I was going to college. I was going somewhere. I was not going to work with steel any longer. It had begun to get in my blood. It was in my brain. I couldn't get away from it. Steel followed me day and night. I packed my clothes and a few books in a suitcase. I got ready. I would leave on September the twelfth, 1926.

I wondered what my folks were doing at home. I wondered how my father felt toward me now. I would not go home to see. I was going to stay away. I would like to go back and see how they were getting along without me. But I would not go. I was going to a strange place. I did not know where. But I was going.

When I told Flannery I was going to college, he laughed. "Going to college with no money. Going to college!" "Yes, I'm going to college." "You ought to be ashamed, leaving me this way. I've took an interest in you. Me and Mr. Whitley both has. We was going to make a blacksmith boss out'n you. And now you quit on us." "Blacksmith boss. What is it? You are one. What have you done? I hate the name of steel. I'm leaving. I don't expect to return. I'm through. I hate the whole damn works. I'm tired of it. And you get mad because I want to get out of it. Well, you'll just have to get glad. Good-by."

"Let me feel of your muscles before you go," said Flannery. "I told you I'd put 'em on there. Now let me show you where I got plugged once." He pulls up his shirt and shows me a big red scar on his side. "He didn't get by with it," says Flannery, "I got 'im. I don't show this scar to everybody—just to the fellows I trust and like."

I walked out of the shop. It was farewell to steel. Farewell to the Cool Memories of Steel forever.

Mules and wagon, in town for supplies

Chapter VII
Beware: Books Hurt the Flesh

I shipped my trunk to Berea College, Berea, Kentucky. I followed on the highway. I had thirty dollars in my pocket. I carried a dollar suitcase in my hand. It was pasteboard. I got it at a dry goods store in Ashland, Kentucky. I had a couple of changes of clothes in the suitcase and some sandwiches Mattie fixed for me when I left the boardinghouse. I had my books in the trunk, a sweater, an old worn-out overcoat, two quilts and a pillow. I did not have a suit of clothes. I had a blue coat that I combined with a pair of blue sailor pants for a suit.

It was fun thumbing my way across Kentucky. The open air of the shaggy eastern Kentucky hills blew on my face. It tasted clean to my lungs. I loved to breathe it. It was different from the filthy air at the steel mills. It was an air slightly tinged with the smell of autumn leaves. The leaves had begun to color now. The white clouds floated over the high blue skies. The buzzards sailed in circles over the heat-glimmering old pasture fields. The crows flapped their wings and cawed in trees by the roadside. This reminded me of the freedom I had once known. It was great to be out again and feel the wind and sun on one's face. Life was great. I loved life.

It took me two days to reach Berea. I was not an artist at thumbing my way. I soon learned this. I slept in a haystack the first night that overtook me. It was out in a small meadow by a creek somewhere west of Morehead, Kentucky. I felt fresh the next morning after I washed my face in the stream and cleaned my teeth. I went back to the highway and at a little country store I breakfasted on a couple of eggs and a cup of coffee. I took the eggs raw and the coffee hot. Then I stepped out on the highway.

I never knew it but what I needed then was a couple of signs on my pasteboard suitcase and a freshman cap on my head. Or a sweater with a big G or a big F across the front would do. Just something for identification to show that I was a schoolboy. But it was hard for me to get a ride. I was too brown to pass for a schoolboy. I looked like a man used to work. I looked like a farmer tanned in a hayfield.

At five o'clock that afternoon, I was at the depot at Berea, Kentucky. My trunk was there. I went up on the campus. It was the first college campus I had ever been on and the first college I had ever seen. It was a swell place to me. Now the next problem I had was getting in. After I had seen the place, I thought Harvard or Vanderbilt University must be wonderful places. They were so much better known. But I didn't think about them now. I wanted to stay at Berea. A thought came to me: "I will see Will Sears. He is a senior in Berea now. He passed through the hills of Kentucky three years before and sold me a Bible. He was selling Bibles, he told my mother and me, to pay his way through school. She bought a Bible and so did I. I think Will can help me. He is from Tennessee. I'll look him up."

The first boy I met on the campus had only one arm. "Hello, Buddy. Say, can you tell me where Will Sears rooms?" "Will Sears? I don't know Will Sears. How is he classified, do you know?" "He's a senior this year if he hasn't flunked any courses," I said. "Well, I'm only in the fifth grade. I don't know any college seniors. You meant he was a college senior, didn't you?" "Yes." "No, I don't know him." "Well, this is none of my business, but how old are you?" "I'll surprise you, I guess. But I'm coming twenty-seven this October." "How did you lose that arm?" "I don't guess it's none of your damn business nohow." He moved on.

I went up to the Y.M.C.A. building. It was a little house set over under some oak trees. I went in and called for Will Sears. "Will is down in Georgia selling Bibles this year. He hasn't come yet. We're looking for him most any day now. Is there anything I can do for you?" "Yes. I want to get into Berea College. Can you help me to do that?" "Have you ever sent in your application?" "Yes. I've tried three times. Three times I've been rejected. Now, I want to talk to the president of Berea." "Maybe the reason you didn't get in was because you don't live in the mountains." "I live far enough back in the hills that the hoot owls holler in the daytime. They mistake daytime for night, the hollow is dark and deep. The sun never shines on our house except for a couple of hours in the afternoon. They always write and tell me the college is crowded." "Wash some of the dust and sweat off your face and put on a clean shirt, and we'll go over and see the dean. The president isn't here. He's on a business trip up east. Get him a towel and some soap, Charlie."

After a general cleanup, we walked out across the campus toward the dean's house. Squirrels played under the oaks. A lazy wind dragged through the dying leaves. Boys and girls laughed and talked to each other on the byways. They were all happy, it seemed. "College is a great place and tomorrow I may be one of the group," I thought. I knew I would never go back to the steel mills. I would never follow another street fair. I might never go back to the farm.

"Dean, here is a boy that wants to enter Berea College." "Stuart is my name." "I'm glad to know you, Mr. Stuart. Where are you from? Sit down there in the rocker—or on the sofa. Just any place." "I'm from Greenup, Kentucky." "Why is it you want to come to Berea College, Mr. Stuart?" "The first reason is, it is a place where a man can work his way when he doesn't have money and just has to pay a little when he does have money. The second reason is, it is a good school." "Mr. Stuart, do you place Berea College above all other schools?" "No, Sir, I do not. I put Harvard, Vanderbilt

University and the University of Virginia above Berea College."
"Well, Mr. Stuart, why don't you attend one of your favorite schools?"
"I don't have the money. And I prefer Berea College to any of the
small schools." "Well, Mr. Stuart, to make a long story short, we
have one-hundred and five students on our waiting list, and we
can't use you until next year and maybe not then. But I'll tell you
a place where you can go. I have a very dear friend teaching there.
He was at Berea for twenty years, and now he is president of
Lincoln Memorial, at Harrogate, Tennessee. If you go there, you
tell him I sent you. His name is Chitwood Langley. Make the best
of life. I'm sorry we can't keep you here. Good-by." "Good-by."

He closed the door. I went back to the little plank Y.M.C.A.
house under the trees. I got my old paper suitcase with the end
mashed out of it where I had sat on it waiting for rides along the
highway for the past two days. I started to leave. I went out of the
door. "Have any luck?" asked the boy who had taken me to the
dean's home. "Not a bit." "Too bad. You're not leaving, are you?"
"Yes, I'm going to Harrogate, Tennessee, tonight." "You are going
to Lincoln Memorial then, I suppose." "Yes, I'm going to try."
"You've got three hours yet before the train runs. You can just wait
and go to chapel with us."

The chapel was a big place to me. The college students got
the finest seating section in the auditorium. On one side of the
college students were the academy students, on the other side were
the foundation school students. Up in the balcony were the normal-
school students. The auditorium was crowded. It was hot inside.
The bugs flew in at the windows and swarmed around the lights.
The orchestra played "My Old Kentucky Home." A violin string
broke and the temperamental music director flew into a rage. No
one laughed. They all took it seriously. A man spoke a few words
in the high-tenor praise of Berea College. A woman from Ireland
got up and said: "I'm glad Berea is my alma mater. It is known all
over the world—in Ireland as well as over this great land of
America." The children in the foundation screamed in applause.
The college students, normal students and students of the academy

clapped their hands. A man led in prayer and we were dismissed

When I went out of the chapel door, I was tapped on the shoulder. I looked around. Here was the one-armed boy, the first man I met on the Berea campus. "Say, I thought I'd ask you how you expect a fellow to know Will Sears when they's twenty-six hundred students here. Found him yet?"

The train left Berea at 10:30 that night. I rode in the smoking car and talked to three boys that had been sent away from Berea for smoking. "Hell, they can a man up there fur purt' nigh anything. Old Baldy even gets out at night and crawls around on his hands and knees looking for cigarette butts. He finds 'em too under the boys' windows at Hanley Hall. Then he goes up and smells in the rooms. He's got a nose like a hound dog. He shore does get the boys. We throwed a cigar down on his head that had fire on it. He come up from on his hands and knees a-whooping and a-hollering. I say he did." The boys laughed then.

The train rattled on into the night. The wind, filled with small cinders, blew alongside the moving train. At a distance from Berea College, one could see from the train window long blue lines of hills in the moonlight. The corn was cut in the fields and one could see the shocks of corn in the moonlight. One could also see the moonlight on the coloring leaves and on the old pasture fields as the train moved on into the night.

Morning came and I got off at Harrogate. There wasn't any depot at Harrogate. It was a wide-open country place. "Where is Lincoln Memorial?" a girl asked me. "I don't know. I'm hunting for Lincoln Memorial too." "Right this way. This way. Bring your baggage and get in for Lincoln Memorial." A freckled-face boy drove a ton Ford truck. We all piled in. The girls, two of them, rode in the front seat, and the boys stood up in the truck bed. It was only one mile to Lincoln. We were soon there.

"Say, Jim, a body would have to use a microscope to find Lincoln Memorial after he gets here. Where is the place anyway?" "You see this tall grass around here, don't you? Lincoln is hidden in the grass. You'll soon find her when we get all this grass cut and all that mountain of corn you see over there in the valley cut. We've got forty acres of hay to rake and God knows how many potatoes to dig. We've got to build some new henhouses over on the chicken farm, paint the dairy barn and lay three miles of water pipes. You'll find out where Lincoln Memorial is when we get all this done."

We formed a line at the auditorium-gymnasium combined, on the very day I arrived at Lincoln Memorial. It was registration day. The line was about three-hundred and fifty students long. It extended from the double doors of the auditorium-gymnasium to down under some locust trees on the campus. I was at the end of the line. I didn't have any money, and I didn't want other students to hear me tell Chitwood Langley that I had none.

It was eleven o'clock before I reached the dean. "Are you able to pay all your expenses here?" "I'm able to pay ten dollars for this quarter and that is all. I want work. I figure I can work a half-day and go to school the other half." "I know, but that is very little money for you to expect to start your first year's work on. Can't you get any from home?" "No, Sir, this is all I can get." I didn't want to tell him I had run away from home and had never been back there. "Where are you from, Stuart?" "Northeast Kentucky." "I'm from Kentucky too. I grew up in the mountains of Kentucky— back where the hoot owls holler in the daytime." He laughed.

"I'm from that land too, where the hoot owls holler in the daytime," I said. He laughed again. "Does anybody here know you? I have never gotten an application from you. When did you decide to come here?" "No one here knows me. I have never sent you an application either. I never decided to come here until ten o'clock last night. I made a futile attempt to get into Berea College last evening. The dean sent me here. He said he knew you well. He said that I was to tell you to enroll me as a student here and give me a job." The dean had never told me that at Berea. But, anyway, maybe it helped to get me enrolled as a freshman at Lincoln Memorial.

"What kind of work have you done?" "I have done farm work, taught school, cut timber, worked for contractors, dug ditches, spread concrete. I can do mostly anything. By trade I'm a blacksmith." "We don't have any blacksmith work around here. We'll find a place for you on the farm. Wait a minute until I call Anthony."

That afternoon I went to work. I worked in a hayfield with seven men. The tractor windrowed the timothy and clover hay across the long field. Each boy took a pitchfork and stacked the hay in what Anthony called "doodles." The field was long and the hot September sun came down and burnt where our shirts fitted tight across our shoulders. The smell of clover hay and the flying dust from the tractor wheels filled our nostrils. There was a spigot out in the middle of the field. The other boys kept going for water. Once I saw them all get together and I heard one say, "Let's work that damn Yankee to death. What do you say?" "It suits me." "Me, too." "Now, let's move a little faster with our windrows. Then we'll make him follow."

They hurried their work along faster and faster. I increased my pace and stayed with their lead men. They went for water too often. I soon took the lead. I could stand the heat better. I was hardened, too, by the hard work at the mills. Forging steel was not playing around like the students usually did under a boss from their own midst.

The boys got together again and talked. I could not understand what was said for the tractor was straining up the west slope of the hayfield. When we had started back to work, a tall, sweaty, long-faced boy came over to the outside windrow I was working on and said: "Say, Feller, there's a boy over here by the name of Claymore Jones. And this boy Claymore takes fits. Old Claymore is a good feller. He's all right when he gets over one or before he takes one. If he takes one, you just get outen his way. I just thought I'd come over and tell you about Claymore, for he usually makes for a stranger when one of them fits come on him." And the boy went back.

It was getting near quitting time. I thought it was a made-up piece of work. I knew what I was going to do when Claymore took his fit. I was going to sober him with a pitchfork. It was a sure cure for frame-up fits.

I heard a noise. It was first like dogs a-barking, then like a mad bellowing bull—spittle was flying from Claymore's mouth as if he was having a fit. He came right toward me. His hands were spread and he was clawing the wind. I stepped back. He thought I had started to run. The fellows were laughing. I hit Claymore with a nice swing of the pitchfork. The steel part of the fork hit him alongside the short ribs. He fell to the ground. The boys came over. "No prongs went in me," he told the boys, "but the lick has shortened my breath." I walked off the field. No one followed me. They remained with Claymore.

Lincoln Memorial stands at the foothills of the Cumberlands. The scenery of the place is the finest I have ever seen. It is not

Jesse, helping stack hay in rick   (Courtesy *Lincoln Memorial University*)

surpassed by any place in all the eastern United States, I have been told. Grant Lee Hall is located on a spur of a Cumberland foothill. On the south slope is an apple orchard. On the east slope that runs down into Democrat Hollow, grow many tall elm trees. On the west slope, a blue stream of water runs and sinks into an underground cavern that takes the waters from Democrat Hollow. North of the Hall is a water tank. It is painted gray with blue letters standing for Lincoln Memorial. North of the water tank are the wooded mountain slopes, and at the edges of these woods are fields of pasture daisies. They looked like blooming fields of white cotton.

At Lincoln Memorial dining hall, ten students ate at each table. The tables were made by students at the woodworking shop under the supervision of Anthony. These tables were made of poplar and pine planks. They never used cloths on the tables at Lincoln Memorial. We ate at these bare wooden tables. When we went in for dinner, breakfast or lunch, we gathered in our regular places. The matron tapped the bell at the faculty table, said the same blessing at every meal, and after the blessing was said, we sat down, and the first ones that got the food were often the only ones fed. I almost starved my first two months at Lincoln Memorial. But I got used to it. I learned to slip a little bread into my pockets and reach and grab like the other students did at the tables. Three-hundred students ate in this dining room. Many of us boys worked hard. We ate heartily. We were always hungry.

There were approximately seven boys to three girls in Lincoln Memorial. The matron of the hall managed to get at least one girl to every table to make the boys behave. If a table was filled with boys, they threw bread, they stuck their forks into the soft pine wood—they nearly wrecked the table—they threw pepper into each other's eyes; but a girl at a table made a difference. She was the hostess and passed the food. It stopped the boys from hogging over the food and kept me from putting bread into my pockets. But I soon learned to find a table where there were more girls than boys. Girls ate less. I found a table where there were seven girls and three boys. Then I began to get enough to eat.

One night at a table in the dining hall, I heard a girl cry out, "Let loose of my leg, you damned old fool, Paul Sykes." Everybody laughed. Paul Sykes had reached under the table and pinched Primrose Halton's leg. The boys stuck their forks into the soft pine tables and laughed and threw biscuits across the table.

My classwork was rather stiff and the work I did in the fields helped to make it stiff. I attended classes during the forenoon. In the afternoon I worked for four hours. On Saturdays I worked all day. At noon, morning, or night, when a student wanted off in the kitchen, I asked to do the work and make something extra. I also wrote themes and history term papers as a sideline. I wrote themes for my roommate and in return he helped me to understand algebra. I wrote a term paper on Mary Stuart, Queen of Scots, that served its purpose in both English and history classes. It made two B's for me and six A's for other students. Once, a student handed in one of Woodrow Wilson's speeches copied word for word, for a term paper. It came back filled with corrections. "You will have to rewrite this paper. You don't have the right angle on your subject matter. Your English is terrible." The student flunked the course. I studied all day on Sundays. I tried to make good. I tried to make what the teachers called "good."

At the end of the first quarter, I stood fourth on the honor roll at Lincoln Memorial. My grades were not high. But good grades were hard to make at Lincoln Memorial. I had worked for all I got. I was in line for a scholarship if it took grades to get them.

My work got harder all the time in the fields. One of the boys I raked hay with on the first day I arrived at Lincoln Memorial told Anthony that I had taken a fit and hit Claymore with a pitchfork. I never knew it then. I learned this later. But I noticed that Anthony would never get near me. He always put me to work in a place by myself. The first work I did was dig potatoes, then help to fill the silo, cut corn and rake leaves. After the leaves had fallen from the trees and the corn was all cut, I helped to lay the water line from the mountaintop to Harrogate, Tennessee. It was zero weather and a water pipe often broke loose at the joint and wet us from head to foot. We had to dig the ditch for the pipes. Often we had to go many feet down through the frozen earth and the hard clay soil and the rock. It was half a winter's work for fifty boys working one half-day a week and all day on Saturday.

When the water line was laid, I went to work at a stone crusher. At this stone crusher, we dynamited the limestone rocks out of a small cedar-covered hill, beat them with sledge hammers and crowbars, and then we wheeled them in Irish-buggies to a crusher. We put them in the crusher, crushed the stone into a fine powder to fertilize the Lincoln Memorial farm and put on the walkways over the campus. We used different burrs in the crusher and crushed a coarser limestone and sold it to the State Highway Commission of Tennessee as ballast to use on their highways.

I had written and told my mother, in the meantime, that I was in Lincoln Memorial, at Harrogate, Tennessee. She told the neighbor women about it. She told Brother Tobbie. Brother Tobbie told her to bring me home. "Write and make that boy of yourn come home. That college will send him right to Hell. He was a right pert boy before he left here. Get him back. Just write and tell 'em you'll git the Law after 'em. Hoss that boy right back here. This world don't need no eddicated people. What this world needs is more people with salvation."

Many of the neighbors talked it over. I had run away from the hills. I had left my home. There was not much to me. I was a runaway. I wasn't anything. Mom told them that I was in college. She told them she was proud of me. They could not understand why she was proud of me. I had run away. I had never returned. When Mom wrote to me, she would always tell me what these neighbors had been saying and how she would defend me. Her letters, poorly as they were written, read like the best parts of a good novel. She could express herself in words that I could understand.

One day Ike Leadingham walked up to me and said, "Here, Freshman, buy a 'campus ticket.'" "What do I want with a 'campus ticket'?" "Well, you know the night watchman on this campus is a bad egg. And if he catches you out here at night on this campus, without any business to be out, you'll certainly go home. A letter will follow you to your Pa and Ma, telling just why you left Lincoln Memorial." "I know all about your fake stuff. You go and bring me a two-by-four six inches wide, will you? I heard you tell a freshman that the other day. What do you think I am? A damn fool, I suppose."

"Now I am not kidding you. You know there is a night watchman here, don't you? You know he is a bad fellow too, don't you? Well, there is an old house out here where we meet girls and have a big time about twice a month. We are meeting out there tonight. Wouldn't you like to go along?"

That night ten of us fellows slipped down the path through the apple orchard on the south slope. "Now, Stuart, if that damn night watchman does happen to get after us, you fly for Grant Lee Hall. And if he catches you, for God's sake don't let him know about our secret."

The moon shone on the coloring apple-tree leaves. The red fruit had not been picked. It weighted the apple-tree branches. We stopped under the apple trees and filled our pockets with mellow apples. I had an idea as we walked under the trees. I would bring a sack and come back to the trees. I would lay in a nice wardrobe full of picked apples. I didn't say anything to the boys about it. But I thought of it. I could hardly wait. I wanted to get them before the farm boys picked them. We went across Democrat Hollow and started up the path towards the Old Tower, where we were to meet the girls.

When we had got about midway of this orchard, a man cried out: "Stop, or I'll shoot every one of you!" "Night watchman!" cried Ike. "Follow me—come on, let's go!" Ike took the lead. I followed. The gun went off again and again. I passed Ike and was soon in the lead. I was headed toward Grant Lee Hall. It seemed the runner behind me got fresher, stronger and closer all the time. I was breathing hard but not winded when a fellow tackled me around the waist. We both fell sprawling on the dewy grass in Democrat Hollow. And when he got his breath, he said: "What in

the hell are you doing out here, anyway? I am the night watchman.
I've got a right to know. And I'm going to know." I never answered.
He made a point of pulling his pistol out and putting it into the
holster on his hip again. "You be on the first floor of Grant Lee
Hall tomorrow night. We'll try you before the Dean of Men, Rodney
Findley. Now you be there and there may be some possible chance
for you to get out of this."

During all the hours of the next day, the boys came and told
me to be very tactful when I was cross-questioned by the Dean of
Men. They said the whole thing was a serious matter. I began to
think I would have to leave Lincoln Memorial. And then there was
the indictment against me, slipping out to see girls at night. I would
not tell it. I would leave the school first. It would get all the boys
into it. Ike would be deep in the whole matter, and after he had
invited me I couldn't get Ike into any trouble.

Friday night came. All the boys in Grant Lee Hall came down
to hear the trial. Old Claymore was there. I wondered if he remembered the day I hit him with a pitchfork. The boys I had been eating
beside at the table were there. The fellows I had worked with on
the water line were there. There were over fifty boys to hear the
trial. The Dean of Men, Rodney Findley, came in wearing a cap
and gown. The boys all stood when he entered the room. He told
them to be seated. Dean Findley looked to be thirty-five to forty
years of age. He wore a serious expression on his face.

"I believe, Boys, the fellow we have up for loitering on the
campus at a late hour is Mr. Stuart. Mr. Stuart, will you rise?" I
rose from my seat. "Walk up and take this seat, please. Now, I hear
that there were many boys with Mr. Stuart, and he was the only
fellow the night watchman caught. I hope it was none of you
schoolboys. You fellows know this is against the rules and regulations
of Lincoln Memorial to be out at this late hour so near the girls'
dormitory. Now, Mr. Stuart, will you get up and tell the student
group assembled here tonight just why you were out there in that
orchard and who all were with you?"

"I shall answer neither question. Do with me what you will."

"Ambrose, did you have much trouble catching this fellow? Will you swear that this was the fellow you caught in the orchard last night?" "Yes, he was faster than an old workhorse to catch. And I will swear he is the fellow." "Now, I would like to hear some testimony witnesses swear for or against this man. I feel convinced that he is guilty." "Dean Findley, I'd like to say that I know this fellow Stuart. He's a good student and a hard worker on the farm. If you can let him stay, I think it would be a fine thing for Stuart. He's new here and didn't know the rules and regulations of this institution. I think he would be a different fellow if you would give him another chance."

Then old Claymore arose. "Dean Findley, I believe this fellow Stuart is all nuts. The other day we were working in the hayfield and Stuart had a fit. He hit me across the ribs with a pitchfork. I thought to my soul I'd pass out. It was a long time before I could get a long breath. I think he is a dangerous fellow myself. He'd better be sent away from Lincoln Memorial. I am in favor of sending him away."

The question was debated among the students for at least a couple of hours. "Gentlemen, let us adjourn. I shall take Stuart out and put a couple of propositions before him tonight." I went with the dean. He took me to a room in Avery Hall. "Now, Stuart, I believe you are a nice fellow. And doing my duty as the Dean of Men at Lincoln Memorial, I want to give you a chance. I'll either send you home or fine you. Either one you prefer. If this was at a lot of Southern institutions, they would kick your tail out too quick to even think about it." "How much will the fine be?" I thought to myself: "Not less than fifty dollars surely." "I'll let you off with five dollars. I don't think that's too much, do you?" "Not at all." I gave him five dollars.

I went out of the room thinking I was a lucky fellow to have five dollars. It had just saved me from going home in disgrace. I would always keep a little money around for fear of a fine. It had come in handy. I would stay off the campus at night from now on. But it seemed as if there was something fishy about it all. I'd never got any rules to the effect of staying off the campus after nine o'clock. I was a man, anyway. I ought to know what I was doing. In my estimation college was a funny place to be. I didn't know whether I wanted to stay or not. I was afraid of getting chased every time I stepped out after dark. I was afraid of the dean. I was afraid to turn around at the wrong time. I was afraid of everything.

When I went back over to Grant Lee Hall, Ike was waiting for me on the steps. "Well, Pal, how did you come out?" "I got out of it for five bucks. Lord, I didn't expect to, either! I thought I was gone sure. Bring a two-by-four six inches wide. What do you think I am, a damn fool?" "Well, Stuart, you are a damn fool. We put one over on you tonight. This is our secret at Lincoln Memorial. You got your initiation tonight. Now let this be a lesson to you." "Yes, and I lost five bucks in that deal too. And lordy, how I do need it." "You just keep quiet about that five. Keep quiet about the whole thing. We have about thirty freshmen yet to get. We'll get 'em all too. I've never seen one yet that wouldn't bite on the women proposition. If we can't sell 'em a campus ticket, we let the night watchman do the rest. Stuart, we take this money and throw a big party every spring. It is the finest event of the year with us. Dean Rodney Findley is treasurer. He isn't a dean at all. He's a student here. Just started college a little late in life."

We chased boys one night each week until Christmas. One cool October night we chased one into the sewage pond. He waded out into the water over his shoulders. Only his head was above the scum of oil, sprayed on the water to keep the mosquitoes away. We chased another fellow into the state of Virginia one night. He never returned. We set fines all the way from one to ten dollars. It all depended on how much we thought the fellow was worth.

I met one fellow on the campus of Lincoln Memorial called Ron East. Ron was a leader among the students. He was a young minister and wrote poetry. He was six feet three inches tall and was a powerful athlete. He was elected to more offices of organizations than he could fill. We exchanged poetry with each other that we had written. We went onto the mountaintops and walked at night.

On Sunday afternoons we went out on the mountains and across the old fields. Ron would preach at the little mountain churches and I would go with him. Autumn in the mountains of eastern Tennessee is beautiful. One cannot find autumn elsewhere that equals the splendor of the autumn in eastern Tennessee. I thought Ron East was the finest man I'd met in Lincoln Memorial. He was working his way in Lincoln Memorial too. He dried dishes.

When December came, I wanted to go home. I was homesick. It had been a long time since I'd seen my people. Seasons had come and gone. I wondered about home. I wondered how they were getting along without my help. I would go home this Christmas. I did not have the money--how could I go home? It was all I could do to stay in Lincoln Memorial. I had thumbed part of my way to Lincoln Memorial. I could thumb all of my way back.

The Christmas holidays came. I wanted to go home more than I had ever wanted to go when I saw the students leaving Lincoln Memorial for their homes. I could hardly stand it to see them go. I wanted to go too. But it would be hard to thumb rides on the highways. A cold December rain was falling, and muddy water ran across the highways and in little ditches by the highways. But that was not going to stand in my way. I was going to try it anyway.

I went to see if Ron had any money. "I have one dollar, Stuart. It is every cent of money I have. You are welcome to it." "I don't have a cent. I hate to take the last penny you have. But I'll need a dollar on a trip like this, three-hundred and twenty miles and the rain still pouring down." "Yes, you'll need a dollar all right and then some. I've done a lot of thumbing. I have gone that far on a dollar but I'd hate to do it at a time like this. You can try it if you like."

I took the dollar from Ron and the old paper suitcase, and through the cold gray December rain I walked out onto the highway. Around me were mountains with their tops hidden by the clouds. Sheets of fog lay in the valleys. The sides of the mountains were drab-colored. The trees that had worn many-colored robes when I first came to Harrogate, Tennessee, were now barren, and the wind and rain beat through their bare branches. The huge rock ribs in the sides of the mountains looked like scaly monsters getting soaked in the rain. But the holly bushes were green, the pines and the mountain ivy were still green.

I caught seven rides before I made the first twenty miles. One of the rides was in a jolt wagon for three miles. The other rides were in feed trucks and coal trucks. But I didn't care what I rode in or how wet I got. I was going home—going home! All the touring cars that passed me were loaded. And those that were not loaded would not stop.

It was getting late now, and I had started at nine o'clock that morning. I had only covered twenty-seven miles. Darkness came early on that short gray December day. I was standing by the highway and a quarter-ton Ford truck rolled up by me and stopped. "Which way you going, Buddy?" His voice was rough. He spoke broken English. "Going north." "Get in out of the rain and let's go." I wanted to put my arm around him. A ride at last! We went moving slowly northward.

"The roads are bad and I can't drive fast. And I am afraid this truck will go fluey on me. It ain't a very good truck. Where are you from, what is your name, and where are you going?" "My name is Stuart. I am in Lincoln Memorial at Harrogate, Tennessee. My home is in northeast Kentucky. I am trying to get there." "Son, you ought not to be on the highway at a time like this. Can your people pay your way home?" "Yes, I got a letter some time ago saying that they were sending me money to come home with, but it never came, so I thought I'd try thumbing my way back."

We passed two fruit trucks going north. Each had "Florida Fruit" in big black letters written on the yellow side. We reached Corbin, Kentucky. We asked a fellow on the street which was the highway leading north. He pointed it out to us. We took this road, and soon we met two large fruit trucks going south. They were exactly the same kind of trucks we had passed earlier, and I remarked to my friend that the driver of one of the trucks was fat and had a light mustache like the fellow we had overtaken less than an hour ago. "The mountains are getting higher. This shouldn't be true and us going north." "Now you are young and restless and excited. I am an old man. I have had lots of experience. I know what I am doing. You leave it to me."

When we had two blowouts at one time and had to stop, we were at Four Miles, Kentucky. We were within twenty miles of Lincoln Memorial. "I thought we were going south all the time. I could tell by the mountains getting higher." "You never thought anything of the kind. I should not have picked you up. I was talking to you and made this mistake. Now we are in a mess." He went around to the back of the truck and got us a couple of apples apiece. "Well, let's drive her back up the road a piece and park. I have blankets in this box here in the back of the truck. We can take them out and wrap up together in them. The rain can't go through them. I have an old oilcloth I can spread over the blanket. It would be fine if we could find a barn someplace." We drove up the highway on two flats. We stopped by a little plank house by the side of the road. We parked the truck. We got out and investigated the house.

We found that chickens had once roosted in this house but now there were none. The manure had dried on the shaky floor. He held a small flashlight while I took a board and raked the dry manure off the planks. We knew that the wet blankets would dampen the dry manure and the heat of our blankets against the manure, after our bodies had warmed them, would create a terrible smell and the manure would stick to the blankets. I was a little afraid of a light in a henhouse. I thought somebody might be living close by and shoot into the building. We got the blankets from the box in the back of the truck. They were damp. There were four of them. We put the wettest blanket on the floor. We put a dry one on top of that to be against our bodies. We put a dry blanket over our bodies and on top of that dry blanket we put another wet one. I pulled off my coat and shoes. My friend pulled off his coat, pants and shoes. We rolled up close together.

"You know I got a girl about your age and four boys older. But me and my wife, we separated, and she ruined me. I had some money but she sued me and got it all. Now I am an old man ready to die. I am very tired too. And I don't have anything but this old truck and these blankets and five dollars. And I've got to go back to Michigan on that." "Where have you been in the South? And what is your name?" "My name is Frederick Menkovitch. I have been down in Florida. I have been following the boom. I am a carpenter by trade. I made good money for two years. Then I turned round and invested it in land. The price of land dropped to the bottom. The bottom fell out of the price, I mean, and I was left without anything. So I am on my way back home." We went to sleep.

That night at about twelve o'clock, Menkovitch woke me up with threats and curses. "I'll kill ye. Ye damn right I will. By God, I'll do it!" I got out of bed and broke off a piece of a rail the chickens had once roosted on. I made up my mind that if one had to die it would be he unless he shot me with a gun. The skies had cleared now. The stars had come out into the blue December sky. And the moonlight and the starlight shone through the broad henhouse window, screened over with chicken wire. Menkovitch dozed off to sleep again. His curses got softer and softer, even down to a whisper. But I did not go back to bed. I stayed up the rest of the night, wrapped in a blanket with a piece of the chicken roost in my hand.

At daybreak, a farmer walked into the henhouse and introduced himself as Tillman. I told him who I was. Menkovitch told Tillman his name. "Boys, this is my henhouse and if I'd a-knowed you fellows was up here, I'd a-come up here and got you and tuk you down to the house and give you a better bed. I am a man of the Lord, and this is a shame for me to let two fellows sleep in my henhouse. Come on down to the house and git you some breakfast."

We followed Mr. Tillman down the path that led from the highway to his house. We went into the mountain home. It was very much like the home I was from. "Here, meet the better part of my life. This is Mr. Stuart. This is Mr. Menkovitch." "I didn't quite get the last name." "My name is Menkovitch." "Wash your faces. Here is hot water in the teakettle. Here is a bar of soap, and over there is a clean towel. Breakfast will be ready for you when you are ready for it. I ain't fixing anything extra. I didn't know I was going to have company. I guess you can stand for one meal what we have to live on all the time."

We sat down at a table filled with food. We had coffee black and strong. The steam rose up over the table, from the pot and the coffee cups. We had hot fluffy biscuits. They were white as cotton inside. We had apples, berries, peaches, cherries and pear preserves. We had butter, ham and brown gravy. We had sorghum and a dish of honey, white in the comb, stacked upon a plate. I never sat down to a breakfast like it. "Martha, I guess Mr. Stuart is used to more than this to eat. He told me up there in the henhouse awhile ago that he was from Lincoln Memorial." This food tasted good. It was all I had had since the morning before except a couple of apples.

I had one dollar but I did not intend to spend it. "Now, Boys, reach and help yourselves. Just feel like you was eating at home. You know you are welcome here." "Have some ham, Mr. Menkovitch, and some gravy." "No, Madam. I don't eat meat on Friday. It is against my religion. I am a Catholic." Mrs. Tillman acted like she had been hit above the eye with a brick. Mr. Tillman sat silent. Then Menkovitch said: "They tell me the Kentucky mountaineers are ignorant. They tell me they don't have any roads and I believe it. Look at all this desolate country and only the one road in it. It is one poor place. They tell me that Georgia niggers made that road up there on the hill and they did it under the whip. Kentucky is one poor place." Mrs. Tillman hit Menkovitch on the temple with a heavy cup filled with coffee. He fell from the chair. "Now say some more about us, will you?" He got up on his knees first, then he arose and went out. He went up the hill to the truck. I offered to pay for the breakfast. Mrs. Tillman refused money. "Son, I wish you didn't have to travel with an old tramp like he is. I believe he is a crazy man."

We fixed two punctures. It was eleven o'clock. We loaded the blankets in the truck box and were on our way again. The skies grew dark and the rain began to fall again. Before we reached the top of the mountain, we had another blowout. The rain beat down against the drabbish Cumberland mountain earth. The wind blew through the naked trees. It was the day before Christmas. I wanted to be home for Christmas.

As we were fixing the flat tire, a Ford rolled up and stopped. "Do you need any help?" asked the driver. "Yes, an inner tube if you have one. An old one if you can spare it." "Here is one that may do you some good." He pitched it out and I caught it for Menkovitch. "Are you loaded too much for an extra passenger?" "No. How far are you going?" "I'm going to east Kentucky. I must go as far north as Lexington and then turn directly east." "I'm going to Cincinnati. Get in and go with us."

I took my suitcase and changed vehicles. "You're not going to leave me, are you, Buddy? I need you. I have helped you this far." "Good-by, Menkovitch." I left him fixing a flat tire on Cumberland Mountain on Christmas Eve day.

I told Ward Milton about Menkovitch and the fight at the table. "I'm glad you got away from him. I am a Klansman and I don't mind letting you know it. I wish I hadn't given him that inner tube."

It was six o'clock in the evening before we reached Lexington. A tractor had to pull us through three water holes on the highway, where small streams had flooded the low places. The water was touching the floor of the bridge over the Kentucky River. It was a terrible journey. We were tired when we reached Lexington. I wondered how I would go on. I still had the one dollar bill that Ron East had let me have at Lincoln Memorial.

I bought a train ticket from Lexington, Kentucky, to Winchester, Kentucky, and that took sixty-seven cents. I had thirty-three cents left. I intended to ride that far on the train and then hide in the toilet the rest of the way to Ashland. I could not catch a ride on the highway on a wet December night so near Christmas. It was Christmas Eve. I went back to the toilet but the conductor found me hiding after we had passed Winchester. "I'll kick your damn tail. I'll stop the train. I'll throw you off—you scum of creation!" I explained where I was trying to go. I told the circumstances I was trying to make the trip under. "That don't matter a damn to me. I'll put you off here. My troubles ain't your troubles. I am hired to work for this company and not to let bums ride in the toilet. That's a penitentiary offense. I'll road you if you talk back, too."

Allie Young, a boy from Morehead, Kentucky, was riding in the smoker. He heard the racket. He came out. "Don't you put him off this train. I got the money to pay his fare first. But why don't you let him ride on in to Ashland? If you don't, I'll get my old man to get a hold of you and you'll wish you'd let him ride." "I don't care for your old man. Who is he anyway?" "He controls the Governor and the Governor controls this state. The state controls the railroads; therefore, my dad controls you." "He'll pay or get off." All the time the train was carrying me on. I had ridden at least thirty-five miles since the quarrel started. I thought if we could keep up quarreling I could ride on. There were only a few stops between Winchester and Ashland for the night train. "Here's your damn money. How much do you want?" "Here's my thirty-three cents." I pitched it in against Allie Young's will. "I want three dollars and sixty-four cents." The debt was paid. "Young, I'll send you that money as soon as I get home."

I rode that night without food. I drank water to keep from feeling weak. At Ashland, Kentucky, I waited on Christmas morning from four until seven for daylight so that I could catch a ride to Greenup and then walk out the old ridge path home. I caught two rides. They put me back in my old hometown.

It had been a long time since I had been to Greenup. Seasons had passed and some of the fields I noticed had grown up in sprouts. I was on the path that led me home. I was glad to go. Home again, going home, old friends, pine trees, oak trees, hound dogs, plenty to eat, lonesome water to drink—home again! Lord, I could hardly wait. Just four miles and home again! It was more like a dream than a reality. Winter oak trees and the gray December skies! Wind in the barren oak trees had a whipping sound. Wind in the pine tops had a lonesome sound. The church bells of Greenup sounded out across the desolate country. I remembered how they used to sound when I first went out this path into the big life in Greenup High School. That high school was only a little life now, I thought. But the bells kept pealing softly over the land, and the rustling of the dead leaves—all this seemed to say:

> "Hie away to Greenup,
>   Hie away to prayer;
>   Hie away to Greenup,
>   I shall soon be there."

I would soon be home. There was the shack in sight now. I would not make any noise. I would slip up through the chip yard and go to the kitchen window and see what Mom was doing. I would surprise her. "I don't believe he's coming home. Now put that chicken in the box carefully. Put in a couple of backs. He always liked backs of chicken." "Yes, and I'm right here to eat them." There was a family reunion in our kitchen. James showed me his .22 rifle he had got for Christmas. Glennis brought me her doll. Mary showed me her new dress. Pa showed me his leather coat.

"How do you like college? Tell me something about it." "How are you paying your expenses, and how do you like Tennessee?" "How did you come home? Why didn't you come sooner?" I could not answer the questions. There was not one word said about me running away from home. It was all forgotten. "Now you let Jesse alone. I want to take him out and show him the corn and the stock. I guess it's his Pa's right to talk to him a little while." "Now hurry back. Dinner is nearly on the table."

"You see, Jesse, this is a right good crop of corn. We just got this crib full this year. It was a good season. We missed you a powerful lot last summer. God only knows what a time we had without you. I plowed at night when I come in from work on the railroad. I worked in the moonlight. I worked by lantern light." "I think you have done mighty well. This is a fine crib of corn. And look here what a stack of Irish potatoes! How did the sweet potatoes do?" "Not so good. The damn craw-dads cut the plants down faster than we could set them out. You see, your Ma worked awful hard, and Mary and James worked out in the fields like grown-up people. Them kids are workers, let me tell you. I hate to see your Ma go out to the fields but, Jesse, if I was worth a million dollars, she'd go out just the same. W'y, when the trees begin to leaf out, she's gone. She just lets the house go. She won't stay inside at all. And she knows every kind of a weed that grows. Did you see all them flowers she's got out there at the house? They're a perfect damn nuisance. But I help her with them just because she likes them. Anything she wants I try to get it for her. Your Ma's worked mighty hard, Jesse, and I have too. We're both getting along in years and hard work is getting us."

I could see deeper lines across my father's face. I could tell that he was going down the hill. He would never go up again either. Age would not let him. Hard work had gotten him. I knew it. Hard work in the hills and exposure to bad weather had put marks across his face. "Say, this is a nice pine here in the yard." "Yes, me and your Ma, we had a little racket about that pine. I wanted to cut it down. She wanted to leave it standing. You know it is a pretty shore sign if you leave a pine standing in the yard or set a pine tree in the yard and it gets big enough to shade a grave, it's a sign of death in the family. But she would let it stand. I told her about it." "I heard you bought fifty more acres of black-oak hill land?" "You heard the truth. I bought all that hill over yonder running back with Wilburn's line." "What do you need with that? Work yourself to death to pay for one fifty-acre farm and build a house on it, then go and buy another farm. You'll kill yourself paying for it." "I am older than you. I know what I am doing. I need that land. I love land. I can't get enough of it. I'm going to get all of this in grass. I'm going to raise tobacco. I'm going to quit working on the railroad section. I'm going to die on this farm. I like it here. And let me tell you, I've made every penny I paid on this land by the sweat of my brow. I work for all I get. You know, Jess, your Pa is an honest man."

"Sit down over there at your old place. We are so glad to have you with us. Guess who was asking about you the other day? I saw her in Greenup, and it was Maria Sheen. She is a pretty girl if I ever seen one in my life. But she wears her dresses a little short, don't you think? Now reach and help yourself. Remember you are at home. Don't be bashful." "I guess he gets so many good things to eat at Lincoln Memorial he can't stand the old home grub any more." "If I'd see a table like this at Lincoln Memorial filled with so much good food, it would scare me so bad I'd run off and hide." "Now you don't mean that, Jesse." "Yes, I mean it too. I fill my pockets full of bread, for often I don't get enough. Good night! Look what a table of food—spareribs, ham, gravy, sweetmilk and buttermilk, roasted goose, chicken, blackberries, strawberries, cherries, apples, huckleberry preserves, wild-grape jelly, honey, biscuit and corn bread, pickled beans, pickled corn and kraut, pie, cake, and quail meat extra. What more do you want?" "This ain't 'food' here, Son. This is old country grub. Take this from your Pa." "And just think, you put up this food from the fields. Mom, you are more industrious than a honeybee. You certainly can turn off the work." "Yes, I get the fruit while it is on the vine. I know it won't always stay there. I only canned twenty-five gallons of blackberries this year. The people from town got our field of berries. Mitch got mad about it and I said let them have the berries. They needed them." "How many peaches did you can?" "I canned thirty gallons of peaches. I would have canned more but Mitch grumbled about me using too much sugar and I had to quit." "Yes, that is the way. Lay everything on Mitch. If I's away from this place, I'd like to know what you'd do. When one of the kids does something good, you say: 'Yes, he takes after me!' That's what you said when you found out Jesse was in college. When James took the gun and slipped off to the woods, well, he takes after me. Jesse, that's the way things go around here."

"Pa, how is old Black-Boy? I forgot to ask." "That dog is the best dog in these hills. I ain't saying it because he belongs to this family, but we couldn't live without him. His teeth ain't very good but he can whip any dog in these hills. He's just as good as he was when you hunted with him. I went out Wednesday night and got four possums and three polecats. Then I had to tie him to bring him in. He'd a-hunted polecats and treed possums the rest of the night. But I had to get a little sleep for I work hard out on the railroad." "And don't you know Black-Boy killed a copperhead just before it got under the floor? It was the biggest copperhead old Black-Boy ever killed. It bit Black-Boy in the head and we had to give him snakeroot and whisky in sweet milk. His head swelled up as big as two heads, but he got all right. Mama said that snake might have bit me when I crawled under the floor to get the eggs." "When I went to get the cows the other morning, Black-Boy killed two vipers up yonder in the newground pasture by that twin chestnut stump. He went down the hollow on a track like he was running a rabbit. But he was following another snake. It was a copperhead. There's more snakes here than anyplace I ever heard tell of. He killed that last copperhead in October--that late, what do you think of that?"

"Jess, the leaves are damp and old Black-Boy is in good trim. Let's go out and knock down some cottontails. I'll beat you a-shootin'." We walked out by the barn and into the second-growth black-oak timber. Pa gave me the old Columbia single barrel. He took a double barrel he borrowed from a neighbor. A covey of quails flew out of a saw-briar nest. I raised my gun to shoot. "Hah—a—a don't shoot them birds! Don't shoot them birds! I don't allow them killed on this place. A quail is an innocent bird. I'd just as soon shoot a dove as a quail. I can't stand to kill one. I can't stand to see one killed. I kept them on this place and they come down at the corncrib and eat with the chickens. They don't harm a thing. They help catch the flies and worms and they eat the weed seeds. I can't kill one." "Do you want me to kill rabbits a-setting or do you want me to scare them out and shoot them on the run?" "This is Christmas Day. Give the rabbits a chance. Don't shoot one asleep. Shoot it on the run."

Black-Boy jumped a rabbit. It came toward me. I shot and

missed. I shot again. The rabbit went on. My father shot. The rabbit rolled over and over. My father got it on the run. He laughed and laughed. "I think books hurt the flesh. You ought to come back to the hills. You ain't a good shot like you used to be. Here you have missed two good shots."

"I think it is the fault of the gun. Surely I can beat this." But another rabbit and another miss. My father got it. A third rabbit and my father got it. He killed five rabbits and I killed one. He laughed as we started home. "Boy, your old Pap can put it over on you. And I ain't no shot at all. Nothing like my Pap used to be. He killed running rabbits with a long flintlock rifle. He could knock them too. When we went squirrel huntin' he had Jim, my oldest brother, to spit ambeer in his eyes. He said it made him see better. Jim hated to do it for Pap squirmed around so, but he knowed better than not to do it when Pap told him."

I used to come into these same woods and get more rabbits and birds than any fellow in the crowd. I do believe books hurt the flesh. I don't care about hunting and killing as I used to do. I am thinking about Lincoln Memorial and the things I learned there. I am thinking about red-hot steel, smoke and steel, and dead men. I am thinking about merry-go-rounds and gay crowds. I want something different. I was happy here until I went away to school. I was dissatisfied because I was so ignorant when I measured my ways with other people's! And I want to know more and more and more. I can't learn enough facts to suit myself and my teachers. What good do they do? They make me dissatisfied. They help me to know that these quiet things I left are the best after all. There is something good about the old country life that is passing. It is the real sweetness of living down against the soil. And that life will never come again.

We walked across the sedge-grass lands and through the blackberry briars to a cow path. We walked under the black-oak trees and the gray drops of rain dripped off the barren boughs. The wind swished through the wet pine tops. The dead oak leaves were wet and they stuck down against the bosom of the soil. Black sticks were on the ground, clumps of greenbriars and tufts of wild goose-berry briars and last year's ferns. And in one of the tufts of wild gooseberry briars was the blood of one of the rabbits my father was carrying. He shot it just as it leaped over the bushes. The warm blood spilt out upon the dead oak leaves and mixed with the rain. But the stain was still left. Oak leaves, rabbit blood and gooseberry briars mix well.

We walked slowly home, around through the pasture and by the crab-apple trees and pine grove. We went out behind the corncrib to skin the rabbits. My father had a nail driven in a back log of the crib to hang the rabbits on when he skinned them. He cut the flesh through under the leader of the hind leg and hung it over the nail. Then he jerked off the skin and threw it to Black-Boy. Black-Boy knew what his share was—the skins, heads, guts, livers, lights and paws. He always cleaned up the scraps but then he never had enough. My father put the cleaned rabbits in a crock and put salty water over them and let them set overnight. Then he hung them up in the smokehouse to let them freeze. Then they were ready to be cooked.

"I want you to finish college and come back here and run for County School Superintendent. I'd rather you'd have that as anything in the country. Wouldn't you like to have it?" "I don't care about that. I don't know what I want." "Well, I was talking to Ike and Brady and Uncle Rank Larks and we aim to run you anyhow. They say you are the man for it. And I think it is a big thing. You can keep that job and stay right out here on the farm."

"What grade is James in now?" "I forgot to tell you. But that James is in his first year of high school. He's too young to be in high school. He was only ten last August. But your Ma would let him go. I thought about it a long time first. I remembered how it changed you, and I didn't much care about James gettin' that a-way. Now that boy can really handle a gun. He's killing rabbits right along. He hardly misses a shot. He can beat you. He's a fisherman too."

"Mom, I've been here eight days now. I must get back to

Lincoln Memorial. I am ready to go back." "Do you have money to go back on?" "No, I do not." "We'll rake up some money someway for you. I have seven dollars I've saved selling eggs and cream from the cows. You can have that. Mitch can give you five dollars. That will be enough, won't it?" "Yes, that is enough but I hate to take it from you." "You go on and take it, Child."

I went back the ridge road I came. I patched the old suitcase while I was at home. I pasted Lincoln Memorial stickers on the sides to let people know I was a college student. But Lincoln Memorial and so many people were not like Kentucky hills and so many sprouts. I didn't want to tell people about it, but I loved the Kentucky hills and the trees on them, especially this December, more than I had ever loved them.

Back to Lincoln Memorial. I was glad to get back early. I thought a student that worked in the dining hall might possibly drop out, and I would be there to ask for the job inside, in the dry. I wanted one there. I registered for the second quarter. I was going in debt sixty dollars. I must work hard to keep the debt down. I was not making extra money to buy clothes. I would have to make arrangements someway to buy clothes. I did not have a suit. And all the clothes I had were patched. The elbows were out of my coat and sweater. The seats were thin in my pants. I bet a boy my old overcoat that I could cut fifty shocks of the heaviest corn the university farm had grown, twelve hills square, and do it in ten hours. I bet him the coat against a new pair of shoes. I lost. I cut forty-seven and the ten hours were up. I lost my old overcoat.

I was sent to the rock quarry. It was the hardest work at Lincoln Memorial. I went to the rock quarry every day. Because I hit a boy with a mud ball one day, Downing Allbright, a straw boss for Anthony, put me on the Bull Gang. I worked as one of the four who drilled holes by hand with a forty-pound drill. We churned the holes from four to six feet deep. Then we put black powder in them and blew the rock loose. Each day Downing Allbright measured how deep we had churned the hole. We were supposed to cut thirty-six inches in five hours, sixty inches in nine hours. It was hard to do.

Then the boys cleaned out the hole, filled it with black powder and attached a fuse. They set fire to the fuse and yelled: "Fire in the hole!" At this shout we always got a rest. We went over on the backside of the hill and sprawled out on the ground and waited for the shot to go off.

The shot would go off. Rocks would fall among the cedar tops like heavy rain. We would lie there, our faces to the earth, flat on our stomachs, until the fragments of rocks quit hitting the cedar tops above us and the earth about us. Then we would walk back to the quarry and take our hammers and crowbars and start breaking the rocks so that we could get them in the crusher.

One day at noon in front of the dining room, I heard a sophomore say: "It's time we's a knockin' a little of the cockiness out of these freshmen." A freshman knocked him down. A sophomore hit that freshman and knocked him down. A free-for-all started. The freshmen outnumbered the upperclassmen. The whole two-hundred boys were in a fight. Fists were skinned and noses were bleeding. "Don't use sticks! Don't choke! And no fair gouging!" One could hear these cries. "Who in the hell's a-gouging?"

The boys trampled the shrubbery under. The deputy sheriff was called. He couldn't stop the fight. The faculty members were called. They couldn't do anything about it. The dean was called, and he had to let them fight. They fought until they gave out and all agreed to stop. The fight lasted over an hour. From this date on until school was out, it was dangerous for boys to go about unless they were in groups. Freshmen waylaid the upperclassmen. Upperclassmen waylaid the freshmen.

The fighting became so intense between the freshmen and the upperclassmen that clubs were kept in the rooms at Grant Lee Hall. Grafton Meadows brought a hatchet from the woodworking shop and kept it in his room. "I'll split the first damn freshman's head open that comes to my door to call me out and beat me up. I'm just waiting for 'im." Groups of freshmen lurked in the dark behind the buildings for the sophomores, the juniors and especially for the seniors. One senior was beaten up and acid poured on his face. The authorities of Lincoln Memorial took action to prevent further war on the campus.

The meeting was called at chapel. All students were requested to be there. Many long prayers were prayed. The president made a long speech. "Students of Lincoln Memorial, this class war has gone on long enough. Students are coming to classes with blacked eyes, cut lips and smashed noses. You must bury the hatchet." We were dismissed from chapel. A representative from the upperclassmen and one from the freshmen group met and decided upon peace between the two groups. One night when a big yellow moon was in the autumn sky, we marched down to the apple orchard on the south slope from Grant Lee Hall. We built a fire from the dead apple-tree branches. We sat around this fire and sang songs until the moon went down behind the clouds. We had speeches from both sides: "Let there be peace." The freshmen's representative and the upperclassmen's representative there, in our presence, buried a brand-new hatchet.

It was agreed further that the initiation, in the future, would involve a flag placed in the top of a tree. The upperclassmen would put eight men up among the branches of the tree to defend the flag and forty men under the tree to defend the tree. The freshmen were allowed fifty men to go up the tree and get the flag. The trouble was, we couldn't get a tree on the campus to hold us. Each year, when the initiation was over, only the trunk of the tree was left. The branches would all be swept away. Boys would be lying on the ground unconscious with their teeth knocked out and bones broken. As the freshmen had tried to climb the tree, they had been kicked down by the upperclassmen above them. Oftentimes a freshman would get up the tree and catch an upperclassman's foot and swing on it. They'd both go down from the tree fifteen feet to the hard earth, and the mass of almost one-hundred boys would fight over their bodies lying senseless there on the ground. The fight would go on regardless of the wounded. It would be a fight to a finish.

In spite of these annual brawls, the work went on at Lincoln

Memorial. One day when the land began to thaw and spring came to Tennessee, Fort Miller and I were the only two fellows using the forty-pound drill at the quarry. We had blistered our hands through our gloves. We sat down to rest. I said to Fort: "Fort, what is your aim in life anyway? Why did you come to Lincoln Memorial?" "I came to Lincoln Memorial because I can work my way here. Before I leave Lincoln Memorial, I'm going to be straw boss of this quarry. I'll work the hell out'n a lot of damn lazy fellows I don't like."

The day came when Fort gave me orders. He was a student the same as I. He was a poor student. He had made three D's and one F. There were not many men at the crusher that Saturday morning. Fort lined us out at different jobs. I had to break the rocks with a hammer and haul them to the crusher. I was doing the work of two. He put a youngster at the crusher that was not able to stand the limestone dust. He made him stay there. One boy said to me: "Stuart, you are the biggest boy out here. Can't you stop Fort from this?" "Fort, why do you stand down there and oil the tractor when it doesn't need it. Why can't you help with this work? You are none too good." "I'm running this place. You'll do as I say." I picked up a flat-stone rock and when Fort stooped over to oil the tractor, I threw it flatwise against his ribs. Fort rolled on the ground. He got up and cried: "I'll tell Downing Allbright on you as soon as he comes." It was my last time at the quarry.

Near the end of my freshman year at Lincoln Memorial, I took this sonnet to an English teacher in the college.

> Muddy waters, how I have loved your crying
> Night and day—forever past my open door,
> Down through the reckless channel breaks along the shore
> Where winter wind in ankle-sedge is sighing,
> And the infant moon circles low above the hill.
> I have gone down at midnight, sat beside you
> In woven reeds when winter winds whistled through

Your lonesome bank-side trees—Your pulsing will
Was surging your body down one lost way.
Like some deep singer in the void you fling
Futility to the wind and flow and sing
New songs, perhaps, for new youth molding clay
While I return to where my candle flame
Burns low and the world will never know my name.

"I don't like your sonnet at all. Get away from sedge and muddy waters and the night wind. Write high beautiful things like Shakespeare, Keats, Browning, and Longfellow. Don't waste your time on such low vile things."

School was over. I left my trunk with a few books, quilts and one pillow. I thumbed my way back to northeastern Kentucky.

My mother was proud to see me when I came back from school. All of the family were happy. They all wanted to talk to me at once. They wanted to know about Tennessee—if Tennessee looked anything like Kentucky, if the people were as poor in Tennessee as they were in Kentucky, how I liked college life. "I'll bet you someday I'll be going to college and come back and you'll all be as proud of me as you are of Jesse," said James. "Well, I'm a-going too if you go, James," said Glennis, "and when I get back, William Everett Holbrook will come around to see me, and he'll ask me where I've been. I'll tell him all about it. He'll be the proudest to see me, too, when I get back from college."

That evening after supper, my mother and I slipped away from the house. We went down through the garden. "Now here, Jesse, are my beets. They are put in two rows lengthwise of the bed. Don't you remember the way you used to want me to plant them. You always said you could hoe them faster that a-way." "Did I? Oh yes, that's right. It was just about to escape my mind. But I remember now." "Here is my early corn. See how pretty it is? It's that little early sugar corn. It won't amount to much when it comes to ears. But you know it comes in right handy in the middle of the crop when everything else is scarce." "Yes, I remember that mighty well. You know sugar corn raised in the garden is fresh and good when a man comes in to the table and sits down hungry. Yes, good old sugar corn! Mom, how much sugar corn do you think James and I have eaten raised from this garden?" "You and James! Well, you know James is small but he is as big an eater as your Pa. I know you boys have eat enough to fatten a hog off this garden." She laughed. "Say, Jesse, I didn't tell you about Brother Tobbie preaching the other night against education, did I? Well, don't you know he got up and preached a sermon on mothers sending their children away to college where they would be educated right for Hell. He looked right at me when he said it. He knowed you was away, you know. Oh, he just made me so mad! I wanted to tell him to go on and preach about the Bible and God Almighty so bad I didn't know what to do. Yes, he did go over that old story again about the Lord calling him to preach when he was a-cuttin' hay on that piece of ground back of the barn. I got tickled when he said he just fell off the mowing machine like he was shot when the Lord called him."

I stood in silence for a minute. I thought: "What if brother Tobbie could get up in the chapel at Lincoln Memorial. The boys would hoot at him. They would surely throw rotten eggs at him. Brother Tobbie wouldn't be at Plum Grove. If he'd tell that mowing-machine story at Lincoln Memorial, people would say he was crazy." Mom and I went down through some young field corn. We went through between the rusty barbed wires of the pasture fence. We went silently. She held the wires apart for me to climb through the fence. I spread them apart for her so that the wires would not catch her dress and tear it.

The evening dew was settling on the grass. The shade had come over. The shade spread as the sun sank over the green hills. The shade spread in an uneven line, uneven as the poplar tops on the hilltop were uneven. The thin crab grass growing in the pasture caught in the eyes of our shoes and between the crosses of our shoestrings. I thought of the days when I went after the cows and pulled the ragweed seeds from between my toes. But now my feet were shod and I was a college student. I had come back to the little shack among the hills and I had got to be something. I was looked up to by all the family.

The night insects were singing down in the lowlands. The whippoorwills were calling, it seemed to me, from every hilltop. "Mom, you know I think the whippoorwill is the lonesomest bird I ever heard. It makes me want to cry to come back among these hills and hear a whippoorwill." "They're not half as lonesome as a nighthawk when it screams."

We went down past where the cows were swishing flies beside the fence. When old Star saw my mother, she bawled. "You know, Jesse, that old cow will follow me anyplace. She is gentle as a dog. But let me tell you, Mitch tried to milk her and she kicked the bucket out of his hand and splattered milk in his face. He wanted to hit her. I wouldn't let him. I give him my apron. I said: "Here, Mitch, put this on and she won't hurt you. Well, he put it on and don't you know that cow stood as still as a haystack."

We went through the fence again and up past some little crab-apple trees that were now in full bloom. Mom lit her pipe and smoked. Crab-apple blossoms have a sweet odor. We stood and breathed the air off the crab-apple blossoms and then went on towards the horse pasture. "My, Mom! That smell of crab-apple blossoms was sure sweeter than the smell of the snowballs in the backyard, the bleeding heart or the lady's finger." "Yes, I try my best to keep your Pa from cutting the dogwoods and crab apples. But you know how he is when he takes a notion. There's no doing anything with him. But he's got to letting the dogwoods stand. He uses them for sled half soles. I tell him crab apples make good jelly, but you know, Jesse, it takes too much sugar. I never do make any. I just tell him that to keep him from a-cutting the trees." The blue smoke goes over Mom's shoulder from her pipe.

The horses came to the fence and poked their noses over to us. "I guess they are wanting salt. I told James to salt them, but you know James. He slips around to keep out of doing little things you used to look after yourself." "Mom, I believe old Fred knows me. I don't know whether old Kate does or not, but I believe old Fred does. Now watch him when I slap him on the neck." "I've often wondered just how much sense a horse has."

There we were back in the old pasture land again. The stars glittered above us in the sky. The wind blew through the pine grove where I used to come and hang a lantern up on a limb and write my high-school themes one night a week. The teacher would brag about them and say they were of the flavor of the soil, and something about them being like the sky. Every time I looked at that pine grove on that yellow clay bank, I thought about Cousin Rile Johnson telling me that when he was in France, he saw a German soldier, dead and leaning against a little pine—as if he had sat down and leaned back against it to rest. He said the fellow had a smile on his lips and the ants had eaten his eyeballs out. He said there were two lines of black ants crawling from his eyeballs, down across his face and off onto the ground. Rile said he thought the man was caught without a gas mask and had been killed by gas. Well, I always thought of this little story when I passed the pine grove.

The whippoorwills kept calling from the hilltops: "Whip - poor - will—whip - poor - willie—whip - poor - will—whip - poor - willie." A slow wind moved the needles of the pines and stirred the thin leaves on the poplars. The moon came up above the light green hill. It was beautiful to see the moon rise over the pasture field. "Mom, you know this was the field where James and I were plowing corn when I left home." "Yes, your Pa caught a snow on in February and he sowed it in grass. The grass growed so fast— I mean the crab grass, your Pa thought it would he a good idea to turn the horses in on it when they wasn't in the harness." "Well, everything changes on a hill farm in a year's time. The sprouts grow up and take the place or the farmers have to cut them down." "Yes, that's about right. It don't take sprouts and youngins any time to grow up. The sprouts stay and the youngins run away."

We had now turned and were walking back towards the house. We were walking on a white dry path, worn that way by the hoofs of the horses when they were taken to the barn from the pasture and from the barn to the pasture. The road wound through a little patch of sumacs and then under the pine trees. "Where the black shoe-makes grow, the land won't sprout black-eyed peas. But where the red shoe-makes grow, I'll tell you it's the land to slip a few beans in with your corn and a few pumpkin seeds in around the old stumps. I tell you that red shoe-make land will certainly grow the corn, pumpkins and beans."

The cold stars of May glittered in a starry sky over our heads. When we looked through the pine tops at the stars, we were silent. We walked up across the pasture and out by the hog pen. The hogs heard us walking and grunted a few times. Then they lay back down on some old sticks they'd gathered for a bed and were perfectly still. I had another thought as I walked through the silence of the night with my mother. I could remember butchering day at this very hog pen. That was when I was a high-school student. I got out of bed early in the morning and fed the hogs before the chickens got off the roost. Then I slopped them later. I fed the hogs until they were my pets. They would follow me all over the pen.

Then there would come a frosty morning in November, a few days before Thanksgiving, and we would have to gather good sound dry oak wood that had long been seasoned. Then we would have to build three fires. While the fires were getting under way, we had to carry three kettles of water and put them over the three fires. We had to get the knives ready and see if the scaffold, with one end resting in the forks of an apple tree, was stout enough to bear up the weight of three good hogs. Then we knocked the door out of the hog pen and the hogs came out rooting their noses in the fresh earth. I would have to take some corn and toll them away from the pen out in a nice place to shoot them. My father could never get me to shoot them with a rifle. I never could do it after I had raised the hogs and knew what pets they got to be. They would follow me and I couldn't lead them out and shoot them after they were good enough to follow me. "Jesse, do you know how my Pap would kill one of them hogs? He would not shoot one—he'd just straddle its back and cut its throat with a sharp knife and let it bleed to death."

"Well, I'm not straddling any hog's back, if I raised it or if I didn't, and cut its throat. There's nobody on this hill big enough to make me do it either." "Son, I wouldn't even try to make you. I feel the same way about it."

"When I raise anything, I hate to kill it. I often think how men raise flocks of geese and call them off down the country road each autumn to the city. The geese follow. They don't know that they are going off to die. And look how old Fred Harris does. He raises hundreds of sheep. He takes them off down a country lane each year to town. They are loaded on a train there and are killed in Cincinnati. I always thought it looked pretty hard. I always hated to do it. I never said anything. I just went on and killed them. I think God Almighty put them here for some purpose."

Mom and I are passing a hog pen in the moonlight. There is dew on the sticker weeds around the hog pen. There is a sour smell there, the smell of sweet-breathed hogs on a pile of sticks in the moonlight. The sour smell of a wallowing hole. Thoughts in my brain of sticker weeds, man, hogs, death and the moonlight.

We are out at the scaffold by the apple tree now. There is an old sled sitting under it with a barrel on the sled. Hog hair is left unburied under the tree. There are drops of dew slowly running down the hog hairs. Here was where the hogs I'd fed had hung, right on this scaffold. Here was where we had to watch the dogs to keep them away from the clean sweet-smelling hog bodies, hanging to a scaffold with a gambling stick sharpened on both ends and run under the leaders of each hind leg and resting on top of the scaffold with the weight of a hog swinging below. Blood dripped from the hogs' noses onto the black ground beneath the apple tree. "Gentlemen, if you want to see purty meat, go up there and look inside that hog. It's shore a purty thing. Looks bad a body has to kill a thing purty as that hog." We walk on silently to the house. We slip in quietly to keep from disturbing those already sleeping. The moonlight comes in at my window and shines on a broad strip of my floor.

This is my old room. Over there on the wall plate is where I kept my books, but they are gone now. I burned them. I wish I had them tonight so that I could go over the places I had marked and turned the corners of the pages down. "Don't ever mark a book. It is a disgrace. And don't turn the corners down. Keep your books in good condition. See, mine are nearly in mint condition." I want to say, "How would you like to go straight to hell and stay when you get there? My books are my own. They are not things to keep in mint condition either. They are mine—and sure as pencils leave traces of where they have been, you'll see mine traced and retraced. My books are to be used and I use them, though I don't have many of them."

I feel the quilts on my bed. They must be the same old quilts. The bed is turned the same old way. Everything in the room is placed just like it was when I left. There is the old battered shotgun without a sight. There is my old fox horn on the wall, the wooden table and the old dresser Grandpa Stuart gave my father. Everything's still here but the books. They were burned under the wash kettle. Well, it is fine to be back home again. I shall go to bed now. The moonlight streams in across my bed. I have been sitting up two hours in the room thinking about days and nights I have spent in this room.

May in the Kentucky hills. A boy a-sleeping in the upstairs of a shack. Moonlight in bright floods pours in at his window. He gets up and takes a rag out of a pane so that more can flood in before he goes to sleep. Dew is on the grass and the leaves of the trees. Moonlight on the dew that's on the grass makes a thousand little stars down on the earth. The fields have been plowed for planting again. And in many of them the little green blades of corn are twisting through the earth. The whippoorwills are calling from the edges of these fields and out in the pasture. One will start calling, another will answer. Soon the whole countryside will be made into a mournful song. The frogs croak in the pond. The katydids are noisy and the beetles drone and drone. Kentucky night and ten-thousand stars swarm in the sky over the green hills.

I had taken the road homeward to the low shaggy greenbriar

hills around Greenup. Here was a Silence I could love. Silence under me in the great Earth, the mother of creation, and Silence above me in the starry heavens. I could love the two great Silences I lived between. I went out and touched a rain-washed, wind-bent black-oak tree. I got the coffee-colored stain on my hands. It had a sour smell, the smell of wet oak leaves. I was so damn tired of books, books, books. More and more they had become a weariness to my flesh.

I worked in the kitchen my second year in college. My job was to dry the pots and put each pot, skillet, lid, fork, knife, big spoon, and meat slicer in its place. It took me a month to learn the work. Spence Fillis was headwaiter. He was thirty years old. He was a short, stocky, strong man. His word was law among the students. They were afraid of him. He tried to tell the dining-room matron what to do. He sparked one of his cooks. Spence fired the students when he got ready. He was the big boy of the dining room.

This job paid my board and room rent. I worked on the campus on Saturdays for my tuition. I was faring fine. My grades were good during my second year. It was the golden year in college for me. My poetry was accepted by many small poetry magazines. I became a candidate for the editor of the school paper. I had always wanted to be on the paper but I was too unpopular to get it. I had been nominated six times and I had been defeated six times. I got my roommate to nominate me. I was nominated twice for freshman issues. I was nominated for the summer number of the paper. I lost by a big number of votes. During my sophomore year, the faculty met and chose me editor and let me choose my staff. I cut off all the clique staff members and tried to make a decent paper out of it. I chose boys and girls for the staff who were interested in trying to make it a college paper. It took two years but we did it. We got papers from other schools and we modeled ours by them. We exchanged with colleges all over the East and many in the South. We got comments from other schools that our paper was one of the most original papers in the country. Poetry was copied from its pages in many Eastern papers, with comments on the originality of the poetry and the paper.

My job in the dining room had grown from bad to worse. Spence had gotten to the place where he was unbearable to work with. He told me one day that I was fired. I told him that I would not leave the place until he gave his reasons for canning me. I

LMU Glee Club 1926-28. Seated, Jesse Stuart, 2nd from left; Don West, 4th from left   (Courtesy *Jesse Stuart Collection, Forrest C. Pogue Special Collections Library, Murray State University, Murray, Kentucky*)

asked the matron if I was canned. She said I was not. She and Fillis stood face to face and quarreled. The next day Fillis told me I was fired. "I'm not leaving here until I get good and ready, Spence Fillis. I've taken all I care to take off you." "You are a goddamn liar. You are going now."

He drew a chair across his shoulder to hit me. I beat him to the first lick. I hit him under the ear. The fight had started. It was after the noonday meal on Sunday was over. All the students had gone. The matron of the dining room was there, and the cooks. Fillis was strong. I knew it. I would not let him get hold of me. He lost his head. He ran into my licks. He swore viciously. He was a preacher. His arms were shorter than mine. He could not reach me. I kept him off at arm's length. I pounded him. We stopped. He pulled off his glasses. Then he grabbed a bread knife. He hit me across the guts the first lick. It was turned broadside. He hit me across the heart. The back part of the blade hit me. I hit him with every ounce of weight there was in my body. I stood on my toes and tore my shirt across the shoulder. I hit him under the eye. He hit the table and knocked all the dishes off it. He twisted down to the floor. The matron he had been fussing with brought a poker up at this time. "A man fighting a boy! You ought to be ashamed, Mr. Fillis." But Spence was on the floor. I dared him to rise again. The matron called for the dean. He wasn't there. She called for the business manager. He was at home. She called for the sheriff. He came but he should not have come. The fight was over. My hands were burst open and my wrists strained. Fillis's face was bruised. His eyes were black.

The fight was discussed on Monday morning on the Lincoln Memorial campus. I was watched until then. I packed my trunk. I knew it would be a trip home. I was called to the office. "We have decided to let you decide whether Fillis can stay on and finish his work here or not. It is left up to you. He is a preacher. He swore time after time and tried to cut you with a knife, the matron said. He has six weeks to stay. Do you want him to finish or not?" "Let him stay. He won't bother me. He won't bother anybody." "Don't let this go to your head. But Fillis was a hard man to fight. He chased his own brother out of Lincoln Memorial. I tell you he was a mean fellow when he first came here. He ran eight of the boys away from the dairy barn. He was the boss down there and he ran them away one night. He came in with an ax. He ran them off like they were children." "Why didn't you fire him then?" "He's the best worker we have at Lincoln Memorial. He's the first man that ever made expenses at the dairy barn. He is the first man that ever made the dining room pay. That is why we held him."

Ron East had gone to his home in Georgia. His mother was sick. While he was there, a telegram was sent to him telling him to stay. He was expelled from Lincoln Memorial. "You are not allowed back on the campus," the telegram stated. But Ron East came back without money. He thumbed his way. He stayed in the woods in a cabin. I didn't have money to buy food for him and I stole it out of the college storeroom. No one knew Ron East was there. He kept it a secret. I took the telegram he had received down on the campus and showed it to the students. "Ron East, you are expelled from Lincoln Memorial. You are not allowed back on campus." The boys would ask me why he was expelled. I repeated to them the exact words Ron said to me—"I made a speech down in the chapel one day. I told them too much about this place. They didn't want to hear it. I told it to them anyway."

The students rose in revolt. "We are going to have Ron East back. We'll wreck the damn school if we don't. Ron East was right when he said Lincoln Memorial was a cheap place. It is cheap, and cheap as hell too. We are going to have Ron East back." Before trouble started, a telegram came from the chancellor in the North reinstating Ron East.

When I was carrying food to Ron in the woods, there was a tree down in a dark hollow I met him by. I gave him the news on the campus and I carried letters from him to his girl. She sent letters back by me. I met him in this secluded spot where I knew no one would be near. Mabel Adams sent him a message in one of the letters that Spence Fillis had insulted his sister. "I'll whip that Spence Fillis if it is the last thing I ever do in my life." "No use to whip him now. I gave him enough. See this bandage on my hand. Well, under that bandage is a fractured bone. And it gives me much pain. That was done the last lick I gave Fillis. He got a good whipping. He'll not bother your sister any more."

Once Clayton Jarvis said, "Things are going to be popping round the school soon. Mind what I tell you. There's been a strange man on this campus for three days now. Just walks around and looks things over. Don't know just who it'll be this time. But a lot of the teachers will have to go. It's getting about time; we're due for a housecleaning here."

Jesse Stuart and friend Don West at LMU   (Courtesy *Jesse Stuart*
                    Collection, Forrest C. Pogue Special Collections Library,
                            Murray State University, Murray, Kentucky)

The housecleaning came. Dean Chitwood Langley had to go. "Why does Dean Langley have to leave here? He's one of he best men I've ever known." "Don't ask me, Bert. There's a higher power over this school. When the higher power cracks the whip, boy, they clean house around here and never give a reason." There were Barry Laws, the music teacher; Stanley Cauldwell, a math teacher; Alicia Dixon, a history teacher; Harry Kroll, a writer and English teacher; Lytton Tells, instructor in psychology; Morton Dent, instructor in math; and Dr. Leith Morton, instructor in French—all forced to resign or they would have been fired.

It hurt me to see these teachers go. I had had classes under many of them. Dean Langley had taken me into the school and had given me a chance when I didn't have money. Harry Kroll was the first flesh-and-blood writer I had ever seen. I had borrowed money from him many a time in a pinch. And didn't he give me the job to wash his car every week? Didn't I get the job cutting the grass in his yard? Didn't he tell me I could write and for me to keep it up? Didn't I get him out of bed and show him poems and he didn't bawl me out? I worshiped the ground he walked on because he was a writer. Didn't he even sell short stories, for he showed me the first check I'd ever seen for short stories. And didn't he say: "I'll see you don't leave this school over whipping Spence Fillis. He hit you with a knife, didn't he? You are underage and he is a man. I'll get a lawyer and pay him with my own money and take it to court first." Why was he leaving? It was sad to see them pack and move away. The place seemed empty after they had gone. I went to Professor Kroll's home to say good-by. He said: "Someday this school will bloom like a flower. That day will be when a few are pushing up the daisies. I love these mountains. I love the fight in these students. We must leave without reason and there's nothing that can be done about it."

My third year at Lincoln Memorial was my hardest year. I carried the mail from the post office, worked in the dining room, edited the college paper and carried a heavier schedule of work than the college was supposed to allow. I was called to the president's office. He said: "Mr. Stuart, by a mistake in the office

Harry Harrison Kroll   (Courtesy *H. Edward Richardson Collection,
Ekstrom Library, University of Louisville*)

*"Harry Kroll was the first flesh-and-blood writer I had ever
seen.... I worshiped the ground he walked on because he was a writer."*

you have been allowed to take three hours too many. To improve the standing of this institution, we must deduct these hours." "I cannot graduate then. I'll have to stay another quarter. I hoped to get out this year." I left his office. I was called to the office a week later. The president said: "Mr. Stuart, we have decided to give you three honorary hours in English for your good work on the college paper." The three hours deducted were B grade, the three honorary hours were grade A. I made three honor points in the deal but, honestly, it was something I could never understand.

At Lincoln Memorial, I wrote about five-hundred poems. They were experiments of a student in verse. I still wanted to write verse. The urge was a part of me. It would not leave. I wanted to put thoughts into words. Words were living things. Verse was living words combined to make a living body and a living force that would be felt. I wrote this sonnet for Bonnie before we parted at college.

> Do you remember April evenings when we
> Tripped side by side on tender orchard grasses
> Beneath the spreading cloud-white apple tree?
> Do you remember night birds' fluttering passes
> Into the shower-drenched wind-quivering leaves?
> And the cloud-patched sky, the wry-faced moon,
> And sleeping valley mists, do you remember? It grieves
> Me to forget—Our lives broke then—broke soon,
> Too soon we drifted down corridors of time
> With new lovers following after. And now,
> The grass is dead, the winter's rainy slime
> Marks jet-black each leafless apple bough.
> Can you remember a dread that banished?
> A love that faded?
>
> A joy that vanished?

It hurt me to leave owing the college money. I hadn't done what I had expected to do. I expected to work all of my way and leave not owing the college a penny. I owed them one-hundred dollars and fifty cents. The most money I'd got from home was two one-dollar bills my mother once sent me. School was all over now. I had finished in three years. I had bought my own clothes and books. I had made something like a B average. I never stopped to count it up. I graduated but I didn't want a college diploma. I didn't get one. I was the first of my father's people to finish college.

I was ready to move on from Lincoln Memorial. I had done all I could. I was ready to go. I took the old suitcase and put more

*Jesse's senior LMU picture and
biographical note, 1929*
(*Courtesy Lincoln Memorial University*)

signs on it. I was ready to travel. I said good-by to the teachers and the students. I said farewell to Ron East. He smiled and wished me well. It was the road again. My first ride took me somewhere in Kentucky. Darkness overtook me among the mountains. I couldn't get another ride. A heavy black cloud arose and a storm came. I remember the lightning flashes and how I ran by their light down the highway until I saw a church house upon the bank among, it looked like by the lightning flashes, a thousand white tombstones. I had slept in many church houses before, and I would sleep in this one for the night.

I tried to open the door. It was locked. I walked around to one side of the building, raised a window and slid inside. I took the organ cover from the organ and rolled up in it. I made a pillow out of song books I found on the organ. I was lying there and watching the lightning flash and the tombstones glare at me like a thousand ghosts that had risen from their graves.

Soon the hailstones tattooed on the windowpanes and water streamed down them and shut away my visage from these ghosts. As I lay there, a sadness came over me and I had serious thoughts about the school I had left behind: "It is among the mountains there that a part of my youth lies buried. It is gone and will not return again. Ron East is gone now. I wonder if he'll keep on writing poetry? Jimmie Still, the shy sensitive youth, with the finest looking eyes I have ever seen in a human head, is gone. I wonder what will become of him and if he'll keep on writing poetry? Bonnie, Margaret, Julia and Louise—I wonder who they'll marry? What will become of old Claymore Jones and Rodney Findley? Will they teach school in the mountains of Tennessee and tell their students what a hard time they had getting their education? What has become of Dean Langley and the teachers forced to resign from Lincoln Memorial? I wonder if I'll ever be the writer Harry Kroll is?" Such thoughts raced through my mind until sleep came and all was nothingness.

Grant-Lee Literary Society, LMU, 1928. Second row down: Donald
West, second from left; Jesse Stuart on far right

(Courtesy Lincoln Memorial University)

Chapter VIII
Back Drinking Lonesome Water

"I knowed you'd come back to drink of lonesome water. Once you get a drink of lonesome water, you always come home. Now old Pete Perkins would say to you: 'Chickens come home to roost,' but I like to think of you coming back to drink of lonesome water. I tell you, lonesome water is good. I drunk of it when I was a little shaver and I never left the hills. I seen you over there one day when you was a little shaver down on your knees and bending over drinking water out'n th' crick. I said to Sam: 'Sam, that boy's not goin' to leave these hills. Look at him there with the ferns around his eyes. He's drinking lonesome waters.' And Sam says: 'Uncle Rank, that don't amount to a hill of beans. My grandpap drunk of lonesome waters and he went away and stayed thirty years. He went to Texas.' And I says to Sam: 'Look here, I knowed your old grandpap. He did come back to drink of lonesome waters before he died. I was right over there when he taken sick. I knowed what your grandpap said to me right before he died.

"He said: 'Rank, I have come home to die. I never could forget the lonesome waters. Fetch me a glass of that water. Go dip it where the crick runs over the gravels. Dip it from under the shade of a willer tree. The gravels clean it and the willer shade flavors it. Wade down through that patch of ferns by the old sugar tree. I want to drink of lonesome water before I die. I couldn't forget the old Kentucky lonesome waters. I had to come back home to die. Hurry, Rank, and bring me the water.'"

"But I've not come back to die, Uncle Rank. I've come back to stay a little while and go again."

"You may come and go but you'll come back here to die. It was here your life began. It was back here where the lonesome waters run. You'll be like Sam's grandpap. When he was a young man, he went away and said he'd never come back. But he did come back. And I was right there when he died. He died in a heap of misery. Poor old Daddy Strickland! I helped make a sugar-tree coffin for him. He wanted it made out'n that big sugar tree down yander by the side of the road. He wanted a horseshoe nailed on both ends for good luck. I took a couple of old Moll's shoes and put them right on the ends of the coffin lid. You know Daddy Strickland had a heap of faith in horseshoes. We put Daddy away right nice. He looked like he did when he was a-livin'. Just a little paler was all. We put him away in the old brown suit he wore. He looked natural. Hall Shelton's mules pulled him out on the hill. The road was awful muddy. And the mules had a load with big fat Seth Warren ridin' and drivin' and Daddy, a right big man in that heavy green sugar-tree coffin. And the boys go around a-singin':

> Old Daddy Strickland died on the fifteenth of April,
> And they made his coffin out'n sugar-tree and maple.

And 'pon my word and honor they wasn't a drop of maple about that coffin. I made it like Daddy told me to make it before he died.

"Did you know this has been a bad spell on the old people? They've been dying like weeds. The old people just keep a-drapin' off. A lot of them you knowed are not here any more. They've took a lot of 'em out to Plum Grove since you was a little tad and went to the funerals there. Old Part Jenkins is dead now. They hauled him out there about three weeks ago. I guess you knowed that old

Annis Bealer, the man your Pap used to borrow corn from, is dead. I believe he's gone to Hell too. He laid right there flat of his back until his face got so bony Jarvis Thompson couldn't shave him. And right before he died, he said: 'Goddamn it—I said turn me over.' Then there was a struggle for breath and the old Devil took him. Old Harmon Manley is dead. He died cussing the Lord, too. Old Harmon took little things that didn't belong to him. I knowed he was the man that took Part Jenkins' coal-buggy wheels. Old man Slackburn is dead. He was a good worker of the Lord's. I ain't a bit a doubt of where old Charlie's gone. The Lord needs a man like old Charlie. He can help the Lord a lot. Old Brother Rankwood's dead. He died a-clapping his hands and saying, 'Glory to God. They ain't no doubt now. I'm bound for the Promised Land. All you people meet me there.' And I know Brother Rankwood is saved.

"I ain't told you about Brother Tobbie, have I?" "No, Uncle Rank. Is he dead too?" "Yes, Brother Tobbie has been dead nigh about six months." "You don't mean that, Uncle Rank!" "Yes, Brother Tobbie wasn't nigh right with the Lord. You know what he done? He put a double-barrel shotgun to his temple and pulled both barrels. He blowed the whole top of his head off. The paper said he worried because he had a cancer of the stomach. But that wasn't it. He had a cancer of the heart. Brother Tobbie lied to the Lord some way. The trouble got heavier than Brother Tobbie could bear. And he just hurried his life right on to Hell. Some people said his wife wouldn't have anything to do with him. But I know that didn't make any difference. That woman of hisin is a little funny. If she'd meet you in the road, she'd go away out around you like a strange dog. I remember one time when she hit him over the head with a skillet.

"I always thought there was something wrong with him. When he spoke the Lord's name out there in the Grove, there was something about his looks I didn't like. I told my wife that Brother Tobbie wasn't nigh right. And she saw something wrong with his countenance too. When he said the Lord's name, he kindly trembled."

"Well, Uncle Rank, go over the hill with me. I got to get over and see them all. I'm anxious to get home. Back to Kentucky again. You'd better go along. Well, if you won't go over, come across the hill sometime and see us."

"Before you go, I want to tell you Granny Flaughtery is dead. She died over two months ago. I would say she went to that Heaven she told people about seeing. You ask your Ma about it when you get over home. Your Ma was right there when Granny died. She died at ninety-three, and she wouldn't a-died then, but part of the cellar rocks fell in on her and broke three ribs. They wouldn't heal, wouldn't knit together, the cracked ribs wouldn't. And one, they say, had run into her right lung. She wouldn't let your Ma leave the place long as she lived. Your Ma fixed her pipe for her long about three hours before she died. Your Ma smoked with her right before she died. She couldn't draw in but little smoke and I told Carrie then that she was gone. We was over there a-settin' up, you know. Yes, if ever there was a saint in Heaven today, it is Granny Flaughtery. After she died and went to Heaven once, she read her chapter in the Bible every day. And some days Granny read two chapters in the Bible. And now Granny is one of God's angels. They took the good old Soul back out on the Hill where all of her people that's passed away are sleeping."

I left Uncle Rank standing by the barn. I went across the hill toward home. It was getting late. August had gone. The first days of September had come. The leaves had begun to color on the trees. Some of the leaves had begun to fall. They fell along the path. And the leaves hanging on the trees were stirred by the wind. I was back to my land again—dogwoods, oaks, pines, poplars, beeches, and maples. And there were many streams of water running over this land, water beautiful to see, blue water in the setting September sun but treacherous to drink. It had put me flat on my back twice. It had made me so sick that I had wished to die. Water, blue water, in the September sun, and typhoid germs. I knew about the lonesome waters. And Uncle Rank had just told me I would come back to drink of lonesome water before I died. Why didn't he say I would come home and drink of lonesome water and die? It would be more like the truth. Here are these old people coming home to die. Shall I ever come home to die, or shall I die at home? It doesn't matter. Uncle Rank is somewhat of a prophet in the hills. He goes to see the sick. He has helped to make the coffins and bury the dead.

The leaves fall around me. Only a few whippoorwills are calling. The stars have come into the sky. I am going home. I shall soon be home. The trees I love are all around me now. The desolate sweep of land lies on every side. I am through Lincoln Memorial and I am coming back to the hills for all the hills may offer. I am coming back for all the good I can do in the hills.

Home was good to see again. My folks were glad to see me there. We talked over the past. We told stories about earlier days. We popped corn. We roasted potatoes. We made lassie-popcorn balls. Here was the life I liked. I knew it. But I kept it to myself. I didn't want people to know how much I loved the hills and how much I had hated them. It took life beyond these hills to make one love life among the hills. I had gone beyond the dark hills to taste of life. I found it sour when I went beyond where the blue rim of hills touches the sky. I had wanted to go beyond and find out all that was there. I wanted to taste of life. I tasted of it from books and steel and the merry-go-round. It was not sweet like the life in the hills.

In the hills a man goes forth to sow his grain in the seasons and a man reaps his own grain. There are no parasites sucking the blood from his veins to live, like I found beyond the dark hills. Though his lot was hard among his hills, it was his own lot. Life in the hills would make one sturdy and independent. The handles of the plow make one free. The sod puts one close to nature. Call it God, if you will. The leafy trees in springtime, the early meadows, the old orchards white in apple-blossom time, ridges of green Irish potato vines, the blue streams running between the dark hills, the lonely sounds at night, the wind in the oak tops and the wind playing in the dead September corn and running through the persimmon trees on the broken pasture fields. Great fields of corn and cane and pumpkins scattered over the cornfields. Rabbits in the dead weeds and foxes barking from the ridge tops at night.

Call it God if you will. And I can't bear to let God pass. The worship of God is something too beautiful to pass. But it has gone from the land beyond the dark hills already. And when I went away and learned about God and that all my early training was time wasted, that men said there was nothing in this game of God, I was dissatisfied. I wanted to make myself believe that there was no God. But when I went back to the hills, I saw as my people had seen. I found the great consolation of God in the beauty of the hills. Call God a God of love or a God of beauty. Say that God is in the wind, that God is in the dead leaves flying over the September hills in Kentucky, but don't leave God out. I once heard something about the ancient song passing deathward mournfully. It seemed to me that God was an ancient song among the minds of many people, and that he was passing deathward mournfully. But the hill people still saw God. He was the great force that drew them together. He called to the inner something of their bodies, greater than flesh and bone, to walk out under the trees and pray.

"Jesse, Mr. Blair has a job for you. And you make a hundred dollars a month. It is teaching back out at Warnock, Kentucky. What are you going to do with that much money?" "Mom, that isn't any money at all." "It's more than any of us has ever made in this family. It's big money. I'm glad to see you make it. You can get out of debt on that and save a little money." "I don't see how in the world I can do it. It looks impossible to me." "Well, I could do it. Your school doesn't begin until after Labor Day is over. You have two days to be at home before you go out to your school. Now I want you to get out within these next two days and look around over the old places where we used to live. You are tired. It will be a good rest for you."

I went the next morning through the cow pasture. I stopped at the pine grove where I had written my themes when I was in high school. That had been nine years ago. I could remember coming there at night and hanging my lantern on a broken branch of a dogwood tree that grew among the pines. I would sit there and write and rewrite a theme. I took my time and tried to do it well. I wrote about pine trees then, the stars, the sound of the wind and the evening sky. I didn't write about people for I didn't know about people. The pine trees had been thinned out by a fire and the land around the pine grove had been cleared of its oak timber. Some pines had been left because the land was too sterile for cropping. The big oak logs that wouldn't burn in the clearing and the old wet soggy chestnut-oak logs that had lain on the ground for years were hauled under the pine trees. My pine grove had been ruined.

The shoe-makes in the pasture field had leaves of scarlet red and yellow gold. When the dry September wind blew, the leaves dripped off like drops of rain. Slower than rain, they zigzagged to the ground. There was just something in the shoe-make that reminded me of the Kentucky mountain soil. Blood-red dripping shoe-make leaves in the fertile back hollows. Yellow shoe-make leaves dripping on the yellow clay banks of Kentucky mountain soil.

I went to an old house where we had once lived. The hills we had cleared had grown up in sprouts again. The windowpanes were gone. The roof leaked. The bats clung to the upstairs roof. The logs were rotting and the house was sinking lower and lower. The ground hogs were denning under the hearth. The rats were living in the smokehouse. The birds built nests where the chinking and daubing had fallen from between the logs. Ragweeds had grown above the paneless windows and had died and fallen over. It was a tract of desolation now. I went on across the pasture where I used to get the cows. I remembered the old scenes and the dreams about Robert Burns there.

I didn't want to write like Robert Burns now. I wanted to write like myself. I wanted to be myself. I didn't want to be a tree like another tree in the forest. I wanted to be a shoe-make with a little different color of leaves, a different kind of bark and different arrangement of limbs, so when the wind whipped through my body, I would sing a different song to my brother shoe-makes. I wanted to be different whether it was for better or for worse. I wanted to be different, not for the sake of being different but being different for something.

I went on to the house where I was born. The coal bank where my father had once dug coal and wheeled it out in a jump-the-track buggy had now fallen in. The rats didn't warn the last two men that worked there. They killed the rats. They put poison on fried potatoes and put the potatoes in one of the mine entries. The rats ate the poison on the potatoes and went down to a blue stream outside the mine that flowed between two shoe-make-covered hills. They drank of the blue water and died. They never got back to the mine. There was no rat stench left in the mine. And one day the left entry roof caved in and Andrew Gurton was crushed beneath a piece of slate, and Ennis Gurton got his back broken by a piece of slate. When the farmers dug them out of the mine, they had to wade in a puddle of blood shoe-tongue deep to get to Ennis.

The tall tree that once had a martin box upon the topmost branch was now a dead, trimmed snag. Crows came and lit on it and wiped their bills and caw-cawed to each other. They seemed to say: "Where is the family that once was here and moved away when snow lay on the ground? Where are the oxen that pulled everything they had on a sled? Where are the children now? Where is the drinking father? Where is the praying mother? Where is the working mother? This place has changed since they moved on. The squirrels have been killed out. The timber has been cut. Fields have been cleaned of red brush and worn out and grown up in black shoe-make and sawbriars. The coal has been dug out of the hill. The mines are done for now. The old road that leads away from the mines has grown up in weeds. The rain has washed ruts where the wheels cut last into the hard clay earth. We are the crows that lived here in the olden days and we know. And now if any team driver could return:

> "He would return to a hollow he once knew—
> Follow the road to where the last house stands,

Six drawbars and a gate he must go through
And cross three hills of worn-out sedge-grass lands,
The road that's grooved with many a rain-washed rut
Over this road the teamsters used to ride,
And give their mules the long keen rawhide cut,
And now both mules and ruts the ragweeds hide.
He would go back this old, old trail at night,
And look for ghosts of horses he once drove;
He'd see a ragweed road in the moonlight
A-winding through the honey-locust grove;
And he would see an ulcerated hill
Where slate dumps in moonlight lie blue and still."

If I could talk to these crows wiping their bills and caw-cawing to each other on the old snag martin-box pole, I would say: "My father and mother used to live here. I was born in this house. And that was many years ago. You remember it, you long-lived Crows. I used to see you come over when the ground was white with snow. You would fly down in a cornfield and help yourselves. There would be long black trains of you flying over the snow-covered land. Sometimes you would obscure the winter sun. And now, Black Crows, I'd like to ask you where many of you have gone since I've been away? You used to help the buzzards and hound dogs eat Long Winston's horses. Who cleans up the carrion now? There are not enough of you to do it. Crows, if you could understand, I'd tell you my father used to dig coal in the sunken-in coal mine you see out there where that tall bunch of black shoe-makes and black-berry briars are growing. That is where he worked. I went back under that hill when I was a baby.

"You see, these old fields were in woods then, and the foxes sneaked up nearly to the door and took our chickens. Black-Boy was a young dog then. Now he is quite old. He is eighteen now. He can't kill the copperheads like he did when we lived here. He's going soon like a lot of your friends and a lot of mine. You see, Black Crows, that tumbled-in cellar is where my mother used to carry fresh dishes of yellow butter. She kept the milk in there where it was cool for the cream to come to the top on it. She kept the milk in crocks. She kept canned peaches, apples, wild grapes and pears in there. She set out a rambling-rose vine in the front yard. Now, Crows, you can write the history of this place. You don't understand what I say, but you can write the history of this place. Be sure to tell about the rambling-rose vines and the coal bank. Tell about the shoe-makes and the greenbriars. You are wise birds. You ought to know about them."

Yes, there are many things the crows don't know about the place. There are many things I don't know about the place. The place is where I was born. And now the wasps build their nests in the comb of the house. A polecat lives under the floor. He chased the mice out of the place. And out in the fields I see where he has dug out the yellowjackets' nest. The bats come back for the dark corners of the shack, and the house wren builds her nest in one of the fruit jars that hangs over a sharp-pointed garden paling.

I can hear the water falling over the Cedar Riffles. It sounds like it did when I was a child here, maybe a little more haunting. And I can hear the wind blow through the shoe-make bushes and rattle the dying leaves. They fall like red drops of rain on the old fields. The big trees have been cut away and the timber line has been pushed back to the hilltops.

I must go on to the Plum Grove church house and the old schoolhouse. And behind the schoolhouse, I must walk down among the moss-green slabs that mark the places of the sleeping Plum Grove dead. I am on my way. Here are the old meadows. Hay has been cut and stacked in high brown stacks at the edge of the fields. The chestnut trees in Wheeler's fields have burrs cracked open and gleaming in the sun. And the oak trees—oak trees! I want to walk up and put my hands on them. I want to feel the bark. I want to rub my rough hands over the bark. I want to tell them that we are both a part of the same soil. But it would be worse than trying to talk to a crow. I want to tell them that I want a box made from their tough fibers when my time has come to take a long sleep with the Plum

Grove dead, or with the dead on my grandfather's farm. These oak trees would not understand. I put my hand on the rough bark, and I gather the oak leaves in my hand. They are good to touch. Oak trees and September, red-flannel skies and red-flannel shoe-make tops out on the old dried pasture fields. Kentucky, you are a book to me, and I never grow tired of turning your pages.

Before I get to Plum Grove, I must stop at the old Buck Harkreader place. I must take down the facts of the place. I used to know them before I went beyond the dark hills. Those facts are gone now.

Desolation

I
The Buck Harkreader Farm

The farm's asleep, must be the house is too;
So lonely here, sleep's all they both can do.

Smokehouse is sunken, the barn is unkept;
Yard's dry as desert bone and clean wind-swept.

The slow uncertain shadows cross the place;
White thunderclouds go drifting out to space.

The empty rooms are dark as ghostly sin;
The windows gone, the whistling winds drive in.

Some lanky cattle bawl and hound dogs howl,
And for the backyard grapes slim foxes prowl.

The hungry rats from under floors have scrawled
Their names on doors and sills and stones high-walled.

Some old stained aprons hang on clothesline rope;
For these the yard-tree fingers seem to grope.

A crow flaps down to gather straw and sticks
And caw-caws: "Where—where are those country hicks?"

The old cookstove is here all rusted red;
The wind laughs where the children cried for bread.

A wren sits on an ash-pile, preens her wings
And says it's on the dust of things she sings.

II

The hands that made the wines and killed the fleas,
Lie warm beneath this bank of chestnut trees.

The man who drank this strong rebellious wine
Sleeps by his wife—Old Buck sleeps like a swine.

His young son Buck who took a risky chance
Smashed in a plane three miles from Verdun, France.

And George and Frank both fond of gun and gin
Now sleep in earth—with what they fought to win.

They got all heady spiked on homemade wines
And tried to end the war in German lines.

Charlie was brought back from a drunken brawl;
He pulled his gun too late and that was all.

And Mag went out one day to fix the fence;
She and Jake Hix were never heard of since.

And Liz and Kate and Will went "west" in haste;
They wanted something new to suit their taste.

They got it for they never have been back
To see old friends and drink the applejack.

They don't come back—they're too, too far away;
Maybe they dream they'll rise again someday.

Maybe return to where their kin have lain
Beneath the tom-tom thrums of windless rain.

A flag floats high above each tall son's grave;
Not for his actual worth but what he gave.

The rest have boards to tell their worldly deeds;
That's less conceit and all a person needs.

I see the little spire of the Plum Grove church house rising above the trees. It sits upon the hill like a paper box in the wind. It is where I once slipped out to get the ball when Professor Iron Hand was not looking. I became afraid of going into the churchyard opposite to the setting sun after I had read a story about Roland going into a churchyard in the opposite direction of the setting sun and the hill swallowing him. I laughed now at my thoughts. I had been beyond these dark hills, and I had tasted life in the world outside them. I found that there was something sweet about the hill life and something bitter beyond. I had to come back to drink of lonesome waters.

I could not laugh at the thoughts I had there many, many years ago. I could not laugh at all when I saw the change that had taken place. The schoolhouse had been torn down and hauled away. The oak trees that grew about the building had been cut and sold. I wanted to go back and look at the old initial-scarred oaks. I remember I cut M.S. and J.H.S. on the side of a white-oak

Jesse in front of old Plum Grove Church, 1936
(*Photo by Woodi Ishmael, H. Edward Richardson Collection,*
Ekstrom Library, University of Louisville)

"I had come back to drink of lonesome waters."

tree. The initials were Maria Sheen's and mine. The logs were gone
where we once sat and ate our lunches. We threw the extra scraps
of bread to the hounds that pilfered about the place. We threw
crumbs out for the jaybirds. But they were saucy sometimes. They
sat up in the tops of the oak trees and stored acorns away and
beechnuts. Everything had changed here. Only the bones of the
old schoolhouse remain.

There is nothing left, only the stumps of the oak trees and the
boys' toilet. It is battered by the fifteen-cent barlow knife. I went
to it and looked the old walls over. And here were the names of
many who were now sleeping with the Plum Grove dead. And in
this privy there were more words said about them than on the slabs
that told where they were sleeping. Many names in the privy were

the names of fellows that didn't have marble slabs with dates and epitaphs but old field-rock markers and board markers without names and dates at all.

I could tell the spot of ground beneath where my old seat used to be in the schoolhouse. There were two graves there now. Some well-to-do relatives had left a nice stone to tell people of their work on earth and where they had gone. The epitaphs read:

MICHAEL SUMNERS   DOLLY SUMNERS
                       Wife of Michael Sumners
B. Dec. 17, 1856   B. May 5, 1859
D. Mar. 6, 1926   D. Aug. 6, 1924
He has found rest   Safe in the arms of Jesus

There was nothing I could say about it. The dead were now being buried on the ground where we used to play Fox and Dog, Jail, Among the Little White Daisies, London Bridge, and Round-town Ball with a twine ball. We used to make playhouses out of plants and bits of fern and moss and broken dishes. The broken dishes were still scattered over the ground. But all the things that once we loved and kept memories of are gone. And most of all, the children who once came here are gone. I take a postal-card picture of a Plum Grove school group I was in. I check up on them as far as I can. Seven are dead. Four have gone to college. Out of four that entered, two have graduated—the teacher teaching there when I was a student and I. Seven boys were in the pen for stealing, and shooting, and making moonshine. One girl was in the reformatory for misconduct. Thirty married and never went beyond an eighth-grade education, if they got that. Ten entered high school. Six of the ten finished. Three I could not place.

I leave Plum Grove. The sun is setting over the slabs. They gleam in the sunlight, these old slabs turning green with lichen moss. I have many thoughts about the past. I want to say something but I can't. Plum Grove is the home of the Plum Grove dead. For miles and miles around, they are hauled to Plum Grove to take their last long sleep. Nothing can be said to them now. Nothing can be said for them now. They are just dead.

I walk back across the hill through the glow of sundown on the red-leafed autumn sassafras sprouts to the Collins' orchard hill. Fruit trees are hidden among the sassafras sprouts and greenbriars. Once I was whipped for taking two apples from this orchard. But now I walk over and pick up mellow apples from the ground. I pull them from the tree. I eat them. They taste good. I put apples in all my pockets. Professor Iron Hand will never whip me again for stealing two apples. I am a man now.

And now I am back where the lonesome W-Hollow waters run. Here is the oak where my sister used to come, carrying her slippers in her hand until she got out of the wet weeds. She put them on here and wore them wherever she was going. Here is the place she let her beaus come to. They never came all the way home—she did not want them to see the log house. One of her beaus was from the city. She always dreaded for him to come.

I want to recall wading this stream more vividly. I pull off my shoes. I wade in the water. It is September. It is late in the evening. I take a stick and beat the water as I used to beat it and kill the water snakes. I wade along the leaf-strewn water. I bend the weeds apart in many narrow places in the creek bed so that I can go on. I wade up where the old beech log used to lie across the stream. I go up and sit down on it where I used to use a pin hook and fish for minnows. I wade back down the creek. I put on my shoes. I go up the sandy road.

I can remember when I used to see Tim Simpson and Sonnie Simpson and Bill Simpson haul loads of coal down this old road. And I have seen eight teams at one time go down this creek road with heavy loads of lumber. But the hauling is done. And the road is filled with ruts. I go home. And on my way I ask myself, "Where are the people now that used to ride in buggies along this road and sing 'Nellie Was a Lady,' 'Old Black Joe,' and 'Sourwood Mountain'? Where are the trotting horses and the old rubber-tired buggy wheels?" The trees do not answer. The grass does not answer. But

I know. The old-timers have gone. Their blood will not stay in the hills. They go out and stay until they grow old and then they come back home to die. The horses have gone like many of the old people. And the buggies have been replaced by buggies drawn without horses. The songs have grown old. People wanted faster songs. The songs they sang then were sweet and slow as the horse and buggy. Fast songs, the people must have, and ragtime songs! Something about a flat and under the moon and something about us having no bananas or about the old man that stood out at night with his shoes all full of feet.

"Did you know that there will be a funeral on the Hill tomorrow?" "Who is dead?" "Warfield Flaughtery is dead. Your Pa has just told me he died yesterday at two o'clock. He will be buried at two o'clock tomorrow." I could not believe that Warfield was dead. I used to haul him in the spring wagon over the bumpy sweet-potato ridges.

I would ask my father what killed him, when he came into the house. "It was drinking. You know how Warfield used to be—well he got worse. You know after his Ma died, he just tried to kill hisself. He sold the timber off'n his land and he drunk that up. He sold off scraps of his land and he drunk that up. I heard that he borrowed three-hundred dollars off'n Brother Tobbie and he drunk that up. He got awful before he died. He drove that poor old horse to town and would leave it hitched up all day without water. He left his cows at home unmilked and the pigs in the pen unslopped. I went over there lots of times and the milk would be a-running out of the cows' teats. And weeds has growed up about that place until a body can hardly recognize it. And since Granny died, old Warfield has never found her like again. That place is dirty. The weeds grow tall as the kitchen. W'y, I've never seen anything like the way that place has gone down."

"Where did he die? Did he die over there at the house?" "No, Sweet Bird found him down there somewheres along the road. The horse had pulled the buggy out'n the road trying to get water. A wheel caught behind some sweet-gum sprouts. Old Bill couldn't pull the buggy out. You know he's a heap of skin and bones, that old horse is. Well, old Warfield was stretched out in the buggy dead to the world. Sweet Bird knowed that he had been drunk for eleven days now, and he was never knowed to stay drunk over seven days before, and he went over to feel Warfield's heart. It was still beating. He got him out and got a doctor. He rushed him to the hospital. Old Warfield couldn't make water. That was what was wrong with him, the doctor said. But I went up to the hospital to see him. Old Sweet Bird and me went up there yesterday. We stayed up there last night to see if he got better or worse. He took a change for the worse last night. But old Warfield never did know me and old Sweet Bird. And we was all three on a big spree together less than a month ago. The whisky nearly killed me and old Sweet Bird, but Warfield just put it right down him. It never hurt him then. The doctors up at the hospital said his kidneys was rotten. Said they was paralyzed and his bladder was full of pus. They fixed it so he could make water. And last night about twelve o'clock, Sweet Bird said to me, 'Mitch, Warfield is gone, ain't he? I know he is gone.' And then, old Sweet Bird began to cry."

"I have been out today looking over the things I knew yesterday. And some of them I hardly recognized. Haven't things changed here in the last seven years?" "Yes, they change every year. I can see the change. I tell you things ain't like they used to be. And they never will be like they used to be. I can't get used to these new things. Men come right out and say they ain't no God. W'y, it's a wonder to me God Almighty don't strike 'em down with a bolt of thunder and a streak of lightning. Old Warfield drunk a lot of licker, but they's two things a body can say for old Warfield. He took care of his mother till she died. And he read his chapter in the Bible every day he wasn't drunk. I believe Warfield's an angel in Heaven tonight. I know he is, if God takes horse traders. All old Warfield did was the worst to hisself. He never bothered nobody."

"Pa, I hear there's church up at Pine Grove Chapel tonight. Would you like to go up?" "I don't care much about that kind of religion but I'll go along." "What kind of religion is it?" "A bunch of them damn Holy Rollers. They are a-ruining this whole country. People are a-going crazy over religion. Men are going out and cutting their green tobacco down. They've been doing it all summer. That old Brother Hammertight has got a bunch of young girls with guitars, and all the young men around here are a-getting saved."

We lit the lantern and set off over a path across the hill. It was eight o'clock when we got there. The singing had just started. The girls were lined up in the front of this old schoolhouse. They strummed their guitars and sang these words:

I Would Not Be Denied

I would not be denied,
I would not be denied,
Since Jesus come and saved my soul
I would not be denied.

You can't go to Heaven with powder and paint,
I would not be denied;
You'll not catch sight of the golden gate,
I would not be denied.

The Devil wears a hypocrite shoe,
I would not be denied;
If you don't watch out he will step on you,
I would not be denied.

Went down in the valley—went down to pray,
I would not be denied;
My soul got so happy I stayed all day,
I would not be denied.

I would not be denied,
I would not be denied,

Since Jesus come and saved my soul
I would not be denied.

If you'd been there when I prayed through,
I would not be denied;
You'd been a-praying and a-shouting too,
I would not be denied.

You can't go to Heaven and carry a gat,
I would not be denied;
You can't go to Heaven and wear a great big R-A-T,
I would not be denied.

You can't go to Heaven on roller skates,
I would not be denied;
You'll slip right through Heaven's pearly gates,
I would not be denied.

I believe without a doubt,
I would not be denied;
The Holiness has the right to shout,
I would not be denied.

The Devil's here on earth to roam,
I would not be denied;
He'll knock me out of yonder home,
I would not be denied.

The old-time religion—what makes the people fear it?
I would not be denied;
Because the Devil won't go near it,
I would not be denied.

I would not be denied,
I would not be denied,
Since Jesus come and saved my soul
I would not be denied.

Brother Hammertight started shouting. He danced a pretty step across the front of the schoolhouse. He held his head up. He turned his eyes toward the rusty tin ceiling. At intervals he would cry out:

"The Holiness has the right to shout,
    I would not be denied!"

He would dance more and then he would shout: "Whoopee—Glory to God! Selah! Brother, the Holiness has the right to shout!" And then he would jump higher and shout louder. The girls, one by one, joined the fray. They shouted louder. They cried to God for mercy. They wallowed on the floor. They threw their handkerchiefs in the air. They talked in unknown tongues. Babies got scared. They screamed. The men would take them outside. It wasn't safe for the women to go outside.

And one would hear on the outside: "That damned Hammertight has got this whole place stirred up. He's a damn fake, I believe. I don't believe God wants you to do all them things. Just look what kind of people are in his church. They are people kicked out of the Methodist and Baptist churches." "Say, Bill, I've heard it said old Brother Hammertight has some kind of powder he slips on the girls' handkerchiefs and when they smell it they go to shouting. They can't control themselves then. They just do anything Brother Hammertight wants them to." "Harry, I believe he charms them someway. Look at Grace Gardner. She used to be a right good girl until she got to knowing Brother Hammertight. Now look at her. She'll go to the woods with anybody that's got pants on. And did you know old Brother Hamnmertight's wife has left him over the young girls? Well, she has left him. Yes, sir! And Harry, I want to tell you something else, too. You know when a boy gets saved among these Holy Rollers, they take his terbacker, his rings (if he's got any) and his knife and his watch. They say: 'Don't you know you won't have any use for a watch in Heaven? God will tell you what time it is. But you'll be so happy you won't want to know what time it is. You'll never stop to ask God about the time then. There won't be any time.'"

"They say, Bill, you won't need a knife in Heaven. You can just say: 'God, I want this cut. God, I want this opened.' And it will be done. God will do it. God will be your knife. And God won't have a terbacker chewer in Heaven. He won't have any slop jars to spit in or hearths to spit on, or back walls to spit against. The terbacker is an evil weed, and God put it here for the Devil to tempt sinners with. And God don't want anybody with rings on their fingers. God will jerk them off men's and women's fingers. God just won't have them. A diamond ring in Heaven will be like a black rock. It won't shine. Heaven will be too bright for any of these old worldly diamonds. God's children will wear diamonds as big as duck eggs."

"Now, Harry, I know what Brother Hammertight does with all this jewelry he takes. He sells it at a jewelry shop in Huckleberry, West Virginia. That's how he has bought them seven farms he owns over on Beaver Creek. He goes on and preaches and his wife and children take care of the farms. He rents some of them out. He knows what he is doing, that old Brother Hammertight does. He won't take money, but he takes the jewelry. He gets two or three pieces every night." "Yes, and he comes around when a body is the busiest with his cropping. He comes when a feller is planting it in the springtime, working it in the summer, or cutting it in the fall. He knocks a body out of a lot of good time."

The people are shouting. They are jumping high. They are trying to touch the rusted tin ceiling. "God give me wings! God give me wings! God give me wings! I want to fly! I want to fly! Whoopee! God give me wings!" One young man is down on the floor. He is rolling over and over. He is crying: "God have mercy on a sheep thief." The suspenders of his overalls have come off his shoulders. His overalls have slipped down. One can see the boy's buttocks. He doesn't have on any underwear. Another sinner is down on her knees. "God have mercy on me. I slept with Jake Hicks. God, don't let my man hurt Jake." Jake Hicks is there. He leaves the house. He says when he goes out of the door: "You can't fool with women. They'll tell every time. I'm in a hell of a fix. Damn old Holy Rollers anyhow." Another young man, who has a common local failing to confess, yells: "God be merciful to a backslider. I done it in a coal bank!"

Brother Hammertight is trying to climb the stovepipe. He goes up to the elbow. He can't get over it. He tears the whole works down. The soot, pipes and Brother Hammertight all come down together. His face is black. He shouts on. Sinners are not asked to come to the altar. They just fall in line and bring their jewelry to Brother Hammertight, and their tobacco. He pins the tobacco upon the wall. "There's the work of the Devil. See, that terbacker up there! The old Devil has went out of this room by now. He's out there running up the hollow. The old cuss! We've got him on the run. Shout on, Brother. Amen, Sister. Shout on. Glory be to God!" The crowd moves on. The babies leave the brown breasts of their mothers. Men and women break from all parts of the crowd and join the hurray.

There is a mockery on the outside of the house that goes like this:

> "I would not be pop-eyed,
> I would not be pop-eyed,
> Until Jesus come and he saved my soul,
> I would not be pop-eyed."

The men are carousing and drinking. And out on the grass, many are stretched out lifelessly drunk. There are loud curses among the men at the window. "That goddamned old Hammertight had better not give my sister any of them powders." "Goddamned old Hammertight had better not take that five-dollar ring I got for Hattie last spring. He's a damned old hairy beast. A-foolin' with the women. I don't see what they see in him." "Boy's, what'll you give me to go in there and break up that shoutin around? I'll do it if you'll give me a couple more big hoots of that old corn." "Bob Powderjay, you tried that last night. You couldn't do it. You went right up on the steps and shot six times. And that didn't faze 'em. You went in there one night and tried to hold Brother Hammertight. Now how air you goin' to faze him tonight?" "I'll faze him. You give me two hoots of corn licker."

Bob Powderjay went into the church house. He went up and caught hold of Brother Hammertight. Round and round they went. Brother Hammertight kept on shouting. Bob Powderjay cut his suspenders. He went away from Brother Hammertight. Before he got out of the house, Brother Hammertight's pants were down around his feet. He danced right out of them. He kept on shouting. He was now in his shirttail. He didn't wear underwear either—a lot of men don't wear it in the summertime among the hills. The women saw him naked.

The women began to holler and scream. They ran out of the door. Many went out of the windows. Brother Hammertight kept on dancing. He was in his shirttail. Men tried to hold him. They could not. They crowded him out of the door. He shouted out on the grass in the September moonlight. The men crowded him over toward the edge of the beech grove. The last time we saw Brother Hammertight, he went shouting under the tall beech trees. He went into the darkness. We heard his voice get fainter and fainter as if he were going on and on and on.

"I told you, Boys, I had my mind made up to stop him. He's hard as hell to stop. I done all I could to stop him. Now the damn Law'll get me for disturbing public worship." The Law didn't get Bob, for he compromised with Brother Hammertight for one-hundred dollars and a new set of mule harness. The boys all pitched in a part on the compromise. Brother Hammertight said the Lord would forgive Bob Powderjay.

That broke up the meeting for that night. "It's a damn sight how them Holy Rollers carry on, Jesse. A section of that stovepipe hit me across the arm. I thought it was broke for a little while. Did you see me get up and go back there by the door? I looked for you. I didn't see you anyplace. Ain't it awful, Bob has to git a few drinks in him and show off everywhere he goes. I don't want people to know he's akin to us. I don't like that kind of preaching. They ain't no preaching to it. I want you to go up in Carter County with me and your Ma in October. I want you to hear the Baptists preach. And, My Son, you'll hear some preaching!

"W'y, that old Brother Hammertight couldn't preach. All he did was holler and shout. He's a-doing this country a lot of harm. What's them poor fellers a-going to do that cut down their terbacker crops green? They'll starve this winter. Their poor children. And old Brother Hammertight tells them God will provide."

We went down under the beech trees. They stood in the moonlight, and when the wind blew through their tops, the leaves would drift to the ground. Men on horses raced through under the trees. Men in buggies went down the road. The horses' hoofs struck fire out of the flints on the hard clay road. A few old Fords were there. The men went away yelling. They emptied their pistols as they left.

Women and men went over the country roads and up the hillside paths and up the hollows singing:

> "I would not be denied,
> I would not be denied,
> Since Jesus come and saved my soul
> I would not be denied."

The voices got thinner and thinner on the night wind. And finally they died away.

The next morning my father and I went out and got a broadax, a couple of picks, a shovel and a foot adz to take to the Hill Graveyard. We took plenty of tools for there would be many men there to pay their last respects to Warfield. Sweet Bird would be there. He was one of the best gravediggers around Plum Grove. Bill Jardin, Trevis

Jardin, Weston Lester, Horner Lester, Melvin and Roy Hicks, Uncle Pat Murdock and Andy Murdock, Steve, Ennis and Flem Howell, Ropper Cartwell, Bun Snyder, Pug Rister and Hank Hallihan would be there.

We carried the tools down the hollow. My father and I went out early together. My mother would come that afternoon for the funeral. We would go in the morning and help dig the grave and stay in the afternoon and help to shovel him under. My father always liked Warfield. They had taken many drinks together. He wanted to pay his last respects to him. We had farmed his land. We had cleared many acres of his land. We had raised corn and cane and tobacco for him. We had cleared his land and moved on. But we remembered Warfield. My mother always pitied him after Granny Flaughtery died. She would worry about his house, if his clothes needed patching and if his cows had stood all day and had never been milked. She wondered if Warfield wouldn't drink himself to death.

The sun shone brightly on the cane-hay stubbles at the Big-hickory-nut-tree Bottom. The wind rattled among the dead cornhusks where the corn had been topped. The milkweed seeds blew out in a white thinness on the blue air.

We passed the place where Warfield had lived with his wife until she died. There were only the bones of a house there now. There were two tall cedars, and myrtle vines had climbed up and entwined among the cedar boughs. There was an old cellar down over the bank from the house. And there were many shoe-makes growing around the old cellar.

"Why is it that no one ever goes over there and gathers the apples where that old house used to be?" "Son, them murdle vines is just full of copperheads. I brought old Black-Boy out here once and he tracked 'em up like a dog tracking rabbits. He killed six copperheads out there in less than two hours. Some of them snakes was old residenters. They was so old they was scaly. No one ever goes over there any more—not even Warfield would go when he was living. He was afraid of snakes. Warfield would stop here ever'

time he passed and look over there where that house used to be."
"Why didn't Warfield have any children, or do you know?" "All I
know is what he told me. He said he couldn't get 'em. He told me
that he had tried and tried. You know old Warfield tried hard. I
know, for he was the last Flaughtery of the name. That is the last
of his generation. The Flaughtery race is done. We are going to
put Warfield in a place where his seeds will never sprout. We are
putting him back into his own clay soil. And it is too poor to grow
him even if he did sprout. I have farmed it too much. Look at
them black shoe-makes over there. Look at that old life-everlasting.
Look at them old yellow banks. That ground won't sprout black-
eyed peas."

We began to dig the dirt away. We used the mattocks, picks,
spades and hoes. We used a grubbing hoe to gravel out the
sandrocks with. We used the broadax to hew the sides down and
get the grave smooth. Two worked in the grave at a time. They
worked hard for about thirty minutes. Then two more went
down. They relayed the work to get it done by two o'clock in the
afternoon.

At two o'clock the crowd began to gather, and the grave was
finished. While the crowd was gathering, I went over to Aton
Felch's grave. He was a schoolmate of mine. I hadn't been to his
grave since I saw him buried. That was long ago. The place was
almost hidden now. Weeds and myrtle vined around the weeds.
They had covered the little hill over pretty well.

The crowd gathered. Many came dressed in black. Many of
the women wore shawls. I knew most of these good old women.
They had lived close against the breast of the earth. They knew
the hardships and the sweetness of the life among the hills. Some
of them were mothers of many children. They had come to see
old Warfield Flaughtery for the last time.

There was much talk in the crowd about the way he had
lived before he died. And many debated whether he would go to
Heaven or not. Some said a drunkard could not enter the gates of
Heaven. They said Christ had no whisky there. Others said that

Warfield Flaughtery had already seen Christ. They said he was an angel now, walking with his mother and his wife who had been dead nearly forty years.

Brother Osborne said something about a man that went forth to sow, when he was preaching the funeral of Warfield. And then he said something about what the man reaped.

And what did he reap? I saw what he reaped. The old fields covered with yellow clay banks and black shoe-makes. He reaped bad kidneys and tracts of desolate lands.

After the singing was over, people lined up and went to look at Warfield. No one cried. It was just Warfield Flaughtery dead. And what was that? The old women spoke about his mother. The men talked about the auction of his land. They wondered how much it would sell for an acre.

Brother Osborne crumbled some of Warfield's own clay soil and dropped it in the coffin beside him (for he had owned the graveyard) and said something about eternity and ashes to ashes and dust to dust. It was all over then. The heavy coffin lid was fastened down and the men lowered the coffin down on a pair of leather check lines. They drew them from under the coffin and put them back on the harness of the mules that had pulled him up the hill. The crowd went back the way they came. Many lingered around the myrtle-covered graves of friends and enemies that had been buried there.

The crows will fly over here. The wind will blow. The rats will make footprints on the logs, and the wind and the rain will change the rat prints. They will smooth them over and the rats will make them again. And thus it happens in the wasteland. They are the symbols of the desolation. The crows don't know about Warfield being planted here, and the wind doesn't know about the footprints of the rats. The wind destroys the footprints of the rats. Fight each other in the wastelands, you copperheads and wind and rats and crows. You symbols of desolation, fight each other over the grave of Warfield Flaughtery.

The sun is sinking now over the wastelands. The sun is

sinking in the west, and the trees are sharply etched against the red sky where the sun is going down. And I think to myself as I carry a broadax and a mattock back from digging the grave: "What does it profit a man if he gains the whole wastelands but loses his own life?"

And I look at the red sky and the setting sun. I look at the red leaves on the black shoe-makes. I hear the wind rustle the dead white-oak leaves. I see them going to the ground. They will lie on the ground and rot and there is beauty in them. And the same wind that blew these leaves to the ground will blow across my face and feel it with soft fingers and then go on and blow over the grave of Warfield Flaughtery. And the trees will shed their leaves when the wind blows and the rain falls and the frost comes. It is their season. And everything has a season on this hill, the weeds, the trees and the vines. I look again into the sunset. I say something that I love to repeat. "The heavens declare the glory of God." Oh you fellow by the name of David, I see why you wrote that. "The heavens declare the glory of God." I have always said it. But I never saw it and felt it until now. The Kentucky heavens declare the glory of this land of desolation.

Labor Day is a big day in Greenup. Greenup has two big days. One is the Fourth of July and the other is Labor Day. Christmas Day isn't half as good to the country people as either of the other two. People can't dance out on the streets during Christmas. It is too cold. The children can't come to town barefooted very well. The sunny days are the days when dancers dance—crickets, grasshoppers and men. Summer is the time to laugh and sing and dance on the village street. It is not winter. Winter is the time to cry if one cries at all, the winter of time, the winter of life. "Young blood and old blood, go spend your summers freely. Dance while you may." No one needs to be told this in Greenup County. Everybody knows it. The crowd has gathered. The streets we made, long, long years ago, are filled with people. The streets are roped off. Here is a place for the horses and buggies. Here is a place for the people. Here is a place for the automobiles. And here is a place for the dance. The music has begun. The people are wanting to go. The dance has started.

First Set

All balance!
Swing your partner once and a half.
El mend your left,
Right your honey, go right and left.

First couple go around behind
And swing where you meet;
Back to the center
And oh, how sweet!

Lead up and circle four
In the middle of the floor.
Left hand Lady by the left hand round;
Partner by the left as she comes around.

Elbow Jim and elbow John,
The mule ran away with the harness on.

A hickory log and a poplar stump,
A hole in the floor and everybody jump.

Second Set

Half waltz to the next one,
And go around behind,
And swing when you meet;
Back to the center
And oh, how sweet!

Lead up to, and circle four
In the middle of the floor.
Left hand Lady by left hand round,
Partner by the right
And go whirligig around.

Half waltz to the next one,
Around behind and swing when you meet;
Back to the center
And oh, how sweet!

Lead up to, and circle four,
Left hand Lady by left hand round;
Partner by the right and
Go promenade around.

Third Set

El mend your left!
All at home, fall in line;
You swing your girl
And I'll swing mine.

Right you are, Honey;
Go right and left.

I chew my backer and spit
Against the wall;
Meet your Baby
And waltz the hall.

Promenade and circulate,
Swing your lady,
Like swinging a gate.

The music gets faster. There is more spirit put into the music. There is more juice put into the twisting of legs, the clapping of hands and the swinging round and round.

A hickory log and a poplar stump,
A hole in the floor and everybody jump.

There is a greasy pole to climb. There is a two-dollar bill pinned on the top of the pole. There is a sack race. There is a wheelbarrow race. There is a foot race for the old men around the courthouse square—a dollar for the winner—and something hidden over on the riverbank in the weeds. A prize is to be given for the prettiest girl—ten bars of soap and eight yards of silk. The prize of two barrels of flour is to be given to the man with the biggest family by one wife. The father of seventeen children, all living and up on the platform with their parents, gets it! Two other children in the family are dead. A prize of one barrel of meal is given to the most loving couple. Rufus Mingus and his wife Clara Belle get it every year. A prize is given for the man with the biggest foot. He gets a new pair of shoes. Antis Winton gets it every Labor Day. He wears eighteens. There is the nail-driving contest for women, the hog calling contest, the cow-calling contest. "Pig - - ee, pig - ee - - pig - ee, pig - - oo - ee." It sounded far above the din of the crowd. "Swouke cow - - - - swouke cow - - - swouke cow - - - swouk - - ee - - - - - swouk - - - - ee." The cows and hogs would come home to the calls, but the cows and hogs are not close by. The winner of the hog-calling contest gets a six-weeks-old pig. The winner of the cow-calling contest gets a Jersey heifer calf. Three prizes are to be given among children for dancing. It takes a long time to let so many dance. A prize of three dollars, one of two dollars and a one-dollar prize is given.

After the children dance, Lester Warren walks out on the truck bed. "I aim to show you these young shavers can't beat the old when it comes to dancing." Everybody laughed. He took from under his coat a china plate. He pulled off his coat and threw it down in the truck bed. He rolled up his sleeves. He weighed two-hundred and five pounds. He put the plate down on the truck bed. He danced on top of the plate. It was a feat. The men and women clapped their hands. "More juice in that music, Boys! More juice! Give her to me fast! I am a-rearing to go!"

This is a day when there is a smile on the lips of everybody up around the courthouse square. Men out on the riverbank and down in the alley by the jail have got a little too much. Some of them are crying. Others are wanting to fight.

Everybody is happy. Men and women are having a good time. The people from the country have put everything aside and driven or walked to Greenup to enjoy the day. This is their day. The uncut corn can wither one day longer on the hillsides. Tobacco can stand another day, another night. Maybe two more days and maybe three—when Bill, Harry and Tom get sober and get into shape after the rotten whisky and the fight on Labor Day. Yes, Jailer Adams locks many of them in the crib. And the tobacco then is subject to many frosts, waiting for the tobacco daddy to come home and take care of his hand-children. The good wives often take care of the tobacco when the men are put in the Greenup crib for "disorderly conduct." The cane can be left over until Tuesday. The juice will keep. The "lassies" will be just as good. It will bring the same forty cents a gallon. Winston Salyers will give that much. If the people peddle it from house to house in the river towns, they will get more.

The music goes on. The dancing goes on. People have come to Greenup to have a good time. They are having it. Money doesn't stand in the way if they have it. It doesn't stand in the way if they don't have it. Greenup people and Greenup County people are out for a good time. They are going to have it. Why not have a good time? There is the time to cry, the time to weep, the time to work, the time to love, and the time to have a good time. "Good time" is on the lips of everybody. This is the time to enjoy one's self. I am with the crowd. People are happier here than they were where I went to school. Their lots are hard. They laugh in the face of hard knocks and hard lots. They are all having a big time. This is the time to have a good time. It is the season. Soon will come the winter of Time and later will come the winter of flesh.

"Look over there at those women fighting. They got into it over a man at the dance. Listen to what they are saying. Goodness—the Lord Almighty ought to send lightning and strike 'em to the ground. 'I'll knock the god-durned hell out'n you! I'll scratch your damn eyeballs out, god-durn you! You old Bitch!' 'Don't you call me a bitch! I'll pull every hair out'n your head. I was dancing with that man first!' Watch them! There goes Rance Chester and Wheed Thomas. They'll get 'em. Look—she slapped Rance right in the face. But Rance's got her now. Old Wheed's got the other one. Watch him swing. She's got her teeth in his shoulder, See! Look, Zebra Wilkerson is helping to take them to jail. They're on their way now. Wonder how they'll like jail?" "Old Wash Adams feeds 'em pretty good. They'll like it all right. The only thing is, he can't put them in together. He'll have to give 'em separate cells to keep 'em from fighting."

"Look out there a-comin' down the E.K. what the Law's got. He rode a-past on his horse and smelled it. The weather is warm, you know. And good corn licker smells like rotten mud turtle. Now what if old Bill Ludlow had got in here with all that stuff? He ought to've put more hay over it so the Law couldn't see. But the Law has a good nose. The Law smelled that licker. It's a damn shame they're a-goin' to pour that good stuff over the riverbank. Boy, put all that loose in this crowd, wouldn't we have a good time!"

The Law and his deputies part the crowd. Two teams of horses with two wagons loaded with whisky pull over by the riverbank. A man drives one team, his son drives the other. They take out eighty-six gallons of whisky in jugs from under the hay on the wagons. They pour it over the riverbank. A stream runs from the top of the bank down to the river. The men line up along the stream and drink the dirty whisky. The Law tries to stop them. There are too many drinking. The Law can't get to them all. They drink and drink. The whisky is all poured out. The jugs are rolled into the river. Bill Ludlow wants the jugs back.

"Say, Sheriff, I'll have to go to old Atlanter, Georgia, now, won't I? The Law's got me. They ain't no way gettin' out'n it."
"Bill, you ought to knowed better than to pull a thing like this under my nose. I get 'em all, Bill, that go agin me. You and your gang fit me like tigers during last August primary, two years ago. I thought you was a-doin' this. I kept my eye on you. I wanted you."

"Yes, but Sheriff, you know for the past two croppings terbacker ain't netted me seven cents a pound. Lassies has been down to twenty-five cents a gallon. And all the corn I raised jist laid out there in the crib, save what little my stock et. I fed them mostly roughage and saved my grain. I couldn't even give my corn away it was so cheap. I thought if the Lord would be with me I'd make it up in corn licker. I ain't no law-breakin' man. I jist had to have the money. My land is a-goin' to be sole next Court day for taxes. I ain't paid my taxes yet. I jist keep gettin' 'em put off from one court to the next. And Sheriff, I got to keep that boy over there on that. I got to keep him in school. I don't want him to grow up like I am. I want him to go to college so he can make a livin' with a pencil behind his ear. I don't want him to have to make licker against the Law and lay in old Atlanter jail like his Pappy will have to. I want him to be a man. I want him to get away from these old hill farms. They ain't nothin' to 'em. They ain't a livin' in 'em. I want my boy to be more 'n I am. I have to make licker to pay my taxes. And Sheriff, did you know there is a bigger Law than your Law? God has a bigger Law then you have. My old Bible is a-layin' out there where I made this. You can go right out there and see. And if I go to old Atlanter jail, I want to take that old book with me."

The men come up the riverbank. They are the men that drank of the water that quenches all thirst for the time being. It was the stream of corn that Bill Ludlow had sweated over to make and pay his taxes with. Bill Ludlow didn't drink. He made the whisky and sold it. His people had done it in the hills for years and years before him. He didn't think it was wrong in the Law of God to make the whisky. He knew it was wrong in the sight of the Law the Sheriff had, the Law of the State, the Law of the Nation, but Bill thought the Law of God was above the Law of the State and the Nation. His Bible was back at the still. He went to jail.

His child was too young to arrest. The boy drove one team back. He hitched the other team and wagon to the back of his wagon. He hauled back two wagonloads of people that had walked into town. The men that drank Bill's whisky from the gutter said it was the best stuff they had ever tasted. They said it was the pure corn. "That licker makes a man feel good. It don't burn a man's guts. If people are a-goin' to make licker and drink licker, I don't see why the Law don't let a man like Bill make it. He makes good stuff. Wouldn't be so many people pizened to death and going blind on good licker like this. I feel like a two-year-old mule. I could dance on top of a china plate if I had one. I could climb the greasy pole. I could catch the greasy pig. I could call home the hogs. And I can whip the damn Sheriff that got Bill Ludlow. Let me to him. Hell, let's go down there and take some crowbars and pry the jailhouse down. We don't need it nohow."

The Labor Day celebration is over. It will go down in the history of the community to be talked about for years and years to come. Tomorrow the men will start cutting tobacco, digging potatoes, cutting corn and making "lassies" down in the cane field. I shall start teaching school. I shall make my living with a pencil behind my ear like Bill Ludlow wanted his boy to do.

I would love to tell Bill Ludlow a secret. I shall not put it on paper. "But, Bill Ludlow, don't leave the soil. Live right down against the soil. Be envious of the snake because it rubs the soil closer than you. Bill, if I were to tell you that from the bitterness of life among the hills there is the greatest sweetness in the world, would you believe me? Look at Robert Frost. But Bill, you don't know him. You can't read. You ought to know him. He is a farmer. But he tells you something about the soil in poetry.

"There is a beauty in the soil that is unsurpassed. There is tragedy, too, in the dark hills, Bill Ludlow. I would like to tell you about the man that went forth to sell his corn whisky to pay the doctor's fee for his wife. His wife was going to have a baby. He did not know when the baby was coming. He took the whisky away to a city. It was thirty miles away. He put the whisky in half-pint bottles and put rags around them. He filled a meal sack with half-pint bottles of whisky. He threw the sack over the mule as if it was meal. He rode the mule to the town. He sold the whisky. He brought the doctor back on the mule. But it was no use. It was too late. The mother of her first-born had tried to have the baby herself. She had died and the baby had died. The unfed hound dogs and the unslopped hogs had come into the shack and had eaten part of her flesh and nearly all of the baby. This is dark tragedy, Bill Ludlow, that is found among the hills. No, Bill, these are the things I would tell you. And I would tell you to watch for the beauty of the leaves falling in the mountains. Now is the time, Bill Ludlow, to watch. It is September now. 'The heavens declare the glory of God.' Bill Ludlow, you haven't read this. I never knew what it meant until I got away from it. I remembered reading that sentence. But I never felt it. I never saw it.

"Look out now, Bill Ludlow, and you will see it. The geese are flying near the sky. The leaves blow hither and thither over the dusty country roads. The leaves blow through the air and the martins and the swallows are gathering to go South. Mellow is the wind and yellow are the leaves and yellow is the mist about the pools of leaf-strewn water. Scarlet are the leaves and scarlet are the patches of shoe-make woods in the pasture lands and the sawbriar stools. Almost yellow is the tobacco and yellow is the corn, but scarlet the cane tops and the cane blades. The earth is scarlet and yellow. Look at it! The whole earth around us is scarlet and yellow, the waters and the mists and the briars and the trees! Yellow the noonday September sun, scarlet the setting September sun and scarlet is the sky around the setting sun. 'The heavens declare the glory of God.' I'll tell you this, Bill Ludlow. But this is not the secret. The secret is about your son."

My schoolhouse attic was filled with bats. Tall weeds grew around it. Wasps built their cones in the eaves. Spiders had strung white gossamer ropes from siding to siding. Birds built their nests in the woodhouse. Rats lived in the woodhouse and ate the corn from Dan Tull's corncrib. I would begin school there the next day. I had one small blackboard. I found some old dried last year's switches in the corner. It was all very amusing.

I found a place to board. "Now if you can stand the grub poor people lives on, you can stay here." I knew when I sat down and put my feet under the table there would be grub on the table. It was a white house on a hill. Fields of grain were in the valley below it, almost as far as the eye could reach, wooded hills were at the back of the house. And this was the place to live. One could hear the foxhounds running at night. One could hear the waters falling over the rocks a stone's throw from the house. One could hear the guns cracking and see the rabbits tumbling in the weed fields.

Ott Taylor was a good neighbor and a good farmer. He worked in the cane, tobacco and corn. He owned a big farm and raised his food to use and to sell. His good wife, Lucy, took care of the berry canning and the apple-butter making. She was a thrifty housewife. It was a great place to stay. Ott would work hard during the day. At night he would try to cut the pigeonwing when we got the Potter boys over with the banjo, fiddle, harp and guitar.

The first thing we did was clean the schoolhouse and kill the bats and knock down the spider webs, the mud-dauber nests and the wasp nests. We arranged the chairs in order and threw the switches out. "Billie Linkous, where do you live?" "I live up on Three Prong." "How far is it, Billie?" "Seven miles." "What do you want to be when you grow older?" "I want to be the governor of Kentucky." "Snookie Taylor, what do you want to be?" "I want to be a barber. I'm cutting hair right along now for ten cents a head." "Robert Baker, what do you want to be?" "I'm going to be a schoolteacher like my dad." "Burton Waters, what are you going to do?" "I want to write histories."

When a funeral occurred in the hills, even if it was three miles away, the children wanted to attend. I let them. The people would hold it against me if I did not let them go. There are not many places to go in the country. They always attend funerals in the hills.

First, it is respect for the dead. Second, it is some place for people to go and meet each other and talk.

I brought books for the students to read. We didn't have a library. I let them read all the books I had and all the books I could borrow. I could not get enough books for them. On Court days I went to Greenup to meet more people. On Saturdays I tramped the

Court Day in an eastern Kentucky town
(Courtesy David Greene Collection, Special Collections
and Archives, Eastern Kentucky University Libraries)

hills but I found Court days in Greenup more interesting.

It is Court day in Greenup. The town is filled with people. The musicians flock to the street corners and play the old-time songs. There is dancing in the street. There is preaching at the street corners. Salesmen from Ashland are selling clothes from a truck at the street corner. The clothes are old. The people buy. It is a busy day in Greenup. The merchants are busy filling orders. The country women bring butter and eggs and trade them for sugar and salt and dry goods.

I go to the courthouse. Upstairs in the big Circuit courtroom, there is a foul smell inside, of tobacco smoke and the tobacco and whisky breaths. The wet dirty clothes of the men smell. Their shirts are unbuttoned at the bosoms and hairy chests are showing. The men spit amber spittle on the floor. They talk and the Judge pounds on the table. There is order in the room. The lawyers whisper to each other. The jurymen have assembled. They are seated in front of the witness stand. They chew tobacco. They twist in their seats. They are uneasy.

Downstairs in the County courtroom, the clerk comes out and reads: "Here are the cases set down for trial on the misdemeanor docket of the Greenup County Court. Willard Boswell, drunk in a public place; Less Hartwell, operating motor vehicle on improper tags; Tibbie Barr, common nuisance; Allan Stewart, carrying concealed weapon; David Marsh, selling liquor; Henry Dodsworth Jr., breach of peace; Buster Wattles, breach of peace; Lillard Hallighan, reckless driving; Norman Loften, possessing liquor; Drew Ashburn, operating a motor vehicle while intoxicated; Charley Raggs, breach of peace; William Raggs, common nuisance; Ennis Cartwell, carrying concealed weapon; Steve O'Toole, carrying a concealed deadly weapon; Jim Henderson, possessing liquor; Wayne Benton, possessing liquor; Tom Hartwell, disturbing church; Horace Hadmann, possessing liquor; George Roper, breach of peace; Jess Barr, operating motor vehicle while intoxicated; Henry Benton, selling liquor; Luke Culty, permitting and suffering gaming; George Bliss, selling liquor; Sam Dodson, possessing liquor; T. W. Bart, possessing liquor; Ram Burts Jr., possessing liquor; Pug Hendrix, selling liquor; Roy Fizzle, breach of peace; Clara Peters, breach of peace; Jim Murdoch, breach of peace; Rob Crown, pointing a deadly weapon; Rob Crown, drawing a deadly weapon on another; Obie Hallie, possessing liquor; Bill Jays, disturbing religious worship; A. A. Foster, suffering and permitting gaming; Cud Plaster, disturbing religious worship."

The Judge pounds the table for order in the courtroom. The windows are filled. The seats are filled. People stand in the aisles. Women sit on the long benches. Many of them are letting their babies suck. Their dresses are open. Their breasts are showing. The babies cry. The men talk. The women mutter. The Judge pounds the table for more order. "Say, Bert, old Cud ain't a-goin' to git out'n here this time. Ain't this about his third time disturbing public worship?" "Yes, Cud'll git out'n it." "You damn right he will. He's from back up yander in the mountains, ain't he? Old Cud always has come out'n it, ain't he?" "Boy, that old Rob Crown is a bad 'un." "Hell, them Crowns'll knock you off." "Old Fidis Waymore won't take any chances on Rob when he gits him out on the country road." "You bet old Fidis'll grip them .44 handles." "It pays him to with one of them bad Crowns."

Men on the outside of the courthouse curse the lawyers. "That goddamn rascal, all he's out fer is the money! Wait till he starts to run fer somethin' in this county. Damn him, I'll see him in Hell afore I'll vote fer him. I'll do ever'thing I can agin him. The low-down son." "By God, I hope he gets old Ram Burts out'n that. 'Pears like Ram gets in so much trouble these days. Damn, I hope Lawyer Stan does something for him. What will his little wife Birdie do with all them four children? W'y, the youngest is might' nigh big as the oldest. All 'pears to me like they are the same size. All sucking their Mamma. Then old Ram goes out and gets into this trouble. I feel sorry for little Birdie."

There is singing at the street corner, "If you're goin' go to Heaven, You can't wear a great big R-A-T." A man is shouting from the truck at the street corner, "All right, all right, Old Tightwad, if you ain't going to give me anything for this pretty tam, I'll give it to you." The old-time musicians are playing:

"Frankie and Johnnie were sweethearts,
  Lawsy, how they did love;
  Swore to be true to each other,
  True as the stars above."

The day is done. The people leave the town. They go back into the hills.

I got a letter from Elmer Heaberlin. "Stuart, we are having hell down here at Lincoln Memorial. We are on another big strike. Ninety-eight percent of the students this time. The lid blew off the teakettle to let the steam out. The spout wasn't big enough to let it out this time. The Higher Power fired three of the teachers without giving any reasons. We are asking reinstatement of the three teachers or reasons why the Higher Power fired them. It's a great life, Boy. We've all taken to the hills. We are climbing over the mountains and riding on the lake. Please send me a little money, fifteen dollars will do, to buy my food with. I am staying at the Cumberland Gap Hotel. I have been expelled from Lincoln Memorial and arrested four times. We are fighting this thing through. We are going to win."

In October the roads got bad. One going to Greenup had to ride on horseback or walk. An empty wagon could not be pulled by a span of horses or mules. But this was late October and November. During the middle of September, I could see great wagonloads of tobacco going over the rough road to Greenup. There would be two teams of mules hitched to each wagon and sometimes three. I could hear the drivers crack their buckskin whips and curse the mules for being lazy. But it was a long drag to Greenup over the muddy road. I could see wagonloads of hay, of corn, sweet potatoes and late sugar-melons. I could see wagonloads of chickens and wagons loaded with barrels of sorghum leaving the valley. Many of these products would sell for less than it cost to raise them. The people received little or no profits. If there were any profits to be made from these products, the middlemen got them. I know the farmers did not. They had plenty to eat, but they could not make enough money to buy their clothes and pay their taxes.

The men would go down the road driving large droves of cattle. They were going to the slaughter pen. The cattle went away contented. The drivers never whipped them. It bruised the flesh. People didn't want bruised beef to eat. And many of them would be on the meat market the next day. They would be cut up on a block and sold out to the people. A man would go down the road and a flock of sheep and lambs would follow their shepherd. He would lead them to their death. They did not know it. He was the shepherd. They were the sheep. But they would be on the market too. Students would say: "I hate to see a sheep killed. I just can't stand to see a lamb brought in and its head cut off over a wooden block. I can't stand to see the blood. And lambs look so helpless. They look so innocent."

During that autumn, I went to cornhuskings, bean stringings and apple peelings. I went over among the hollows from the valley and heard the old-time fiddlers play, the old people sing, and saw the children dance. It was a great place to live. The hills were dark after the scarlet and yellow leaves had fallen. The woods were dark and the trees were black, barren, hard wires in the winter wind. The whole earth was in the sad season of winter. It was the winter of Time.

In the evenings by the fireside, we popped corn, roasted chestnuts, made popcorn and lassie balls; we read, listened to old-time music and stories. Darkness would come early. Many nights when the stars shone, I would go out and walk beneath the stars. I would go through the woods alone. I always wanted to go alone. The woods were my own. I knew the land for miles and miles after I had been there for the autumn. I remember the trees. I could not forget.

My mother wrote me a letter and said that my father had seen Elmer Heaberlin's trunk at Wurtland. "Elmer has come home. The boys up around Wurtland said he was kicked out of Lincoln Memorial. And they said everybody had been kicked out, teachers and all, and the place would start all over again."

"Say, did you know Randall Woodrow and Hattie Snowfield got married last night? Randall's Pap married 'em. I knowed they would marry right soon. They have been courting four years or nigh about it. Randall is eighteen now. Hattie is seventeen. I guess they'll live up there in that little boxed house on Ethan Woodrow's place."

And that night was Christmas Eve. We put the harness on the mules and hitched them to the sled. We put about a doodle of cane hay on the bed of the sled. We tied cowbells on the sides of the sled bed. We got our shotguns and plenty of shells. We climbed into the sled, pulled straw over our feet and went to the Snowfields. Randall and Hattie were there. They heard the bells ringing and the sound going out over the white frozen earth. The bells broke the stillness of the night. When Randall and Hattie heard the bells, they hid upstairs. We went in and asked for the man and his wife. We started searching the house for them. Everybody laughed as the hunt went on. We found them. We brought them downstairs. "We ought to put Randall on a pole and ride him around for hiding from us." Then we took the cowbells, the fox horns and the shotguns and we began. We beat dishpans and plow points. We shot all our shells away. The noise went far out over the white countryside in the stillness of the night. After the belling was over, Randall gave us cigars and candy. We wished him well and got in the sled and rode off over the snow—home through the moonlight and the starlight.

Every Monday morning the boys and I would take a coal bucket of water and a broom and scrub the obscene pictures and the vulgar writings about the girls and boys in the high school off the walls of the schoolhouse, the doorsteps and off the inside walls of the privies. "Mr. Stuart, it is outside people that come here over the weekend and do that writing. They think the girls that go to high school are all bad. They are boys that live over on Hog Branch and round about there. They are boys who won't go to school."

It was January and the weather was cold. I heard a student say: "Mrs. Waters has gone crazy and killed herself." "Do you know why she went crazy?" "Yes, she has a young baby, you know. That was her ninth child. Burton is the oldest and he is just seventeen. The birth of the last child made her nervous. Then they only got seven cents a pound for their tobacco. They have a mortgage on their place. They have a lot of debts that are coming due right now. They can't pay them. She got to worrying about the debts and losing their home and she got nervous. She tried to kill herself. She tried to do it with a butcher knife and then a rope. Mr. Waters took her to a doctor in Greenup. The doctor said she was crazy. They didn't have any place to put her that night. They were going to send her to the asylum the next day. They put her in the jail that night. She wrapped blankets around herself and set fire to the blankets. She burned herself to death. She died and left nine children. The oldest seventeen, and the youngest about two months old."

They made a coffin for Mrs. Waters. It was made out of Kentucky oak and poplar that grow in the eastern part of the state, the oaks and poplars that grew from the earth where she milked the cows. The coffin was padded with quilts, and sheets were used over the quilts. Lace was put around the edges for trimming.

The team of mules that pulled Mrs. Waters for the last time off Clay Creek, the creek where they had always lived, were the mules that had helped to grow the crops of tobacco and the mules Mrs. Waters had often driven to Greenup. And there about the Waters' home were the mattocks, the spades, rakes, plows and hoes and the implements they had used in cropping. She had used these things. The children had used them with her. Her oldest boy had used them. They had tried hard to redeem the mortgage and save the home. But Mrs. Waters was going now for her last long sleep. She had left a great heritage behind, more than a book, more than a farm. She had left nine children. They were strong children. They were the smartest children among these hills.

There was a train of wagons moving over the muddy road and through the January icy wind. The grandmother kept four of the Waters children at home. They were too small to stand the four-mile trip in the cold icy wind over a rough muddy road in a jolt wagon. They would not see their mother buried.

About them were the old muddy harvest fields. It was winter now, the winter of Time. The tobacco stubbles and the corn stubbles were white on the old fields. The woods were naked and the wind whistled through the woods. The dark outlines of the hills cut sharp against the cloudy January sky. The tall dark hills looked barren and desolate. It was the land of tobacco, the land of God, the land of oak trees, the land of beauty, the land of desolation, the home of tragic living and the home of the sweetness of life. Great dark hills, with life among them, with death among them. Great hills, formed millions of years ago, that give us food, shelter, and warmth in life and take us back to their bosom in the end.

The mules forded the Tiger River with the casket. The water was up in the wagon bed. The teams forded the river. The water was swift and many of the teams were nearly swept downstream by the current of swift clear water. Many of the people got their feet wet. The front team that pulled the spring wagon with the coffin in it followed a man on horseback that led the way. We were soon at the graveyard out on the hilltop. Fresh dirt was piled high where the men had come and dug the grave. It is the best act a man can do in the hill country. It is always done freely and with a good will behind it.

Brother Osborne was called to preach the funeral. He is the shepherd to the flock of hill people in Greenup County. He preaches to them. He marries them. He preaches their funerals. He comes to their bed in time of sickness. He rides on horseback or walks. He goes to them in their time of need. He is the shepherd of the flock.

And he said something like this: "The apple trees bring forth bloom in their season. This was like unto this woman's life. I knew her then. She was beautiful in youth and in spirit. And then the fruit of the tree was abundant and the fruit was rich fruit. And this fruit of her life is in her children and the way she has lived among the people in the Valley. This was the summer of her season. And then the autumn came and the winter of Life and called this Sister, still beautiful in spirit, home to rest."

The men with hats off and heads bowed in reverence and grief stood over to one side. The women came up by the grave and sang:

> There's a land beyond the River
> That they call the Sweet Forever,
> And we only reach its shore by Faith's Decree;
> One by one we'll gain the portals

There to dwell with the immortals,
When they ring the golden bells for you and me.

Don't you hear those bells a-ringing?
Don't you hear those angels singing?
'Tis the glory hallelujah jubilee—
In that far-off Sweet Forever,
Just beyond the shining River,
When they ring the golden bells for you and me.

And then they sang this chorus:

Safe in the arms of Jesus,
Safe on his gentle breast;
There by his love o'er-shaded,
Sweetly the soul shall rest.

Brother Osborne crumbled clay upon the coffin lid and said something about dust to dust, ashes to ashes and something about eternity. The children cried. The old women and the old men shed tears. They lowered the heavy homemade coffin down into the grave with the leather check lines. The men threw in the dirt and tramped it down with their feet. The wagonloads of people moved off towards the ford.

I was made principal of the County High School for the next year. "Now you can have the school on trial. If you can handle the boys and make them know their places, we want you. If you can whip them, we want you. If they whip you, we don't want you. It is a big job we have up there. And next year there will be nearly three-hundred students. They are mean. You've got to watch them. One might hit you across the head with something. One boy come nigh as a pea whipping the coach last year. They come out of the windows on you and do everything else. They go fishing over at the river. I want you to break that up. They have jugs of corn liquor over at the pond, I'm told; ride in boats over the pond; drink corn liquor and fish. You must break that up."

Summer again at home between the handles of the plow. There were the fields to plow and plant. And the grain to be gathered in the autumn. There was a stillness out among the hills. The wind in the trees was the most impressive noise, and the dog barks and the bird calls.

I plowed the soil. I planted the grain. I read books. I wrote poetry. My father and I would take long walks through the woods. When he found a sprig of bluegrass or of clover, he drove a stake up by its side for protection. He loved a blade of grass more than I did a line of poetry. He loved the soil. He loved the trees. He wanted to own more land. And before the summer was over, he annexed another fifty acres to his hundred. He wanted to take other farms. He wanted to clear a farm and get it ready to live on and then buy another farm and get it ready.

"Old Black-Boy is gettin' mighty old. When he gets down, he can't get up. But when he is on his feet, he's still ready to fight strange dogs and copperheads and skunks. But his teeth are all gone and his head is white with gray hairs. He won't be here much longer. That old dog has been a great dog. If he'd a-been a man, he'd a-been the governor of Kentucky. But now he is only an old dog and he is very tired. He ain't much longer for here. And I can't hardly stand to see him die. About the next copperhead he tries to kill, it will do him in. For when he bends to get the snake, he will fall over and the snake will get him. Old Black-Boy never did lie at a tree until the other day. I went to him when he barked. It was only a big bunch of leaves lodged in the limbs of an oak tree. Then he barked in a hole. I went to him. It was a big bug he was scooting around with his paw. He acts like an old childish man now."

The last copperhead did get Black-Boy. He found it in the oat field. He ventured in and fell. He was too old. His teeth were worn off into the gums. The snake bit his head several times. It was swollen as big as two heads. All we could do did not save him. He went to the Happy Hunting Ground.

We carried the faithful mountain cur to a knoll over from the house. From the top of the knoll, one could see all the land for miles. James and I scooped out a hole for him and buried him where the cracking of hunters' guns could be heard for miles away. We buried him where the fox crossed often. We buried him in the land he had hunted over often. Not ten paces away, he had killed two skunks. He had killed rabbits near and caught snakes and weasels. But the old warrior among the dog world of his hills was laid to rest. And at the grave of Black-Boy, I had to shed tears at the loss of a friend and write poetry in his memory.

> We laid him here to rest a warrior done
> Upon a hill that shoulders to the sky.
> We knew if he could only speak he'd ask to lie
> Where he could hear the thunder of my gun.
> To us no man had been a better friend
> Than old Black-Boy, and when we laid him here,
> Above his grave we paused to shed a tear,
> Knowing he'd gone unto his journey's end.
> We hear his midnight howling at the gate
> No more when strangers pass; the rabbits play
> Around the house, the foxes have their way,
> In tall damp backyard weeds snakes writhe in wait.
> He took the wrong trail when he took the track
> Of Death—We called but he could not turn back.

The drought came that summer. The crops burned in the ground. The tobacco crop soon turned yellow and then scarlet. The corn grew only high enough to be bumblebee corn. "Pa, why do you call the corn bumblebee corn?" "Because a bumblebee can suck on the tassel and its tail touches the ground."

I could stay at home and teach the County High School. It was only a three-mile walk. September came and I had passed my twenty-second birthday. I was ready for the school. "Are you the new principal? I heard you was. I just wanted a look at you. Wanted to tell you too that when a high-school principal does me a dirty trick, I'll take my knife and cut his guts out." "What would you do, Smith, if he were your friend and did you a favor?" Smith only smiled. He was as big as I was and better muscled. I knew if he got the first lick it would be too bad. My intention was to see that he never got it.

On the first day of school, I saw a student with a familiar walk coming up the street. He walked in. He was Burton Waters. He had followed me to my new job. He said: "Could I stay at your home and do some work to pay for my board?" "Go out with me tonight and we'll see Mom." Mom took him in and made him a member of the family. She washed his shirts and darned his socks the same as she did for James and me.

The students in the County High School laughed at the strange actions of Burton Waters. They did not laugh when they later knew him in the classroom. His big mouth spread from ear to ear, his pimpled face, his shaggy head of unkempt hair, his long, narrow, half-shut eyes were admired by the students. His remarkable mind placed him first among his classmates. My brother James was my student. I had to reinstate him. He had been suspended the preceding year. At the half-year, when I called for book reports, I checked the class members to see if they had read the required three novels. Burton Waters had read 103, James had read 100. In the meantime, they had gathered the corn at home, chopped and split the firewood, and possum hunted at night. Burton made one of the highest records ever recorded at the school.

Smith came to me one day and said: "Mr. Stuart, there's a boy here I am going to kill. It is Jimmie Archie." "Do you have his burial ground picked out yet?" Jimmie Archie came the same day. He said: "Mr. Stuart, there is a boy here I'm going to kill. It is Troy Smith." "Jimmie, I want you and Smith to meet me this afternoon at four o'clock in the office."

At four o'clock Jimmie Archie and Troy Smith, two youth tremendous in size and powerful in strength, stood in the office and snarled their lips at each other. "Smith, you think you are a better man than I am." "Archie, you think you are a better man than

I am." I said: "Boys, come out behind the schoolhouse with me. I'm going to see who is the better man." The football coach went with me. These boys were his best football players. We drew a circle, searched the boys to see neither had a knife, and told them to get in the circle and mix them up.

They were red with blood. Smith spit out a mouthful of teeth and went back to fighting. Finally they both quit, walked into the shower room together and washed the blood off each other's faces. It ended an old grudge and was the only way to settle it.

Once in a football game, I saw Smith get the finger next to his little finger on his left hand broken off at the first joint. He put the piece of finger in his mouth and made a swell tackle. Later a doctor sewed the finger back on.

One morning when I walked into the schoolroom, a boy came to me with his lips burst open. "That new boy that's just come in here did it. See him over there." Another boy came to me. He said: "That new boy cut me with a knife." He showed me his finger. "Said he wasn't afraid of no teacher around this place. He jerked Bill Tremper's pants down out there too. Then he knocked Bill down. Bill's out there now behind the house a-crying." I walked over to where the boy was. I said: "Did you hit this boy, cut this one, and pull another boy's pants down." "Yes, and what of it?"

I took him by the shirt collar to the office. I laid him across the table. He squirmed and I put him across my lap. I used the board on him. He never flinched. I let him up. I said: "Just what is your name, anyway?" He said: "Houndshell is my name." I said: "Where are your people from?" "Big Sandy." I said: "Get down across my lap again." When I got through, the tobacco pipe in his hip pocket was sawdust.

The next day his father came to Greenup with a gun. He was coming up to the school to get me. He was turned back in Greenup by my friends and his friends.

Thus the season passed. When the weather got bad, I had to board in town. I drew one-hundred and thirty-five dollars per month for my work. All the teachers on my staff were older than I, and all but two had far more teaching experience. This was one of the hardest year's work that I had ever done. I had to teach four classes and be principal in a school with two-hundred and seventy enrollments. With Burton Waters our school won the scholastic contest in eastern Kentucky.

Mr. Blair, the county superintendent, would come up to me and say: "You are getting pretty well known over the county. I hear you are going to run for superintendent against me." "It might be talked about, but I haven't planned anything like that. I don't want your job." Then, to show that he was the boss, he would advise me to do things about the school. I was supposed to do what he said. He wanted me to teach the school and black his boots. The latter I refused to do. I would not teach under him again.

One day when I came home from teaching, I told my father and mother: "I have been to look over a house in Greenup. It is a very fine house. I'll get it and we'll move to it if you two will leave the hills. Why not leave this old desolate farm? There is not much to it. Pa, you are getting like Warfield Flaughtery. You love land too well. You are getting land poor. It will make you too poor to pay your taxes. You own far too much of this old hill land now. Don't you want to get out of this mud and this drudgery work for a while? Don't you want to move to town?" There was silence. "Give me and your Ma time to think it over. You have asked us too quick."

The next week when I went home: "No, we don't want to move to town. We have thought it over. Town ain't no place for us. We have lived among the hills all our life, and now we are going to die among the hills. Town would kill us both. Your Ma couldn't get out and run around among the trees and work in her garden and work with the strawberries. You know how she gets every spring when the leaves come back and the whippoorwills start hollering. She just goes out and stays. And then we would have to leave the place. We would have to leave all of our stock. We couldn't take it to town. I think we might as well stay where we are. We could only take a few chickens and leave them in a fenced lot. They would get out and mix with other chickens and ruin the pure gray game stock.

I don't believe we want to go."

"You'll live right here until you die. You'll die here or you'll die someplace among the hills. You will never get out. You have seen nothing beyond the hills. And I guess you are just about as well off. But if you want to move away, I'll get the house. You are still working hard and buying more of this old land. It looks foolish to me. You go out with a lantern and work in your cornfields at night. You work by lantern light around the barn. I hate to see you do it. People ask me about the light that they see moving upon this hill every night. They say they see it moving far into the night. I tell them I guess that it is you doing up the work. I hate to see you work like this. I hate to see Mom work the way she does. If you'll let me, I'll stop it."

"Let me tell you something. I have raised you and you're no boss over me yet. I aim to stay right here. I aim to give this farm to you two boys before I drop off. And I want you to carry on. I want you to run this farm like your Pap run it. This is a place where you can do as you please and there's not a boss to look down your collar and watch you sweat. The girls don't need it. Their men can keep them. And they don't carry on." "Carry on what?" "Carry on the name of Stuart. And you see that little knoll up there where that hickory stands, I want to be buried there. I want your Ma to be buried there beside me. I want us to rest together. I want us to be up high, overlooking this farm and above the cornfields, the strawberries and the tobacco fields. I want a coffin made out'n black oak. You see them black oaks right up there on that rocky bank, cut one of them oaks and take a hammer and maul and split it into puncheons and get boards to make me some sort of an old box. Have Sweet Bird to dig my grave if he is a-livin' when I am gone. And bury me on this farm. Now you see this is done. I want to tell you this. And you see your Ma is buried by my side. And I want you to carry on."

Jesse, as a young educator

*(Courtesy H. Edward Richardson Collection,
Ekstrom Library, University of Louisville)*

Chapter IX
A Stranger Was Afraid

At Greenup, Kentucky, Uncle Rank Larks helped me to rope my trunk and strap my suitcases for shipment to Nashville, Tennessee. "Jesse, it's a plum shame that you are leavin' here. You know I hate to see you go worse than if you was one of my boys. I've knowed your Ma since she was a little girl wearin' ribbons on her hair. They ain't no better woman than your Ma. They ain't no better man than your Pap. Your Pap's the hardest-workin' man in this county. He grumbles a lot but he's a good man. You know I hate to see you go."

"Well, Uncle Rank, I don't mind to go but I can't see my way through. It's going to be a little hard, you know, without money, and work so hard to get. But you can't blame me for leaving here. This county is not big enough for Trevis Blair and me. He won this time. When I get a thing to move along, Blair steps in and tells me to do it another way." "Jesse, Son, I don't blame you. I've been interested in knowin' how all this thing is goin' to work out. I don't blame you for leaving him." "I'd face starvation before I'd stay." "You'll be back here again sometime. You know boys always come back to drink of the lonesome waters they left at home."

"Well, Uncle Rank, the bus is coming. Won't you go along with me?" "No, Jesse, the Old Woman is a-makin' apple butter and

I promised her I'd be back to stir it for her by nine o'clock. It's nearly ten now. She'll comb my hair, Jesse." "Well, here, Uncle Rank, let's shake good-by for a while." The old man turned away with tears in his eyes when he saw me go. That is the clannish brotherhood we have among the hill people. It is great to live among people like Uncle Rank Larks.

On my way to Vanderbilt University, I thought of such names as Davidson, Wade, Mims, Curry, Warren and Ransom. They were all well-known teachers and writers. I would rather be with them than be principal of a county high school. I was tired of teaching school anyway. I was tired of everything. If I lived always in Greenup County, I could never get anywhere writing. I needed contact with men like Ransom, Davidson, Curry, Mims, Warren and Wade. I was afraid, for I didn't have the promise of work. I had only $130. It would not go far in Vanderbilt University.

I didn't know anyone in Vanderbilt. But I said to myself: "You're turning to be a damn coward now! Have you got clay feet? W'y hell, go on and meet things like you have met them before!"

All that I told myself didn't matter. I was afraid and didn't know why. I was a stranger and I was afraid. When I registered at Vanderbilt University, I told Doctor Mims the circumstances. "It looks as if you've got something big before you, Stuart. I don't see how in the world you can do it and do yourself justice." He was right. But I was not turning back. I was going through with the ordeal. Hell, stand up and face the thing like a student should. Why show clay feet on the spur of the moment when the whole tryout was coming off? Well, I was going to stay.

As I was walking up Wesley Hall stairway, I saw between me and the murky September light the familiar outline of a tall rugged man sitting at the window. His face was turned toward the smoke-clouded city. I had almost passed him when he glanced round. It was Ron East! "Stuart, what in the world has brought you here!" "More education... my M.A. What brought you here?" "I'm getting my D.D. this year, preaching and working in the slums." "Same old Ron East!" "In flesh and blood but not in spirit. I've been kicked out of three churches since I preached in the mountains. I've seen so much human suffering, Stuart, that I've grown bitter. I've been trying to save human beings on earth instead of preaching to them of a reward in Heaven."

Strange the paths of destiny where they cross and recross. Ron East, six feet three, a great cross-country runner, a great high jumper. His heart big as all-out-of-doors. Didn't he used to work his way at Lincoln Memorial and send his poor parents money to support a big family? Didn't he carry baskets of grub that he bought with the money from his own pockets to the mountain people in Poor Valley? Didn't he often go there and preach the funeral for one of the mountain dead and do all the singing too at the funeral when there was no one to help him? Hadn't I found a friend at Vanderbilt University! Didn't he always tell me on the cross-country runs that the man a step ahead of me was just as likely to fall as I was, and to vomit and keep going? Didn't he always lead the pack of us and come in first at the end of the five miles, hurdling the fences a mule couldn't jump? I always felt as strong as a mountain alone, and as strong as two mountains when with Ron East.

Wesley Hall, Vanderbilt University campus, 1930
(Courtesy Photographic Archives, Vanderbilt University)

"Why don't you register in the School of Religion, Stuart? You can get by there on the money you have." "Hell, I can't preach. I don't ever intend to. If I were called on to lead in prayer, I'd sink through the floor." "That's not the thing, damn it! Others are doing it and they're not ministerial students. You could too." "Yes, but do you know what they are when they use religion for a blind like that? They are a bunch of cheats. That's exactly what they are. I don't intend to do it unless I have to leave Vanderbilt University. Then I'd have to drop two of the courses that I'm taking in the English department for a couple of courses in the School of Religion. Well, I don't intend to do it."

I spent all my money for registering the first quarter and shipping my trunk and typewriter and bringing myself. I had four dollars I held out when I registered, but at the Business Office I had to make a note to the university for eight dollars. Well, there was nothing left to buy books with. I'd have to borrow or do without. The first quarter I had mostly to do without. I took examinations and never studied for them. They made flat impressions on the faculty members—a graduate student to do no better among the undergraduates of the university! But I couldn't do any better. Vanderbilt was so much bigger than Lincoln Memorial. Everything was different. My mind was in a muddle. If ever I could get lined out just right, I'd show them I wasn't a fake. But I could never get a chance. I was with many very bright students.

One day I stepped up to Oscar Boswell and said: "I think you had a very good poem in the university magazine, last issue. The poem was about the ghosts of dead leaves following you on the street." "I'm glad you think it was poetry. I do not." But I knew he did think it was poetry. He only said those words for false modesty. "Well, I try scribbling verse too. I've placed a few poems in one-horse magazines." He only smiled.

I believed that he didn't believe me. I think that he thought I was a faker.

I went down the corridor of the hall and up the street. I thought if I were to tell these teachers at Vanderbilt University that I wrote over five-hundred poems in three years and did regular classwork and worked my way in Lincoln Memorial, they would not believe me. They would think I was a newspaper crooner—a poem-a-day keeps the doctor away.

It was just in me to write poetry and I did not suppress the desire. Poetry took me along. It made me its servant. I couldn't handle poetry. That is funny to say but I heard Lum Dryasdust say something funnier at Vanderbilt: "I'm reading the sonnets of Shakespeare now. I'm getting inspiration from them to write. I'm reading Edgar Allan Poe's *Poetic Principles*, about how to construct verse. I'm going to sit down and write poetry when I get my term papers off and have a little time. I want to be a poet. I want to write novels too."

Oh, dear Lum Dryasdust! You are taking poetry along with you. It doesn't have you by the heels and drag you everywhere you go, through the steel mills, and the leaves, through the pasture fields and the cornfields, through the tie-timber woods, at the plow and everywhere you go. No, you are going to sit down and write poetry, when you get ready. All I have to say is don't tell everybody about it. Poetry puts you down and makes you write. Edgar Allan Poe is not going to tell you to do anything He is only a human being too. You have to be your own self. Poetry will tell you to let the term papers go to hell. It will make you lie to your teachers.

For three weeks I went daily to see the university Y.M.C.A. man for work. He found me a job. It was selling tickets for an automobile concern on High Avenue. I sell the book of tickets for a dollar. I get fifty cents of the dollar. But the head of the fellows selling these books at Vanderbilt University gets a nickel out of my fifty cents. But forty-five cents isn't half bad. I work me up a sales talk like this: "Hello, Mister. Would you be interested in a bargain for your car repairs?" "No." "Oh, now wait here just a minute. Look at this! Two car washes absolutely free. That's worth a dollar of any man's money. Now over on the little blue ticket—look at this! A free rim inspection. Two of them." "That don't amount to nothing. I can do that myself." "All right then. Over to the little green ticket, two green tickets. Look at this. Two free greases with a change of oil each time, that is, you must pay for the oil." "Oh, yes, I thought there was a catch to this." "Now just a minute. You've not seen all of this. Over to the two yellow tickets. Within a radius of five miles, if your car runs out of gas, all you've got to do is call this garage, and they bring it to you at the regular price. Now what do you think of that! Over to the orange tickets. Now here's the fine thing about this ticket book. Here's the best thing in it. You get two flat tires fixed free here with this book of tickets. Now you just think about it." "Say, how much is this book of tickets anyway?" "Only one dollar." "Here's your money. I thought it was ten or twelve dollars the way you was showing me through it." "I didn't want you to miss a bargain like that."

I had no faith in the bargain myself. I wanted the forty-five cents. I had faith at first, but once I went and stood in front of this garage and the manager chased me away. "I'm selling your own products. I'm helping you and I'm helping myself." "But hell, you'll ruin our trade." "Well, what did you put out any such thing for? My heavens, put out a bargain and then be afraid to let one of your agents sell it in front of your garage." "Yes, but don't argue with me. You go now. Don't you know you are going to ruin us standing here?" "Before I go I'd like to leave something with you. It isn't a stick of dynamite either. Here, take this damn pack of 'bargains' and keep them for yourself. But be sure and don't put them off on the people. I want to keep one of them." I pulled one out and stuck it in my pocket. "What are you doing that for?" "To show my authority." The truth was I wanted to sell one more and go to the Paramount to a show. I sold that one and went to the show.

I was ashamed to ask the university teachers I knew to buy one. What would they think of me? But I sold them to the fellows at Wesley Hall. When I thought of a possible sale to a friend, I sent John, the boy that sold with me, to him. It doesn't pay to sell bargains to one's friends.

Then I went back to Mr. Hart at the Y.M.C.A. for more work. "Mr. Hart, that job's played out." "What job, Jesse?" "Oh, selling the garage bargains." "Garage bargains!" He laughed. "Yes, I've got a job in mind for you. It is big enough for two good fellows. You know this man Horton that sweeps Science Hall?" "No." "Well, he is a preacher from Wesley Hall and he's keeping a wife and baby on that job. It pays fifteen dollars a week." "Good. Can I get it? Where is Science Hall anyway?" "You pass it every day. See that brick building over there." "Yes." "Well, that's it. Now, there is a lot of work about it. It is supposed to keep one man busy all day long. Two boys are supposed to spend twenty-six hours a week there. I mean twenty-six hours apiece. Will that hurt you much, Jesse, in your graduate work?" "Yes, that'll knock a big hole in my time but I'll try to do it. You know I've got to have money and I can't get it." "Well, you and Easton go down and see Mr. Abernethy right now. Six fellows are trying for the place."

Mr. Abernethy was a pleasant fellow to talk to. He told us he had worked his way at the university. We got the job. We started work on Wednesday. I think my clothes helped me along as well as my tongue. He saw my worn shirt with split places around the shoulder.

Well, for nearly three months, I worked seven hours a day and did graduate work. I went out at six o'clock and worked until seven. Then I went back at two and worked until five. I worked an average of two hours each day in the cafeteria. I went to the football games and I took a notion to get a job selling programs. I was told I could not get that as all the boys had been selected to sell the programs. I remembered the time I was fired for hitting a boy in the face with a piece of watermelon and how I went over and began working with the second gang of men and it was never noticed. Well, I would just go down and get myself an armload of programs and start selling. It worked beautifully. I made a little money and saw all the games free.

But the work at Science Hall with a fellow as slow as Easton was getting to be monotonous. Of the thousands of men I have worked with, at fifty or more different kinds of work, Easton was the biggest ass. He had gone to the Hall and Horton took him around and showed him how everything had to be done. When I began work the next day, Easton started showing me, and he tried to keep it up for weeks afterwards. At first, we started sweeping all the rooms together. I swept three and sometimes four rooms to his one. He was slow and he was lazy. Finally I said: "Easton, I'll clean half the building and you clean the other half. Now I'll divide the building and give you your choice, or you divide the building and give me my choice. Just the way that suits you."

When we did this, I had plenty of time to spare. Rister was our boss. He was the boss over fifty-eight black janitors and two white janitors. He told us to put in our time. He told us to stay there twenty-six and one-half hours each week. I told him I could do my half of the building in one hour. "You can't do it and do it right." "You stay with me and see." One night I did it in forty-six minutes. I cleaned the floors and the blackboards of six rooms, two halls, three offices and two flights of stairs. I talked to Mr. Abernethy about leaving early. He said it was all right if I did my work well. Easton always watched for me to leave the building. He went then and told Rister that I'd slipped out. Rister went about trying to find more things for me to do. When I left early, he went about looking for me. He thought I had a hiding place in the building. But I was going to the dormitory and studying.

He examined my timecard over at the powerhouse, where all the janitors and campus laborers checked out in the afternoon and in, in the morning. He found it was punched very inconsistently and sometimes had not been punched at all. I always took a pencil at the end of the week and fixed the card in good order before it went into Abernethy. Rister came and told me I'd have to check in and out on time. He said he was afraid he'd lose his job if I didn't. I didn't want to see him lose a job where he felt as if he was president of the university.

One morning he sent me to the supply house to get eleven rolls of toilet paper and a gallon of antiseptic to drench the commodes with in Science Hall. He came down a few minutes after I had reached the supply room. I ran a wire through the roles of toilet paper and then wrapped them up with a wide piece of brown wrapping paper. I was ready to cross the campus now. "What are you wrapping that toilet paper up for?" "I don't want those girls standing up there on the walk to see me carrying it across the campus." "Oh, you don't? Well, all the other janitors do it." "Well, here's one sure as hell not doing it, Rister. I am a janitor but I'm not going up across that campus with an armload of toilet paper." Rister looked at me. He said: "Well, ain't girls seen it before?" "That may be true, but don't we have a certain amount of decency between us and self-respect? If we didn't we'd all use the same toilets." Rister didn't like the attitude I took toward him. He wanted to say things to me, but by the way he approached me I knew he was afraid.

The job only lasted till January the first, then Horton was to take it back. Easton had quit now. I had one distinction. I was the only white janitor at the university. It was during the Christmas holidays that I made my last trip down to Science Hall. I went down to work. I was going over the woodwork and polishing it with wax. I had got seven dollars per week instead of seven and a half like the colored janitors got. I asked Rister about it. He promised me seven-fifty hereafter. But when I went down this morning to work, I threw my broom across the room and kicked a light bulb out with the toe of my shoe. I had been trying every morning to break that bulb, but I could never kick that high before. I don't know whether Rister was hunting for me or not. I know that was my last job at Science Hall. I left the clothes there that I had worked in.

And now I went again to hunt for work. I tried to get a job at newspaper reporting. I tried both city papers. I went all over Nashville trying. One night I stood at the corner of Church Street and wrote this on an envelope:

Courage Be With Us All

Be with me, courage, for I walk alone,
Although I have no fear of night and gloom.
The earth is wide and there is spacious room
For human creatures on her streets of stone.

Be with me, courage, in this trying hour
When stars are hard to barter for thin bread,
(Be with us all in this dark hour of need)
The lonely poor with dreams, the rich with power.

The leafless tree in winter stands alone
Dreaming of leafy days and sunny Spring
When birds alighted in her boughs to sing.
Now somewhere out by changing winds I'm blown,
A yellow leaf to drift with time away
The silver moments of my swift brief day.

It was Christmas time now and people in Nashville were buying presents. The city was a busy place. The windows were decorated with Christmas tree trimmings. I wanted to go home for Christmas. But I had used all the money I made sweeping at Science Hall as fast as I got it. I couldn't go home. The cafeteria was not getting much trade, and for three days it was closed entirely. The workers there were cut to one-third of their regular time.

With two dollars in my pocket, on January 4th I caught a ride through from Nashville to Ashland, Kentucky. I was going home to spend one day. I had to make the trip. A note at the bank was coming due and I wanted to talk to the banker and get him to renew it. I didn't want the man and woman who were giving my security to have to pay it. I hadn't intended them to. The note was for the money I had borrowed to enter Vanderbilt University.

When I reached Greenup, I thought no more of stars being hard to barter for thin bread. I was among people like Uncle Rank Larks. I'd get to help him eat some of the apple butter he had helped his wife make last September when I left. But only for a day. The time was too short. On Monday, January 5th, I was in Greenup. My friends would say: "Say, you're looking good. Getting plenty to eat, I suppose." "Oh, yes, I'm getting plenty." "Well, we don't have very much and don't expect you can stand our grub, but if you can come around and stay a week with us, we'd be glad to have you." Then another would say: "Say, ain't you got enough education yet? That head'll be a-bustin' open the first thing you know. You'd better quit a-goin' to school so much and get the benefit of your education. Run for County School Superintendent. This county's a-wantin' you. Blair can't be elected again. W'y, everybody I've heard talk is for you. Youngins shore liked you up there at that high school last year."

The first Monday in every month is sales day in Greenup. Men from all parts of the county and from the adjoining counties come to buy, sell and trade. Horse trading is very popular. "Look at that mare, Bill. She's a plum good 'un. She's not a day over seven years old. Look at her teeth. Hell, Bill, she's a plum good 'un." It's hard to find a horse over seven in Greenup on sales day. Plenty of them are over seventeen. "Look there. See that feller a-goin' with that string of old plug horses. That's Rufus Yellowhammer. He comes down here every sales day and buys 'em like that, and he gets them for around a dollar apiece. Then he takes them back out here on town ridge and kills them for their hides. You know I think a man ought to be swung up to a limb when he gits that onery."

I remembered old Rufus when I was a youngster in Greenup High School. He was buying horses then and killing them for their hides. One day when I was on the town ridge, I saw Rufus driving nine plug horses out on the ridge. He had his brother Cy with him. One of the horses stopped to get a drink at a spring. "Cy, hit that horse across the tail and start it on. It won't need water anymore." The horses were eating the dead leaves and the old dead stalks of life-everlasting as they went along. They were hungry horses with bad teeth.

The fox hunters' hounds would get fat on horse carrion. They would get lazy. They wouldn't hunt for the fox. When they did start the fox, they were so short of breath that they couldn't run far until they fell out of the chase. The crows would blacken the trees around the slaughter grounds. The buzzards would sail above and wait for the hounds to leave. Then they would fly down and get their share. Soon there would be many white skeletons gleaming in the winter sun. Cy Yellowhammer would come and haul the bones away to sell for fertilizer. Greenup is the dumping ground of the county for plug horses. The Rufus Yellowhammers and the Alec Stubblefields are there to get the give-aways. Horses under seven! Farmers had got the best of these horses on their rough Kentucky farms. When the horses were old, many farmers let fellows like Rufus Yellowhammer have them to take out and kill and skin for their hides and let their bodies be eaten by the crows, buzzards and the hound dogs, and their carcasses would whiten the autumn hilltops.

Horse traders are running their horses up and down the streets. Men are buying winter onion sets at a corner grocery. Down at another corner, men are selling clothes from a truck. They are bidding them off to the bystanders. The truck is from Ashland, Kentucky. "All right! All right! Who'll buy this nice pair of pants? Ten cents! Do I hear a better bid? Ten, fifteen, twenty, twenty-five, thirty! All right, thirty cents now! A nice pair of moleskin pants! Any higher? All right, come up and get your pants! They are dirt cheap—thirty cents. Here is a woman's coat. [He lifts it up from the truck bed and everybody laughs.] It looks a little bad, Folks, but there's shore some good stuff in that there coat. Who'll buy? Who'll buy? Who'll give me a nickel for it? All right, Tightwads. Now see who wants the coat."

He throws the coat out into the crowd and two women grab it. They quarrel over the coat. The quarrel brings madness. The town policeman steps in and takes the coat and the women off toward the jail.

In the courthouse square, there is a crowd and each person is trying to peep over another person's head. They are all trying to gather closer into a huddle. I hear the fiddle and the guitar. I hear long-drawn-out sentimental voices. It is Blind Hartley and his blind wife:

> "In London far city a lady did dwell,
> Concerning her beauty no tongue can tell.

"He courted Pretty Polly the livelong night,
  And then just to rob her before daylight.

"'Come home, Pretty Polly, and go along with me,
  Before we get married some pleasure we'll see.'

"He led her over hills and through valleys so deep,
  At last Pretty Polly began for to weep.

"'Willie, Oh Willie, I'm afraid of your ways,
  I'm afeared you're a-leadin' my body astray.'

"She trusted him a piece farther and what did she spy,
  But a new-dug grave and two spades a-lying by.

"'Polly, Pretty Polly, you're guessing just right,
  I've finished your grave I was digging last night.'

"She threw her arms around him, she trembled with fear,
  'How can you kill a poor girl that loves you so dear?'

"'No time for to talk, no time for to stand,'
  He came with his knife all in his right hand.

"He stabbed her to the heart and the heart blood did flow,
  Down in her grave Pretty Polly must go.

"He threw the sod over her and he turned to go home,
  And left little birds to weep and to mourn."

The men and boys, one by one, walked up and dropped
something in the blind man's hat. There was silence in the crowd.
"Now play something purty lively, Doc; I want to get these old legs
of mine limbered up. I've been hauling crossties all week. I 'spect
I'm a little stiff." "What do you want, Jim?" "Oh, I always liked that

'Old Sourwood Mountain' piece, and tell your wife to kindly hold that guitar down so I can hear the fiddle. All right, let her go now."

> "Chicken crowing on Sourwood Mountain,
>   Hey ho diddle dum dee-ay.
> Get your dogs and we'll go a-hunting,
>   Hey ho diddle dum dee-ay.
>
> "My true love she lives in Letcher,
>   Hey ho diddle dum dee-ay.
> She won't come and I won't fetch her,
>   Hey ho diddle dum dee-ay.
>
> "My true love she's a blue-eyed daisy,
>   Hey ho diddle dum dee-ay.
> If I don't get her I'll go crazy,
>   Hey ho diddle dum dee-ay.
>
> "Big dogs bark and the little dogs bite you,
>   Hey ho diddle dum dee-ay.
> Big girls court and the little girls slight you,
>   Hey ho diddle dum dee-ay.
>
> "My true love lives up the river,
>   Hey ho diddle dum dee-ay.
> A few more jumps and I'll be with her,
>   Hey ho diddle dum dee-ay.
>
> "My true love lives in the hollow,
>   Hey ho diddle dum dee-ay.
> She won't come and I won't follow,
>   Hey ho diddle dum dee-ay."

"Boy, Jim, you shorely rested on them plow handles a lot if that made your legs stiff. I couldn't see them working." "Jim, Old

Boy, that's the way we used to step it off back in them good old days. People can't dance like that nowadays. They just get up and belly-rub a little. Ain't I seen 'em right down here at this garage of Charlie Bennett's get right in there and belly-rub. They had a lot of old tinhorn music and called it good music and good dancin'." "Jim, that's fine for an old man like you." "Say, I ain't old. I's only sixty-eight last March." Everybody laughs with Jim Washburn. "Say, don't let the music stop. Waitin' on money, Doc? Well, here's a half dollar right out'en my old terbacker money." "Thank you, Cy. What do you want us to play for you?" "Can you play 'The Hangman's Song'?" "Yes, Sir. Wait till I get a little resin on my bow."

I was waiting for the song too. I had heard it from infancy. I loved it as much as any hillman. I thought: "If getting educated makes me hate old-time music and old mountain ballads, then I'm not getting along very well with my education." I could never lose my love and appreciation for them. I didn't want to. The mountain people are the happiest people in the world. Go off to college and get educated and lose appreciation for things you loved before you went away. Go away and live in the air, forget the earth; come back home and put your feet on the earth again. See how you feel. You'll know a lot of the stuff you've been taught is damn tommyrot. Get educated so that you can know God. Oh, my heavens, how foolish! I cry out against it all. I know it is all different. It's foolish to get educated to know God. Get close to the soil and know Him. Get educated and forget life. That's what you'll do if you're not careful.

I shall be silent now. I shall not dream. I shall listen to the words my uncle sang to me in the long ago:

The Hangman's Song

> "Hangman, Hangman, slack up your rope,
>   O slack it for a while,
>   I looked over yonder and I see Pa comin',
>   He's walked for many a mile."

"Say, Pa, say, Pa, have you brung me any gold,
  Any gold for to pay my fine?"
"No sir, no sir, I've brung you no gold,
  No gold for to pay your fine,
  But I've just come to see you hanged,
  Hanged on the gallows line."
"Oh won't you love and it's hard to be beloved
  And it's hard to make up your time,
  You have broke the heart of many a truelove,
  Truelove, but you won't break mine."

"Hangman, Hangman, slack up your rope,
  O slack it for a while,
  I looked over yonder and I see Ma comin',
  She's walked for many a long mile."

"Say, Ma, say, Ma, have you brung me any gold,
  Any gold for to pay my fine?"
"No sir, no sir, I've brung you no gold,
  No gold for to pay your fine,
  But I've just come for to see you hanged,
  Hanged on the gallows line."
"Oh won't you love and it's hard to be beloved
  And it's hard to make up your time,
  You have broke the heart of many a truelove,
  Truelove, but you won't break mine."

"Hangman, Hangman, slack up your rope,
  O slack it for a while,
  I looked over yonder and I see my sweetheart comin',
  She's walked for many a long mile."
"Sweetheart, Sweetheart, have you brung me any gold,
  Any gold for to pay my fine?"

"Yes sir, yes sir, I've brought you some gold,
 Some gold for to pay your fine,
 For I've just come for to take you home,
 From on the gallows line."

I wish my professor Donald Davidson could be in Greenup. He could hear plenty of the old songs now. Only drop a nickel, a dime, a quarter into the hat. "Doc, I want you to play and sing, 'The Little Mohee.' Can you play that?" "Oh, yes."

The Little Mohee

"As I went out walking all by the seashore
 The wind it did whistle, the water did roar.

"As I sat a-musing myself on the grass,
 O, who did I spy, but a fair Indian lass.

"She came and sat by me and took hold of my hand
 And said, 'You are a stranger and in a strange land.

"'But if you will follow, you are welcome to come
 And dwell in the cottage where I call it my home.'

"The sun was fast sinking far over the blue sea,
 As I wandered along with my little Mohee.

"Together we wandered, together we roamed,
 Till I came to the cottage in the coconut grove.

"She asked me to marry and offered her hand
 Saying, 'My father's the Chieftain of all this fair land.
"'My father's a Chieftain and ruler can be,
 I'm his only daughter, my name is Mohee.'

"'Oh no, my dear maiden, that never can be,
  I have a dear sweetheart in my own countree.

"'I will not forsake her, I know she loves me,
  Her heart is as true as any Mohee.'

"It was early one morning, Monday morning in May,
  I broke her poor heart by the words I did say.

"'I'm going to leave you, so fare you well, my dear.
  My ship's spreads are now spreading, over home I must
  steer.'

"The last time I saw her she knelt on the strand,
  Just as my boat passed her, she waved me her hand,

"Saying, 'When you get over with the girl you love
  O remember the Mohee in the coconut grove.'

"And when I had landed with the girl that I love,
  Both friends and relatives gathered around me once more.

"I gazed all about me, not one did I see
  That really did compare with my little Mohee.

"And the girl I had trusted had proved untrue to me,
  So I says, 'I'll turn my courses back over the sea.

"'I'll turn my courses and backward I'll flee,
  I'll go and spend my days with my little Mohee.'"

The music is smothered by the cries of horse traders. I wish
they'd trade down around the jailhouse in Greenup. That's where

they're supposed to trade horses. This part of the town, the courthouse square, is for loafers, judges, tired farmers on Saturdays, lawyers, insurance agents, housewives waiting for their husbands to drive the teams around from the hitching places, anybody that is tired and wants to rest. For anybody that is lazy or anybody that wants to be seen, the Greenup County Courthouse Square is the place. "Say, Tom, don't you know I got fined five dollars for hitching my horse to Poker Mullin's fence. What you know about that? This damn town's getting more like New York every day. But Tom, I went and talked to Burton Bailey about it. Old Burton said: 'Alec, now don't you worry, Old Boy. They can't run the law over me. I'll get you out of it. You remember me when election time comes around.' And Tom, I'm goin' to remember old Burton, don't you worry."

A preacher is preaching at the corner in front of the First National Bank. Some old gray-headed men are standing there with their hats in their hands. The man and his wife and daughter sing. The woman plays a guitar, the girl a tambourine. The man begins to preach. His preaching drowns our music. We have a crowd. He has only a few followers. He says: "Lord God, you see the little crowd I have here. Here are Thy patriarchs, Lord, these old men before me. Here they are, Lord. They are nearly ready for you to receive into Thine own hands. Oh, I wish I could call more of them unto You. Now, Lord, right over there, look at that old man. He can't get to Heaven on dancing feet. [Jim was dancing again to the tune of "Turkey in the Straw."] Lord, he is an old man and his hair is turning white. And, Lord, right over at that corner is a couple of men cheating the widows, the orphans and the poor people, selling them old clothes. Jar them, Lord, with a thunderbolt. You can do it. Let us make Greenup a new Jerusalem. We can do it. Now I want to ask for a little offering here, Folks. Just a little offering. Play 'Nearer My God to Thee,' Rosie." "We don't pay for our religion. We get it free. What air you, one of them Holy Rollers?" "You ain't paying for my religion, either. You are just paying the cost on it." "Well, in Baptist Church, by-grabs, you don't have to do that. I'll go back to

them old Baptists. I know they air right." The preacher doesn't get
but a few nickels and dimes. He, his wife Rosie and their daughter
leave. We can hear our music now.

Loving Nancy

"The heart is the fortune of all women kind,
  They are always controlled, but are always confined;
  Controlled by their parents until they are wives,
  Then slaves for their husbands the rest of their lives.

"I've always been a poor girl, my fortune has been bad,
  I've often been courted by the wagoner's lad;
  He courted me daily by night and by day,
  And then for to leave me and going away.

"My parents don't like me because I am poor,
  They say I'm not worthy of entering their door;
  I work for my living, my money's my own,
  And if they don't like me they can leave me alone.

"The cuckoo is a pretty bird, she sings as she flies,
  She gives us glad tidings, she tells us no lies;
  She feeds on sweet flowers to make her voice clear
  And never hollas 'cuckoo' 'til spring of the year.

"'Go put up your horses and feed them some hay,
  Come and sit you down by me, while you have to stay.'
  'My horses are not hungry, they won't eat your hay,
  So farewell, Loving Nancy, I'll feed on the way.'

"'Your wagon needs greasing, your bill is to pay,
  Come and sit you down by me, while you have to stay.'
  'My wagon is greasy, my whip's in my hand,
  So farewell, Loving Nancy, I've no time for to stand.'"

The Sheriff is taking two men to jail. His deputies are helping him. The men are trying to fight. "Too much corn," says one of our crowd. It must be three o'clock and I have not started out home yet. I have four miles to walk. I must soon be going. Now is the time. I see Doctor Torrey coming across the street. He sees me. I shall miss him. I know what he is going to talk about, and I don't want to hear it. He's going to say, "Well, how do you do, Young Man? When did you get in? I've just been telling the boys around here that I was once a boy like you. Like you, I got my education out yonder on that hill first in a little log house under some oak trees. The boys laughed at my grub, which I took in a split-bottom basket. They laughed at my clothes. But I beat them all. Yes, I beat all them boys. Purt' nigh all of 'em dead now. I beat them, I want you to know. I taught three months of school each year, and then I went to college. I went to college for three months every year for three years. Then I began to practice up there at Brighton. You know where that little place is. Well, I starved out. I couldn't even shoe my horse with what I made. The seat was out of my pants and the elbows out of my coat sleeves. But I got my education. And I went back and took three months more work to make me a heart specialist.

"Ah, but times are changing nowadays. Boys go off and stay years to be a doctor, and they come back and don't know nothing. I made my money when I left Brighton and come to Greenup. I went day and night. I made good money. I got mine out there on that hill just like you did, and I got mine in college like you did. I just went off and my Pap didn't want me to go. He wasn't able to send me. But I went anyhow. And you see I've got mine and you can get yours, if you'll come back here and take that school up there and buckle down to it." I saw him coming. I left the town.

I went up Hungry Hollow past Uncle Rank Larks' place. He was not at home. I went up through an old apple orchard and then through a dogwood thicket. The sun was setting over town ridge about the spot where Rufus Yellowhammer killed his horses. I could see the white bones gleaming in the setting sun. I could see the scars winter had left on the soil. I was happy to be back among the Kentucky dogwood trees and the long black outlines of hills with smoke settled down in the valleys. Dark hills tinted by a setting sun, going down over January oak treetops and horse bones. It was great to be back. I wanted to forget that I'd been away.

I walked into a patch of black-oak trees at the edge of a cornfield. I used to walk this path to school and look at these very trees. I wanted to put my arms around them. I wanted to touch the bark, the rough black bark. I did put my hands on it. I wanted to put my face down against the dead leaves on the ground. I heard the wind rustling a few of the dead leaves that still hung to black outlines of trees. It was getting dark now. The stars were coming out. The moon was coming up. I had stayed from sundown until moon-up among the dogwood trees and the black-oaks. They were my friends. I couldn't go back home and not see them. But the wind sang lonesome-like in the bleak treetops. The January wind was bending the treetops and rattling the fodder blades in the shocks standing in the cornfield at the edge of the woods.

Oh, but it was great to be back again! I could forget school life. I could be free. I could run with the wind. I could act crazy out there on the ridge. There was no one to see me. And right there by the side of the road was the white-oak stump, where I sat and wrote:

The Trail

This trail that leads me to my mountain hut
Has lonely breaks, strange turnings down the wild;
And weeds are growing in the wagon rut.
These country splendors cover mile on mile.
Nights, I have gone this way through mud and mire,
Wet cornfield winds sang with a lonesome sound;
The tilted moon, a strip of yellow fire,
Threw a dim lantern light on sodden ground.
With these strong legs and rapid mountain stride;
With blood strong as the mountain waters flow;

With heart of sumac clay, with rustic pride
I move into the hillside world I know.
I know my supper's waiting for me now,
And seven strong, we'll soon be gathered there
To eat and drink, forget the field and plow—
Let hills be stubborn here, we do not care.

Then after supper's done we'll sing and play,
And dance and tell the tales of warriors old;
For many times I've heard my grandsires say:
"Live happy now for soon you're sleeping cold."
We do live happy, don't you ever doubt,
We drink our wild-grape wine and apple gin,
We hear the storm winds blow the leaves about,
We wonder if the cattle are housed in.

Dear path of earth, lead me the olden way,
Give me the lonely break and road-run rut,
And let me keep a heart of sumac clay;
And in its core an image of my hut.
I am no better than my fathers were
Who now sleep on a dark Kentucky hill,
And once they tilled that soil, these first pioneers,
Now in its bosom lie forever still.

I'll follow on beneath white swarms of stars;
I'll follow black-oak stubbornness that's free;
Within these hills there are no prison bars
To cage the wiry flesh and mind of me.
Then beat, you winds, against my barren breast;
Fall, moonlight, on this trail that leads me on,
I am the blood of those now seeking rest,
Pioneers now gone to meet and conquer dawn.

It had been five years since I sat on that stump and wrote the poem one December night that I came home when I was a student in Lincoln Memorial.

The orchard I had set out in 1926 stood out in the moonlight. There were many dead weeds around the trees. I saw a rabbit run out through the dead weeds and sit down. The wind whipped through the fine peach-tree branches. It shook the stout young apple trees. January and home again, the house in sight! They were all up. I heard their voices. Home again! Just across a little pasture field and I would be there.

"Well, my heavens, look who's come! Pa, get out'n th' bed, Jesse's here! Well, we're all together again." It is a great time for us. We are all together again! "James, I thought you would be gone back to Berea College. Stand up there and let me look at you." "I'm tall as you are now." "How tall are you?" "I'm six feet and weigh one-hundred and forty-one pounds." "It can't be, and you fifteen! You went away weighing one-hundred and three pounds. You were just a kid." We made a comparison of grades we had made. He was working his way at Berea College.

"Well, Jesse, don't you know schoolwork has softened me. I can't hunt like I did. I can't shoot like I did. I don't care as much about hunting as I used to care. I've only killed fourteen rabbits and eleven birds since I've been home. I missed a couple of times at the birds. I aimed too low when they were flying up into the air. That's why I missed. I got all the rabbits on the run. I never missed one rabbit."

"Supper's been waiting so long it's got cold. We heard you's in town. It made me kindly mad you didn't come right on out." "Mom, I heard 'Loving Nancy' played and sung the sweetest I've ever heard it. A blind man and his blind wife played 'Loving Nancy' and a lot of other ballads I've heard all my life. I just couldn't get out of Greenup. It was so warm and pretty today and everybody stirring around in Greenup at the sales day."

"Yes, but didn't you know we wanted you to stay all the time? I have had so many things I wanted to talk to you about. Now, get you a chair, get your feet under the table there and help yourself. I guess you've been having so many good things to eat you can't eat this old rough grub we have here." "Yes, I've been having a lot of good things to eat, but I never get tired of your cooking. Reach me over another piece of that chicken. Yes, I'll take a pickle. What about a piece of that sausage? Has it got sage in it? You know, the way you used to fix it. Was this ham smoked with green hickory? I thought it was. You know that is the way I like it. Yes, I'll take another piece of hot corn bread. I want some of the butter down there at your end of the table to go on this bread. Mom, you know that buttermilk is just good and sour, just the way I like it. I'm ready for another piece of chicken and a pickle.

"Pa, how are you? You look like you went to bed before I got in." "Yes, I laid down in there to take a nap. I know when you come in. But I wanted to let your Ma talk to you a little while. You know I've got to kindly let her have you. In there's the boy that takes after his Pap, that Jim. Now, that boy looks like the Stuarts. You look like your Ma's people. Well, how you been gettin' along at school? Having plenty to eat and making good grades, I guess." "Oh yes—I'm doing both." "I told your Ma if anybody could take care of hisself you would. You know she's been worrying around about you boys, mostly James. He's so much younger, you know. Neither one of you got any money."

"Don't worry about either one of us. We'll take care of ourselves. You've got enough to worry about here at home. You owe on the place yet. You have plenty to worry about." "But a man will worry about his children some, even if he does have debts hanging over him. Your Ma sells cream and eggs and sends James a little every week. That's a lot of help to him down there. I got kindly uneasy about him when he first went away. I sent for him to come home. He quit writing to me. So we just left him alone. Only got one of you here now. Glennis, and she is learning mighty fast. She went up a grade in November. Miss Hisel said up until now she had the best record at Plum Grove."

"Say, Pa, pass me a piece of chicken." "Just take you off a

couple of pieces. You'll eat 'em if you eat like you used to eat. Look at the bones around your plate now. Throw them under the table if anybody comes in." "You know this old country grub sticks to the ribs, don't it, Mom? Another sausage and glass of buttermilk and I'll call it a good meal."

"Now, Jesse, is the best time you could run for County School Superintendent. I want you to have that once in your life. Everybody is for you in the county that I've heard talk. Now, I want you to run. You can get it." "Pa, how's your corn holding out?" "We're not talking about corn. We are talking about the County School Superintendent."

James and I go to bed in our old room upstairs. We lie awake. We look out at the stars. We talk. "Jesse, when I was in the grades at Plum Grove, I thought it was a big place. When I went to Greenup County High School, I thought that was a wonderful place. Now since I've been away at Berea College and come back, Greenup County High School is a small place. I was down there Friday and saw all the gang. When they saw how I'd grown, they all laughed. I was glad to see them all. But I don't want to ever go to school there again. I just about read that library through there, but I can't read the library through at Berea."

"James, I felt the same way about Plum Grove and Greenup being big places when I went there. And you graduated from Greenup County High School three days younger than I was when I started down at the old building in my first year. You are leaving the hills and you are very young. Do you feel like you want to come home and farm again?" "No, I want to stay in Berea. I want to stay there until I finish. If I can get the money, I shall stay there that long. I shall never return home and farm unless something happens that I just have to do it."

We talked nearly all night about hunting trips and fishing trips and about the school days we had spent at the same schools. The clear January sky was bright with stars. They glittered like bright jewels in the big blue bowl of night sky. The moon came up above the pine tops on the hill and like a strip of crescent yellow raced swiftly among the white clouds in the big, big bowl of blue. The white clouds were fish, the sky was blue water and the yellow moon was the scaly monster after the fish.

James was going back to Berea College on Tuesday morning. I was to leave for Vanderbilt University on Tuesday afternoon. The next morning I said farewell to him and watched him walk out of sight across the pasture, through the orchard and out the ridge toward the oak grove. He swung a heavy suitcase at his side.

I could see that college had changed him. When he went away, he had never stayed over a week at a time away from home. At Berea College he had stayed four months. When he came home, he was so changed, he had grown so tall that his mother hardly knew him. He wore his clothes better. He was careful about choosing words when he spoke. He looked cleaner and his face looked keen and bright. He was not the same boy, only in a physical sense. The dry hard seed that was James Stuart was bursting into a very reticent masculine flower.

That day at noon I left. I had gone away many times before. But this was the time I hated to leave home most. I said a farewell to the hills and the woods and the old house there, farewell to the pines. I said a soft farewell to the land I cursed once and left, not to return.

When I got upon the hill and started to cross the fence into the peach orchard, I dropped my suitcase on the ground and sat on it. I wanted to look back on things that would stay in my mind like the pages of an old memory book, scenes I could cherish long afterwards. I had once called this place the Kentucky Highlands, a place similar to the land of Robert Burns. I looked back now and thought of this as a dream. I thought of poetry and people and plowed fields, plum trees, cherry trees and oaks.

What my father had said about being buried on the little knoll at the back of the house overlooking his hill farm wasn't a bad idea after all. At least, one's heart should be buried in the place one loves the most. If I were to die, I thought, I'd want to be hauled up here on one of these hills to take my last long sleep. Why think of

Death? One should not dream about Death in an orchard. It is the place to write. Before I left the orchard, I wrote:

Return

Kentucky, I shall return to you some day
To live out in your wind and rain and sun
And watch your trees and fields together run
And orchards whiten with the blooms of May.
I shall go back and sit before the fires
At home and tell tales with a fellow rover,
Before I'm cold and the best of life is over;
We'll tell of drinking days and fighting sires.
I shall go back to tramp the crimson leaves
That spread like quilts upon the frosty ground.
I'll take my gun and faithful hunting hound
And be alone where wind in treetops grieves.
Kentucky, your dwindling autumn streams
Flow out across old meadows of my dreams.

It is somewhere between twelve and one o'clock. The bus plunges by long leaps into the night. I have had a rough nap of sleep—on and on the hum of the motor, straining up the grades, taking it easy down the hills, on and on. The bright lights flare around the curve. The bus is a clumsy greyhound on the hills, but it leaps on the long stretches of concrete across the Bluegrass section of Kentucky and down over the low flat hills in the western part of the state. Morning—Tennessee and Vanderbilt University.

When I received my first grades at Vanderbilt University, my legs weakened. I knew they were coming, but I wanted to make myself believe, I must believe they were passing. The time taken up in the sweeping of Science Hall, the selling of "garage bargains" and football programs, and the work in the cafeteria had robbed me of too much time. And I had bought only a few books, too. But I had worked hard and it hurt not to climb the hill. I'd have to try it all over again. I tried to forget it. I wrote a sonnet about the grades and then I felt better:

To Three Low Grades

My hands and brain created you dream stuff.
They fashioned you, but not to my desire;
For now I wish I'd thrown you in the fire
Or taken time to build you strong enough.
God knows my time was spare and timber rough—
Deceptive things that made of me a liar
Trying to raise you dull pavilions higher.
Must I sit down victim to scorn and scoff?
Not I … though in steel corridors you lie
And bony fingers sour as drainpipe rain
Will turn you over once, but not again,
And catalogue against me your old cry:
"Not good enough. We'll choose a higher grade!"
Better for me if you were never made!

Would I register the second quarter with such grades? W'y hell, yes. Why stand up and take a beating? Why not hand back a few blows? I was afraid of myself. Everybody was a stranger to me. My mind was in a muddle. I was afraid. Would I ever step out and be myself again? That didn't matter as much as fighting back now. I should fight back. Go away with both eyes blacked and be afraid to speak? I tried to make myself do better. But I could not. I was afraid.

Why didn't I take the time I spent on sonnets and poems and spend it on my regular classroom work? I had a little spare time I'd been using for writing stories. I could use it all to a better advantage. No one ever saw the sonnets I did. I wrote them and hid them away in a notebook. I had the notebook half full. I could have used this time learning facts. But facts didn't stay with me.

I registered for the second quarter in Vanderbilt university on trial. If my grades were not better, I could borrow no more money from the university. I came back with a determination to be a better student. I intended to conform and study all required subjects.

It is somewhere between eleven and twelve. About twenty of us are listening to Robert Warren talk about Elizabeth Madox Roberts. He goes on lecturing. I don't get it all. My stomach keeps on bothering me. It is empty. I forgot to drink water before I came to the class. Drink plenty of water for water is good drink. The head is dizzy and the whole body feels sick. Drink good cool clear water and drink plenty of it, for it makes the sickness leave the body. Drink water when you are hungry so that your guts won't growl and the girls next to you won't hear and laugh. I don't mind a boy hearing but I hate like hell for one of the girls to hear. But their guts would growl too if their stomachs were empty. I only forgot to drink water. My stomach has ripped out a long growl. I bend over and press my hand on my stomach. It ceases slightly. My arm grows tired pressing down on my stomach. I remove it for a rest. My guts let out another long growl. Damn guts, I'd like to put my hands on them and squeeze them in their emptiness and confusion. I'd stop them from embarrassing me. I didn't quite get all that Warren said. It is only five minutes until the bell. I can see the clock in the tower from my window. I'll be glad when the five minutes are gone.

A man ought not to get hungry on eleven meals a week. One on Sunday, two on Monday, one on Tuesday, two on Wednesday and Thursday, one on Friday and two on Saturday. The weekends were the hardest. I walked more then. The cold spells were a little hard. It took more food then to keep the body supplied with heat. Plenty of food for a strong body. How funny and how strange! Plenty of water for a strong body. My body was as strong on eleven meals as it would have been on twenty-one—still one-hundred and ninety-two pounds and never stopped going. I know a little about food. I've worked a whole shift overtime in the steel mills without it, from eight to ten or fourteen hours without it. I drank water. Why not drink water at school? It is much easier to drink water and study books than it is to drink water and hook hot slabs of steel

Robert Penn Warren, born Guthrie, Kentucky, 1905
(Courtesy Special Collections, Vanderbilt University)

"...I would take my work to Robert Warren, and he would say it was good and for me to keep it up if I had to throw everything else aside."

with a long rod of iron with a hooked end.

I have known hunger on a Kentucky hill plowing. I had to plow a piece of corn. I could not quite finish in one half-day. I would not go in to dinner until the field was finished. I always felt sorry for the mule. He pulled the plow and I only guided it through the roots. He knew as much about plowing as I did. I didn't have to drive him. A mule knows right where to step. But he can't tell his driver whether he is hungry or not. And food, for the mule, is all he lives for. Give it to him. I don't live for food alone. I live on food and dreams. Give me mostly dreams—some day, you to whom I'm speaking, I hope you'll see them changed into reality. And you remember water is good to drink too. Cramp your guts when they growl. Push them against your backbone with your hand flat against your stomach. But don't cramp your dreams.

I have an appointment with Donald Davidson at seven this evening. He has passed me often walking through Wesley Hall. Sometimes he spoke, at other times he did not. He is a strange man. He is a man with dreams. There is something very fine about his face. I love to look at it. I think a lot of that silent man who slips quietly through the corridors of the hall and seldom speaks. But once I heard a deep laughter outside the hall. I went to the window. It was Donald Davidson laughing. He was bending over and slapping his knees with his hands and laughing. There was a tall man with him on the street.

I have talked to Donald Davidson. I didn't tell him half what I wanted to say. I wanted to tell him that I was a damned ass for not passing my schoolwork. But I hated to use that word to him. He would think it was unnecessary exaggeration on my part. But that is the way I felt about it. I should have passed all my schoolwork.

"Here was one of the greatest, if not the greatest, teachers I had ever known.... He changed my life."

Donald Davidson, born Campbellsville, Tennessee, 1893
(Courtesy Photographic Archives, Vanderbilt University)

He would say to me when I tried to explain, "Oh yes, I understand." I wondered if he did understand. There was a lot to be understood that amounted to trivial dreams. What was I down there for, anyway, bothering Davidson? I had no business telling him my troubles. Davidson had a use for his time. He could write poetry. He could grade papers. He could sit in silence and forget teaching school. I could go on and be myself and get out of a spell of cowardice and fear I was going through. Hell, forget three C's. What were they? I was standing at one end of the class, Boswell was at the other. Somebody had to be last. But I felt better by talking to Donald Davidson. "You don't have to get an M.A. before the sun goes down. Take your time about it. You are capable of an M.A. from this university. Don't get tense about it. Don't worry. I understand." I got something off my chest when I talked to him. I had told somebody something and felt relieved.

I could not write a term paper in Vanderbilt University that would pass. I hated to write one. When I started to write a term paper, I would write a poem. I wrote a term paper for Doctor Mims on Carlyle. I thought now: "This will be an A paper. I have spent a week on it." Doctor Mims looked over the paper and couldn't find a single thing about Carlyle. He wouldn't take the paper. One day I got the paper out of my bureau drawer, and I couldn't find anything about Carlyle in the paper, only in three places I had imitated his prose.

I began to think about a thesis. I had to write one before I could get an M.A., so I must write a thesis. I went to both Vanderbilt University and Peabody College and looked over the small steel corridors of thin black theses. They were all covered with dust. The only time they were ever used was when a student wanted to see what one was like before he wrote his. He wanted to look at one for a pattern to cut his by, not for the dry contents, no, no, my heavens, no! Theses and hard work, reading and pounding a hard table with your fists for nothing, saying: "God help me! God help us all! God help this dry educational system! God give it a backbone to hold to and not dry theses, dust-covered, happy and contented in their steel corridors on a shelf at Peabody College and Vanderbilt University or anywhere. God! Can't you hear my prayer, and my thesis is undone? My fists are sore. I am still beating on the table."

"No, the gods of education have not heard your prayer but it will be heard fifty years from today. Go on and write your thesis. Measure your education in bushel split-bottom baskets like your mother used to make."

"The contents are cane seed. Put a paper inside so that the seeds won't sift through the cracks of the basket. Then stack on a few extra pints of bright red cane seed, a couple of extra quarts— maybe a gallon. Run it over and tell the people to look at your golden heap of education. Show them how it is running over, cane seeds and education. They walk hand in hand. Can't you see them! God, give me cane seeds and education. I have to have them. I have to eat. I have to carry my bushel split-bottom basket around to show my cane seed. Education, you know, is measured on dusty shelves. If you don't believe me, go wipe away the dust and read for yourself. Don't strike matches around theses or wear tacks in your shoes."

I intended to fill the basket by the fifteenth of April with golden cane seed. But one day in Wesley Hall, when I was near the top of the building, running the fingers of my brain through the seeds I'd gotten at the university, I heard a fire siren. I looked down and the men were throwing on water. "Oh, it won't amount to much. It can't. Now I'll take out a little stuff and put it under that green tree in the yard." I took out three shirts and a picture. I put them in a suitcase. When I stood in front of Wesley, where I could see the fire, I thought that Wesley was gone, at least my room was right under the fire. I knew it was certain to burn. I ran back upstairs and the smoke came in and blinded me. The building burned all night. The next morning only the brick walls stood, with smoke oozing from the pile of ruins. I lost the job where I had been able to eke out eleven meals per week, enough rations to keep strength in my body. I lost all the clothes but the suit I had on my back, and the crotch split in the pants when I was trying to save a few of my books from the burning building. I lost all I had, but the greatest loss was not the few old clothes I had—I lost my thesis, and the term paper I had rewritten for the fifth time, fifty sonnets, part of a novel and several poems.

How could I stay in Vanderbilt University with everything gone? Hell yes, I would stay even if the place where I worked out eleven meals each week did burn, even if the term papers, the novel fragment and the sonnets burned, my textbooks and clothes and everything! Let them be in ashes. I would arise from the ashes and be stronger than when I fell among them.

I marched away from those ashes on February 19th with seventeen-year-old Bill Chandler, and each of us promised the other that we would hang together. He carried his little bag of belongings thrown over his back in "turkey" fashion as if he was going to a lumber camp. I carried mine in the same style. But it didn't look as if we would be able to stay in the university. I thought I would have to go home and lose the year at Vanderbilt University. I resolved again to stay. Clothes were gathered over Nashville for us, and there was one suit too big for anybody else but it just fitted me. I let it hang for a long time because I didn't intend to take anything given to me secondhand or firsthand. Finally, my pants went from bad to worse and the colored maid said they could be patched no more. I went over and got the big suit. It was a fit. It looked very good on me but I always felt guilty in wearing that suit of clothes.

I was able to obtain a free room in Kissam Hall. Bill Chandler was my roommate. I took a sonnet prize in *Muse & Mirror* and got five dollars. I got five dollars (donated) to buy textbooks with, but I saved this ten dollars for food.

I made four B's in my second quarter in Vanderbilt University after the turmoil of the fire. In the meantime I sent to northeast Kentucky and borrowed a suit of clothes from Lewis McCubbin, one of the teachers at the Greenup High School, so I would have a change. Then I went to the registrar and begged him for another loan so that I could register the third quarter. He asked me about security. I told him about a friend I had at Vanderbilt University. He accepted him and I took the note out to get him to sign it. Ron East signed his name to it and I brought it back within an hour. I got the money and registered.

The last quarter in Vanderbilt University, Doctor Mims asked for an original paper written about our own selves—a short autobiography, so to speak. I decided to make mine eighteen pages at first. But that pleased me very much—the idea of writing an original term paper—something that concerned our own lives. I heard many of the students laugh about their very important lives and say it was an old-fogy idea Doctor Mims had—and the students had to do this every year. I did not think the idea was old-fogy. I had failed every term paper up till now but one, and I got B minus on that. The paper was written for Donald Davidson. I had written two before this time for Doctor Mims—on the first one I did not even get a grade. The paper was too poor to grade, but he marked one little paragraph in the paper I had written about my experience in the steel mills. He said it was interesting and fairly well written.

After Doctor Mims had rejected my term papers, I wanted to write one that would stick. I would tell him how we lived in the hills of Kentucky and how I got to college and how I had been disappointed by finding colleges were not what I thought they were. I had a dream of going to Harvard once, and then the University of Virginia—and then Vanderbilt University. But I landed at Lincoln Memorial without a recommendation or an application or knowing a single person there. That was when I was hungry for knowledge. I wanted to write all this up and give it to Doctor Mims.

Ron East came to my room while I was working on my term paper. "Stuart, I hear you're having it pretty hard, Old Boy, since Wesley burned. Did you get registered all right?" "Yes, I got registered all right. Getting a little grub to eat's been the worst trouble. Bill Chandler and I have been getting moldy loaves of light bread, two big loaves for a nickel. We've been cutting the mold off and eating the bread. Sometimes we have cheese to go with it. Sometimes we have water. But we are staying in the university." "I just came over to tell you I've paid for you a meal a day at a boarding house on Highland Avenue. Sorry it couldn't be two meals but I have to stay in the university and I've got my wife to keep. I don't make much with that job I have down there in the slums." "Ron, I'm happy to have a note with your name signed to it. If I'm dead, you will have to pay that note. If I'm living, remember I'll pay it if I have to crawl and work to do it."

I started the term paper toward the last of March and finished it about the first of April. It took me eleven days to write it. I worked at night—sometimes all night long—and attended classes during the morning. I remember one day I did thirty-seven typewritten pages on that paper. Nearly every morning, I would take my work to Robert Warren, and he would say it was good and for me to keep it up if I had to throw everything else aside.

Ron East came to my door again. He said: "Well, how are you faring now?" "All right, Ron. I'm on the last chapter of my term paper that I'm writing for Doctor Mims. I'll have it finished tonight sometime. I've worked eleven days on the damn thing, but I've enjoyed writing it a lot more than I have enjoyed writing about dead authors. East, I've never made an A in this university. The first one I make I'm going to frame in the school colors and send home. I've had one term paper pass and I got a B minus on it from Davidson." "I hear the poems you slipped under Davidson's door are going well here. I heard he read them to the class." "It's been a new Vanderbilt to me since Donald Davidson got those poems. Boswell, who made fun of me when I told him I wrote poetry, has been my friend since Davidson read those poems to his class."

The paper is done now. I shall not come back again and add to it. Blindly, I've beaten these words out. They fell like drops of blood on the eardrum. I beat them with a hammer and forged them with heat cleavers to make them undouble the small pictures I have gathered in the album of my brain. Some of the words got cold too soon, and I could not twist them into the shape I wanted them. And you will not care for many of the pictures I have saved. I hope you like what I have had to say about the trees and the horses and skies full of stars. It won't matter much about the bread and onions and my grandfather hanged in the old house. It does not matter about a family moving from place to place and clearing the land and moving on. And the snakes, and the buzzards, blackberries, and copperheads, and dead horses by the blue stream and bones in the sunlight don't matter very much. But since I have gone beyond the dark hills, I think of a pasture field and pines, and a strong woman with hair turning white now, who goes there with a hoe and a basket of flowers on Decoration Day. And this good lady of the hills, unaware of the world beyond the dark grim jaws of the hills where the rims of ridge trees touch the sky, is living there and dreaming of the blood and flesh she has sent beyond the barrier. She has grown older now and does not want to go beyond. She has grown old and given her strength so that her flesh and blood may have a glimpse of a new light, a new sun in the sky, and a new sunset where there is no white glitter of horses' bones and cornstalks in January fields. Two sons have gone beyond the dark hills and two sons will lie forever in the lap of the dark hills.

When I handed Doctor Mims my term paper—"Beyond Dark Hills," I called it—he sucked his pipe harder than I ever saw him suck it before. I let everybody get out of the room before I handed it to him. Then he said: "You write all of this for me to read. Stuart, you aggravate me—you are not passing my work and then you go and write all of this." I humbly handed him the manuscript that I had bound down on a piece of cardboard with three heavy rubber bands so that he would not think it was as large as it was. I was really ashamed of imposing on him in the spring of the year when all the term papers were due and a group of theses must be approved by him—and there were 322 closely written pages in my paper. I knew he would read it, for Doctor Mims was to be complimented on the way he handled his written work. If he required a student to write a paper, he read every word of it. He was one professor who read every word of a paper, whereas a lot of the college professors, I had been told, threw their papers in the wastepaper basket. He grumbled as he walked out of the room tapping his cane every alternate step and smoking his pipe. He muttered words I could not understand and did not want to hear. But he had the huge term paper under his left arm, and the last time I saw him he was turning in at his office door with it under his arm and grumbling.

"...I have never read anything so... beautiful, tremendous, and powerful as that term paper you have written."

Dr. Edwin Mims
(Photo by John Hood, Photographic Archives, Vanderbilt University)

Approximately one week from that time, I passed by his office door. I had just finished a four-hundred and seventy-nine-line poem that I called "Whispering Grass." I was taking it to show to Robert Warren, and Doctor Mims came to the door and waved his cane at me and asked me to come in. He never spoke—he just looked at me. His eyes pierced me and finally I let my gaze pierce him. I looked hard at him. He looked hard at me. If he was going to start a row with me, I thought I would not stand it any longer. And finally he said: "I have been teaching school for forty years, and I have never read anything so crudely written and yet beautiful, tremendous, and powerful as that term paper you have written." And then he smiled a hard smile. I couldn't believe that he was sincere. He floored me as if I had been hit between the eyes with a bullet. "Do you really like it?" I said. "I took it home and let the family read it. It is a great piece of work—I can't go out with you to lunch today but I am paying for your lunch—here, take this dollar and eat on me today." He handed me a dollar bill. I didn't want to take it but I could not refuse. I had work pending with him and I couldn't afford to raise a row.

When I got the dollar, I broke for the pie wagon to eat baked peach pie and drink coffee.

> There is a pie wagon down on Broad Street
> That keeps good pies and coffee black as ink,
> The place where intellectuals used to meet,
> Survey their scanty food and eat and think.
> I was no intellectual, but I went
> And listened to the silly things they said.
> I got more for the money that I spent
> Is why I went—I drank coffee instead
> Of listenin' to Will Shakespeare's "Tragedies."
> And now I think I shall go back and meet
> The intellectuals there and discuss fleas,
> Order my lunch with five baked pies and eat
> And drink black coffee with white rings of cream,
> Discuss Shakespeare and fleas and eat and dream.

I shall never forget the thoughts I had about Doctor Mims when I walked across the campus. "If he flunks me, I deserve it. I haven't done anything for him. I should not try to bring pressure enough to bear on him by doing other things and make him pass me in my schoolwork. If he passed me, he would not be the teacher I thought he was. If he flunked me or held my work up, he was a teacher. But he was an old fogy with regard to what he said about the work in the term paper." I really thought he knew the subject matter he taught but he was not up on creative work. I had been told so many times my prose was as rotten as dead leaves and my poetry would pass as fairly decent stuff that I could not believe now that I had ever done a fairly decent piece of prose.

The dogwoods are in bloom now that I saw last January when I was home. They stand out among the thin-leafed oaks like white spreading sails. The redbuds are redder than patches of red clouds when the sun goes over the horse bones on town ridge on summer evenings. There are crab apples in bloom and crows flying to the pine woods to hide a nest in the deep branches, and I am not there.

The time has come when the green is getting back to the hills. I feel that I should be plowing. I would love to follow the plow and see the cool damp sod roll over from the silver moldboard on the plow. Plowing two mules on a hill in Kentucky. Plowing under the apple trees. A redbird sits on the twig of a tall poplar at the far end of the field. Uncle Rank Larks says: "When a redbird sings like this one is singin' in the tall poplar tree, there is goin' to be rain."

My dreams must not turn back. April has come to this city. And I have many books to read before the spring is over and many papers to write. They hurt the flesh too. There is a place to go to here where there are a few trees and wild birds and tame flowers. It is Centennial Park. It is a nice place to walk. The ducks play in the water. The weeping-willow trees have little thin blades of leaves on them. The stars come out and shine like jewels in the sky. The honk-honk of the ducks is lonely. When I am there, I like to think about Lum Dryasdust lying on my bed and shouting about the wretched poetic mood of which Poe's poetry has made him a victim. It is very strange.

I am in my room now. The April wind is moving the green elm branches at my window. It looks to me as if the crescent moon has been caught in a branch of this windy tree. The sky is bright with stars. The shutters on my windows bang and bang.

> April is but a night-flying shadow
> That comes as people come
> And goes as people pass.
> April is a thin moon on the meadow,

A thin moon on the grass.
Destiny beats her drum
And all the people come,
And all the people pass—
White petals on the grass.

There was one place in Nashville, Tennessee, that Ron East and I used to go to. But many times I went alone. I was a welcome visitor at any time. I would take whole sheafs of poetry there to show to Sidney. He never censored my work. It was always praise and encouragement. His home was filled with good books. His place was home to me. In addition to the bread of dreams he gave me, along with the other youth of the land who would come and stay a week or longer with him, he gave me big plates of potatoes, big slices of cheese, green onions, milk, bread. . . . Ah, those feasts there when I ate food until I was ashamed, and then he stacked more on my plate! What a home! What a haven for youth trying to write university term papers and trying to conform to the course of study. Once Sidney said to me. "Your teachers used to come here. Donald Davidson came to me when he was just a boy in Vanderbilt University. I have many of his youthful poems now. He was the handsomest youth I've ever seen. When the war came on, he enlisted and became an officer. Once he captured five Germans single-handed. The war didn't do him any good." Religious leaders of India came there, Robert Frost had been there, and G. K. Chesterton, Clarence Darrow, Edwin Markham, George Russell, Vachel Lindsay and T. S. Eliot! It was great to hear about these people.

We would walk back many mornings at three o'clock in the morning and hear the ducks quacking in Centennial Park. We would hear the soft Tennessee winds of spring combing the white hair of the spirea and the sweet-scented blossoms of the magnolia trees. A moon would be leaving the sky, and the hoofs of heavy horses drawing milk wagons would be pounding emptily on the stone streets, breaking the silence of the morning.

The year at Vanderbilt University was over now. The classwork was finished. I would not wear the cap and gown even if my grades were good enough the last quarter to bring up my three C's the first quarter. We waited for our last quarter's grades in Calhoun Hall. It was in the literature class, where I had stood at the very bottom of the class the first quarter, that the grades were read. I had made the highest grade by two points out of a possible two-hundred and

Sidney Mttron Hirsch, born Nashville, TN, 1885
(*Courtesy Photographic Archives, Vanderbilt University*)

"His place was home to me. [He gave me] the bread of dreams...
along with the other youth of the land who would
come and stay a week or longer with him...."

twenty-four points. It was a victory, a victory! My two next reports were A's. Only one class now to hear from and whether I passed or failed in it, I had passed my residence work at Vanderbilt University. I had to hear from Doctor Mims' class. I had not brought up all the assignments. He was the teacher I thought he was. The report was: "Work unfinished. No grade." There wasn't any grade on the term paper, only handwriting one had to interpret: "I've told you before what I think of this." I'd not made an A on any term paper throughout the year.

Wasn't Vanderbilt University a great school after all! Wasn't it strange to be in school where teachers and students were writing books! If one wrote a book there, what of it? One was just in company with the rest. It wasn't anything to get excited about, as we got excited at Lincoln Memorial when Mr. Kroll wrote his first novel. Didn't they smoke in the classrooms at Vanderbilt University—long cigars, pipes and cigarettes? Such evil practices! And if you got stewed at Vanderbilt University, wasn't that your own business too? If the University Law found you meandering lifelessly on the campus, didn't he take you to the dormitory and put you to bed, and if you hugged his neck and wouldn't let him leave didn't he sit on the side of your bed and tell you what a good man your father was when he came to this university, until you fell into a drowsy slumber! And the city police force that tried to undo these doings of the university, weren't they rotten-egged until they left puking and screaming!

Wasn't one of the ministerial students one of the best poker players in the university? But few would go to the Wesley Hall garret with Anton Abernathy. "Don't catch me playing poker with that damned preacher. Believe the deck is marked." Didn't many of the professors keep jugs of corn liquor made in the Tennessee hills in their homes because they couldn't get legalized whisky? "I've got a real moonshiner now," says Warren, "and I hope he doesn't get too much trade so he'll continue to make good corn." It was strange that the students would go up before or after a class and fill their pipes from the professor's tobacco pouch, but they could not drink with him until after they had graduated from Vanderbilt University. That was a tradition there. And when I asked Doctor Mims if I could get an M.A. without writing a thesis, didn't he refer me to the dry pages of the catalogue and ask me to read for myself, and that was that. Vanderbilt University, upon a little hill, overlooking the city, unmolested throughout the years, going on quietly and watching the students come and go.

I borrowed a dollar from Ron East. As we stood there, the long line of students passed us in caps and gowns. "What's the matter, Stuart?" "Got my thesis burned, all I had done of it. Wouldn't rewrite it. It will have to wait, along with my 'unfinished assignments' in Doctor Mims' class. I'm going home to farm. I'm going back to the hills. Tomorrow night I'll have my feet under the supper table at home, and I won't have to worry about something to eat. I'll remember you with a great big slice of hot bread, yellow-buttered, and a great big glass of buttermilk."

I could take all my belongings home in one suitcase. My typewriter and trunk were in ashes. It was a hot day to hitchhike on the roadway. The tar oozed from the road and it was smelly. Rides were hard to get and there weren't any ripe tomatoes or apples along the highway. I had to spend forty-five cents of the dollar, but I covered two-hundred and fifty miles of my journey. That night there was a rainfall and I couldn't sleep out in an open field. I got a tourist cabin and spent fifty cents more of my dollar. I felt in my pocket for the sheaf of poetry—"Whispering Grass," a group of sonnets and poems. They were gone. They were gone forever too, for I didn't have another copy. They were planted eternally on the asphalt highway.

The next morning, after a cup of coffee on the last five cents, I caught a Memphis, Tennessee, dynamite truck and rode on the loaded cargo for one-hundred and thirty miles across Kentucky to Olive Hill, where there is a brick plant. But I was going home. I would easily get there today. I would see the old home!

> Deserted now you stand with lichened walls
> Moldering into dust. Your window panes
> Are shattered by reckless winds and rains.
> Your birds and bats will come when darkness falls.
> Once we gathered in your eerie halls
> To share life's meeker gifts of joys and pains,
> But now your folks have gone, still your remains
> Abide with me when your haunting spirit calls,
> Even your yard-trees whisper from their height.

They see my eyes heavy-lidded, wet with dreams,
They see my candle-soul send forth its beams
And wonder if I shall share the coming night.
But oh, this place is lonesome, lonesome here,
And no one, oh, no one any more goes near.

The pastures are growing up in locust and sassafras sprouts and many fields have been left fallow. They are covered with tall dark waves of weeds. The wooden plow is resting under some oaks at the end of the field. The ax has rusted in the chop block. The buzzards laze up in the sky. The crows build in the pine trees near the house and caw-caw lonely songs. "Let us revert back one decade," they sing. The horses need new shoes. The hound dogs lie asleep upon the hill. And the house is leaking now. Two older people live in this house now. When I knock, the door will be opened.

The second Greenup County Courthouse—location of
the county school superintendent's office
(Courtesy Frank Dunn Collection,
Kentucky Historical Society, Frankfort, Kentucky)

"Stuart, Old Boy, you're going places. Boy no older than
you got a big office up there in the courthouse."

Chapter X
Man with a Bull-Tongue Plow

The old house in May moonlight looks good to me. I step quietly onto the back porch so that I won't wake the dogs and get everybody out of bed. I open the kitchen door and walk over to the pie safe in the kitchen. I know where Mom keeps everything. I light the lamp from a stick of kindling that I put into the embers left in the cookstove. Just the same old way she used to keep everything when I'd come in late at night and eat from the safe before I went to bed. Here is a plate of cold biscuits. Here is cold ham meat. Here is plenty of milk. I help myself.

I slip quietly through the corner of the dining room to the stairs. I go upstairs to my old room. The moonlight falls across my bed. I can see a long object lying in my bed. I light the lamp and carry it over to see who is in my bed. It is James. He's certainly grown long enough. I blow out the lamp, undress, and crawl into bed beside him. I didn't know he'd got back from Berea College this soon.

I feel good to lie in my old bed once more. From my window I can see the poplars below the hog pen. They are dew-covered and when the wind rustles their leaves they look like a silver cloud in the moonlight. I can hear the whippoorwills calling from every hilltop. I can hear the beetles in the dewy grass. I can see the light of fireflies on the meadow. I can hear hound dogs running the fox over on town ridge. It is peace again. It is home. No more worry about food. I shall have food here and three meals a day instead of one. I lie here and look out of the window until comes the nothingness of sleep.

"Roll out'n there, James," I hear my father say. "You can't get anything done and sleep all morning. Get out'n there, I say, before I come up there with a bucket of water!" James says: "Just in the minute. Just in the minute." Then he turns over and lies perfectly still. Ah, that old familiar voice of my father's! How many times it has rolled me out of bed! How I used to hate to hear it. Now I am glad to hear it again. I say: "James, let's get up!" "You here! Well, fine! We've got plenty of work to do. You've just come in time. Got more work here than five men can do. It's about to work me to death. Pa sold the horses. Got a span of mules, Jack and Barnie. Horses couldn't stand the newground plowing."

"What time is it anyway?" I ask. "Three o'clock in the morning, of course. You know the time Pa makes us go to bed and the time he gets up." Eight and nine to bed. Three and four of a morning we roll out. The moon is getting low over the town ridge. A few whippoorwills are calling from the hilltops. A swarm of white stars blink at a dew-covered world.

When we walk downstairs, we meet my father. He is coming with a lard bucket of cold water for James. "How would you like to hire a new workhand?" "W'y, when did you get in? Never did hear you come in. Never needed you so, Jesse, in my life! Weeds taking the corn and terbacker. Just James here steady to fight 'em. Your Ma helps him all she can. I got four days a week now on the section. I work two days here a week and of a night when I come in off the railroad. I do my gin work on Sunday."

My father puts the bucket of water back on the table. He says: "Get to the dabbling-pan, you boys, and wipe the wrinkles out'n your faces." "Good morning," says Mom, when I walk into the kitchen. "You're getting to be a stranger here. Jesse, I'm glad you've come. There's no end to the work to do here. James can't do it all by himself. I'm glad you're home to stay."

Mom carries the coffeepot to the table and pours us cups of hot black coffee. She says: "You're looking good. Looks like you've had plenty to eat." "Oh, yes, you know me. I'll always manage to get plenty to eat." "You look natural now," says Pa, "in them clothes. They suit you better. Looks like old times."

We eat breakfast. The stars are still shining. My father gets the lantern to light his way across the hill to the railroad. He says: "Eyes not as good as they used to be. Got to take the lantern any more. Now, you boys had better get that corn out'n the weeds down there on the bluff today. It's a foul piece of corn. Hate to put you to work, Jesse, before you look around a little, but we need you. Jim's been going through the mill a couple of weeks now."

I can see my father's lantern across the pasture and over the fence, a lantern light beneath the starlight. I can see it far out the ridge and then it fades from sight behind the brush and sprouts. James says: "Well, let's get our hoes and try some college algebra down there on the bluff." "What about the feeding? We'll have to do that yet, won't we?" "Now, you know better than that. Pa does that the first thing after he gets up of a morning and puts a fire in the stove. Just like he's always done. No one on this place ever built a fire in the morning but Pa. No one feeds in the morning now but Pa. He's an early bird, believe me, after me being in college."

This bluff is a newground piece of corn. After the brush was burned, it was just laid off, double-furrowed, and planted. We have to hunt in the weeds and sprouts for the corn. It is light enough now for us to see. Black-oak sprouts are tender after a fire has burned over the land in the spring. Just tap them the right way with a hoe and they'll sliver from the stumps. The sawbriars are the worst things to get rid of. The sourwood sprouts are easy to cut. A few ragweeds grow where a big heap of brush has been burned. In these spots we find the biggest stalks of corn. The sprouts have not smothered the corn. The corn is dark and pretty in these spots.

When I hoe a row of corn, I have to stop and rest. James says: "What's the matter? Trouble with your college algebra? Boy, come right out'n college after you got your master's degree and get back in the old sawbriars and sassafras sprouts with a big one-eyed grubbing hoe! Getting somewhere, aren't we, Boy!" And while I rest he starts back to the other end with his row. He is hatless, shirtless and the legs of his pants are cut off above the knees. All he wears is a pair of trunks and a pair of shoes. "I'm weak or something, James. I just can't take it. I'll get back on my feet after a while."

James says: "Used to be you took the bottom row of corn on me and told me to come on. Now I take the bottom row of corn on you, and I'm a little better to you. I let you sit at the end of the row and rest. If you can't stand this, wait until you get to digging post holes." "Have we got fences to build at this time of year?" "Have we got fences to build? We've got to run a five-strand barbwire fence from the hog pen to the Burns' place, got to re-fence the meadow and put a division fence between the woods pasture by the barn and the wheat field by the Burns' place. That's not all we got to do. After this is done, we've got to cut the oats and the hay and get 'em in the barn. We've got to paint the house and fix the leaks in the roof and get this crop laid by. After that, we've got forty acres of sprouts to cut off the pasture. That's the way Pa's got the work lined out for us."

"I'll be here all fall," I say to James, "and I can take care of the tobacco. You'll be in school then. My school work is over." "Mine is too," says James. "I've never told you but I didn't make it at Berea College the last semester. Mom never got my final grades. I beat her to the post office." "You mean to say you didn't pass?" "I mean to say a lot of things happened. Look at this, won't you."

James takes a letter from his pocket that says: "You will not be allowed to return to Berea College. We don't think you are the type of boy to finish college."

"That makes my blood boil too," says James, leaning on his hoe handle. "I smoked down there. Had a fight with a boy. I had to take a Bible course and I didn't like the way they taught it. I couldn't write a theme that would pass. I've written the whole story. I'm going to send it to a magazine. I flunked English composition too.

English teacher said a comma was worth ten-thousand dollars. I'd like to sell a bushel of commas at that price in these hard times. I'd pay some of my debts. It's all right to leave the college but when they tell me I'm not the type to graduate from college, they are a pack of dirty damn liars. I've seen a lot worse jackasses than I am get through college and strut around with their diplomas for pedigrees."

"What are you going to say when I tell you I didn't get my master's degree? It doesn't make my blood boil." "You didn't! That's fine! Both in the same boat and I'm not so bad after all."

Before Mom rang the dinner bell, I was ready to eat. My hands were sore already, and the tender skin started hooving with blisters as big as nickels and dimes all over my fingers and the palms of my hands. I would have to wear gloves to hoe the corn. How funny! At the table I didn't wait to have anything passed to me. I reached across the table and helped myself. Mom says: "Now, Jesse, eat something that will stick to your ribs. Don't start mincing on a lot of sweet stuff." "Don't you worry, I'm helping myself to the corn bread and buttermilk. I know what stays with me. I've eaten too much of it before."

The whole week long it was go and come through that field of corn. At the end of the week, we had it clean as a hound dog's tooth. I threw my shirt aside, cut the legs out of my pants, wore gloves on my blistered hands and went hatless in the boiling sun. I could feel the strength coming back to my body. The flesh that I gained at Vanderbilt University that made me look well kept was not good flesh. It was bloated on my stomach. My soft flesh started going down as air leaves a balloon. I gradually started creeping up on James with a row of corn until he stepped up and let me have the bottom row of corn again.

In the morning while it was cool, I would plow until ten o'clock. It was good to walk between the handles of a plow again behind the mule and watch the fresh dirt turn over. It was good to see the growing corn and hear the caw-caw of the crows winging their way in pairs from hill to hill. It was good to hear the cackling of the chickens around the barn and the hogs grunting for their slop and corn. This was the life, the only life. It was the only life for me. I just could not escape it. I was not cut out to study books, I was patterned for the farm.

I would turn the mule back into the pasture after I'd plowed in the morning, and then I'd help James hoe the corn and chop the weeds and sprouts the rest of the day. About nine o'clock each morning after Mom had got the work done up at the house, she would bring her hoe to the field. I'd say: "Mom, we can do this work. You have enough to do at the house. If you are going to tend the crop, James and I will go to the house and start wearing aprons and do the cooking." She says: "Remember, I've raised you boys. I've done this all my life. I am not too old to do it now. This corn must come out'n the weeds." She would work for a couple of hours in the field and then go to the house and get dinner.

"You can't do anything with her," says James. "She's just like the rest of the Hiltons. She has to have her way. I've tried to keep her in the house. I can't do a thing with her." In the afternoon along about two o'clock, Mom would come to the field and work until four, smoking her pipe and wearing her old slat bonnet, and then she'd go to the house and cook supper for us.

My father would come in and eat supper and he'd go to the field and work until dark. He would look at the clean corn on the hill below us and say: "Tearing up the place around here now. That's the way I like to see corn cleaned. Look at that corn how pretty it is! Look at them old stumps showing after you got the sprouts cut. W'y, this corn was gettin' about bad enough to snake before you got it out'n the weeds."

The two days each week that my father worked with us, he did the plowing and let James and me use the hoes. Either of us was much faster than he was with a hoe. "Now if my terbacker hits this year, I'm all right. If it don't I'm a goner. I'll lose this end of my farm. I owe seven-hundred dollars on it. I can't make it at two dollars and eighty-four cents a day, and only four days a week at that on the section. We've had a drought, it looks like, every summer and that's made it hard. Have to buy more than usual."

We waded through patch after patch of corn until we were through the first weeds and had the corn clean. "Now," says my father, "the corn crop is just what you might as well say is made. When you get it cleaned out the first time like that, you'll have no more trouble. You and James can take a mule apiece the second time you go over it and run two plows. Just need to cut a few sprouts with your hoes and straighten up the hills of corn around the end of the field where the mules step on them. The next thing is to get into that terbacker and get it worked over before this is ready for the second working."

The early corn in the garden was ready for roasten-ears now. We had beans and beets and young corn. When we would go in for dinner, Mom would have each of us five pints of cold sweet milk. She would put the buckets of milk down in the well and tie them with a rope. The milk would be as cold as the water in the well. She would have us seven big roasten-ears apiece. We would eat more corn than the mules for it only took six ears of hard corn apiece for them. We were brown as autumn black-oak leaves. I was the strongest that I'd ever been in my life.

When we finished a day's work in the tobacco field, James and I often took the dogs and walked three miles to the Ohio River. We would swim across the river and back with the dogs. Often old Don would get tired and want to climb upon my shoulders or James' shoulders to rest. We would let him. Rex would always swim on ahead. Bob would lag behind. Don would swim right along with us. After we swam the river, we would walk back home and go from there to Door's to a square dance. "A square dance in crop time," James would say, "is good for a man. Just have to get out once in a while." We would dance all night long and get home in time for breakfast. We'd never go to bed. We'd go back to the tobacco field and work all day. We did this time after time and didn't think anything about it, except the next day in the tobacco field we'd talk about the girls we danced with.

One night out of the week, one of us, and often both, went

with Mom and Glennis to Plum Grove Church to prayer meeting. "There's where you boys need to be instead of kicking up your heels at them old square dances. It won't hurt you to go to the house of the Lord one night a week and to Sunday School on Sunday." Back to the same old church and glad to be back where I used to be in Sunday School and hear Brother Tobbie. He was not here any more. The place didn't seem right without him. Brother Doubty was here now. Often while church was going on, I'd slip out and saunter over the ground where the old schoolhouse once stood and wonder about my playmates who used to come to this school and this church. I would saunter down among the graves and I would think: "What if they could all rise and speak for themselves now? They could tell us where they've been. They could tell us things we'd like to know out at the church house. Brother Tobbie could speak to us, and Warfield and Granny."

We cleaned the tobacco of crab grass and sprouts. Long pretty rows of tobacco just across from the house on the knoll. The small tender leaves would flap in the wind. Many of the plants were very small. The ground was getting dry and the little white clouds that looked like a duck's feather up against the sky would float out to space in the big sun-scorched simmering bowl of blue. "When you see that kind of clouds," says Uncle Rank Larks one night at a Plum Grove prayer meeting, "you can just mark down another drought. It was a black Christmas last year. It takes a white Christmas for a good crop year. It takes a dry June for a good crop year. We had too much rain the first of this month. It's a bad sign. I believe we're going into another drought right now."

Drought or no drought, our plows must keep going. We started through our corn the second time. A trail of dust follows us around the steep hill slope. "It's going to be bumble bee corn," says James, "if we don't get rain. A bumblebee will certainly be able to suck the tassels with his tail end dragging the ground if we don't get rain before this corn starts tasseling and ears start shooting." Each day the white clouds would sail out into a big sea of blue. Only each day it seemed the white clouds were nearer the ceiling of the wind-scorched sky. The dust would get in our mouths and noses. We would hike out the dust from our mouths and blow it from our noses and keep going through the brown clouds of hillside dust. The bottom blades of the corn started dying. The bottom leaves of the tobacco started shriveling fast.

Once I said to James: "I'm going to write poetry to suit myself from now on. I'm in a different university. I don't have teachers to tell me this is good or that is good. From now on, I'm going to be myself and write to suit myself and the way I damn well please. I've failed all my life and I can't do any worse than I have done."

We were plowing the bluff corn above the spring below the house. Under the two little poplars where Mom used to have her wash-kettle, I was letting my mule cool and rest from the bitter dust and hot sun. I wrote:

> Sir:
> I am a farmer singing at the plow
> And as I take my time to plow along
> A steep Kentucky hill, I sing my song—
> A one-horse farmer singing at the plow!
> I do not sing the songs you love to hear;
> My basket songs are woven from the words
> Of corn and crickets, trees and men and birds.
> I sing the strains I know and love to sing.
> And I can sing my lays like singing corn
> And flute them like a fluting gray corn-bird;
> And I can pipe them like a hunter's horn—
> All of my life these are the songs I've heard.
> And these crude strains no critic can call art,
> Yours very respectively, Jesse Stuart.

That day I wrote six sonnets, sitting on the beam of the plow while my mule rested. When thoughts came to me, I stopped my mule and put them down. I would sit on the beam of the plow in the hot sun and write poetry. Before we got the corn plowed over the second time, I had written eighty-four sonnets. I took them to my room upstairs and stacked them on the table. It was fun to write them at odd times while the work went on.

Often when I went to the pasture to get the mules and didn't

Jesse's bull-tongue plow on display in the Jesse Stuart Room at Morehead State University   *(Courtesy Jesse Stuart Room, Camden-Carrol Library, Morehead State University)*

"...I wrote six sonnets sitting on the beam of the plow while my mule rested."

have a pencil with me, something would pop into my mind. I would get a big poplar leaf and write a sonnet on it with a stick. A sonnet to one poplar leaf and room to spare. There were plenty of poplar leaves and sticks in the woods. Sometimes I'd write as many as eight sonnets on leaves and bring them to my room. Before the leaves shriveled with my sonnets on them, I would rewrite them in longhand on rough paper. Many times I would have a pencil and no paper. I would be walking along the road and find a "Red-Horse" tobacco sack. I could get six sonnets on a "Red-Horse" tobacco sack. There is an inside paper in this that I tore out and used. My table upstairs was filled with odd kinds of paper with sonnets written on them. I used the envelopes of all the letters I got to write poetry on. The poems just flowed to me. I was the happiest man in the world.

I owed money that I could not pay. I didn't have a job that paid me ready cash. My job was on the farm at home. If the tobacco got rain and did make good tobacco, I would not get the money. My father would have to have the money to pay the back payments due on his land. I owed money at the bank. I could not pay. I had borrowed money to pay the interest and had kept the notes renewed. I could not buy a pair of socks for I didn't have the money. I could not mail a letter unless I sold eggs. Mom let us sell the eggs to mail letters. We got seven cents a dozen. It took three cents to buy a postal stamp . . . two stamps and a penny postal card for a dozen eggs! What if the hens had known their eggs sold for only seven cents a dozen!

My father brought me a letter from the post office. It is a thin letter from the *American Mercury*. I open the letter. It is a $25 check for a poem! The first poem I've ever sold for money! Donald Davidson told me to send this poem to the *American Mercury* when I was in Vanderbilt University. I'd even forgotten about sending it . . . "Elegy for Mitch Stuart" . . . A check with H. L. Mencken's name on it! Just a short time ago, didn't I see where H. L. Mencken had said there wasn't any worthwhile poetry written in America? What was he doing buying a poem from me?

I proudly showed this check to my friends. It was the same as three-hundred and fifty-seven dozen hen eggs with one egg left over. Not fair to the hens, when I wrote the poem in less than an hour. I take the check to Ashland and buy me a new suit of clothes. I get a blue serge double-breasted suit for $16.00. I buy me a pair of shoes, a couple of shirts and socks and handkerchiefs. The most money I have had since I borrowed at the Greenup Bank. Now I can have a new suit of clothes and throw away the old suit that was given to me at Vanderbilt University, the old brown suit that I never liked to wear because it had been given to me.

James says: "That's the place I'll send my story. I'll send it to the *American Mercury*. If you can do it, I can." He sends his story to the *American Mercury*.

James and I took scythes and cut our oats. We mowed them on the hillsides for the land was too steep and filled with too many stumps to use a mowing machine. We would cut a swath of oats to the top of the hill. Then we would walk back to the foot of the hill and take another swath to the top. "Save all the young locust sprouts, Boys. Don't cut a one of them. We're going to need them for fence posts one of these days. A blight has killed all the chestnuts. Not any left anyplace." We left the locust sprouts that had grown up among the oats. The oats were short but they had headed fairly well. We hauled them to the barn. We didn't have to rush for fear a rain would fall and get them wet. The sun shone like a ball of molten pig iron from the sky. The rain crows croaked for rain. The wind burned our faces.

> Water is all we want, water to drink—
> To moisten lips and dust between the teeth,
> Water is all—water is good to drink—
> And men and plants are thirsting near to death.
> The roots of corn and goldenrod are dry.
> The juice is drying in the stalks of cane.
> The wind and grass and silking cornstalks sigh
> For water and the rain crows cry for rain.
> "Oh, heavens, send rain to our dusty teeth,"
> They cry, "and send cool water for grass roots.
> Send water soon—we're thirsting near to death.
> Send water soon—water is good for guts.
> Our guts need water and our roots are dry—
> Oh, wash our dusty teeth before we die!"

We put a mowing machine on the drought-scorched meadow. Before we cut the grass, it would have been dangerous to have smoked in the hayfield. I honestly believe the grass would have burned standing there. We raked the hay and hauled it to the barn.

"Save every little bunch of grass. We'll need it this winter for the mules and cows. This is going to be a hard winter. I'll tell you times are blue. Little trains going down loaded with coal. A big Mallie locomotive used to pull a hundred and fifty loaded cars. Now it pulls from twenty to twenty-five. So many tramps along the railroad we got to watch where we put our dinner buckets. A bum hooks one off the handcar with a long wire hook every once 'n a while when a freight train passes. The rest of us men divide with the fellow that lost his dinner. Trains carry bigger loads of bums than coal."

The corn has now been laid by. We have plowed it the last time. We just have to plow the tobacco once more and chop the few sprouts from it. It's too dry for the weeds to grow. "Boys," says my father, "we are going to be up against it. Another year and another drought. When are we going to get a good crop year? Middle of July here and no rain. I see the corn out there on the ridge has started tasseling and shooting. Blades dying at the bottom. Dying right up the stalk. Looks like it is ripe enough to cut. Terbacker's gone too. I'll lose the upper tract of the farm."

"Well," says James, "corn's burnt to the ground. All of our work lost. We've got the hay and oats in the barn, corn laid by. We have to make the fences this month and get the pastures sprouted off in August. You can be sprouting the pastures while I paint the house and fix the roof. The roof doesn't look that bad, but after the drought's over we will need a sound roof to catch the heavy October rains."

I go over the hill to the post office. Minnie Lartmore comes out and says: "Too bad for your poor old Ma about James gettin' sent home from Berea College. I was just talkin' to Ellen Sperry this mornin' about it. I heard he just fit and scratched and clawed and bit like a wildcat among the children down there. I heard he hit a teacher in the face with a dry horse pill. Heard he driv all the sows to the boar and they drapped pigs before killin' time and the children didn't have any meat."

"James, did you know Minnie Lartmore knows about your

trouble at Berea College? She's telling everybody. Said you hit a teacher with horse manure, bred the fattening sows, and fought like a wildcat. You'd just as well tell Mom about it. No use to hide it now." "How does she find out everything about me? I can't turn around but what she knows it. She slips around like a snake. She's got an eye like an eagle's and her tongue is long as a hoe handle."

Mom says: "James, I know about your low grades at Berea College. Every time you got a letter, I got one. I know you can't return. I didn't want the neighbors to know it. I've been waiting for you to tell me about it. I don't uphold for one of my children in the wrong. I don't know what all you've done at Berea College. I didn't want your Pa to find it out. You know I skimped for little things here and sent you egg money and cream money, all I could spare."

We started digging post holes below the barn. We first had to take a briar scythe, ax, mattock, and grubbing hoe and cut a right of way for the fence down through the hollow. It was hot, and the briars scratched our naked arms and shoulders. We cut the right of way to the Burns' place. Then we cut a measuring stick eight-feet long. We used it to mark the distance to dig the post holes. We never used a line like a lot of people to get our fence straight. We sighted across the handles of our post-hole diggers. The digging was hard. The ground was dry as dust as far down as we dug. Many places we would strike a shale stone and couldn't get the holes two and one-half feet deep. In many places we had to cut through the shale stone with a spud. We dug enough post holes for over a mile of barbwire fence. Then we went into the woods with axes, wedges, a crosscut saw and sledge and cut enough dead chestnut posts to fill these holes. We hauled them to the fence lines with the mules and put them in the holes, tamped them and braced them ready for the barbwire.

Next came the hard job for hot July. It was stretching the wire. We had a lot of old wire to restretch. Many times it would break and the rusted wire would wrap around our bodies and cut us. We carried a bottle of iodine to smear on the cuts, and we went on. It was not so bad to stretch the new wire. There was less danger of it breaking. At the beginning of August, we had the fences finished, and we could change the cows from the old pastures to the new pastures. There was a good crop of drought-scorched grass on them.

"I sold eggs and cream and bought that paint," says Mom, "and your Pa can't paint and make it look like anything. I've waited for you boys to come home and paint the house. The roof has to be coal tarred to stop the leaks. We'll surely need the leaks fixed before fall."

James started painting the house. I started cutting sprouts from the pasture. My father would come home from his work and walk out to the pasture and help me. "If you cut sprouts in dog days, they bleed to death and rot out of the ground. All but the persimmon sprouts. I don't believe anything can kill a persimmon sprout or a pawpaw. They just keep coming no matter how many times you cut them in dog days."

I would cut the clumps of blackberry briars with a briar scythe. I used a light mattock for the sprouts so as not to leave sharp snags over the field. I cut them close against the earth. Often while I cut sprouts from the pasture, I would think of a sonnet and write it. Sometimes I would go for a week and not write a line. Then in one day I would write twenty sonnets. The leaves had started turning now. I felt stronger than one of the hills I cut the sprouts from. I weighed two-hundred and seven pounds. I was browner than any of the leaves on the sprouts.

The creeks became as dry as a bone. We dug water holes for the cattle. The water in our well ran so low we could not draw a bucket of water without stirring sediment in the water. Rabbits died in the woods for want of water. Birds died for want of water. Minnows died in the creeks. One could follow the creek and find in some of the deepest holes a little puddle of water with a pile of water snakes, mud turtles and poor minnows still clinging to the last breath of life by breathing dirty warm stagnant water.

When James finished painting the house, I had one pasture hill sprouted clean. He and I double-teamed on the rest of the work. We did not sleep in the house anymore. We slept out in the yard on a quilt. Above us was a dry quilt of stars. We would lie there and talk far into the night and tell each other stories. When James had left for college a year before, he was small and spindly. Now he was long as a beanpole and still spindly. His feet stuck over the end of the bed and his head bumped our ceilings. It was strange to have a brother who could wear my shirts and socks. It was a disappoint-ment to look in the dresser drawer and find them all gone. It was strange to have one to work beside me and crowd me working with a row of corn in the field, a brother who could dig one-hundred and eighty-two post holes in one day, two and one-half feet deep.

We sprouted the pasture hills as we had cleaned the corn the first working. Before the end of August, we were through. Our pasture hills had been sprouted clean and our fences had been mended.

Autumn is coming now; plowing is over.
Pastures are sprouted clean and gardens tended;
The cane is thinned and all the fences mended;
It's cool for bees to gather for late clover.
And we must gather now the rakes and plows,
And mattocks, spades, pitchforks, and garden hoes,
Stack them away just as the summer goes;
And we must watch the water for the cows
And keep the holes cleaned out, for land is dry
And pasture grass is short this time of year.
The martins gather and the autumn's near—
And August clouds go floating slow and high.
When it's too cool for bees to work on clover,
It's time to gather tools, for summer's over.

II

September comes to the hills again. The leaves start turning on the red oaks, poplars, sassafras, sourwood, beeches, sugar maples, birch and ash. The green world of summer is turning now to a golden world, a world of light gold, scarlet, yellow and light yellow. The corn is dying and the lazy winds of autumn moan through the dry blades of fodder on the steep hillsides. There is something lazy about the whole earth. It is good to smell now and beautiful to see.

> I hate to see the lazy summer pass
> And blackberry leaves curl off the thorny briars;
> I hate to see cows taken off the grass;
> I hate to see the death of cornfield flowers—
> The phlox must shed its petals to the ground
> To wither with the phlox leaves bedded there;
> The shoe-make leaves will fall without a sound,
> For now they flaunt their banners to the air.
> I'll say I hate to see this summer pass
> And see white blossoms dying with the year;
> I'll hate to hear the wind blow through the grass
> When it is dead and autumn days are here.
> Autumn is sure to come and summer pass,
> And many of our dreams die with the grass.

We do not have a good crop to look back upon. Our work for the summer is over. Our crop has burned to the earth. The corn is bumblebee corn. The tobacco is spindly and has died before its time. Ah, the rain comes now but it is too late to help. Our summer's work has been in vain.

My father comes in from work and says: "W'y, word was sent to me by Work Riddle that Trevis Blair wants to see you right away. Said he had something interesting for you. Said for you to be in his office Monday morning bright and early." "Trevis Blair wants to see me! Surely there's some mistake! He doesn't want to see me! Trevis Blair—well, did you ever!"

"Yes," says Trevis Blair, "you've always wanted this job. Now it is yours if you can get your superintendent's certificate in time. People don't seem to appreciate me any longer. I hope they appreciate you. You're a nice young man from out here in the hills. Got life before you. Now just a minute though, you might not like the salary. Just recently, due to hard times, the salary's been reduced to a hundred dollars per month."

Trevis Blair smiles. Then he says: "Just two applications in for the job. One is a lady's application. She has no business with a job like this. The other application is Ernest Sandburn's. He can't get it!" Trevis Blair smiles again. "You know he ran against me once. Didn't beat me though, did he? I'm going to the Greenup City School System. I'll be principal of the Greenup High School and supervisor of the grade school."

"I've never wanted this job. If I had wanted it, you know I would have tried to get a superintendent's certificate. I don't have one." Thoughts race swiftly through my mind. "The county is a broken-down horse. It is not as good to pull for Trevis Blair as it has been for the last seven years. He is discarding it and getting a new horse. He more than doubled the salary that is left here for a new man. Wonder why there is such a sudden drop of salary when Trevis is getting ready to leave? Why cut this salary below the principal's salary of McKell High School, the west-end county high school? He makes $160. The subordinate making more money than the superintendent! That is illogical. Rubbing it in on me again! I'll show him! I'll take the job!"

I say: "Hand me a piece of paper. I want to write out my application for this job. I'll have my certificate here if I can get one." Trevis Blair smiles again. He hands me paper and a pencil. I put in my application.

I apply for my certificate. The County Board of Education meets. I have my certificate. I am hired as Superintendent of Greenup County Schools at the salary of $100 per month, the lowest salary the State of Kentucky allows a county to pay a superintendent of rural schools.

"I told you, Son," says my father, "if you'd quit writin' over everything on the place you would amount to somethin'. Now you are going places. Me and your Ma is proud of you. Everybody will be proud of you here in the deestrict." "Might not be so proud," says Mom. "Nearly every man yet that's gone in one of these offices has come out with more enemies than friends."

Trevis Blair worked every day he possibly could with the county before he took his position with the Greenup City High School. He took only two days vacation between his old and new jobs. Those days were Saturday and Sunday. Saturday was Greenup County School Board meeting day. It would be my first day to meet with them.

When I walked into town that Saturday morning from out home, I met many of my old friends. W'y, yes, didn't Blaine Felch walk up and say: "Stuart, Old Boy, you're going places. Boy no older than you got a big office up there in the courthouse. Get to set up there with a pencil behind your ear and me out on a Plum Grove hill pounding my daylights out making crossties. Wish I'd a-gone to school. Ma ought to a-taken a four-year-old club and beat the stuffins out'n me. Had the same chance you had. I'll tell you a little dab of education makes a powerful lot of difference in this world."

Uncle Watt Womack walked up and shook my hand. He says: "Son, I'm glad to see you get a job after the time you've had getting through school. I have seen you come in my store many winter afternoons without enough clothes on your back. You always acted to me like a steady boy." Uncle Watt Womack had credited me from one hunting season to another for shirts, shoes, socks, and sweaters when I was in high school.

On the courthouse square, I met a fellow who got up from a bench and walked toward me. He said: "Young Man, I've heard about your success with your new job. How about taking a old codger over and buying him a drink?" "What has the success of my new job got to do with buying you a drink when I've never seen you before?" "Never even seen me, huh! You wouldn't since you got that big job and the swellhead. You'll remember me when vote-gettin' time comes around."

I walked on thinking: "Well, if it takes such buzzards as that fellow sitting around and waiting for a piece of carrion to drop, to hold me in the superintendent's office, I don't want it."

I went upstairs in the courthouse to meet my board members. Three were talking in one group. Two were talking over at one side by themselves. Lawrence Loftin, Talburt Hauflin and Mooner Bentworth were board members who had been elected for, and had favored, Trevis Blair. Benton Dangerfield and Josh Montberry were board members elected by the people in two of the five county districts who opposed about everything Trevis Blair did, wrong or right.

"Well," says Benton Dangerfield, a big man six-feet-four, weighing two-hundred and sixty pounds, walking over to me, "so you are Jesse Stuart and our new superintendent. I thought you was an older man. You are a boy going into some mess. I feel for you."

I meet the other four board members and shake their hands. I see the board has split. The group who favored Trevis Blair is in the majority. Benton Dangerfield and Josh Montberry are glad to see a new superintendent. They are my friends. Yet, they are in the minority. Without the help of one of the other three, I cannot do anything. My hands are tied.

"It's time for the board to meet, Gentlemen. It's nine o'clock."

"I'd like to have just a word with you, Mr. Stuart," says Benton Dangerfield. He steps to one side. I follow him. He says: "There's something strange about this setup. Three men in there are Trevis Blair men. They put him in the office and they hated to see him go. I was elected agin him. I've fit him ever since I've been in the office. I expect to fight him every move he makes. You know his brother Timothy Blair tried his best, as Prosecuting Attorney of this county, to send me to the pen over killing two men in my chickens. I know Trevis Blair didn't like you. Then, he sent for you to come and take his place. You was a fool for ever gettin' in this mess. It will break you and wreck you. After the County Board sold their half-interest in the east-end high-school building to the City Board, he got the job didn't he? You watch for a trap laid for you here." "Thank you for the warning."

We walk back to the meeting. "Now," says Mooner Bentworth, "I don't see how we are going to pay anything. Everybody wanting their money and we ain't got no money. Ain't got a dime. Just have to put 'em off. That's what Trevis always done."

"What are we going to do," says Josh Montberry, "about the children up in the east end of the county? We don't have a high school for them this year. You know we've sold our interest to the city."

"That's right," says Mooner Bentworth, "Trevis said we couldn't keep two a-goin' and the best thing to do when you had a hot tater in each hand was to drop one and work the other hot tater from hand to hand. We had to sell it. Now we are out of a school. But Trevis said he'd take on a new teacher and be prepared to take care of all the students and the county could pay their school tuition."

It ran through my brain like a missile. "I can see the whole thing. Never while I am Superintendent of Greenup County Schools will we pay him tuition. Sell the high school and then force us to pay the town tuition! A nice scheme if it would work. But I'll throw a monkey wrench into it so big it'll crumble all the wheels of the machinery!"

"Gentlemen, as your Superintendent, I have some advice to give. That tuition for all the east-end county students will cost us too much. Why not put an extra bus on the road and haul them to the west-end county high school. It's only a distance of thirty miles. We can hire our unemployed county schoolteachers and give a bus driver work. I suggest this instead of giving it to the Greenup High School."

"It's not a bad idea," says Lawrence Loftin. "I make a motion we do it."

"It will wreck Trevis Blair's plans," says Mooner.

"Who are you working for, Mr. Bentworth, the county or the city?"

"W'y, the county, of course."

"It doesn't look that way to me," says Benton Dangerfield.

The motion was made, carried, and recorded in the minute book, to transport the east-end county high-school students to McKell High School in the west end. A motion was made for an auditor to audit the books and for me to try and find credit for the Greenup County school system.

This move of the county had hurt the attendance of the city high school. It was rumored over the city what the county had done. "Jesse Stuart did a thing like that when he finished high school up there in that building! He's turned against his own people!"

After the board meeting had adjourned, Benton Dangerfield says: "Looks like, Boys, we're going to get someplace now. We got more done today than we have in the past six months."

"Going someplace!" Mooner shouts. "If you ask me where we're going, I'd say as straight to hell as this county can go. We're on the road to hell and damnation with that boy in there. He ain't got good school sense. He's got wild ideas."

The men walk out of the courthouse. Josh Montberry and Benton Dangerfield wear broad smiles. I walk into the main office to have a talk with my secretary. "Mrs. Riley, how much does this work pay you?" "Forty dollars a month." "How many hours do you work?" "I've been going from eight o'clock in the morning until sometimes midnight. Mr. Stuart, this job means everything to me. My husband is dead. I have a boy and a girl in college. I have to send them money and keep myself."

She has an open honest face. She has a straightforward eye. "Well, I would like to hold you as my secretary. You know this work. You've been here about five years, haven't you?" "Yes."

When I leave the courthouse, Pert Jenkins stops me on the street. "W'y, Jesse Old Boy, you want to rescind that move you made up there today. Let us have them students back. Keep our old school going. You're from here, you know. No use to act that a-way." He pats my back and winks at me.

"W'y, Doctor Torrey wants to see you, Stuart," says Mike Austin. "Have you seen him yet?" "No, but I'll go right over to his office."

"Young Man," says Dr. Torrey, "you are a disappointment to me. You have started a battle here. It's against the laws of health to transport students thirty-five miles by bus over these bad roads. The whole town is hot. They'll be after your scalp. You, a young man with great promise for this county, and do a fool thing like you've done today! By God, you are not worthy of your mother's milk you nursed. I know she's a fine woman." "Not worth my mother's milk I nursed, huh! Well, you can get this! The one disgrace I've had in life was when you came to deliver me on a stormy August night and got there too late. You are still too late to know what's going on!" I walk out of his office.

Going home, I meet many people on the streets of Greenup whom I've known. They will not speak to me. They snarl their lips when they pass me. Many speak to me with pride. I walk four miles over the hill to home. I tell Mom about Dr. Torrey. "W'y, he's always been our family doctor and there's not a better man in the county." "That's what you think. I understand this whole setup. I'm fighting it until hell's not bigger than a gnat. I left this county once because of Trevis Blair. This time I'm staying. I know I'm right and, believe me, I'm fighting. I'm in for a long fight. I've been appointed for a year. W'y, he even said I wasn't worthy of your milk I nursed as a baby."

That night I walked among the black-oak trees at the back of our barn. To amuse myself and to forget the day, I sketched rough bits of poetry. I thought earnestly about the whole situation. I was sworn to work for the county. I was the representative of the hill people. If I betrayed them, what would they do? I could not betray them. I would not betray them no matter if I had to swing by the neck. A rope of slick persuasive tongues a mile long couldn't make me betray them! Let the fight go on! I was ready to meet them and fight!

Monday morning I saw a bus heavily loaded with east-end county students going to the west end for McKell High School. The Greenup High School was sadly reduced in number. Down this same road, I saw a ton truck coming with a tarpaulin over the top. It was loaded with students. When they passed me, they jeered at their new County School Superintendent walking down the highway. One says: "Where's your hat, Big Boy?" My hat was gone but I still had my head. They were students whose parents were still faithful to Trevis Blair.

The fight had started all right. Neighbor beside neighbor started quarreling over the school situation. The people of the city were divided. At least half of them didn't want Trevis Blair. "W'y, he got the county school system all messed up. Now he leaves a white elephant in our hands." "It's not Trevis Blair that ruint this county. It's that Stuart fellow. He's just a upstart! Too young to know what it's all about! Come from Vanderbilt University with big ways. Guess they teach big ways down there for us poor folks up here. The county quit paying the minute he took the job over."

"W'y, Mr. Stuart," says Mrs. Riley, "somebody is trying to get me kicked out of this office as your secretary. Mooner Benworth says you don't need a secretary." "That's just it, Mrs. Riley. I see through the whole thing. Josh Montberry saw Mooner coming from Trevis Blair's home. He's taking orders yet. If you leave me with all this work and little as I know about the detail work of this office, then my hands are tied good and proper."

I see Lawrence Loftin down on the courthouse square. I know I have two votes that will always stand by me. One is Benton Dangerfield and the other is Josh Montberry. I need another vote to have the majority of the board. I walk down where Lawrence Loftin is. I say: "Mr. Loftin, may I speak to you a minute?" I call him to one side. "Do you have anything against me?" "W'y, not a thing in this world, Stuart." "Then you will do me one little favor?" "If it's in my power." "That's just it. It is in your power. There is a move to dismiss Mrs. Riley from my office and leave me without a secretary. I don't know all the detail work in the office. I need her. I have to have her. She knows that work from A to Z. She's a good, loyal, honest, intelligent worker. Your vote will decide. I know one board member has made a suggestion we dismiss her." "It will never be done, My Boy."

The auditor works at his report. "The county is $144,000 in debt, including its bonded indebtedness. There is a $3300 deficit in the treasury. The property taxes and the state appropriations total approximately $100,000. It will take all of that and more to maintain the schools, run buses, buy coal for the rural schools and other expenditures. You are up against it. You owe the Greenup Bank $54,000. Twenty-six thousand dollars of that amount was borrowed on the promise by this school board that it would be paid out of this year's taxes, the first that came in. Besides, Trevis Blair didn't get all his money and his checks are made out, signed, and waiting over there in the bank to be cashed out of the first tax money that comes in. Presently, there won't be money for stamps. The budget will have to be remade. It is as efficient in this school crisis as a sieve is to hold water."

"We cannot raise the taxes either. Taxes are already as high as the state will allow them. The people can't pay their taxes now. All I know to do is make a new budget. I've tried every big bank in Ashland, Kentucky; Huntington, West Virginia; Portsmouth, Ohio, and all they tell me is they are scarce of money and thousands are asking for credit. They ask me about collaterals for security. We have nothing to offer. I can't get the money."

"For the past three years," says Auditor Heaberlin, "this county has overspent its budget."

"We'll have to hurry and do something or the whole county school system will collapse. Approximately five-thousand students will be sent home and the doors closed."

Harder-than-plowing-corn days spent in the office … staying behind closed doors while my secretary sends away teachers and county workers trying to collect old debts from the county. I gave her orders to tell them I'd see them later. I am trying to work out a budget to take to the State Department of Education personally and explain. I don't want them to think I am responsible for the predicament of the Greenup County schools and the task we are facing.

I could not escape the long line of people waiting to be paid. When I walked out of the office at noon one day, a long line of people was waiting. One big man walked up and said: "I want my money for the coal I hauled to Blackwoods School." I said: "I'm sorry but we don't have the money." He said: "When are you going to get it?" The fire was dancing in his eyes. Many of the others smiled at the way he was talking to me. "When the people pay their taxes and when we get the money." He said: "I'm going to get mine before that. Trevis Blair told me I'd get my money this month, to go on and haul the coal." "Trevis Blair is principal of the Greenup City School. It's about a mile up the road. If you want to collect from him, the road is open." "No, by God, he always paid when he was in here and you are going to pay. I'm going to take it out of your hide right now. That's the way I collect old debts." "That's just fine. If you want to take it out of my hide, I'm ready. I'd like to pay all the county debts like that, especially the $54,000 we owe the bank. Remember, when you take it out of my hide, it's marked off the county books."

The crowd moved back. He, a mountain of a man with piercing black eyes, shrugged his shoulders and looked me over. I was waiting and looking him steadily in the eye. I intended to block his legs hard enough to break them and dump him on the floor and beat the hell out'n him or let him beat it out of me, but not if I could help it. He never made a move. He turned, still eying me, and walked away. The crowd followed him, all but a few who talked to me about the debts, when they would be paid. I explained the situation the best I could.

The state was slow about sending in its appropriations. These appropriations and half of the county property taxes made up the teachers' salaries. The superintendent's salary, the salaries of board members, janitors' and bus drivers' salaries, the maintenance of buildings, playgrounds, and the construction of buildings, coal, brooms and all other expenditures came from the other half of the property tax. The highest salary paid in the county, and that was to any college graduate who had four years of teaching experience or more, was seventy-nine dollars. The lowest salary paid, to older teachers who were without high-school training, was less than fifty dollars. The minimum was forty-four dollars, the maximum seventy-nine dollars.

When the first money came from the state, we sent the first checks to the teachers. Those checks meant as much to them as rain would have meant to our corn and tobacco in the drought last summer. They took their checks in these dark days and were glad to get them. Thus the days dragged by. The leaves fell from the trees swiftly as the frosts came and the heavy autumn rains beat down upon the dry-crusted autumn earth.

Once, a teacher had gone home and had a baby. Before her resignation had reached the office, a teacher was there to take her place. She was from an adjoining county. Three trustees had hired her. I had recommended a young Greenup County teacher to fill the place, and my school-board members approved. Yet, the three school trustees had more power than the Greenup County School Superintendent and the Greenup County Board of Education.

It made me wonder: "What kind of a setup is this, anyway? Three school trustees for every little district. Fights between the three trustees over who the teacher shall be. Five board members and a superintendent on top of these trustees, all with power over the poor teacher! One worker with nine bosses! Who in the rotten hell ever heard of a system like it!" It was not only in our county, it was all over the state! How could a teacher do good work under such circumstances? Have to cater to her trustees, who often could not write their names, yet told the district, above the voice of the superintendent and the county board, who should teach their schools! If a trustee wanted the teacher to board with him before he'd promise her the school . . . very well! She had to do it or some other teacher who would board with him got the school! He could tell the superintendent to go straight to hell, as he often did! Why not let the superintendent recommend his teachers and the county board of education hire them or reject them! He ought to know about the schools, since he was superintendent!

I recommended this change to my board. They sat silently, even the men who had fought for me. They were for the century-old trustee system they had in Kentucky when they were boys. I had to sit with my hands tied and watch teachers come in from other counties and take the jobs from the teachers at home! Another thing, married women had taught school in the system right up until the time to have their babies, dismissed school, went home and had them and were back at their jobs in a couple of weeks! How could a thing like this be practiced! Oh, for the seventy-five millimeter guns I'd seen at Camp Knox! How I would have loved to have these unfair educational practices for my targets so I could have blasted them into a thousand hells! That's the way I felt! I had to fight against them! I had to speak out! I couldn't help it! I had to write articles about them to be turned down by our state educational journal! Another thing, the older teachers, too old to teach, still clinging to life by teaching—where was the pension so that these teachers could retire and new blood take their places? Ah, for such idle dreams!

I would walk home at night after a day's work in the office. I would help James feed the cows, and Mom, James and I would milk them. I would then walk out among the black-oak trees and hear the wind swish through their bare branches. I would see the autumn moon ride in the sky above the barn and the sky's big autumn bowl fill with white swarms of stars. I would hear the loneliness of the night wind in the pine tops. It would make me forget the day of toil. I would walk and walk through the woods at night over the old hills that stood by me as faithful friends. Then I would walk to the house, go upstairs to my room and ponder far into the night over the next moves to make in the County School Superintendent's office.

My father walked into the house one morning and said: "It's a funny thing, Sall, about that sow out there. I went out to the lot to slop the hogs this morning and she had seven pigs. She's mashed the eighth one to death. Was just getting ready to pen her up and fatten her. Don't see how on earth she could a-got to the boar. James said last spring she'd make a good brood-sow. That'll make us short of meat this winter. Wouldn't had it to happen for a twenty-dollar bill." "You know James never liked to see a sow killed. He's always loved hogs. He worked at the piggery at Berea College."

We couldn't pay bus drivers any longer from the county funds. We didn't have them. Why couldn't the students pay a small fee and this go to the driver? It would make him a small wage. The county could keep the buses repaired. It would relieve the county of a great expense. Cut one month's salary from all the teachers to pay the last month's salaries of last year. That would cut off a bad winter month of school and a big coal bill for the county.

The budget was remade. The County Board of Education met and appropriated me fifty dollars for expense money to visit eighty-four rural schools over our county, where schools were often many miles apart. They appropriated me twenty-five dollars to visit the State Department of Education at Frankfort . . . a distance of approximately one-hundred and eighty miles. One of the garage men, to whom the county owed a big debt, loaned us a car free of charge. With this twenty-five dollars, I was to pay Auditor Heaberlin's expenses and my own. We roomed at the Y.M.C.A. in Frankfort. We got our rooms and beds cheaper there. We spent two days in Frankfort. We ate our food at the cheapest restaurants to make the money last.

The state approved of our cutting one month from the schools. They approved our new budget and, in fact, helped us rearrange many things in the budget. "It's a mess," says the State Inspector, S. N. Taylor. "That place over there is one of the worst messes in Kentucky. It's the seedbed of rebellion." "Not seedbed rebellion now. The seeds have sprouted."

I spent the last sixty-five cents of our twenty-five dollars in Greenup to pay for cleaning the carburetor on the loaned vehicle. At the board meeting the next morning, Mooner Bentworth openly accused me of embezzling twenty-five dollars of the county's funds. When he did this, Benton Dangerfield jumped to his feet and ordered an investigation into the activities of our school-board chairman, Mooner Bentworth. Benton suggested we go to the garage and find where Mooner had bought gas on the county's credit, to use the school bus as a family touring car during the summer. "Yes, he got the gas here last summer." "What did you use the bus for?" "Went up on Big Sandy to a baseball game."

Mooner Bentworth was removed as chairman of the board but remained as one of its members. It would have taken court procedure to oust him from the board. We had enough lawsuits pending already. Talburt Hauflin took his place. From that point on, Mooner Bentworth and Benton Dangerfield did not speak. It was rumored that both men toted pistols for each other. I feared trouble at every board meeting with the two men not on speaking terms and eying each other viciously, and neither one afraid of the Devil.

I went to Sunday School with Mom on Sundays at Plum Grove. Uncle Rank Larks would always be there. Once, Uncle Rank and I did not go into the church house. We sat out on the old rail fence that runs down the hill from the Plum Grove church house. I told him the situation. He said: "You know, Jesse, anymore I don't worry a great lot about things like I used to. A little older, you know, and the hair I have left is getting whiter. I give the weeds a little better chance to grow in my corn now. You know all the rakes and furrows we give this old earth, the green grass in the spring will always hide last year's scars. Mind you, this will blow over in the end and they'll be your friends much as they have ever been. Just remember the grass of spring and Time will hide all sores and bruises among human beings."

The days go on, dropping one by one like the leaves drop one by one from the shaggy tough-butted oaks on the rocky hills. Once when I walked to my work, the Sheriff met me and handed me a summons. A man from the county, Greenleaf Noe, was suing the County Board of Education to make us pay the bus fare and tuition of students who had entered the Greenup City High School without the County Board's permission or my advice. A Greenup city attorney was backing up the suit. The lawyer handed me the petition, stating what they were asking for, and the names of the students whose tuition we were to pay. I asked Mrs. Riley to check the names of these students with the names of the students who had passed our exams to enter high school. Very few of the names were on our list. It was obvious, then, that they had gone out and solicited our unqualified students, or else the students had just come in and asked to enter high school and they had admitted them into the Greenup High School and expected eight dollars a head per month for their tuition when the county's purse already was so flat that this demand was like trying to draw blood from a turnip.

"We'll not pay it as long as I'm Greenup County Superintendent of Schools. If that is right, I'm a suck-egg mule!"

"If the Judge decides agin us," says Mort Hargis, "we'll beat him the next election in spite of hell. We've got the votes in the county and we're going to win this fight." When the lawsuits started, the old men came from the county and offered their services. There was Mort Hargis, Jason Spleeves, John Conway and Burton Bailey. "Tell me about this, Boys," says Jason Spleeves. "Who sold that building up there nohow? Damned if I won't have somebody in the penitentiary over this. I'm back of this county and I'll give the land and put up a building right in the middle of this town. I own that Weston property there. By God, I'll put a schoolhouse on it." Yes, Jason Spleeves had money. He was the man my father owed for the farm. He had memorized a kind of signature for his name. He couldn't read or write.

When the first trial came off, the old courthouse was filled with people. There wasn't the glory in the trial that the people expected, just hearing the lawyers put their petitions before the Judge in an orderly manner; two petitions were read and a few words were spoken. "W'y, it wasn't worth listening to. Thought it would be something. When I hear a trial, I like for it to be one." We got our lawyers from Ashland, Kentucky. "Get away from the town," says Jason Spleeves, "by God, go out and get lawyers. All the Greenup lawyers live in the town and they might lean a little. We're going to win this thing, Son. I'm with you a hundred percent."

"Mr. Spleeves, have you got anything against me?" "W'y, no, Son, who said I had? Ain't I sticking right by you in this school war?" "Will you do something for me?" "Yes, if it is in the bounds of reason." "You know that seven-hundred dollars my father owes you? He can't pay it. Since I've got a job, I'll pay you if you'll wait long enough." "That will be all right with me, Son, I ain't going to take that farm. I got twenty-seven-hundred acres too much nohow. I'm land poor. I never crowded your old Pap for a penny in my life. I won't crowd you."

When that suit was over, another petition was filed against us. Bent Harwood filed the petition in his name. "By God," says Jason, "I hate to send you to the pen, Bent. But damned if you don't remove that petition—go over there and scratch your name off—I'll send you to the pen. You know you are making licker out there. I hate it for your wife and children but we are fighting. You are undermining our rights."

In three days Bent's name was withdrawn from the petition. When the Judge was rendering decisions in our lawsuits, Jason Spleeves sat on the front row where he could look the Judge in the eye and hear every word that was said . . . a big man of two-hundred and sixty pounds, sixty-five years of age, with every tooth in his head as sound as a silver dollar, and a man who could, just a few years ago, run on his hands and feet like a horse with a man on his back and jump a ten-rail fence and never tip it. He would get two men on his back who would try to ride him like a mule. Men would bet on Greenup County's best mule-punchers riding Jason. They would gouge their heels into Jason's ribs. He would run on his hands and feet, crack louder than any mule when he kicked up his heels and throw both men high into the air, and they hit the hard earth on their tails, nearly jarred to pieces. No one ever lost money who bet on Jason throwing the men.

Didn't Jason keep his barrel and dipper throughout the whisky drought for himself and his thirsty friends so that they might sip the fragrant mountain water unmolested by the Law? Wasn't Jason a good soldier? He didn't fear man nor the Devil. He was just suspicious of the Law—that was all.

Jason was one of our eager enlisted soldiers. Mort Hargis, John Conway and Burton Bailey were just as eager and also sat on the front row at every trial.

If my recollection serves me right, we had thirty-two trials, over debts and with the Greenup City School group. We moved to different places to have our trials. Court weeks didn't come often enough in our county to take care of all our lawsuits. We felt the city sentiment was too strong against us to render fair decisions. We went to Catlettsburg, Kentucky; Grayson, Kentucky; Vanceburg, Kentucky. We would take a school bus and it would be loaded with people from the county, board members, and our old fighting soldiers. We would go with people hollering and banners flying. Jason would always be with us on the front seat. We would make the day a holiday when we had a trial. The trials turned out to be great holidays.

When a summons was handed to me now to appear in court, it didn't hurt me or scare me like the first one did. I just accepted it as a seasoned soldier would when he had served an autumn on a battlefront and screaming shells had begun to mean less to him than when he first heard them. I was getting seasoned to my schoolwork now. I was getting experience giving orders as an officer and fighting side by side with my men.

John Kenyon came to my office one morning and said: "Mr. Stuart, I'd like to have a talk with you." We walked into the back room to talk in private. He said: "You don't know how much danger you are in. I've heard men talk. When you start visiting schools, you'd better be prepared. I believe your life is in danger. I've heard talk from people you take to be your friends. They're after your scalp at Argeal. You know I've always been your friend."

"Yes, John, you've been my friend. You either belong to the Lord's camp or the Devil's camp. Some say my camp is the Devil's camp. Others say Trevis Blair's camp is the Devil's camp. I can understand now why the Lord said something like this: 'You are either with me or you are against me. You cannot serve both God and the Devil at the same time.'"

So far the city had not won a single thing from us. Our schools were still in session. If Greenup city schools got judgment from the court for the tuition they asked, then we couldn't pay our teachers. This tuition money came from the same fund from which we paid our teachers. If they got judgment, we were doomed. In many situations where we couldn't furnish coal and the coal had run out, the students went to the hills and cut wood to burn. The schools did not stop. We had kept the morale of one-hundred and twenty teachers. They had received half of their small salaries and they were still working. Often they came to me and asked about the next money . . . I didn't know when they would get it. I would always say: "It's due here anytime now. You'll soon be getting your money." I lied like a dog. I never knew when the next money was coming. Why not lie? Why not say anything, for the schools must go on!

I had seen droughts come to the hills. I had seen years of plenty. I had seen the lean years. I had never seen a summer like the past summer, and I had never seen the sturdy hill people and the people from the city crying for help as they were crying now. Long lines of people thronged the courthouse stairway until Jailer Wash Adams had to usher them aside so that Mrs. Riley could get to the office. He made them stand only two abreast on the old courthouse stairway for fear it would fall, as it was too weak for such loads of people. They had come for free cloth to make clothing and for Red Cross flour. They would get sacks of Red Cross flour and turn the red crosses downward when they walked out into the streets, so that the people couldn't see they had asked for alms. They had been a proud, high-spirited group of people, but famished stomachs and children crying for bread with their naked bodies exposed to the autumn weather had reduced their pride. Day after day this lasted. It wore on my nerves so much that once I got the key, went into the storeroom where we kept supplies, and cried as hard as any child. A sturdy race of hill people, with farms where they had once raised plenty, were now reduced to hunger and want by a dark Depression and the evil forces of the elements.

I hired Uncle Rank's boy, Possum Larks, who had a dilapidated Chevrolet roadster, to drive me over the county to the schools. I paid him three dollars a day for his services and the services of his car. I bought the gasoline. Our lunches never cost us a penny. I knew too many latchstrings over the county which I could pull. If I'd ask them to take pay, it would have been an insult. They would have quit fighting for me. They would have taken me for an enemy. I was a welcomed guest at these homes, and Possum Larks was just as much a welcomed guest because he was my friend. My friends were their friends.

We visited school after school. This was a requirement by the Kentucky school law that "the Superintendent shall at least visit each of his schools during the school term." Inside the car, under the seat and in the pocket of the door, lay two settlers of differences between the forces of men, handy if they were needed in any decisive moment. Thus we traveled from one school to another—the one-room and two-room weatherboarded, initial-scarred, dilapidated school-houses in the oak groves, the pine groves, by the roadsides and out on the faraway lonesome hilltops where the wind whipped lonely through the brown autumn broom-sage and the leafless trees.

It was here where the hill children must come from the farms across the swollen creeks in autumn after the boys did the feeding and the milking at home and the girls swept the floors and cleaned the dishes. It was in these schoolhouses, cold in winter when the wind whistled through the loose constructions, that the children, poorly clothed so many of them, gathered up around the big stove, where their faces froze and their backs burned. It was here the students were getting six months of school while the city children got nine. Boys and girls from the hills and the hollows, whose parents eked out a living from the old clay slopes even in the best of seasons and suffered in the time of drouth and bad seasons. I wanted to stand on a stump for once in my life and tell it to the world! Why the difference in school terms for the poor county children and the city children? State of Kentucky Educational Department, I'm asking you, "Are we not all of one flesh and blood in our Commonwealth, and do we not speak the same language and breathe the same air and feel the same sun and wind and see the same stars? Do not the children of the hills move to your cities and take up your jobs there? I am as much Kentuckian as any man and as loyal to my state and my people. But this is not fair! My heart is bigger than this, and my principles."

"Speak from a cornfield stump on the hillside," says the Wind, "I hear you. Your old desolate hills hear you. You are a little cheeping bird not worthy of your mother's milk you nursed when you were a baby. Your trees hear you . . . your mighty oaks . . . but they are too dumb to speak. Besides, it's late autumn now and they are asleep. Go home and spend your days dealing with little baskets of education . . . your nights writing articles on the unfairness of education. Forget what you have seen, for the fluffy grass in spring will hide all scars in the end."

We park the car. We cannot drive to the schoolhouse. We have taken the old roadster over roads it looked impossible for a horse and buggy to get over. We've just had five flats, bent the steering gear, and knocked a hole in the oil pan. Now we walk two miles through the woods the rest of the way. It is Hill View School. It is noontime and there are no latchstrings for us to pull. The students divide their lunches with us. It is late in October and the ruddy-cheeked boys are barefooted here. Yes, the first sharp frost has fallen long ago and the corn is shocked on the hills and the tobacco is hanging in the barns. Many have only corn bread to eat . . . a dry hunk of corn bread and nothing with it. Better to have just dry corn bread than no bread at all. The bread tastes good, and Possum and I eat with the children. We are glad to get it. Besides the corn bread of life which has grown from these hills, their teacher is giving them the bread of books under difficult circumstances. These youths are eager youths, sturdy as their hills and without their mothers' kisses when they leave over a two-mile path to school each morning across the swollen streams and slippery hillside paths. There are no automobiles here to take them to school and bring them back. Six months of happy school days this year and maybe seven next year. After this, they clear the earth, use the mattock, hoe and plow. The children work in the fields with their mothers and fathers, for it takes all hands of the house and the cook to make a living!

I spend my fifty dollars and do not visit all the schools. The school board appropriates me twenty dollars more. Trevis Blair had been allowed three-hundred dollars expense money. I visit the rest of the schools. I could tell the Wind from atop a cornfield stump: "Here is something for you, and you might listen. I have received all the money I'll get for my services for this county. From now on I must work without pay. My secretary must work without pay. The Greenup Bank has been tottery and even our big bulk of C. & O. tax money could not fill its starving stomach. It doubled up and collapsed anyway."

Teachers come in and ask: "When are we going to get our money? We need it. We can't pay our board." Mrs. Riley would say: "We are looking for it just any day now." Many of the women would quarrel. Many of the men would row. Our tongues had grown slick from lying. Buses would plow through seven miles of mud on one end of the road, and the other twenty-three miles of rough-surfaced road was filled with chugholes. Students would leave by starlight and get home often when the stars were shining on the short winter days. Greenup's Law Chore stopped pounding away at us when they found that our money was exhausted. Trevis Blair had gotten his money, since his checks had been issued and endorsed before he left the County Superintendent's office. He cashed them out of the first tax money that came in to the Greenup Bank. He had had a good job for seven years and needed his money. The rest could wait.

L. N. Taylor comes to visit the county school system. We visit schools one day together. He is Supervisor of Kentucky Rural Education. He says: "You are in a bad mess here. You are a young superintendent with one of the big counties. You are the youngest county school superintendent Kentucky has had. Keep in mind great growth is slow growth."

I work all day in the office and go back and work at night. Many nights I work at school problems. Since I have a typewriter to use, many nights I type poems I have been writing during the summer and autumn. I seek refuge from teachers asking about their checks. Now that the rural schools are over, I see a few familiar faces every day. I slip to the toilet and spend a few minutes peacefully. If they know where I am, they'll have to wait until I come out. Here I write many sonnets. I put my indignant feelings, or the insults I've gotten, into a sonnet. The stack is over four hundred now.

Many nights I stay at the hotel when the winter rain is pouring. Then the sun comes out and dries the roads. Through the winter wind I walk out home. My father and James are hauling corn nubbins on a sled, pulled by the mules, to the crib. James says: "I've done it, Jesse. You know that story I wrote on Berea College. The *Mercury* took it and paid me seventy-five dollars." "I tell you," says my father, "we're all into it here. I hear them talking in town about getting you mixed up in the Law and sending you on a trip. James is getting in another mess. He's getting letters from foreign countries. Got a letter from France. Some of the letters are good. Yet he's got a lot of people all riled up. A lot of cussing in some of the letters."

"What did you do with your money?" "W'y, I bought me some guns."

"Yes," says Pa, "got a new pump gun, a automatic, a pistol and a old muzzleloading rifle that blowed up down there the other morning and nearly put Bill Hillman's eyes out. His face is powder-specked as a guinea egg. Shooting at a lizard. Bill says: 'Put another gram of powder in, Jim, and I'll blow him away.' Jim must a-put three grams of powder in for Tid Fillson heard the top of the barrel, she said, wheeze over their house a half-mile away. The rifle went back over Bill's shoulder and stuck in the ground. James had to dig it out. I had to run down there to Bill . . .

down on the ground moaning like a stuck hog and asking if his face was blowed off. James working with 'im and telling him he was just scared a little."

"Did you spend all your money on guns? I want to borrow twenty-five dollars from you. The county has stopped paying me." "No, I spent the rest of it for shells." "Where did you get that old muzzleloader?" "It's the old Crump gun. Wouldn't sell it to nobody but me and wouldn't sell it to me until I agreed to keep it." "No wonder it blew up. It was made by a gunsmith in 1820 and was used for deer and Indians."

Sold an article to the *American Mercury* at sixteen! I couldn't make it with prose. Money coming into our house for both poetry and prose! Mine had gone for a suit of clothes. James' had gone for guns!

Minnie Lartmore says: "Hear your brother James sold a piece on that college where he went for seventy-five hundred dollars!"

The days pass. I plow home through the rain, sleet, snow. Many times I come home in the dark night when I nearly have to feel my way. Some nights I come home after working late in the office, and my father is up building a fire at three o'clock to get breakfast. I sleep until seven, eat breakfast and go back to Greenup. Many mornings I go to the office and thaw the ice out of my hair. "This will kill you, Mr. Stuart," Mrs. Riley says. I often show her a new group of sonnets and they are wet and the ink has blurred the lines. I wrote them while the snow was falling.

The rural schools are out now. Only the high school is going on. Another new suit has been started against us by Trent Easton. "No way to get him off that I know of," says Jason Spleeves. When I walked up the street one day, a man came to me and said: "You are the man that has caused all of this. You have caused us to have more teachers than we needed by taking away the county students from our city school. There's going to he a suit filed against you for talk you have had of malicious intent." "Let me tell you something right now. The sweet little woman to whom you refer, you'd better tell her not to contemplate a lawsuit to sue a beggar and catch a louse. What about the little baby doll her husband slept with? Wonder if she knows that? Not my way of fighting but if this method is fair for one it's fair for the other." He went his way. I went mine. I never heard any more about the suit.

The winter days were dreary days. Snow covered the earth and the people came to the town for alms. One midnight when I stepped outside of my office door into the dark, I stumbled over something. I walked back and turned the light on. It was a coffin at my door. It had been dragged out and left for someone who had died back in the county. The next morning I saw a whole stack of county coffins in a garret of the courthouse extension. "Well, it looks pretty bad," says Ike Splevins, "all them coffins in there to get us when we starve to death." I understood the County Judge had bought a shipment of these pauper coffins at reduced rates.

The big fight had simmered down now. Time was bringing the grass of spring that would hide all the scars. The darkening skies hung lead-colored above the hills. The swollen streams emptied terrific loads of water into the rivers. Then from the lead-colored skies, came drenching downpours of rain that soaked the earth. The water in old man river started him rising, inch by inch and foot by foot until the people were shut in. Water had them cut off from all sides. The Greenup people at first take a flood as a sort of a holiday. They have been on the flood-front a long time, and there's not a great deal to get excited about. Just so long as it doesn't get up in the second stories of the houses.

Next the boats were landing in Main Street and the brown swirling water kept coming. Gas lines were shut off. No heat for the buildings. People of the little town started moving their belongings up to the second stories again. Johnboats delivered coffee sacks of coal through the upstairs windows and life went on just the same. Lovers plied in their canoes above the old familiar alleys of the town. It was a New-World Venice now, only no sweet singers and gondoliers!

Yes, the moonlight shone on the crisp wintry night when all the stars from the heavens, it seemed, were anxious about the flood and swarmed in the sky to look down on this Ohio River flood. The siege lasted days, the battle with this mad river. People from the county came in and worked for the people of the city. After all, hadn't the elements brought us together? Those elements that had been so cruel last summer, that had burned the crops to the earth and caused the people and the cattle to go hungry, had come again and made man mourn for man. The people I had disliked and who had disliked me—I felt for them now. I wanted to lift their furniture, pull their boats and help them. It was a hard time for them, for time and again in previous floods they had lost all they had. This was just another flood.

"W'y," says Jason Spleeves, "I guess you heard about Trent Easton. At the first big shock of thunder, he passed out. Died right in that big storm the other night. That relieves us of another lawsuit. God Almighty is with us, Son. Just when the thunder and the lightning was waking up the snakes and the frogs, turtles and terrapins and shaking the mighty hills, Trent Easton went to his long rest, a good neighbor and a good man but in the wrong the way I see the right."

Yes, the grass is here again. The poplars leaf by the hog pen. The fluffy grass hides the old corn rows with their little receipts to show for last year's bread. The birds sing again and the pairs of crows go winging their way across the blue. Men go to the fields undaunted by last year's crop failure. I walk again among the greening hills of my parents' farm. I take long walks over the old pathways. Yes, back to Plum Grove at night. Didn't I have a thought once that the dead would like to speak from their Plum Grove graves? Didn't it say on one tombstone:

> Remember me as you pass by,
> As you are now so once was I;
> As I am now, so shall you be,
> Therefore, prepare to follow me!

Why not let all these dead speak? All the dead I'd seen hauled here and buried. That is what I would do. Flowers blooming now above their graves, the yucca, myrtle, roses, and the larkspur. I go among these graves at night. It is lonely here among these departed ghosts. I let them speak. I write and write and write for them, as the whippoorwills sing in the moonlight from the drowsy Kentucky fresh-leafed hills. On Sundays I come here and write. I let them speak for themselves. It is a recreation to me, unlike the firing line I have been on all winter. I am weary of fighting. I am weary of madness. I am weary of it all. It has been nearly a year now. Dreams have come and dreams have faded, but the people have passed through the pages of a book, all kinds of people, and they have spoken. Even the worst of them had something good in them when they spoke what was in their hearts. I put myself honestly into their places and spoke for them. What would I call these seven-hundred and three poems written for my own amusement, for my people both dead and living, and for the hills that had always stood by me?

"Boy with a Silver Plow," first came to my mind. No, I was no longer a boy. I was past twenty-five now, a man now if I'd ever be one. Besides, I didn't use a silver plow. I used a root-cutter plow. Then I'd call them: "Man With a Root-Cutter Plow." No, that would not work. I would call them: "Man With a Cutter Plow." Now, didn't we use the big bull tongues on the old root-cutter plows? Why not call it: "Man With a Bull-Tongue Plow"? That is what I would call it. So, I took this "Man With a Bull-Tongue Plow" home and wrapped an old hand towel around it, a huge bulk of poems, and laid it away upstairs in my dresser drawer. It was all over. The drought, summer, autumn, winter, school war, the flood, and the great new-life storms of spring. The book was finished, dreams and sights and sounds and feelings that would not come again. I had been eleven months writing the book. In the meantime I had farmed and had served as captain of my forces in a school war that had split us into the camp of the Lord and the Devil. I was feeling weary of it all. It was over and I felt like a balloon with the air slowly let out . . . something that falls flat.

"Mrs. Riley, it's been a long time since we had money. I don't know what a dollar looks like. I'm going to bet on a horse race." I walk to the drugstore, borrow a dollar from Sam Leslie, and buy a card. My card has the name of Broker's Tipp. It is my first bet on a race. But the horses are off. I just got my ticket in time. There is much noise and yelling down in old Kentucky over the radio. At the end of the race, the announcer screams: "Broker's Tipp wins by a nose length and the jockeys are fighting." I picked up a pot of twenty-eight dollars. I pay the dollar which I have borrowed back to the druggist. I pay Mrs. Worthington for laundering my shirts. I have owed her so long. I pay Aunt Mollie the rest of my board bill. I have a few dollars to put in my pocket.

I did not apply for the position of county school superintendent for another year. "Gentlemen of the County Board of Education, as the superintendent of schools has the right to recommend the high-school principals, I wish to recommend myself for that position next year, as you expect to make a change."

I put in my application and all five board members voted for me. I had to make money. I was deeper in debt. It had been the most trying year of my life and the hardest fight. I would go to the west-end high school, McKell High School, and build the best school of its size along the river. I could teach school during the winter and farm during the summer. That would give me enough to do. I could not go on being county school superintendent. Too many were sore at me.

Hadn't I made enemies when I found where a well had been cleaned out and a bill of ten dollars turned in and approved for the job? I would say, "No wonder this county is about to collapse. How deep was that well?" "Twenty-five feet." "Our well is twenty-four feet deep. My brother and I can clean it out in three hours. Think I'll start cleaning out wells for the county. Could make more money than being superintendent."

Then a man would come in and say: "If you'll ease me my money and let the others wait a while, I'll get you twenty votes when you run again." "There's not going to be any running, Brother, and your name goes down right where it belongs. Slip, hell! . . . and let the other fellow wait! I'm waiting and you're no better than I am."

These men would go off mad and say I was a hellcat and had insulted them. No wonder officeholders have spoiled the voting populace, trying to get votes by promising them this and that and doing little favors from the public funds. I wouldn't do it, didn't do it, office or no office. Let all men fare alike. If some man walked from the back of the county for a dollar debt, we knew he needed it and paid him his dollar before we did some of the bigger debts.

The darkest year in the history of Greenup County schools had come to a close. The darkest year in many a hillman's life had come to a close. If the faction who had engaged us in this school war had won, we would have been eternally sunk. Our only victory had been keeping our schools going. It had been expensive to the children of both sides. It would take a lot of tall grass to cover the bruises and scars left by these school factions. It would take a lot of tall grass for many seasons to completely hide them.

III

Peace again between the handles of the plow. The plow handles feel good to my hands after handling bushelbaskets of education and the problems at the bottom of them in Kentucky. The feel of the wind is good to my face. It is sweet to breathe. The sun tans my face. James works beside me on the hills. It is the old life again.

I get a letter from the Greenup Bank. It says my two notes are due. It states plainly that there will be no renewal. They have been renewed too many times. Three-hundred dollars looks big to me. I have to gather eggs again from the barn and sell them to buy postage stamps. Mom spares James and me a little money, sometimes fifty cents and sometimes a dollar, from the cream she ships to Cincinnati. Greenup County owes me, and I owe the bank. The bank closed and hurt the county school system. It is just like a dog chasing himself around after his own tail.

I go down to the bank and say: "Listen, I've got nearly all my salary coming to me for being county school superintendent. As soon as I get it, I'll pay you. Please don't try to collect from the two who have been good enough to sign my notes. I've never tried to beat a debt yet." "We've got to have our money. You must remember this bank owes debts. Look at the depositors who have only received a small percent of their money!" The bank owes money here the same as I do, and the strange thing is the bank can demand its money and get it. The depositors can't. They have to wait and get it as the bank is able to pay them. I think what is sauce for the goose is sauce for the gander. "I'll pay you when I get my money." The newly appointed officials agree to wait.

The rain falls in torrents. It is a wet summer. We had a time keeping the weeds down in the corn. They grow prolifically and the rank stalks of corn and tobacco shoot up rapidly in the open air above the weeds. It's going to be a good crop year. We don't have the dust to plow through that we had last summer. The corn and tobacco are going to be good this year.

Many days I stay at home and work in the smokehouse. My father will say: "Ground is a little wet but we can chop weeds in the corn today. Looks like James is having more than his part of the work to do this summer. You can't quit writing over everything on the place. Weeds taking the corn. You taking days out."

I take days out. I have written so many poems . . . about four thousand now. I'm trying to write stories. I get moods for a group of poems. I put the words in prose. I was told in college to follow a skeleton. When I thought of a skeleton, I always thought of a man's white bones dangling in the wind without flesh on the body, without blood in the veins, without life, color, love, dreams. I thought of a dead snag of an oak tree standing on our hill with the branches chopped off, the bark dead and slipping, no leaves to adorn the naked boughs, no blooms, no sap running through the veins. I just didn't like skeletons and never could use them. The white deposits on the skeleton oak where the crows rested on their long flights was the marked climax.

I did the story the way I wanted to. Why not . . . who was writing the story? Wasn't it my thought? Did I read a story to get inspiration? No, the thought was my own thought. It was a slice of life lived by my own hill people. They didn't live and die by a skeleton with crow deposits for a climax either. I would write as they had lived—to be honest about it. That was my skeleton, and the blossoms for the branches were words I thought would fit. Ideas would come to me like ideas for poems. I would go into the smokehouse and write them. The first one was "Battle Keaton Dies." It was great fun to write these stories and see the living people I had known in words.

> No one has sung for us and may I sing
> As one of us, for all of us, my songs
> Thought futile as the mountain winds that fling
> Their fluffy silver bellies on these throngs
> Of jutted hills oak-crowned against the skies.
> I sing of mountain men, their lives and loves
> And mountain waters and the wild-bird cries,
> The percoon blooming in the late March coves.
> It's fun to run on iron legs and shout
> Songs to the wind my blood has left unsung,
> The tunes at home they never thought about
> Too busy living life while they are young.
> I'll keep on singing long as this blood flows
> And brain keeps active in this living head;
> I'd like eternal spring when this blood goes
> To sing among ghosts of the mountain dead.

I was needing clothes badly, for McKell High School started soon. I took a sheaf of poems from the manuscript of "Man With a Bull-Tongue Plow" and sent them to Donald Davidson to ask his advice, to ask if they were worthy to send away to magazines. A letter came almost instantly. "These are good poems. They are fresh right from the soil. Send a batch to *American Mercury, Virginia Quarterly Review*, and *Poetry: A Magazine of Verse.*"

How could Donald Davidson tell they were from the soil? He had never seen where they were written. How did he know I didn't sit by a good warm fire and write them? How did he know I wasn't one of those gentlemen farmers who is afraid to dirty their damned soft hands? Strange the way Donald Davidson knew things!

I sent approximately two-hundred sonnets to the *Mercury*, one-hundred and fifty to the *Virginia Quarterly Review* and one-hundred to *Poetry: A Magazine of Verse*. Before the summer was over, all three had accepted some poems! My heavens, one-hundred and thirty dollars for thirty-two poems! I didn't know how long it had taken me to write them but at the least calculation not over four moods from one to two hours each! Was that money rain for a drought-stricken stalk of corn needing water! Debts, debts, debts!

> The money that I owe I know I'll pay.
> It comes too slow and hard and easily goes
> To pay for shelter, paper, books and clothes.
> I'm further paying debts from day to day.
> My friends, it's hard to squeeze a cornfield stone
> And earn above the nourishment I get
> For a mammon chaser on his soft taboret.
> He gets my gold, the little that I earn.
> And he can have my copper, silver, gold . . .
> He is the man to take it to the grave;
> Poor fool, he is the kind to skimp and save.
> My words above his coins when we are cold
> My words above his coins, don't you forget;
> Above this lazy ass on his taboret.

I start sending stories to magazines. They start coming back. I take the rejection slips and put them on a wire at the foot of my bed. Soon they reach across the wire. One rejection slip had a personal note pinned on. It says: "There is genius in this story.

Keep up your work. Sorry we can't use the story." I laugh and say: "I'm sorry too." Then I think: "It is poetry that is in the blood in my veins and not the story."

I move to the west end of the county for the autumn and winter. It is twenty miles from home. "Young Man, you will have a time with that school. Not the students so much, but the outsiders come in and tear up the school's games and plays. Last year they pulled a knife on one of the teachers and dared him out. They rushed the doors to the basketball games. Just went in nohow. It's a bad place. I sympathize with the Devil when he takes that bunch home. They'll give him trouble in Hell."

In my office in a chalk-box, I kept a little friend. Just a .22. It would stop any man all right. When he was stopped, it would take two of his friends to drag him out of the way. Therefore, three would be eliminated. My six office girls, working one hour each during the day, knew about this. It didn't necessarily excite them. They understood, for they had seen pistols too often to get excited about them. It was just an accepted thing.

"Mr. Stuart," says Pent Kenton, "they are coming tonight. They are going to tear up the school play." "Are you sure they are going to tear up the school play?" "They said so. All coming lickered up and ready. Elick Preston, Jarvis Conway, Spruce Dunbar, and Spikey Fitch."

The play is started. The crowd is quiet. Two men walk in with tall cowboy hats on their heads. They do not remove them. They start talking out loud and throwing apple cores at the students in the play and calling them by names. I walk over to a board member and say: "Are we going to allow this thing to go on? I sent for the Law tonight but the Law, as usual, never gets to this school. You know the trouble the teachers have had here." He says: "I don't know what to do about it." "I know what to do about it. If there's not any Law here to protect us, there surely can't be any to prosecute us."

I walk over to the boys and say: "Fellows, you will have to be quiet. You are disturbing everybody in here." One says: "Who are you?" "Never mind who I am. Will you or will you not be quiet?"

They get up and move to another seat. They are quiet for a few minutes. The women start moving away from them. They take their toes and gouge the women in the behinds under the backs of the seats. I walk over and say: "You fellows will have to leave." "Who said so?" "I said so." "Will you give us our money back?" "You can have your money back."

They take their money and walk to the back door. They turn and one blackguards as loudly as he can. I throw my coat across a chair and walk out. A small man follows me out. His name is Walter Burke. I don't know what he will do. I find out. He collars one of the men. The other one steps up and I catch him a right someplace on the head, lift him over a row of dead spirea and he slumps against the wall. Bob Wigginton goes a mile to get the Sheriff. My knuckle is knocked down but my man is knocked out. The other fight continues until Walter gets his man down. He chokes his tongue out and the man turns black in the face. Several men have come outside. We have to pull Walter loose. In the dim moonlight the fight goes on. The board member is fighting now. The gravels fly and there are shouts of fighting men. We have the door closed and the play goes on inside the schoolhouse as if there were no trouble. The Sheriff comes and my man is just waking up. The Sheriff arrests him and takes a .38 from his pocket. Good for me the lick counted.

One of my students comes running out after the fight and says: "Why didn't you tell us boys? We'd a-done your fighting. We could a-cleaned that bunch." I say: "You get back in the house where you belong. I'll do my own damn fighting." My troubles at my school were ending. I didn't need my little friend any longer. I returned it to Edd Cross.

Didn't someone keep breaking into the cafeteria and stealing our leftover pies? Mrs. Riggs says: "I can't keep anything." Druggist MacDonald wouldn't sell me croton oil. He says: "Got a powder here just as good. It's tasteless, colorless, and odorless. This little dab is enough to physic twenty cows." "Give me that little dab now."

Didn't Waha Menton vomit on the Tygart bridge before he got home from the basketball game! "Believed I'd a-died if I hadn't. I come nigh as a pea dying. Seemed like fire in my belly. I got upon the eatin' table at home and put a toe under each corner and my hands on the other corners and stretched. All at once a pain hit me like a bullet. I run out of the good warm house to the toilet. Thought I was through. Before I got back in the house out'n the cold, another pain hit. Had to stay in the toilet all night. It's been two days since I got that pie and I'm still goin'. Nineteen times and I've lost eleven pounds. Lew Fraser got just a little piece of it and it physicked him eleven times, and Red just got a bit and it physicked him seven times. It's runnin' their legs off yet. It must a-been high-powered croaken oil or some kind of poison one. No more of that high-school pie for me." Our cafeteria was left alone.

Teaching school! I had never thought about ever teaching school! Isn't this the spring of life that once I saw? Youth, like the Tygart River, a steady stream forever flowing! I, who wanted to be a great track man and a great writer, have failed to do either! In debt and have to do something! But I have always enjoyed life though living in debt. How would it feel to be out of debt one time in my life! Would I enjoy life as much?

I have even sold my blood for clothes to cover my back— $75, $30, $25. Poetry, the very blood of me! It seemed as if I have sold children that belong to me because I needed the money. Poetry so close akin to me. Poetry that haunts me. Poetry that I see in the great prolific earth in Kentucky hills; poetry that I see and smell and feel in the spring blossoms and the budding of the leaves and in the changing seasons of the year. Poetry that speaks its messages to me in the flower-scented winds of spring among the wild crab-apple blossoms and the snow-white percoon; poetry I hear in the winds of autumn sighing among the dry clusters of turning leaves for the summer that will not come again; poetry I hear in the moaning winds of winter in the leafless boughs that moan for the old life lying beneath the snow, creating a womb wherein violets will peep with the first bird calls for spring!

Poetry I feel in the very human beings about me! I see it in the gay boys and girls of spring alive with the blowing wind, the blooming flowers, and in the first burst of their blossoms; I see poetry in the men and women working in their summer of life and growing their fields of grain, having their families and walking hand in hand; poetry I see in the autumn of life when the hair on their heads starts to color as the leaves on the trees, and when the happy pairs who have climbed the hills together start down the other side; poetry, too, I see in the snow-white hair of the men and women who have been through all the seasons and have accepted wisdom and love and life from all! And then I cry out: "Poetry, how can these wonderful human beings pass? Can't we get a few in song? I am just your medium. You flow through my veins and through the gateway of my brain! How can we let them pass, people of my generation I have learned to know and love? Can't we catch a fleeting glimpse of them as they pass from the fluffy green of spring to the dying autumn grass? Can't we do these things while it is my season and my generation and before the glorious or the tragic end!"

When I go home to visit, Minnie Lartmore comes out on the porch and says: "Guess you heard about James?" "No, what has happened now?" "W'y, he's went down there to Lincoln Memorial where you used to go. Went down here in town and had Charlie Murray to learn him how to half-sole shoes with that machine so he could work his way. Took a lot of guns with him and pulled out. Charlie told Sweet Bird, before he'd learn him, James had to promise not to come back and put up a shop against him in Greenup."

"Mom, what's this I hear about James going to Lincoln Memorial? Minnie Lartmore told me he'd pulled out and went down there with a bunch of guns." "God knows what he took down there," says Mom, "but I'd a-sold every cow off'n the place to get him away from this crowd he's running with. Another one of the fattening sows dropped a litter of pigs. Your Pa's taking the top of the house off. He signed a note for him for another hundred dollars to get him away. James said he'd get his basket filled with education this time."

"He'll never get along at Lincoln Memorial. He'll ruin what little reputation I made there." "Well, Jesse, James is gettin' worse. Mrs. Fister and Tessie Fillson and me was all sittin' out there under the hickory tree smoking our pipes, with our faces turned toward the meadow, and I heard something come tearing down through the sprouts and shaking the dead leaves. I looked around and saw James coming just in his shirttail. I was plagued to death . . . didn't know what to do. The women hollered and run in the house. James went in and got in your Pa's bed. I run in and throwed a quilt over him. I says: 'James, where did you get that whisky?' He says: 'Republicans give it to me.' I says: 'What was you doing at the election?' He says: 'I was over twenty-one.' Then I says: 'Mitch, James has even started voting.' Your Pa says: 'He's got to get used to the polls sometime.' I say to him then: 'Mitch, this foolishness has gone on long enough.' Then he flies off the handle and says: 'Tryin' to raise him under a petticoat government. Ain't I been under one for the last thirty-five years? It would a-been alright with you if he'd drunk Democrat whisky!' Then he whiffs off mad as a hornet to the barn."

"Did James ever find his clothes?" "Yes, the next day he went across the hill and found them by that big rock over there in Maddox's pasture field. Found all his clothes but the shirt he wore home." "For goodness sake, don't let Minnie Lartmore know about it. James might want a school in this county some day."

We never hear from James. The days pass. I send stories their rounds. I write in the smokehouse at my boardinghouse. It is a good hideout. My typewriter is sitting by an onion pile. "When anybody calls for me, Mrs. Lawhorne, I'm not at home. You understand? My days belong to the school, my nights belong to me."

A letter comes to me. It is from *Story* magazine. It says: "We are accepting your 'Battle Keaton Dies.' Enclosed is our check for $25." Strange, the first story I ever wrote! Strange, I got the same money that I did for my first poem. Sold a story! It didn't have a plot. Just a man died and wanted to be buried in his shirttail. But it was not the same kind of money the poetry money was. It was fun-money. Poetry was blood-money.

Could I believe it? A letter from a publishing house. It says: "Have you got any more poems like the ones you have in the autumn issues of the *Virginia Quarterly* and the *Mercury*?" "Yes," I write and say, "I have seven-hundred and three in that batch." An answer: "Send them to us if no one else has spoken for them."

Lord, no one had spoken for them. Certainly I would send them. I packed them up and sent them away. A letter came with a contract. It said: "This is a great book of poems. It is like a big river with tributaries of life entering in. It is like a symphony of wind." My Lord, a book contract! It couldn't be that my poems had been accepted to be published in book form. It must be a dream I was dreaming! I walked in the wind for three days. At night I went to the hills and tried to calm myself by walking under the oak trees! I was the happiest man in the world. Just to think, you try to write something to suit everybody and you suit no one. Then you write to suit yourself and be yourself and the people like it! The corn I farmed was burned to the earth. The poetry I wrote there would be included between the covers of a book.

The days pass. I hear from a story I sent away. It is a check for $125. I rush home over the weekend to show it to my father. I say: "This is what I did the day you tried to run me out of the smokehouse

Jesse on his way to mail the manuscript of *Man With A Bull-Tongue Plow*
(Courtesy H. Edward Richardson Collection, Ekstrom Library, University of Louisville)

"A letter came with a contract. It said: 'This is a great book of poems. It is like a big river with tributaries of life entering in. It is like a symphony of wind.'"

to hoe corn. One-hundred and twenty-five dollars!"

My father takes the check. He says: "Read that for me, Sall." Mom says: "It's for a hundred and twenty-five dollars, Mitch. He's telling you the truth." "God Almighty, Jess," says my father, "I didn't know you was that sharp after the way you bumfuzzled the superintendent's office. I'd have to work two months to get that, beatin' it out on the railroad. You made it in a day. You can stay in the smokehouse if you can do that. I'll hoe the corn."

Then he says something he's never said before: "I've come in a one havin' a lot of fights over you when you was superintendent. Old Dan Manburn tried to pop off about you. I told him to shut his damn trap or I'd smash it. I says: 'Dan, he makes mistakes but after all, don't others make mistakes or there wouldn't be any erasers on pencils. He's my boy and you can't talk about him like that in my presence.' Old Dan shut his mouth. He ain't amounted to nothin'. I ain't neither. If he'd die tomorrow, it would be old Dan Manburn dead. If I'd die tomorrow, it would be old Mitch Stuart dead. I hope you boys do better than either one of us in this world." It took a check to show my father what I was doing, for he didn't read. He could make out some of the little words on a tobacco sack by spelling them over slowly. He would never do this in our presence. He felt ashamed. When teachers would tell him we were good students, he secretly felt proud of us.

Superintendent Fred Maynard says: "I've blasted the trustee system. I recommend my teachers. The County Board hires them or rejects them. We are the first hill county in Kentucky to do this. After the storm, we're getting a little sunshine. Seven months of school again and eight months we hope next year. Had to put the old debts aside and start a new paying basis. It may he years before you get your money. Our budget will call for a sinking fund to retard old debts. The reconstruction period has been lawyer fees, soreheads, men wanting their money, dilapidated school buildings, buildings washed away by the floods."

Before the Christmas holidays, James came home. I say: "What's the matter, James, didn't you get your basket filled with education this time?" He says: "Lincoln Memorial is worse than Berea. The cards were stacked against me. It was over the story I wrote on Berea College. The students like me. Lincoln officials got my 'rep' from Berea College. I just popped in on them or they'd never let me be enrolled. They couldn't very well send me away."

"Did you get any rabbits?" asks Pa. "Many down in Tennessee?"

"W'y," says James, "not near as many as we have in Kentucky. I never saw the day I could go out and kill fifteen. Too many foxes in Tennessee. They kept the rabbits caught out. Had a fox farm at Lincoln Memorial!"

"What kind of foxes," says Pa, "red foxes or gray foxes?"

"Two-legged foxes," says James, "old residenters like Cewee Pacenback, who knows when and where to slip around and catch you smoking. Foxes slip through your wooden drawers when you are not in, hunting for your guns and ammunition. Two-legged foxes who watch every move their chickens make."

"I was just asking you," says Pa, "about the rabbits down there in that state. I didn't ask you for a lot of damn foolishness about foxes. Is that what they learnt you down there instead of your books?"

"The quarter's not ending this soon," I say to James. "How did you make your grades?"

"Never made any," says James. "Didn't stay long enough for the exams. I'm home to rabbit hunt. Just to tell you the truth, I didn't like the way they ran that college."

"Too bad," says Pa, "you couldn't show 'em how to run the place. Now you got me hooked on that hundred-dollar note. When, My Son, are you ever going to be able to teach school and pay a few of your debts?"

James and I leave Pa by the fireplace. We walk out in the pasture. We stand under a leafless cluster of black-oak trees and talk. James says: "It's like this, Jesse. I took over the shoeshop. I put soles on their shoes and heels on them. I found out there were as many bodies need souls as there were shoes needing half soles.

Didn't the students put me on the staff of the old paper you used to edit? I was contributing poetry every issue when along comes old Cewee Pacenback and telephones down to Tazewell and tells them to stop publishing my poetry. 'It is dangerous,' he tells them, 'it is dynamite.' I get hot under the collar. The *New Republic* used five of 'em whether they're dynamite or not. Then Cewee comes up smiling to me and quotes the Bible and tells me about bad boys going to Hell. I just wonder what Hell's got to do with a fellow in college.

"So Cewee brings his shoes over for me to put heels on. He pats me on the back and brags about what a good shoe-cobbler I am. He says: 'Now, Jimmie, Old Boy, put me a good pair of heels on these shoes. They cost me fourteen dollars.' And I says: 'I'll sure make an exception for your shoes, Mr. Pacenback.' And about that time a nice-looking little girl comes in the shop and flops her end down in my customers' well-cushioned waiting chair. Up she gets, hollering and screaming, and Cewee asks: 'What's the matter, Honey?' She says: 'Don't know. Had all kinds of a funny feeling up my back.' I say: 'Mr. Pacenback, if you don't mind I'd like for you to make an announcement in chapel about boys slipping in here and sticking a live wire up through that cushion.'

"Ceewee walks out and I put the heels on his shoes. I get me some good cardboard and use leather for the outside. I shine them until you could see yourself in the heels of his shoes. Now Ceewee comes to get his shoes. I say: 'Mr. Pacenback, you see I've fixed them up for you.' 'A fine job, Jimmie,' he says. 'How much do I owe you?' I say: 'Two dollars, since I had to take such pains with 'em. It took me some time to fix 'em up right.' He says: 'Just put it on my bill please.' I put it on his bill. Now Cewee was walking on sixteen dollars—another dollar for each shoe. The first rain came and his shoeheels got soaked and flattened out. He was a heavy man for paper heels. He stayed. I left. I got credit in English and my first A in college. The night I left Lincoln, we celebrated. The boys got a case of Ridgemore. To give it the kick, we supplied it with Tennessee white-mule. I had the honor before I left of shooting every man's gun as a salute and a farewell to Lincoln Memorial. You ought to have seen the guns coming from under the bedclothes. Had to quit keeping them in the wooden drawers because of the foxes.

"On my way home I stopped at Berea College. I knew the hogs would be glad to see me. I visited the old piggery where I used to work. I saw the hogs in the December moonlight. I visited Lon Stanton's room, the boy who closed my eyes with his fists once. He was ready to be my friend. I telephoned headquarters that James Stuart was on the Berea college campus. 'Get him for us!' I say: 'Hold your tater for another half-hour. Have to work him into a trap, get him in a room and close the door.' I got out of Berea College while they were waiting for James Stuart to get in a trap. I was on my way.

"When I got here, I got a letter at the post office with a statement in it that said: 'You owe Lincoln Memorial $37. Will you please remit at once.' I went down to Greenup and put the case in the hands of my lawyer, Ti Fitzgerald. W'y, Cewee Pacenback never even paid me for putting the heels on his shoes. Got all my affairs attended to now and I'm going up on Big Sandy and take a rabbit hunt with Uncle Joe's boys."

"James, why don't you withdraw that suit? Pete Maddon told me that when he got Ti to defend him for making liquor that if Ti had said ten more words he'd a-sent him to the pen for life. He got him to sit down and he just got a couple of years out of it. He just takes little five-, ten- and twenty-dollar cases."

"He's got a thirty-seven dollar case this time. He's my lawyer and a good one. Besides, I'm tending to my own affairs. You tend to your own. Pa thinks I'll never pay my debts. Unless I cash in my checks pretty soon, I'll pay every penny I owe. I don't intend to beat anybody. In addition to that, the day I'm twenty-one, I'm going to beat your damn face into a jelly for helping Pa whip me that time." "You'd better do it now. Why wait until you're twenty-one?" "Celebration on the day I become my own man."

"I know that I helped him whip you. If I hadn't knocked you

cold, what would you have done to him? You know you could
have whipped him. Hard work and exposure in all kinds of weather
have got the best of him. I used to despise my father. Refused to
step in his tracks in the snow. Now I wonder if I'm worthy! Isn't he
an honest, law-abiding, hard-working respected citizen? Isn't that
something for any country? Look at you and me! You're into it
with the schools. I'm into it over putting my neighbors and friends
in poems and stories."

"Oh," says Minnie Lartmore, "too bad for your poor old Ma
and Pa about James leaving college to rabbit hunt. Maybe his mind
won't take a education. You know my boys' minds would never
take it. Just runs in some people. Sweet Bird don't know a letter of
the A,B,C's. Wouldn't know his name if he'd meet it in the road. I
'sign' for him."

How swiftly the time flies! How quickly go the days, the weeks
and months. James and I are at the hayfield again. It is hot. James
says: "I wish for one of the snowy Tennessee days now, like last
December when I rode over the hill on one of the women teacher's
back on a little sleigh at Lincoln Memorial. Nice and cool and soft.
Here we are out in this hot field." It is August and I get the first
copy of *Man With A Bull-Tongue Plow*. When I take it to the house,
I say: "Here it is, Mom . . . here's my book." She takes it in her
hands and fondles it like it was a baby. My father takes the book
and looks at it. "I never thought you had a book in your head. I
want you to read that book to me sometime when we're not so
busy with the work." I leave the book at the house. My mother
looks at it again and again, and she shows it to the neighbor women:
"This is Jess's book." It will be released in October.

With my debts paid now and the farm clear of mortgage, I
stand by my father's side. We lean against a fence. Below us is a
wide waste of land. It has the only possible road into our farm. The
land is dark and fertile. There are twenty acres of bottom land here
and eighty acres of hills. We have one-hundred and fifty-two acres
of land on our farm and only two acres are level. My father says:
"God Almighty, Jesse, if we just owned that land, we'd have bottom

land to farm and a road to this place. All these years and never but one automobile to our house. Had to pull it out four times with the mules. Your Ma has always wanted that place."

My father looks over the land that he has rented by paying a share of the crops. He looks over the land where my mother has worked for twenty-five cents a day and he and his horse for a dollar and a half a day, and I worked from sunrise to sunset for twenty-five cents. It is the land we cannot trespass through. It is the land whereon I played as a youth and hunted the cows. I would love to have it too. I do not tell him, but I start saving money to buy the land and a right of way from our door. The only way to get out is buy our way out. We have been bottled in for twenty years . . . ever since we lived in the head of the hollow.

I save my money from teaching school. I do not buy many clothes. It is for a dream I have. The pay I get on Saturday makes me eight-hundred dollars. On Sunday I contract for the farm, date it for Monday so that it will be legal. On Monday I take possession! The farm is mine! "You got a lot to pay yet," says my father, "and, Son, be careful about your money."

I put every story I had on the road. I put all my poetry out I could. I sold three stories in one week. Five-hundred and thirty-five dollars . . . could you beat it? The county paid me for being school superintendent, the money it had owed so long. It looked as if Providence was with me! Good luck or fate or anything you want to call it! I was going up a high hill and had to pull hard. I braced my feet and made the climb! I had nine-hundred dollars in my pocket on my way to finish paying for the farm. I met my mother and father in Greenup. I called them out by the bandstand on the courthouse square. I say: "Look at this, won't you! This is the last payment on my farm!" "God Almighty, Jesse, you ain't robbed a bank, have you?" Pa asks.

"Have you been bettin' on horses?" Mom asks.

"No, that's for three stories and the County paid me the back money it owed me for being county school superintendent. I've got money for a new hayrake, a mowing machine and twenty bales of barbwire."

My father says: "I'll be damned if you can buy the land, I can build the road."

My father built the road . . . and seven little bridges spanning the winding creek. And the first car came to our house. W'y, didn't brother-in-law "Buffalo" Darby drive right up to the chip-yard! And Pa says: "Son, get in that car and take me over the road I built out of this hollow. Take me to town. I just want to ride around the hills these old legs has clim' ten-thousand times over. I want a glass of beer and a cigar anyway." I cannot tell you what this meant to us. It was the greatest thing I could have ever done for my mother! She always wanted a road. I got the land, and my father made the road.

> The hills are dear to you, my mountain Mother,
> Cornfields are dear to you—green in the sun,
> The touch of wind is dear to you, my Mother,
> The rock-ribs of the hills are dear to you.
> White rain that falls on leaves is dear to you,
> The lightning storm will make no fear to you.
> One of the elements, you surely are,
> With power to love a child, a stone, a star.
> A will to work—one unafraid of life—
> One that loves life and gave her seven life.
> An autumn tree, my Mother, now you are,
> The gold of age is hanging to your boughs.
> And unafraid you stand to meet new life,
> Beneath white glistening beauty of a star.

One day while I was in the McKell High School teaching a class, one of the office girls came in and said: "Mr. Stuart, there's the tallest man out here wanting to see you." I said: "Tell him I'm busy teaching a class. Guess he's a salesman anyway." She came back and said: "He says he must see you now or he'd come in here and drag you out on your head." "He isn't mad, is he?" "No. He laughed and said that." I excuse my class and walk out.

"Ron East, you old long-legged grasshopper! Where have you been all this time?" We walk around together. He says: "Oh, just piddling about. Old Stuart, teaching school! Ah boy, I never thought you would have been a schoolteacher! And your book! I want to thank you for the money you sent me for the meals I paid for you. It just saved me. I was down and out and Mabel had this little lady here." He shows me his daughter's picture. Ron East, with a baby's picture in his pocket! "I just can't imagine it, Ron. Seems like only yesterday when you and Mabel, Bonnie and I, doubled-dated. Now her husband won't let her read my book, so I hear. She's in the book, you know." Ron stands before me now. He is a little thicker around the waist. His heavy crop of coarse black hair is shoved back from his massive forehead like the tree lines are pushed back year by year on the Kentucky hills. Old Ron East, the fighter, the dreamer, the iron man running around with a pretty little baby-girl's picture in his pocket!

"I've read your book and liked it. Haven't been able to buy one. Heard about the brilliant records your brother James made at Berea College and Lincoln Memorial. What's he doing now?"

"He's teaching school at Hill View. Rabbit hunting in his spare time. His superintendent told me he was one of the best of the beginning teachers."

"How did he get a certificate?"

"W'y, he went to Teachers' College at Morehead, Kentucky. Liked it fine. They let him smoke there. He wired me for money once to keep him out of jail. Hit a fellow with a piece of pipe for calling him a son-of-a-bitch. They took fourteen stitches on the other fellow. James hit him with the pipe after he'd nearly beaten James to death. I borrowed the money from Forrest King and went over to Portsmouth, Ohio, and wired it to him. They fined James twenty-three dollars and the other fellow thirty-three dollars. Guess for once he wasn't the aggressor."

"I'd never thought you'd taught school."

"Strange the paths of destiny, Ron. I could never imagine you doing what you are doing. You'll never be the same old Ron East to me until I see you back in the pulpit in that long split-tailed coat. I would walk ten miles any old day to hear you preach. You'll never be the same old Ron East until I see you rolling over the bar again. That is the Ron East I shall never forget. Come on, my boys are practicing the high jump now."

Ron says: "I'm not in any shape. My first tryout since college." He pulls his coat off and lays it on the ground, slackens his belt and lifts his long body across the bar with ease. The same old Ron . . . his feet kicking as he rolls over and hits the sawdust pile with the quick spring of a cat. Not one of the high-school boys comes near his mark.

My thought about the seasons when I was a child, was it not right? Sis with four children now, Mary with two. Uncle Rank climbing swiftly into his late autumn days. "My heart's got to bothering me so, Jesse." Warfield, Granny, Brother Tobbie beneath the green grass of April, and Mom and Pa, Sweet Bird and Minnie going down the hills of autumn.

Grace, Irene, Elinor, Gladys, Jenny, Catherine, Susie, Bessie married, and Kyon dead. Jim, Thurman, Oscar, Elmer Heaberlin married. Their sealing-wax hearts melted by the hot suns of womanly love. Old Elmer Heaberlin . . . "the spout can't let off the steam. We're going to blow off the lid!" "Wear my old Lincoln Memorial belt buckle upside down," says Elmer, "that's the way I left the place. All I got from there was my wife, Scottie. She took to the mountains with me during the strike. Stuart, if you ever want to get a son good as mine, just let me set my shoes under your bed."

Didn't Bert Smith get married! Who would have ever thought it. "Just two snorts of corn from the jug before a game, Boys." Bert would take his headgear off and run in to the old Greenup Flour Mill's brick wall. "All set," he would say. "Didn't do any good in this game. Just knocked out a mouthful of teeth." Didn't Alabama tame this Kentucky wildcat? "Broke a whole damn panel of my ribs, stove-up my hand and tore the ligaments loose at my knee. I got a couple of them, though!"

Could Jesse Larks be dead? Hauled over the floodwaters by boat, then hauled to Plum Grove. Didn't he help me whip the Howell boys at last? When we were picking blackberries to buy our school-books on a high Kentucky hill, didn't he give me my first and last chew of tobacco and told me just to hold it in my mouth to keep from eating more blackberries than I put in the bucket? Didn't I lose all I had eaten and then some! He just couldn't be dead and leave Elizabeth with four children!

Wasn't Uncle Rank right after all when he said the fluffy green hair of April would hide all scars? Hadn't the Greenup Book Club invited me home to speak to them two years after *Bull-Tongue Plow* was published? "After all, Jesse is our boy. If he's good enough to speak in Tennessee, Ohio, Kentucky, West Virginia, Pennsylvania and away up there in New York, over N.B.C., he's good enough for us folks right here at home. There must be something to his book. I've never read it but I heard there was a lot of bad women and cusswords in it. He belongs here and not in the west end of the county anyway. We'll look over all these lies he makes up about us and bring him home."

It might be best to return to the east end of the county for a while since the grass and Time have covered a few of the old bruises and scars. I'm getting letters of threat in the west end now over my stories. "Don't step on our property. [How could I miss it when they own half the west end of the county?] Don't speak to me nor speak your filthy words into my telephone. I'll notify my people in due time."

Could it be that the early spring of Life is passing? What about Jean Torris, Quadroon Mott, Elizabeth, Nancy, Charlotte, Maria, Julia and Jenny? Could it be that we were going into the summer of our season? I've not had time to notice. If it's passing, it's slipped upon me and caught me unaware! Wouldn't it be fun to turn back the clock of Time and live each silver minute over, fight the old fights, love these same Loves, run wild and free over the hills and enjoy the fleeting days! Oh, for the joy of having my first poem, my first story and my first book published! Oh, for the love of life, the ecstasy, the little joys and pains! Oh, for the tender lilting beauty of spring and the fleeting silver minutes of Time! Can't you stay a while longer? What is your rush? I'm not in any hurry for you to go for I must say: "I have loved you, sought you, lived you."

If youth were just an endless flowing river
Born in the world of springtime not to fade;
Youth with its season blossoming forever,
A glorious river young in spring parade!
If youth's strong mansions of quick devilish dust
Would not disintegrate into decay
Only because that Time has said they must,
And who is Time to blow youth's breath away!
And who is he to fling snow into the hair
And blotch the temples with his downy flakes;
A sneak you cannot fight and fight him fair;
Because, Time in the end will get the breaks.
Oh, Youth, forever we must race with Time
For we must quickly bloom in our short season;
One time to work and play and spin and rhyme,
For Time will crumble us without a reason!

Jesse Stuart and his bride, Naomi Dean Norris (Jean Torris in his poetry), pictured here at their home in W-Hollow in 1941

(Photo by James Muncaster, Ashland, Kentucky)

Through the years, Jesse and Naomi made several additions to their home. In 1982, the property was listed on the National Register of Historic Places.

(Courtesy H. Edward Richardson Collection,
Ekstrom Library, University of Louisville)

Glossary

These words and phrases from *Beyond Dark Hills* may be unfamiliar to some of today's readers. They are defined here only as they are used in the novel.

air hammer - see ten-ton air hammer

adz handle - a strong wooden handle with a flattened head (usually made of hickory), used in heavy-labor hand tools

apple jack - fermented apple cider

apple peeling - an occasion when people assemble at someone's home and visit while preparing several bushels of apples for preservation as applesauce, apple butter, jelly, dried or canned apples

a-setten - sitting

backslide - to fall from a state of religious grace by committing an offense such as chewing or smoking tobacco, drinking an alcoholic beverage, swearing, gossiping, or attending a movie

ballast - gravel or broken stone used as a base or surface for roadways *balk* - the space between two rows, as between two rows of corn

bank post - sturdy white-oak posts are stacked on either side of a
coal mine shaft to support the walls

bean stringing - Neighbors often assist each other in the tedious,
time-consuming process of removing the strings from green
beans in preparation for preservation (by drying on a string
or canning in a fruit jar), thus turning the labor into an enjoyable
event.

bed - the flat rectangular area of a cart, wagon or truck, upon
which items to be hauled are loaded

belling - a shivaree. Friends pay a surprise visit to the home of a
newly wedded couple, marking their arrival with noise-making
devices such as cowbells, beating on metal kettles or firing
shotguns. Custom requires the newlyweds to treat the reveling
group to refreshments.

big game - white-tailed deer and black bear

biler of coffee - a boiler of coffee; a coffee kettle or coffeepot

blackguard - to curse, usually using the name of God in vain

"black his boots" - to gain favor with someone by flattery

bleeding heart - a popular perennial garden flower bearing red
heart-shaped flowers in late spring

block and tackle - a pulley system for lifting heavy loads; one or
more wheels with a grooved rim (sheave) mounted inside a
frame of wood or metal (block) whereon rides a stout rope or
cable, used to raise or lower heavy objects

bloodroot - also called red puccoon. A plant which bears a white
or rose-tinted blossom in the spring. Its root contains a red
sap which is sometimes used for medicinal purposes and was

used as war paint by the early American Indians.

blue flag - a blue wild iris; usually grows in wet soil

bottle cork - a stopper shaped like a wine-bottle cork and about twice the size. The cork makes an excellent fishing floater.

bottom - a level field next to a creek or river

briar scythe - also called a mowing scythe; a long curved blade attached at a right angle to a long wooden shaft, on which are two handles

broadax - an ax with a curved broad head shaped like a battle-ax, used for dressing timber

broom-sage - see sedge grass

buckwheat - a cultivated plant, growing about three feet high and having heart-shaped leaves. Its flower produces an abundant supply of nectar. Its seed is used for animal feed and flour.

bull gang - also called a gin gang; workers assigned to general tasks which require good physical strength and endurance

bull-tongue plow - a single-shovel plow. The shovel is small (6" to 10") and shaped similarly to a large tongue. A colter (knife-like blade) is mounted to the beam of the plow in front of the shovel and functions to slice soil and roots in advance of the shovel. Stuart also refers to this plow as a "cutter" or a "root cutter."

bumblebee corn - corn stunted from lack of water. Old-timers joke that bees bump their hindquarters on the ground while gathering nectar from tassels of this dwarf corn.

burdock - a coarse weed with a broad leaf, usually growing two to four feet high *burnt* - having contacted a venereal disease

burrs - steel grating screens used with a rock crusher to filter out the desired aggregate—large or medium crushed rock, gravel, or limestone

C. & O. - Chesapeake and Ohio Railroad Company

can - to be dismissed from a job or to order someone to stop doing something

candy-ankle - someone considered "soft" by another who considers himself to be "rough and tough"

cane - sorghum; also called sugar cane. The stalk is similar to corn in appearance but is smaller. It is used to make molasses.

cane hay - the dried stalks of sorghum (or corn), more commonly known as fodder

carriage - the front axle system of a wagon

"cash in my checks" - to die. Another version of this expression "cash in my chips."

check lines - leather reins used to control a horse or a team of horses

chestnut post - a fence post made from a chestnut tree. In the 1920s, a nationwide blight killed chestnut trees.

chip yard - also called a wood yard; an area of the backyard where firewood is chopped and stacked

church house - Appalachian pleonasm for a church

churn - to drill a hole in a rock with a jackhammer

cleaver rod - the metal handle on a cleaver, four to six feet in length *cleavers* - hardened steel-forging chisels of various sizes and shapes. Each cleaver is welded to a long handle, by which it is placed over a block of hot steel. Driven by repeated blows of a ten-ton vertical air hammer, the cleaver cuts and shapes the hot steel.

clench - to grab or tackle someone with both arms, making him fall onto his back

clim - an Elizabethan past-tense form of climb

coal bank - the surface around the entrance to a coal shaft

coal buggy - a dump wagon built to haul coal for delivery, with 52" rear wheels and 36" front wheels, having a cranking mechanism to elevate the bed. Sheet-metal chutes are carried under the bed.

coal tarred - to spread tar over holes rusted in a metal roof. Tar is derived from coal.

coal truck - a 1 1/2 ton platform truck with an in-line 6 cylinder engine and solid side rails. Many homes are heated by a coal burning fireplace. Archaic.

cockleburs - a spindly weed which grows in moist areas such as bottomland and bears prickly burrs which cling to clothing and animal fur

colored - a word used to distinguish a person of Afro-American descent. Archaic.

Columbia single barrel - a brand of shotgun

comb - a ridge of a roof, the topmost part of a roof

cone - a wasp nest

cookstove - a cast-iron wood-burning stove, consisting of a firebox, four caps (burners) and an oven

corn - slang for corn liquor; see moonshine whiskey

corn-bird - a catbird; related to the mockingbird, this bird's song
resembles the mewing of a cat

cornhusking - also known as a husking bee. Neighbors assemble to
remove the husks from an individual's yearly corn crop, while
they enjoy abundant food and drink and lively conversation.

corn licker - also known as moonshine; see moonshine

corn nubbins - ears of corn which did not fill out well with grain;
the sections of an ear broken into pieces are also referred to
as nubbins. (Cows are fed nubbins because they swallow the
entire piece and would choke on a whole ear.)

corn shock - also called a fodder shock. Dried corn stalks cut and
leaned vertically against a "horse," made by tying together
the tops of four uncut stalks. The stalks are secured by a stout
string tied around the shock near the top, making the shock
resemble a tepee. Ears of corn are harvested from the stalks
at a later date and the dried stalks (fodder) fed to livestock.

cottontails - wild rabbits

Court day - County Court officers—several magistrates and the
county judge—meet monthly to tend to fiscal matters,
usually on a specific day such as the first Monday of each
month. It is a time to see one's magistrate to seek help with a
road, community school or even a personal problem. Misdemeanor cases are heard by the county judge. Archaic.

cow fly - house flies and blowflies which swarm the dried manure on cows

craw-dads - crawfish; crayfish

crib - a building where the annual corn crop is stored (on the
ear), built of wood or logs

crib - slang for the county jailhouse

crosscut saw - a saw designed to cut across the grain of wood

crossties - timbers used in the foundation of a railroad track; the rails are mounted on crossties

croton oil - a powerful purgative

cur - a mountain cur is a hunting dog of mixed breed

currant vines - shrubs which produce berries such as gooseberries and black currants for jams and jellies

"cut the pigeonwing" - to perform a solo, high-stepping dance; to show off

cutter - see bull-tongue plow

dabbling-pan - see wash-pan

deathward - passing deathward; an idea or belief which is dying

Decoration day - Memorial Day; traditionally celebrated by decorating the graves of loved ones with colorful flowers

dinner bucket - an oblong metal container with bail attached for carrying a large lunch. The lid compartment can act as a thermos, holding one and a half quarts of liquid.

dog days - the first two weeks of August when creeks and rivers become stagnant due to a lack of rain

"dog to lie" - a hunting dog circles a tree, barking, thinking it has chased an animal up the tree but is mistaken

doodle - a mounded pile of loose hay or straw (about 5' x 5'), which may be picked up with a pitchfork and thrown into a wagon or sled

double-furrow - a furrow is a narrow groove plowed in the ground for planting. To double-furrow, one runs the plow over the same row a second time (usually in the opposite direction) in order to make the groove deeper.

drag of wood - a sled loaded with firewood

drap - drop; an Elizabethan past-tense form of drop

drapped - dropped. A sow drops (gives birth) a litter of pigs.

drawbars - a type of gate; two or three slender poles rest on blocks between double posts on either side of a fence opening. To operate the drawbars, one simply slides the poles to one side.

drinking gourd - a dipper. A gourd is a squash-like fruit. Its dried shell makes a leakproof container. The bulb of a long-necked gourd can be hollowed out to form a ladle, or dipper, from which to drink.

driv - an Elizabethan past-tense form of drive

drove - a large number of livestock

drowse - sluggish and not alert

"dry-clothes" man - an employee of the state Department of Alcohol Beverage Control

dry horse pill - a clump of dried manure

E.K. - Eastern Kentucky turnpike; a wide two-lane road

el mend - a square dance movement; to lock elbows with person to your side and swing around

express wagon - a fast, lightweight wagon with a bed approximately 86" x 45" and twelve-inch side panels, mounted on leaf-springs.

With 51" rear wheels and 39" front wheels, the wagon
moves rapidly.

feed basket - a bushel or half-bushel basket made of white-oak
splints

feed truck - a 1 1/2 ton platform truck with an in-line 6 cylinder
engine, for delivering livestock and poultry feed to small
country stores. Archaic.

figures of earth - people with various types of personality,
character, and intelligence

fit - an Elizabethan past-tense form of fight

fit - a period of catatonic physical and mental activity associated
with a psychological disturbance

flints - flint rock; a hard stone the early American Indians used to
form arrowheads

flood-front - a field next to a river or creek

fluey - to break down; to cease to perform properly

fodder - see corn shock

foot adz - a tool usually used to roughly shape timbers. It is similar
in appearance to a grubbing hoe, except its blade 6" to 8") has a
square top, which allows one to push the tool with the foot.

ford - a shallow place in a creek where one can cross from one
side to the other

Fords - Ford automobiles

forenoon - before noonday

.44 - a .44 caliber pistol

fox horn - a hunting horn, usually made from a cattle horn

fragrant mountain water - see moonshine whiskey

gambling stick - gambrel stick; a wood or metal device for suspending a slaughtered animal

garret - the attic of a building

get saved - the feeling that one has obtained religious salvation. This feeling may be negated by backsliding.

gin gang - see bull gang

gin work - general physical labor

"going through the mill" - working long hours to a state of exhaustion

gooseberries - a shrub which grows in shady, well-drained soil, producing tart berries that can be used for preserves or pies

gooseneck hoe - a standard gardening hoe, the shank of the blade resembling the shape of a goose's neck

gossamer - very light, fragile and delicate

gouging - to stick one's thumb into an opponent's eye

grained - skinned

grandsires - male ancestors

gravel out - to dig the dirt from around an object

green terbacker - unripened tobacco

greenbriar - a green vine plant with small green thorns. It can run up into small trees and it may be ten or twenty feet long.

grub - food, usually homegrown

grubbing hoe - a tool for digging. A sturdy hoe, with a 4" x 7" blade, mounted on a wooden adz-head handle. Some grubbing hoes are made in combination with a pick.

hand of tobacco - approximately twenty to twenty-five leaves of moist, cured tobacco gathered together by the stem ends and bound ("tied") by a leaf wrapped tightly around these ends

hand-children - for marketing, tobacco leaves are stripped from the dried stalks and tied into small bundles called hands. Children usually help with the task.

he-man - a muscle-bound male

heat cleavers - steel cutting blades, heated in a fire until they turn cherry red

"Highland Mary" - one of the loves of Robert Burns' youth, for whom he wrote the poem of this title

High Sheriff - the county sheriff, who generally holds an inside position with the political party in power. The position of the High Sheriff was an important one in an English shire.

hike out - to cough up and spit out

hog pen - a fenced area where hogs are confined. Inside the area is a small building for shelter, a trough or pond with water, and a trough for feed.

hoot - a drink; usually a swallow of whiskey

hooving - swelling

horseweed - a green weed approximately five-feet high which can be found near barnyards or in rich bottom land. It is often fed to hogs.

hoss - to lift

hurray - a celebration

inner tube - a doughnut shaped inflatable rubber sleeve which
    fits inside a balloon tire

Irish-buggy - a wheelbarrow

jarfly - also called harvest fly or dog-day locust; a large
    cicada that "sings"—makes a loud, shrill, buzzing—in late
    summer

johnboat - a small rowboat

jolt wagon - the work wagon of a farm; a sturdily built mule- or
    horse-drawn wagon with a bed approximately 10 1/2' x 3 1/2',
    used to haul the harvest. The bed is mounted directly upon
    the chassis and can support loads up to three and one-half
    tons.

jump-the-track buggy - a cart for hauling coal out of a mine shaft
    one ton at a time. The bed is approximately 66" x 28",
    mounted on two-inch-wide wheels which run on a track of
    white-oak 2" x 4"s. The cart is pulled by a small mule called
    a bank mule.

K.P. - kitchen police; kitchen duty assigned to soldiers.

katydids - a large green, American long-horned grasshopper
    having stridulating organs on the forewings of the males that
    produce a loud, shrill sound, heard mainly in late summer
    and early autumn

kettle - see wash kettle

kindling - narrow strips of wood, preferably cedar. Kindling is
    used for starting a fire in the fireplace, in the cookstove or
    under a wash kettle.

knob - a rounded small hill; a piece of ground shaped like an inverted funnel.

lady's finger - kidney vetch or woundwort; a plant with kidney-shaped leaves and silky flowers, believed to be effective in the treatment of kidney ailments.

laid by - a cultivated crop matured to a state that weeds are prevented from receiving sunshine and no longer grow. The soil no longer needs to be worked.

laid off - to plow rows for planting seeds, approximately one long step apart

lard bucket - a one-gallon tin bucket with a bail, made to hold ten pounds of lard

larkspur - a wild woodland flower of the delphinium family with a spur-shaped growth at the bottom of each blossom

lassies - sorghum molasses, made from the sap of sorghum (sometimes called sugar cane). The annual making of molasses is a major event in rural life. Archaic.

latchstring - a string passed through a hole in an entrance door so that the latch on the inside can be lifted from the outside. One might extend an invitation by saying, "Our latchstring is always out."

Law Chore - a citizen/citizens temporarily empowered to help the Sheriff serve a court summons or make an arrest

lays - songs

leaf - a tree putting forth its annual spring leaves

lean-to - a structure consisting of three walls and a pitched roof built against an existing side of a house, creating an additional room

licker - liquor

(to) lie at a tree - see "dog to lie"

life-everlasting - sometimes called rabbit tobacco; a weed which when dried can be smoked or chewed

light bread - a store-bought loaf of bread

lights - lungs

long gun - a long-barreled pistol

lot (as a lot in life) - one's fate

Mallie - a Mallet compound locomotive, designed for high-speed powerful freight service

marsh hens - wood ducks

mattock - a combination tool used in heavy work, having a long-bladed grub hoe on one end and an ax blade on the other, mounted to a sturdy wooden adz handle

May apples - a woodland wild flower, having a white cup-shaped bloom located beneath umbrella-shaped leaves. Its fruit is edible and often made into preserves. The plant is also used for medicinal purposes.

merry mix-up - a carnival ride also known as "roller chairs"; the centrifugal force of a spinning circular platform—to which booths on rollers are attached—creates a thrill ride by causing the booths to spin rapidly

middlings - a mixture of ground wheat and bran, used to feed live stock

milk gap - a pasture gate to which cows are accustomed to being called to be milked each morning and evening *milkweed* - a weed that when cut produces a white, sticky substance

milk wagon - a horse drawn, enclosed commercial wagon, 9' x 40", for delivering milk daily to homes and restaurants. The cab is four feet high at either end and has a center portion of six feet, where the operator rides while standing. The milk is kept ice-cold by large blocks of ice, weighing twenty-five to fifty pounds. Archaic.

mincing - having a picky appetite

mind out - also "watch out"; to think before acting

moldboard - the shiny curved plate of a plow which turns the soil over

molten pig iron - red-hot melted iron

monkeying - associating with whores

moonshine whiskey - illicitly distilled whiskey made from corn and sometimes from middlins (cow feed) when corn is not available. The alcohol content ranges from 50 to 75 percent.

mourners' bench - the front pew in a church

mud thrush - a wood thrush; this bird plasters its nest with mud

mule puncher - a person who breaks and trains mules

murdle vine - see myrtle vine

murrain - a plague affecting hoofed animals such as hoof-and-mouth disease

myrtle vine - periwinkle; a dark green ground cover with purple, blue or white flowers, common in old family cemeteries in out-of-the-way places

N.B.C. - NBC radio network

newground - land which has been recently cleared of trees and brush in preparation for cultivation

newspaper crooner - one who sells newspapers on a street corner, chanting a sales pitch such as, "Get the latest news! Read all about it!"

noddled - an up and down motion of the head

normal school - a two-year college program of teacher education. Archaic.

oilers - a machine with a pump and spray nozzles for dispensing oil onto cold-rolled steel, forming a coating which acts as a preservative against rust

oil lamp - a glass lamp burning kerosene (coal oil) by means of a wick

one-eyed grubbing hoe - a long-bladed hoe with a hole at the top of the blade into which a round-head (planters') wooden handle fits

Owl Head pistol - a pistol with the back of the breech (hammer area) shaped like the top of an owl's head

pawpaws - a papaw tree, seven to eight feet in height and bearing a fruit (resembling a banana in taste) which ripens after the first frost

pen- a penitentiary

pert - pleasing, clever, likeable

"pheasant" - In Appalachia, the ruffed grouse is referred to as a pheasant.

phlox -the wild sweet william; a biennial flower with bluish or
   pale lilac flowers

physic - to cause the bowels to empty

pick - a tool used for digging in rocky soil, having a sharp steel
   point at either end. A grub hoe made in combination with a
   pick is called a pick mattock.

pickled beans - green beans fermented in a crock of salt-water brine

pickled corn - sweet corn (on or off the cob) fermented in a crock
   of salt-water brine

pickups - randomly selected temporary workers

pie safe - a piece of kitchen furniture, usually with ventilated tin
   siding, where prepared food is protected from flies

pie wagon - a wagon used for selling pastries, having an enclosed
   cab with windows on all sides. Archaic.

pilfering - someone or something intruding in a vicinity where
   he she/it is not wanted

pinches - difficult times in one's life which require courage,
   action and endurance

pinhead - a person with a narrow head; a stupid person

pint - a point; a place where a mountain ridge narrows into an
   ending point. Appalachian family graveyards are usually
   located on ridge points because of the magnificent view.

pizened - poisoned

plug horse - an inferior, unsound, or very old horse

polecat - a skunk

post-hole digger - a tool with two long wooden handles joined to two half-moon-shaped hinged metal heads, which operate in a jaw-like fashion as the operator jabs the digger into the ground and removes the soil

privy - an outbuilding that houses a toilet

promenade - a square dance movement; to dance forward, either alone or with one's partner, in a lively prancing step

puncheons - heavy boards of timber, roughly dressed

puncture - a hole in the rubber inner tube of a balloon tire

purt' nigh - almost

pursley - purslane; an edible herb with yellow flowers

quiled - an Elizabethan word meaning coiled

ragtime - Dixieland jazz

ragweed - a weed with highly allergenic pollen, blooming in the early fall

railroaded - to work at great speed

rain crow - The black-billed North American cuckoo. A slender, brown bird, about a foot long. Its song is low, mournful and quivering. Frequent rain-crow calls are believed to be a sign of approaching rain.

reach - to hand

rep - reputation

residenter - one who lives in a particular place

rider - a stake or rail used to brace the corners in a split-rail fence

Ridgemore - a brand of whiskey

road you - to throw someone from a moving vehicle

roasten-ears - roasting ears; sweet corn boiled on the cob

Roland - the hero of the French epic poem *Song of Roland* (written about 1100 A.D.)

root cutter - see bull-tongue plow

rotten-egged - bombarded with spoiled eggs—a favorite antic of young boys. A flock of laying chickens is a part of every small farm and young boys have no trouble finding spoiled eggs. Archaic.

roughage - hay or fodder

row - argument; quarrel

rush the corn over - to hoe only the largest weeds out of a crop of corn

sassafras sprouts - the small shoots or saplings of the sassafras tree. The dried root bark is used as a flavoring agent, as in sassafras tea or root beer.

saunter - to walk about in a leisurely fashion

saw-briar - a briar with small but extremely sharp thorns which can cause a long tear in one's clothing or skin.

saw-briar stools - clumps of newly emerging saw-briar shoots where briars have been cut

saw log - a log large enough to saw into boards

scythe - see briar scythe. In Stuart's works, the word "scythe" denotes the briar scythe.

sealing-wax - hard blocks of paraffin which melt when heated, used to form air-tight seals in jars of jelly

section - a particular length of railroad track a group of workers is charged with keeping in perfect order, including track maintenance and mowing the right-of-way

sedge grass - also called broom-sage; a grass that grows wild in uncultivated fields and turns the color of broom straw in the fall of the year

set - situation

settin' up - when someone is expected to die, friends come and sit (visit) with the family

settlers of differences - loaded pistols

seventy-fives - a 75-millimeter caliber field howitzer (cannon) used in World War I

shale - coal containing impurities of various kinds

shale stone - a mixture of shale and hard rock

shocked - see corn shock

shod - to have shoes on the feet; a term generally used in regard to horse shoes

shoe-make - an Appalachian pronunciation of sumac. See sumac.

shoestring vine - a tangled, yellowish green vine which spreads as a thick ground cover

shotgun house - a small, narrow house of two or three rooms, so named because if one opened the front and back doors, he could fire a shotgun straight through the two entranceways

"siff" - syphilis

sinner - one who is not a member of an organized church, or one who has broken the rules of the church. Sinners "praying through" are sinners who gather at the mourner's bench, kneel in prayer with the minister and continue to pray until each feels that he/she has obtained salvation.

slat bonnet - a cotton bonnet with a wide stiff brim and back neckcovering, worn by women to protect from sunburn. The brim is made stiff by cardboard inserts.

sleight - a trick or skill; an easier way to do something

slop jar - chamber pot used in bedroom at night

slopped - to feed hogs their daily mixture of table scraps, middlings and water

smartweed - a common annual weed with a strong odor

smithy - a blacksmith

smokehouse - a small outbuilding where ham, bacon, and sausage are cured with salt and hickory smoke, then wrapped in paper and cloth sacks for storage in a wooden meat box. It is one of the few locked buildings in rural communities.

snake feeder - a small dragonfly of brilliant dark-blue color. An Appalachian folk tale often told to children is that snake feeders feed and nurse injured snakes.

snakeroot - a name given to several plants whose roots look like snakes; several have medicinal value

snowballs - large clusters of white flowers which grow on a shrub

sole - sold

some'rs - somewhere

sourwood - a sorrel tree; a small softwood tree with white bell-shaped flowers

souse - to force one's head or fully-clothed body under water

span of mules - a team; two mules

split-bottom - a chair bottom woven of white-oak splints

spring wagon - a wagon with a comfortable ride, with a bed mounted over three large leaf springs—one over the front axle and two over the rear axle

sprout a hill - to chop and clear the small bushes (sprouts) from a hillside

sprouts - small bushes growing in a field or shoots growing from a stump

spud - a steel rod with a star bit on the bottom end and a flattened top end. It is struck with a sledge hammer then turned and struck again repeatedly until a hole is drilled through rock.

stalwart - stout; strong

stay in - required to remain after school hours as punishment for misconduct

steal - to move slowly and quietly

steel blocks - white-hot blocks of steel, taken from a blast furnace and placed on an anvil, where air-hammer-driven cleavers are used to cut and shape the steel into desired sizes and shapes. Blacksmiths then shape the piece/pieces into the desired product, such as a wagon-wheel rim.

steely marble - a ball bearing used as a taw (the marble with which one shoots) in the game of marbles

stick of kindling - see kindling

sticker weed - also known as stickweed; in Appalachia, the term can also mean horseweed

stole - past tense of steal. See steal.

stool - the metal baseplate of an air hammer

stove-up - to dislocate a joint. ME stave.

stovewood - very small pieces of firewood for use in a wood-burning cookstove

straw boss - a member of the work crew who acts as the boss or is an assistant to the boss

stretching (fence) wire - nailing barbwire to fence posts while keeping it taut

sugar melon - also called a sugar baby; a small round dark-green watermelon, which is very sweet

sugar tree - a sugar-maple; a species of maple from which sugar is made by boiling the sap

sumac - also called shoe-make. A shrub or small tree that produces red seed-like berries and, in the fall, beautiful scarlet red leaves.

suck-egg mule - a term of disbelief. Dogs that sneak into a hen house and eat eggs from the nests are called "egg-sucking dogs." The idea that a mule would "suck eggs" is preposterous.

Sunday School house - a church building. The traditional Sunday morning worship hour is conducted one Sunday per month in many rural churches, when the circuit minister comes; however, Sunday School is taught every Sunday.

supper - the evening meal

swath - the width of the arc made by swinging a mowing scythe

sweet william - a member of the pink family; one of the oldest garden flowers, ranging in color from white to dark red and purple, having velvet-like blossoms growing in clusters

taboret - a plush low seat without back or arms

tater - a potato

team - a pair of horses or mules trained to work together

ten-ton air hammer - a vertical forge hammer, the face of which is secured to a compressed-air driven piston. With a four-to-five feet stroke, the hammer strikes with a ten-ton force.

terbacker - tobacco

tie-timber woods - a woodland tract with black-oak trees (hardwoods), which are good for making railroad ties

timothy - a perennial grass used for hay, or mixed with hardier grasses for pasture

.38 - a .38 caliber pistol

tobacco spittle - also called ambeer; the liquid which forms when one chews tobacco

toll - entice; call forth

tommyrot - something ridiculously untrue

touring cars - passenger automobile

trace chain - the part of a harness which connects to a crossbar (a whiffletree) which is then connected to the item to be pulled. (A whiffletree is commonly called a singletree.)

truck bed - the floor of the hauling area of a large cattle or coal truck, approximately 7' x 10' in size

truck box - an inbuilt metal toolbox located on the side of a truck

trustee - a local Kentucky educational position. A prominent person/persons appointed to oversee a school district, which usually consists of a community one-room school. This person has the responsibility of locating a qualified teacher and recommending him or her to the board of education. Other duties include keeping a record of all children in the district who are ages five to fifteen, and obtaining a box of chalk, a half-dozen erasers, a broom and a water bucket from the board of education. Teachers are required to be eighteen years of age and to pass the qualifying examination. Archaic.

turkey (of clothes) - a bundle tied to the end of a long stick, containing a person's belongings. The outer wrapping of the bundle is often a shirt, coat, or other garment. Men working away from home, peddlers or homeless people often carry turkeys across the shoulder. These are sometimes suspended from an ax handle, freeing the hands to carry a toolkit or other item.

.22 - a .22 caliber pistol. A .22 rifle and a .22 cartridge are also referred to as "a .22."

undaubed cracks - logs without filling material between them. Daubing is a clay-mud mixture used to fill (daub) the spaces between logs in a building.

unknown tongue - an indecipherable language spoken at a religious meeting by someone in a state of religious fervor *unshod* - a horse without shoes

vipers - snakes. Archaic.

wagon tongue - a long wooden shaft extending from the center
     of the front carriage of a wagon, to which mules or horses are
     hitched

wall plate - a mantel above a fireplace

waltz the hall - a man and woman in waltz position dance round
     and round in wide sweeping circles

wash kettle - an iron kettle made to hang over a wood fire in
     which water is heated on wash day. These kettles vary in size
     but an average size is about 10 to 12 gallons. Archaic.

wash-pan - a shallow baked-enamel metal pan kept on a small
     table beside a bucket of water in the kitchen or on the back
     porch for washing the hands and face. Archaic.

water birch - the silver-barked birch tree which grows near
     streams of water

(the) weed - tobacco

weedmonkey - a whore

wench - an Elizabethan word meaning prostitute

whiffletree - a wooden bar about thirty inches long (commonly
     called a singletree) used to connect the harness of a horse or
     mule to a wagon, buggy, or piece of farm machinery

whirligig - a square-dance movement wherein a man and
     woman in waltz position whirl round and round in a tight
     circle

white-eyed - to faint from exhaustion

white-mule - moonshine whiskey

willer basket - a willow basket, woven from the green, pliable
branches of a willow tree

windflower - a spring wild flower having a slender stem and
delicate white, pink or purple blossoms

windrowed - hay in a field which has been raked into rows to dry
and be collected

woods - woodland

work hand - a farm worker; usually a hired person

worms went into ground - during a period of drought earthworms
must burrow deeply to find moist soil

writhed - a twisting movement

yellow flag - a yellow wild iris

yoke of big cattle - a team of oxen

youngin - a young one; a child

yucca - an evergreen plant of the lily family, with rigid pointed
leaves at the base. It bears white flowers.

Acknowledgments

The editor wishes to acknowledge the following people who have assisted with various words in this glossary: Mae Alford, cattle farmer; the late Roscoe Alford; Chester I. Bays, attorney; Jeffrey Bush, auto restorer/builder; Ray Buckberry Jr., attorney; Charley Dygert, blacksmith; Judge J. David Francis, retired federal judge; Dr. James M. Gifford, director Jesse Stuart Foundation; Dr. Joseph Glaser, professor of English; Judge Basil Griffin, retired judge executive; Dr. Jerry A. Herndon, professor of English; Porter Hines, cattle farmer; Cecil Hurst, retired US Army Corps of Engineers, Greenup Lock and Dam; Jonathan D. Jeffrey, special collections librarian; Keith Kappes, Vice President Morehead State University; Wendell Lee, mechanic; Dr. Jim Wayne Miller, poet/professor; Dr. Joseph R. Millichap, professor of English; Era Stinson, housewife; Noble Stuart, retired vocational technology instructor; Bridget Tolliver, Jesse Stuart Foundation; Dr. Wilson E. Wood, retired professor of English.

The editor is grateful to the following people, institutions and enterprises, who have made possible the photographs in this book: Irene Griffith—schoolmate of Jesse Stuart; Sharon Bidwell and Byron Crawford of *The Courier-Journal*; Delinda Buie and Dr. H. Edward Richardson of the University of Louisville; Cynthia L. Cooke and Robin Lamb of Lincoln Memorial University; Dr. Jerry Herndon and Barry Johnson of Murray State University; Keith R. Kappes, Clara Keys and Teresa Johnson of Morehead State University; Dorothy Griffith of the Greenup Public Library; Charles Hay of Eastern Kentucky University; Dr. Melba Hay and Mary Winter of the Kentucky Historical Society; Constance Mills and Jonathan Jeffrey of Western Kentucky University; Lisa Wood of the University of Kentucky; Strawberry Luck of Vanderbilt University; George Wolfford of *The Daily Independent*, Ashland, Kentucky; Dr. James M. Gifford, Ethel McBrayer and Bridget Tolliver of the Jesse Stuart Foundation.

John H. Spurlock, Ph.D.
Western Kentucky University